Simpsonology

TIM
DELANEY

Simpsonology

there's a little bit of SPRINGFIELD in all of us

Prometheus Books

59 John Glenn Drive
Amherst, New York 14228-2119

Published 2008 by Prometheus Books

Inquiries should be addressed to
Prometheus Books
59 John Glenn Drive
Amherst, New York 14228–2119
VOICE: 716–691–0133, ext. 210
FAX: 716–5691–0137
WWW.PROMETHEUSBOOKS.COM

12 11 10 09 08 07   5 4 3 2 1

Library of Congress Cataloging-in-Publication Data

Delaney, Tim.
    Simpsonology : there's a little bit of Sprinfield in all of us! / Tim Delaney.
        p. cm.
    Includes bibliographical references and index.
    ISBN 978–1–59102–559–7
    1. Simpsons (Television program) I. Title.
PN1992.77.S58D45 2008
791.45'72—dc22

2007051693

Printed in the United States of America on acid-free paper

*Dedicated to all those who contribute to popular culture
in a positive manner.*

Contents

About the Author

Tim Delaney holds a PhD in sociology and teaches a wide variety of sociology and criminology courses at the State University of New York at Oswego. Delaney has authored numerous book chapters, book reviews, articles, and books including *Seinology: The Sociology of Seinfeld*, *American Street Gangs*, and *Contemporary Social Theory*. He is currently busy working on his next two books. Delaney serves as a "media expert" and is often quoted in newspapers and interviewed on radio and television. He is a loyal fan of *The Simpsons* and has watched every episode when it first aired and continues to watch old episodes in syndication. To learn more about the author, visit his Web site at: www.BooksByTimDelaney.com.

Preface

I can remember watching *The Simpsons* when it first aired as "shorts" on the *Tracey Ullman* show in the late 1980s. As a resident of Los Angeles and an avid Dodgers fan, I would watch KTTV, Channel 11 (FOX TV) for all the latest local news, Dodgers games, and cutting-edge new television shows. FOX was not a network at this time but KTTV represents its American beginnings. I must admit that I have always been willing to give *any* FOX show a try—kind of as a reward for bringing us such entertaining shows as *The Simpsons* and *Married . . . with Children*. FOX TV (not to be confused with FOX News) has always been a network willing to take a chance on liberal, controversial shows. *The Simpsons* certainly qualified as a controversial show. When it first aired, *The Simpsons* was criticized by religious and family organizations. Former President George H. W. Bush (see chapter 1) once famously stated that he preferred the Walton family over the Simpson family. Well, the days portrayed in *The Waltons* are long gone and the creator and writers of *The Simpsons* were keenly aware of this. A generation later and the Simpson family is still going strong. Today, there are more controversial shows airing on regular TV than *The Simpsons* and they often take the brunt of criticism once directed toward the residents of Springfield.

Simpsonology: There's a Little Bit of Springfield in All of Us is designed to entertain and inform the reader on the social significance and relevancy of the TV show *The Simpsons*. The social relevance of *The Simpsons* is demonstrated by the fact that the show touches upon every major social institution (e.g., culture, romance, marriage and family, religion, economics, politics, sports, health, education, environmentalism, and popular culture holidays such as April Fools' Day and Halloween) found in society. Utilizing a variety of approaches, including sociological, psychological, and philosophical, *Simpsonology* demonstrates the prevalence of *The Simpsons* in popular culture in the United States (as well as in many other nations around the world).

A number of *Simpsons* episodes are referenced throughout *Simpsonology*. (Obviously, it is impossible to discuss every episode. As a result, some readers will undoubtedly think of episode skits that *could have* been included in *Simpsonology*.) For the convenience of the reader, each referenced episode is listed numerically in chronological order rather than by the bothersome method utilized by *The Simpsons* that involves a series of letters and numbers. For example, the first full-length *Simpsons* episode, "Simpsons Roasting on an Open Fire," is listed as episode #7G08 in the credits. (Note: The letters and numbers are production codes.) *Simpsonology* will cite this episode with the number "1" placed in parentheses (#1). Providing the chronological order makes it easier for the reader to ascertain whether the referenced episode is recent or from many years ago. Don't worry, purists! The index will provide both a chronological listing of episodes cited and *The Simpsons* episode identification used in the credits at the end of each episode. The index will also provide the episode title, the original airdate, and the chapter(s) in which each cited episode can be found.

There are more than four hundred episodes of *The Simpsons* as well as a full-length movie (*The Simpsons Movie*), all of which have provided us with great entertainment. As one might imagine, producing a full-length movie after airing so many original episodes presented a number of challenges. Matt Groening explains that this challenge was compounded by concerns with satisfying die-hard fans while appealing to the uninitiated when he says, "We're trying to entertain ourselves. We figure that if we can surprise ourselves, we'll surprise the fans" (*Entertainment Weekly* 2007). To no one's surprise, *The Simpsons Movie* was a huge box office success.

By all indications, there are many new episodes, and perhaps films, to come. *Simpsonology* provides an entertaining path down memory lane of some of your favorite episodes. *Simpsonology* also enlightens the reader to the social significance of this brilliantly written and hilarious animated sitcom. As Homer Simpson might say, "Mmm, a book called *Simpsonology*, you say?" So, before sitting down on the couch to read this book, go to the kitchen and grab a favorite snack and beverage.

Acknowledgments

Particular thanks to Tim Madigan for reviewing an early draft of this book. My thanks also go to all the folks at Prometheus Books who helped in the publication process, especially the editing, marketing, and sales personnel. As always, a special thanks to my continued inspiration, Christina.

Chapter 1

An Introduction to The Simpsons

"As far as anyone knows, we're a nice, normal family."
—Homer Simpson

A brother and sister are pushing and shoving each other in the living room of a modest, working-class family home. Their father rushes in to stop the siblings from fighting. The children explain that they are merely arguing over who loves their father more. Feeling better about himself, the father allows the children to continue their disagreement. The boy shouts, "You love him more." His sister responds, "No, you do." Disappointed, but guided by a greater concern, the father instructs the two children to get their mischief out of their system before they all leave for his company's family picnic at the boss's home. Welcome to one of America's most dysfunctional families—the Simpsons.

From the beginning, Matt Groening made it clear that the Simpson family is anything but normal. The scene described above comes from the "There's No Disgrace Like Home" episode (#4), original airdate, January 28, 1990. As the Simpson family heads to stately Burns Manor, or as Homer describes it, "Heaven on Earth," Homer warns his family, "Okay now look, my boss is going to be at this picnic so I want you to show your father some love and/or respect." Homer's daughter Lisa replies, "We get a choice?" Bart, Lisa's brother, responds, "I'm picking respect." Homer, who is a working drone, needs to make a favorable impression with his boss, Mr. Burns. Homer realizes that he will be judged based on the behavior of his

17

family. Homer is so concerned about the impression that his family might make with Burns that he gives one last bit of instruction shortly after entering the Burns estate, "Now remember, as far as anyone knows, we're a nice, normal family."

Although the company picnic is not a complete disaster, Bart and Lisa run amok throughout the grounds and Homer's wife, Marge, gets drunk. At the conclusion of the picnic, Burns announces that the party is over and that everyone has ten minutes to leave the premises before he releases the hounds. As the Simpsons and other families head back to their cars, Homer admits that he is glad to leave so that he can go home and act in his normal manner. In this regard, Homer reflects the sentiments of many employees who are uncomfortable spending time with their employers outside of work. On the other hand, the Simpson family is hardly the barometer of "normalcy"!

MMM . . . A FAMILY CALLED *THE SIMPSONS*, YOU SAY?

The Simpsons represents one of America's most recognizable families. They are certainly the most famous animated one. The Simpson family includes Homer Simpson, 36; his wife, Marge, 34; their three children, Bart, 10; Lisa, 8; and Maggie, 1; their dog, Santa's Little Helper; and their cat, Snowball (various versions). The Simpson family resides in Springfield—the state is unknown—a fairly typical midsize American city. (Note: Springfield is most likely located in Oregon, the home state of Groening. As Groening states, "Secretly, I've always believed that the Simpsons live in Springfield, Oregon" [Turnquist 2007, E-4].) Springfield is large enough to have its own "badlands," it is home to a minor league baseball team, has its own blimp, a number of cultural museums, an unendingly burning pile of tires, an air force base, and an international airport (among other things).

The Simpson family is headed by Homer J. Simpson. Although *The Simpsons* was first centered primarily on the antics of Bart, it is Homer Simpson who has become the primary focus of many *Simpsons* storylines. Homer is overweight and bald and works as a safety inspector in Sector 7-G at the Springfield Nuclear Power Plant. If Homer were a safety inspector of a nuclear plant in real life, we might all be in great peril! Homer's occupational ineptness is demonstrated by the fact that he holds the plant record for most years worked at an entry-level position.

Homer is known for saying "D'oh!" when he is upset and "Mmm . . ." when tempted. Homer's "D'oh!" expression has become a part of popular culture and his constant use of the word is responsible, at least in part, for its inclusion into the Oxford English Dictionary, where it is defined as "expressing frustration at the realization that things have turned out badly or not as planned, or that one has just said or done something foolish." Matt Groening, the creator of *The Simpsons*, explains that the "D'oh!" sound uttered by Homer was originally written in the script as "annoyed grunt." Dan Castellaneta, who does Homer's voice, created a shortened version of the sound that the character actor James Finlayson made in old Laurel and Hardy movies (*Playboy* 2007).

Homer Simpson loves to drink Duff beer and consume large quantities of food, especially donuts, pork rinds, Krusty Burgers, and pork chops. Homer's unhealthy eating habits have led him to endure a large number of medical procedures, including a triple bypass operation. Homer is just as lazy at home as he is at work. His favorite pastime is sitting on the couch watching television while drinking beer and eating munchies. Homer purchases a great deal of his beer and food at the local overpriced Kwik-E-Mart, owned by Apu Nahasapeemapetilon, a "semilegal" immigrant from India. (See chapter 7 for a description of Apu's residency status.) Apu and Homer have shared numerous conversations and adventures over the years. In the "Homer and Apu" episode (#94), Apu sells Homer meat that has expired for a lower cost, rather than throwing it away. Homer buys the meat, eats it, gets sick, and is rushed to the hospital. Lisa convinces her father to expose Apu and his many health violations to the media. After a successful sting, Apu is fired from Kwik-E-Mart. The only way Apu can get his job back is by going to the corporate headquarters of Kwik-E-Mart in India and meeting with the company's benevolent enlightened president and CEO. Homer joins Apu on his trip to India but manages to foul up Apu's meeting with the enlightened one. Disappointed, Apu returns to Springfield. He saves actor James Woods's life (who was working at the convenience store for an upcoming film role) during a robbery attempt and is awarded his old job back.

Marge Simpson is a homemaker; although, over the years, she

has held a variety of part-time jobs. Her signature distinguishing trademark is her tall blue hair—she uses Blue #56 hair dye. Her hair is so enormous that over the years a wide variety of objects, including a large jar of money, scissors, three puppies, and even Maggie, have, on occasion, been found there. Marge has a vital role in the Simpson family. She must keep this highly dysfunctional group intact. She often grumbles disapprovingly at Homer's antics and schemes. Despite the many challenges that her husband and three children present her with, Marge almost always comes out on top. However, even Marge has had her setbacks (e.g., a gambling addiction and a conviction for misdemeanor shoplifting) and desires to "escape" it all for an adventure from time to time. For example, in the episode "Marge on the Lam" (#87), Marge befriends her divorced neighbor, Ruth Powers. Interestingly, Ruth divorced her husband because all he ever did was eat, sleep, and drink beer. Ruth and Marge, neither of whom are particularly happy with their lives at this point, decide to go out for a night on the town. Homer, who is jealous over his wife bonding with a friend, decides to go out as well. He ends up hitching a ride with Police Chief Wiggum, who later attempts to pull Ruth over for a minor motor vehicle infraction. Admitting to Marge that she has stolen the car from her former husband, Ruth speeds off. Wiggum and a slew of other police cars give chase to Ruth and Marge as they head toward a cliff. This scene and the bonding of Marge and Ruth are a parody of the film *Thelma and Louise*. However, whereas Thelma and Louise wind up driving off a cliff, Marge and Ruth stop just in time. Chief Wiggum and Homer, however, cannot stop on time and sail over the cliff, but land safely on a huge pile of garbage.

As stated earlier, originally the primary character of the *Simpsons* was Bartholomew (Bart) Simpson. The Bart character was inspired by Dennis the Menace from the TV show aptly titled *Dennis the Menace*. Groening recalls watching the 1959 premiere episode of *Dennis the Menace* and being captivated by the idea that there was a menace on TV and that this menace was a kid. Groening states, "I was so excited. It turned out to be this fairly namby-pamby pseudo–bad boy who had a slingshot but didn't ever seem to use it. Bart Simpson is basically what Dennis should have been" (*Playboy* 2007, 145).

Bart Simpson is the eldest child, and only son, of Homer and Marge. For many fans of *The Simpsons*, Bart remains their favorite character. Interestingly, when deciding what name to give their son, Homer insisted that he and Marge choose a name that didn't have any negative rhymes to it. Thus, such names as Louie, Larry, and Luke were passed over because they rhyme with "screwy," "fairy," and "puke" respectively. Apparently, Homer forgot to try rhyming words with Bart! If he had, he'd have realized that Bart could be teased by the word "fart." The name "Bart" was chosen by Groening because it's an anagram for "brat."

Nonetheless, Homer's concern that a "negative" name for his son might cause dire consequences is not without merit. In fact, a study conducted by researchers from the University of California at San Diego indicates that names really will hurt you (McConnaughey 1998). The researchers examined twenty-seven years' worth of California death certificates (over five million people) and found that people with "good" initials (the initials spell out something positive), such as ACE, GOD, HUG, JOY, LIF, WIN, and WOW, live longer (nearly 4.5 years) than people with "bad" initials (the initials spell out something negative), such as, APE, ASS, BAD, BUG, PIG, RAT, ROT, SAD, SIK, and UGH. The researchers suggest that liking your name and liking yourself may be linked to both a positive self-image and better mental and physical health. Conversely, people who are teased all their life because of their names/initials develop a negative sense of self. Death by suicide was nearly thirteen times higher for those with "bad" initials than those with "good" initials. One would imagine that the initials DOH would lead to an early death!

Bart is seldom teased because of his name, but he is certainly a very devious young boy. He regularly pulls pranks and tests the patience of his parents, his sister Lisa, school officials, and law enforcement—both domestic and international. One of Bart's most notable pranks occurred in the 1992 episode "Radio Bart" (#48). In this episode, Bart receives a "Superstar Celebrity" microphone that transmits sounds through an AM radio. Bart tosses a radio down a tight-fitting well. Using the fictitious name Timmy O'Toole, Bart screams out for help. The townspeople rally together in an attempt to save Timmy. Bart's idol, Krusty the Clown, and singer Sting perform a song, "We're Sending Our Love Down the Well" to raise money to save Timmy. Lisa, meanwhile, reminds Bart that he placed a "Property of Bart Simpson" sticker on the radio and that his prank would be revealed once the rescuers found their way to the bottom of the well. Bart attempts to retrieve the radio and ends up stuck in the well for real. He is eventually rescued. This episode was a parody of an October 15, 1987, real-life event involving eighteen-month-old toddler Jessica McClure. Jessica captured the attention of the world when she fell down into a well that was too small for adults to fit into. She was trapped for almost sixty hours. Once she was rescued, she was treated like a "hero." (Note: Scott Shaw captured the moment in a photograph, earning a Pulitzer Prize.) In "Radio Bart" Homer and Lisa discuss what it means to be a hero.

> *Homer*: That Timmy is a real hero!
> *Lisa*: How do you mean, Dad?
> *Homer*: Well, he fell down a well, and (pause) he can't get out.
> *Lisa*: How does that make him a hero?
> *Homer* (not sure how to respond): Well, that's more than you did!

Whether or not Timmy O'Toole or Jessica McClure are heroes for falling down a well and surviving, people enjoy basking in stories that involve children surviving potential tragedy. In "Radio Bart" a street vendor provided onlookers with an opportunity to bask in the heroic saving of Timmy O'Toole by selling T-shirts that read, "I survived Timmy O'Toole's Getting Trapped in a Well."

Bart does not always get into trouble by himself. He has a trusty sidekick in fellow fourth-grader Milhouse Van Houten. Groening admits that the name "Milhouse" was chosen because of former president, Richard Milhous Nixon, whom he viewed as a "cardboard villain." Groening takes a special delight in skewering Republicans. "I have this obsession with Nixon. On *The Simpsons*, Milhouse is named after him. On *Futurama*, we made Nixon's head in the jar president of Earth. George W. Bush seems to me equally cartoony, and we've only barely begun to take him on" (*Playboy* 2007, 60). Of course, as any Republican viewer can attest, *The Simpsons* is just as willing to make fools out of Democrats as it is Republicans; and this is attributable to the fact that some of the writers are rabid Republicans themselves.

Milhouse is often teased at school for being a nerdy type of kid and for wearing glasses. But he is clever enough to have once bought Bart's soul for just five dollars! It is Bart's cleverness, and his use of catchphrases, however, that have endeared him to generations of fans. Among his most famous phrases are:

"Ay, Carumba." (The first words spoken by Bart.)
"Don't have a cow, man!"
"Cowabunga."
"I didn't do it!"
"Eat my shorts!"
"Get bent!"

Lisa Simpson is perhaps the most complicated member of the family. She is highly intelligent and determined to make something of herself, and yet, at times, she is very emotionally insecure and appears to suffer from depression. For example, in the "Family Therapy" episode (#45 of "The Shorts"), the psychologist calls Lisa a "borderline psychotic." In the "Moaning Lisa" episode (#6), Lisa brushes her teeth with Glum toothpaste and refers to herself (in the lyrics to "Lisa's Blues Number") as "the saddest kid in grade number two." Her often sad outlook on life combined with her saxophone-playing ability led Lisa to choose blues artist "Bleeding Gums" Murphy as her musical idol. (It has often been said, "To truly enjoy the blues, one must experience the blues.") In the "Moaning Lisa" episode, Lisa is suffering from an extreme case of the blues. She wakes up depressed and is sad all day long while in school. Her band teacher yells at her in the morning; she does not participate in the food fight during her lunch hour; and she refuses to play dodgeball during gym class. When Lisa's gym teacher asks her why she is not participating in dodgeball, Lisa responds that she is too sad to play dodgeball. In disbelief, the gym teacher states, "Too sad to play dodgeball? That's ridiculous. Now let's see some enthusiasm. Play ball." The class resumes and Lisa gets bombarded by dodgeballs. The principal sends a note home with Lisa for her parents. The note reads: "Lisa refused to play dodgeball because she is sad." Her parents try to bring Lisa out of her funk but to no avail.

Later that night, Lisa hears music off in the distance. She sneaks out of her bedroom window to find the source of this music. She finds a man called Bleeding Gums Murphy playing beautiful, soulful music. Murphy generally plays the saxophone on the streets of Springfield and at the local Jazz Hole club. Lisa tells Murphy why she is so sad by playing a soulful sound of her own. Murphy then teaches Lisa a few notes and the two jam together. Impressed by Lisa's talented saxophone ability, Bleeding Gums tells Lisa, "You know, you play pretty well for someone with no real problems." Lisa replies, "Yeah, but I don't feel any better." Bleeding Gums informs Lisa, "The blues isn't about feeling better. It's about making other people feel worse and making a few bucks while you're at it." The episode concludes with the Simpson family attending a live performance by Bleeding Gums.

Lisa often feels like an outsider in her own family. She is much brighter than the rest of them and often has a hard time identifying with her immediate family members. In the "Mother Simpson" episode (#136), Lisa meets her paternal grandmother for the first time (she was presumed dead) and is relieved to discover that Grandmother Simpson is both intelligent and a social activist. Lisa reasons that intelligence must skip a generation. It is her relationship with her brother, Bart, however, that serves as the primary focus of Lisa's role in the family. Bart and Lisa share a complicated relationship with each other. They do love each other, but as is often the case with siblings, they have difficulty expressing their love to each other. In Lisa's case, she is often the victim of pranks, teases, and jokes played on her by Bart. Often, Bart is more her nemesis than her brother. But Lisa's love for her brother is deep-rooted. In fact, as revealed in the "Lisa's First Word" (#69) episode, the first word Lisa ever spoke was "Bart." Her next words spoken were "Mommy," "David Hasselhoff," and then "Homer" (instead of "Daddy"). In this same episode, Marge recalls Bart's first words as "Ay, Carumba."

The final member of the immediate Simpsons family is Maggie, the pacifier-sucking toddler. Maggie shows signs of being as intelligent as, if not more than, her older sister, Lisa. She can spell out "$E=MC^2$" with her toy blocks and can scribble her entire name, MAGGIE SIMPSON, on her Etch A Sketch. On the other hand, Maggie has also shown, over the years, that she can get into her share of mischief. She was adopted by a family of bears in "The Call of the Simpsons" (#7) after she got lost trying to follow Homer and Bart in the wilderness.

However, it was in the two-part "Who Shot Mr. Burns?" episodes that the spotlight showed brightest on Maggie. Reminiscent of the famous, and highly rated, "Who Shot J. R. Ewing?" episode in the 1980 season cliffhanger of *Dallas*, C. Montgomery Burns was mysteriously shot by an unidentified gunman in the "Who Shot Mr. Burns? (Part 1)" episode (#128). There were numerous suspects, including Groundskeeper Willie, Moe, Grandpa Simpson, Barney, Lisa, Principal Skinner, Homer, and Bart. In part two of the "Who Shot Mr. Burns?" episodes (#129), the suspects were all interrogated. In a hilarious spoof of the film *Basic Instinct*, Groundskeeper Willie, wearing a traditional Scottish kilt, uncrossed his legs in a way similar to Sharon Stone's famous leg-crossing scene. Finally, it was revealed that Maggie had shot Burns. And despite the fact that Mr. Burns had tried to take Maggie's lollipop from her ("Like taking candy from a baby"), the shooting was an accident—Burns's gun fell into Maggie's hands and discharged. Upon learning that Maggie shot Mr. Burns, Marge is relieved that it was not Homer. Trying to defuse a potentially delicate situation, Marge assures Mr. Burns, "If Maggie could talk, I am sure she'd apologize for shooting you." Burns replies, "I'm afraid that's insufficient. Officer, arrest the baby!" Chief Wiggum responds, "Ha. Yeah right, pops. No jury in the world's going to convict a baby. Uhm, maybe Texas."

As with most families, the Simpsons have pets. In particular, they have a dog and a cat. The dog's name is Santa's Little Helper. Santa's Little Helper joined the Simpsons family in the episode, "Simpsons Roasting on an Open Fire" (#1). In this episode, Homer is working as a part-time mall Santa so that he can buy Christmas gifts for his family. Homer is extremely disappointed when he receives his paycheck. After a number of deductions, including one for Santa training and another for costume purchase, his check is a mere $13. His friend Barney, a fellow mall Santa, gives Homer a tip on a dog named Whirlwind. Homer and Bart go to the greyhound racetrack, Springfield Downs. Upon looking at Whirlwind, Homer says that the dog is too scrawny to win. Bart replies, "C'mon Dad, they're all scrawny." Instead of betting on Whirlwind, Homer takes a chance on a long shot named Santa's Little Helper. He reasons that during the holiday season a dog with such a name must surely be a good sign. Much to the chagrin of Homer, Santa's Little Helper finishes in last place. The dog owner is so sick and tired of Santa's Little Helper losing all the time that he chases him away. Santa's Little Helper runs right into the arms of Homer and starts licking his face. At Bart's urging, Homer decides to bring the dog home. He is dejected that he is going home without Christmas presents. However, when Lisa and Marge see that Homer brought home a dog, they assume Santa's Little Helper is the gift.

As it turns out, Santa's Little Helper was one of the best gifts Homer ever gave to the family. Interestingly, this episode, which first aired on December 17, 1989, coincides with the year that Greyhound Rescue, Inc., was founded. Greyhound Rescue is a nonprofit organization with a goal of finding high-quality, loving homes for ex-racing greyhounds and to educate people about the excellent, loving pets that these noble creatures make (Greyhound Rescue 2006). Greyhound race dogs are generally scrawny looking because they are kept thin to run. *The Simpsons* was at the forefront of the movement to save greyhounds. Today, that campaign remains vibrant, especially with the help of Bob Barker, former host of television's long-running *The Price Is Right*. As a strong proponent of animal rights, Barker used his show as a platform. Among the prizes you never saw given away on *The Price Is Right* are fur coats, anything with leather, hunting safaris, and bullfights in Spain. Additionally, once a week, Barker made sure that an animal, sometimes a greyhound, was brought on the show in some sort of setting that came from a shelter. He encouraged viewers to adopt an animal in a shelter near their home. Further, Barker closed each show by urging viewers to "Help control the pet population. Have your pet spayed or neutered." (Note: The beloved Bob Barker retired in May 2007 after fifty years on television.)

The Simpson family also has a cat named Snowball, albeit in a variety of versions. In the episode "Old Yeller-Belly" (#310), Snowball II saves Homer from a burning tree house built by the Amish. In the "Simpsons Roasting on an Open Fire" episode (#1), it was revealed in the Simpson family's holiday greeting card that: "Our little cat Snowball was unexpectedly run over and went to Kitty Heaven. But we bought a new little cat, Snowball II, so I guess life goes on." (See chapter 5 for a further discussion on the Simpson family's pets.)

THE LONGEVITY OF *THE SIMPSONS*

The Simpsons were created by Matt Groening, a comic strip artist best known for the underground cartoon strip *Life in Hell* and not for his portrayal as an elderly, eye-patch-wearing, alcoholic Southerner as he was depicted in "The Simpsons 138th Episode Spectacular" (#138). For thirty years, Groening continued as the sole writer for the weekly *Life in Hell* comic strip that appears in 250 newspapers and magazines. Groening started writing *Life in Hell* when he first moved to Los Angeles from Portland, Oregon, in 1977. The concept behind *Life in Hell* reflected Groening's overall attitude about his early years in Los Angeles after arriving there shortly after graduating from Evergreen State College. Groening also created the Emmy Award–winning cartoon sitcom *Futurama*, which ran for five seasons (1999–2003) and is scheduled to return in 2008. *Futurama* is billed as the funniest show of the thirty-first century.

The Simpson family characters are based on Groening's own family (Dobson 2006). Matt's father, Homer Groening, is a filmmaker and producer of movies and TV shows. Groening notes that his father once told the young Matt, "You can't draw." And now, Groening has made a fortune by drawing cartoons. In an effort to assure his father that the Homer Simpson character was not meant to disrespect him, Matt Groening named his son Homer. Both the Homer Simpson character and Matt's son Homer were born around the same time.

Marge Simpson is named after Matt's mother, Margaret, or Marge, as most people call her. Marge Groening's hair was very tall during the 1960s while Matt was growing up; but it was not blue! Lisa and Maggie are named after two of Matt's sisters. Groening explains that while she was very young, Maggie Groening "did actually walk around in a blue sleep suit, incessantly sucking on a pacifier" (*Playboy* 2007, 58). Matt also has a brother, Mark, and a sister, Patty, whom characters were not named after. Groening admits that the Bart character is a combination of himself and his brother, Mark.

Groening's big break occurred when he was commissioned to produce a number of brief two-minute cartoon skits to break up *The Tracey Ullman Show* in 1987. These episodes are known as "The Shorts." The first "short" ("Good Night") aired on April 19, 1987. There were seven shorts in the first season and a total of forty-eight shorts in all. The last short first aired on May 14, 1989. The original animated characters were very crude compared to the well-known figures that air today. Many of the actors from *The Tracey Ullman Show* provided the original voice-overs for *The Simpsons* characters (they continue to do the voice-overs to this day) (Dobson 2006). *The Simpsons* shorts became very popular. So much so that FOX television decided to convert *The Simpsons* shorts into a full-length program.

On December 17, 1989, the first full-length *Simpsons* episode aired in what is referred to as season 1.

A number of writers have assisted Groening over the years. "The path to becoming a writer on the show runs right through *The Harvard Lampoon*. The bulk of the show's writing staff did time at the renowned humor magazine" (Gonzalez 2007, E-4). Conan O'Brien, for example, is just one of the many writers from the *Harvard Lampoon*. Creating full-length *Simpsons* episodes is very time-consuming. A twenty-two- to twenty-three-minute full-length episode takes about nine months to create, including the animation work completed domestically and in South Korea (Elber 2004). From its humble beginnings, *The Simpsons* is now a global phenomenon and is shown in Europe, Asia, Africa, and elsewhere and watched by over eighty million viewers. As actor Troy McClure proclaims in "The Simpsons 138th Episode Spectacular" (#138), "The Simpsons are America's favorite nonprehistoric cartoon family!" A true testament to the staying power of *The Simpsons* is revealed by the fact that the 2007–2008 season marked the nineteenth season, and more than 420 episodes, for these nonaging characters.

The Simpsons has enjoyed a long stay on television but it certainly has had its detractors and has often served as a lightning rod for controversy. The show is irreverent, cleverly written, and willing to mock or challenge prevailing ideals of family values, religion, and politics, among other topics. Christian organizations in the United States are among the leading critics of *The Simpsons* and have regularly taken offense at the content of the show for its frivolous portrayal of God and Christianity, lack of respect for authority, and creation of bad role models. During a January 1992 National Religious Broadcasters' convention former president George H. W. Bush commented that he would prefer to see the United States as "a lot more like the *Waltons* and a lot less like the *Simpsons*" (Ortved 2007, 94). Cleverly, and quite quickly, *The Simpsons* responded to Bush's criticism. The Simpson family, seated in front of the family television, watched and listened to Bush make his comments and Bart responded, "Hey! We're just like the Waltons. We're praying for an end to the Depression, too." This classic response to outside criticism of the show provides an extraordinary insight as to the popularity of *The Simpsons* and the writers' ability to make immediate responses despite the typically lengthy process of animating an episode.

Such reactionary and unrealistic hopes for a more perfect society (as if people would actually want to live similarly to the Waltons during the Depression) expressed by people like former president George H. W. Bush represent the tip of the iceberg of criticism that *The Simpsons* has endured for two decades. In August 2006, China announced that it had banished *The Simpsons*, *Pokémon*, Mickey Mouse, and other foreign cartoons from television from 5 to 8 PM in an effort to protect China's struggling animation studios. Communist leaders are reportedly frustrated that so many cartoons are foreignmade. Cartoons, after all, like other television programming, present a wonderful opportunity to influence China's 250 million children. Homer Simpson and the gang apparently represent unfair competition in China.

In the Middle East, a censored version of *The Simpsons* is broadcast by the Dubai-based MBC network, an Arabic satellite channel. Homer Simpson is known as Omar Shamshoon. Omar works each day at a nuclear plant owned by millionaire Mahrooey Bey, goes home to a blue-haired wife, Mona, hypersmart daughter, Beesa, and a rambunctious son, Badr. However, Omar does not eat pork products or drink Duff beer. Omar drinks Duff brand juice and instead of hanging out with his friends at a bar, they meet at a local coffee shop. Episodes that are considered too controversial are not viewed, while others are modified with the laid-over dialogue. For example, Ned Flanders, the devout Christian neighbor of Homer Simpson, is simply Omar's annoying neighbor—with no hint of religion. On *The Simpsons*, Mr. Burns has an assistant, Smithers, who has a crush on him. On the Arabic version, Bey and his assistant, Salmawy, have a strictly professional relationship. Although the show is quite popular in places like Egypt, viewers familiar with the original *Simpsons* are disappointed because much of the multilayered dialogue and stinging shots at American society and politics are glossed over or ignored completely.

Despite criticism and dialogue that gets lost in translation in certain foreign markets, *The Simpsons* remains hugely popular. The popularity of *The Simpsons* is a combination of cleverly written satiric humor and the realization that this program is still better than most television shows that have quickly come and gone over the past twenty years. *The Simpsons* characters are among the most recognizable in television history. In fact, many Americans know more about

The Simpsons characters than their five basic freedoms. A 2006 study conducted by the McCormick Tribune Freedom Museum in Chicago found that 22 percent of Americans could name all five Simpson family members, compared to just one in one thousand (.1 percent) people who could name all five First Amendment freedoms. For those readers among the 99.99 percent who do not know the five basic freedoms guaranteed in Amendment I, they are: religion, speech, press, peaceful assembly, and redress of grievances. Interestingly, 20 percent of Americans thought that the Constitution guaranteed them the right to own a pet!

The Simpsons is not only popular with viewers; the show has attracted a huge number of actors and musicians who have eagerly provided "guest" voice-overs for the show. Here is a mere sampling of the long lists of actors and musicians who have appeared on *The Simpsons*: the Rolling Stones, Tom Petty, Elvis Costello, Elizabeth Taylor, Ringo Starr, James Taylor, Bono, Sting, James Woods, Albert Brooks, Dustin Hoffman, Glenn Close, Jon Lovitz, Kelsey Grammer, Phil Hartman, Joe Mantegna, Jackie Mason, Ron Howard, Winona Ryder, Alec Baldwin, Kim Basinger, Kiefer Sutherland, Natalie Portman, and scores of others.

THE ICONIC STATUS OF *THE SIMPSONS*

The Simpsons has amassed a global following. Its massive following is the result of nearly universal characters combined with a massive advertising campaign. Advertisement represents one of the most effective ways to reach a mass audience. Whether it's an individual promoting his latest book or an auto company introducing its newest line of automobiles, good advertising not only provides public awareness, it can also shape public perception. Unique packaging or creating a recognizable brand, or logo, is an important element in advertising a product to the public (Solomon 1998). Brands have been used for thousands of years. Artists branded their names to their art as long ago as 3500 BCE. European guilds, such as master brick makers and bell makers, emblazoned their names to their products to assure that their high-quality work was not compromised by inferior guildsmen who attempted to dupe the public by claiming their work was that of the masters. Silversmiths and cattle owners also branded their work. However, it was not until fairly recently (the mid-1800s) that brands came under federal protection from those who would attempt to infringe on someone else's logo. In the United States, the first brand to come under federal trademark protection was Bass Ale's triangle brand.

Today, logos such as the Nike "swoosh" and the McDonalds "golden arches" are iconic brands in the public world. *The Simpsons* characters are also easily identifiable. Placing an image of *The Simpsons* on nearly any product assures that it will garner interest by the public. Large numbers of *The Simpsons* brand of products (e.g., figurines, board games, apparel, snacks, holiday decorations, and so on) are prominently displayed in a variety of fashions by millions of people around the world. The easily recognizable *Simpsons* image helps to transform this cartoon to iconic status. Further, *The Simpsons* is not only a part of culture, it has helped to shape it.

The Simpsons, for better or worse, has become a symbolic American icon throughout the global community that eagerly consumes US popular culture. Domestically, the twenty years of popularity that *The Simpsons* has enjoyed speaks volumes to its impact on American popular culture.

The Simpsons is certainly entrenched in the world of popular culture. But its relevancy does not end there. As we shall see in the remainder of this book, *The Simpsons* episodes incorporate examples of popular and high culture and seemingly every aspect of our daily social lives. *The Simpsons* reveals a great deal about us because so many of the episodes are intertwined with all the social institutions found in society.

The longevity of *The Simpsons* has led to a generation of fans who first watched the show when they were young and who are now viewing it with their children. First-year college students have never known life without the Simpson family. Here's hoping that the next generation can say the same thing.

Chapter 2

The Culture We Live In

"Would it really be worth living in a world without television? I think the survivors would envy the dead."
—Krusty the Clown

There is a great deal of violence in the world. Ethnocentric thinking and intolerance toward others are among the prevailing factors that lead to global violence. With wars and acts of terrorism commonplace in the twenty-first century it seems hard to believe that the media, in particular television, is blamed as the primary purveyor of violence in society. *The Simpsons* addresses this issue in the "Itchy & Scratchy & Marge" episode (#22). In this episode, Maggie whacks Homer on the head with a mallet. Marge wonders how her infant daughter learned about such violent behavior. She decides to watch the *Itchy & Scratchy* cartoon (to be discussed later in this chapter) with Bart and Lisa. Marge is horrified by the extreme level of senseless violence displayed in the cartoon. She writes a letter of protest to the producers of *Itchy & Scratchy*. Roger Meyers, the chairman of Itchy & Scratchy International, responds to Marge's complaint, "In regards to your specific comments about the show, our research indicates that one person cannot make a difference, no matter how big a screwball she is."

Upset by this response and undaunted from her crusade to impose her sense of morality onto others, Marge organizes a protest outside the studio where the cartoon is produced. Marge carries a sign that states, "I'm protesting because Itchy & Scratchy are indirectly responsible for my husband being hit on the head with a mallet." Forced to join the protest, Homer carries a sign that reads, "Please ban violent cartoons—Next time I might not be so lucky." Marge is invited to appear on an episode of *Smartline*, hosted by newsman Kent Brockman. Joining the panel are Roger Meyers, Krusty the Clown, and leading Vienna psychiatrist Marvin Monroe. Brockman starts the show by saying, "Are cartoons too violent for children? Most people would say, 'No. Of course not. What kind of stupid question is that?' But one woman says, 'Yes'—Marge Simpson." Meyers tells Brockman that he did some research to prepare for his appearance on *Smartline* and discovered that there was violence in the past, long before cartoons were invented. Brockman appears stunned by this "news." Dr. Monroe states that the hijinks of a couple of cartoon characters pale in comparison to the real problems he hears daily from his patients. Impervious, Marge urges listeners to join in on her boycott of companies that advertise on the *Itchy & Scratchy* show.

Marge's protest quickly escalates into a nationwide boycott of *Itchy & Scratchy*. In response to the boycott, the violent cartoon is transformed into a friendly cartoon devoid of humor. The children of Springfield no longer enjoy *Itchy & Scratchy* and start playing outdoors instead. Marge would appear to be vindicated. However, when it is announced that Michelangelo's *David* will appear at the Springfield Museum, many of the same people who joined Marge in boycotting *Itchy & Scratchy* assume she will join them in this protest as well. They are upset that the *David* statue graphically portrays parts of the human body, which, as practical as they may be, are evil nonetheless. Marge refuses to join in on this boycott because she is in favor of displays of art. She then realizes that it is illogical to protest one form of artistic expression while condemning another.

CULTURE

Every society possesses a culture. Culture entails social expectations and ideas that are shared within a society. Culture is the universal, social determinant of behavior. It puts order to our lifestyle and may be viewed as a guide for proper behavior. Thus, culture may be defined as all the shared values, norms, knowledge, behavioral patterns, and artifacts that are passed down from one generation to the next and form a way of life for a society. Culture is a very powerful force in any society. Matt Groening and the other creative geniuses behind *The Simpsons* offer a great deal of social commentary about American culture. They accurately point out that not everyone agrees with the cultural norms and values of society. This is especially true when it comes to such issues as violence in society, the use of firearms, and gun control.

THE SIMPSONS AND VIOLENCE

"Just like in real life."
—Itchy & Scratchy Land Park Attendant

Violence is a prevalent aspect of American culture. It is so commonplace that the expression "bombs bursting in air" is a part of the lyrics for the US national anthem. In "The Bart of War" (#312) episode the American national anthem is referred to as a "hymn to war." In this episode, a riot breaks out at Springfield Stadium during an Isotopes baseball game. The rioting ends when the combatants join together and sing the relatively passive Canadian national anthem. Ten-year-olds Bart and Milhouse, who were on opposite sides during this conflict, reveal that they have already learned about the role of war in their home country.

> *Milhouse*: Well, Bart, we've learned that war is not the answer.
> *Bart*: Except to all of America's problems.
> *Milhouse*: Amen!

Americans typically celebrate their most important national holiday, the Fourth of July, in a potentially violent manner by setting off fireworks—a great deal of which is done illegally. In the episode "Summer of 4 FT. 2" (#153) the Simpsons family is celebrating the Fourth of July at the Flanders' beach house. (Ned allowed the Simpsons to use his beach house because he was called to jury duty.) Homer attempts to purchase some illegal fireworks at the Li'l Valu-Mart convenience store as part of his family's celebration of America's Independence Day. The store employee (presumably foreign-born and very similar looking to Apu) invites Homer to the back room where he sells illegal fireworks. The store clerk tells Homer, "Celebrate the independence of your nation by blowing up a part of it." Homer buys an M-320 (a huge firecracker) and brings it back to the beach house. Disappointed at Bart for not having any matches or a lighter, Homer is forced to light the M-320 on the kitchen stove. The fuse malfunctions and Homer attempts to dispose of the explosive. In a panic, Homer throws the dangerous combustible into the dishwasher, which in turn blows up, resulting in sewage spilling from the appliance. Setting off dangerous fireworks on the Fourth of July is a part of American culture and is reminiscent of some revelers who fire their guns on New Year's Eve. Apparently, these people are ignorant of the fact that bullets fired straight up into the air will quickly fall back to earth at speeds near 90 mph, risking the health of all those nearby. And yet, such acts of violence are usually brushed off as good, harmless fun among the participants.

The *Krusty the Clown Show* is the favorite television show for the children of Springfield. Although Krusty's rudimentary, sophomoric jokes and hijinks are reason enough to watch the show, it is the *Itchy & Scratchy* cartoon shown on *Krusty the Clown Show* that has the greatest appeal to Springfield's youngsters. (The idea of a cartoon within a show mirrors *The Simpsons'* origins on the *Tracey Ullman Show*.) *Itchy & Scratchy* tests the limits of the level of violence allowed to be shown on television. Itchy is an anthropomorphic mouse that continuously mutilates and brutalizes Scratchy, an anthropomorphic cat. On many occasions, the *Itchy & Scratchy* cartoon mirrors the general theme of *The Simpsons* episode itself. For example, when Homer joins NASA and goes off to space in the "Deep Space Homer" (#96) episode, the *Itchy & Scratchy* cartoon gruesomely parodies the films *2001: A Space Odyssey* and *Alien*. Other *Itchy & Scratchy* episodes parody the violence of Quentin Tarantino's films *Reservoir Dogs* and *Pulp Fiction*. Thus, the *Itchy & Scratchy* cartoon reflects the desire of the creators of *The Simpsons* to, among other things, examine the role of the mass media's presentation of violence and its impact on society.

What is mass media? The mass media includes all forms of communication that (generally) permit a one-way flow of information from a single source to a large audience. The mass media is comprised of television, radio, video games, motion pictures, sound recordings, books, newspapers, magazines, and the Internet. The media is such a prevalent aspect of Western society, it is fair to say that we live in a mass-mediated culture—a culture in which the mass media plays a role in both shaping and creating cultural perceptions. The media has been accused of being responsible for a great deal of society's violence. Experts have conducted research for years on a variety of the media's genres in an attempt to prove or disprove a link between societal violence and the media. Proponents of the media will point out that we live in a violent world, one that is filled with war, street violence in most major cities, and disease that kills millions of people every year. The media is not the cause of war, street crime, or disease. It has also been shown that the role media plays vis-à-vis commercial advertising, political advertisements, and public service announcements, has had little effect on people's behavior. In short, most people are not easily swayed by the mass media.

However, some people are influenced by the media, especially young and impressionable individuals. Consider the following sampling of mass media–linked acts of violence and/or research:

- In 1999, a jury found *The Jenny Jones Show* guilty of negligence in the slaying of a gay guest who had admitted to having a crush on another male guest during a televised broadcast of the show. The male guest felt so humiliated he later murdered his intendant (Hyde 1999).
- In 2001, a teenager was charged with the involuntary manslaughter of a nine-year-old who died after the two imitated wrestling moves they had watched on television.
- According to researchers at Columbia University, teenagers and young adults who watch as little as an hour of television a day are more likely than less regular viewers to get into fights, commit assaults, or engage in other types of violence later in life (Vedantam 2002).
- Researchers in Iowa and Texas conducted research on the effects of listening to music with violent lyrics. The results strongly suggest that listening to songs with violent lyrics increases feelings of aggression, at least in the short term (Danton 2003).
- Exposure to violent video games is particularly troublesome. Research conducted over twenty years by psychologists found that, in general, children exposed to virtual bloodshed showed

greater short-term increases in hostility toward peers and authority figures than those exposed to more benign games (O'Connor 2005).

- Kimveer Gill, a twenty-five-year-old man who went on a deadly killing spree at a Montreal college in 2006, had posted pictures of himself on the Internet with a rifle and claimed that he was feeling "crazy." On his blog, Gill stated that he liked to play "Super Columbine Massacre"—an Internet-based computer game that simulates the April 20, 1999, attack by two students who killed thirteen people and then themselves (Couvrette 2006).

Violence has existed throughout time, and certainly long before the mass media was created. To blame the media for all, or even a significant amount, of the violence in the world would be misguided. To suggest that constant exposure to violence desensitizes people to it is not so far-fetched. Further, it seems fair to question the need for ultraviolent forms of entertainment, especially that which is directed at youth.

The Simpsons addresses many aspects of the mass media that are popular in today's culture (to be discussed later in this chapter) and provides examples of the gratuitous violence found in society. Once again, we can look at *Itchy & Scratchy* for examples. Although numerous episodes could be cited to describe the extreme forms of bloody violence portrayed on the *Itchy & Scratchy* cartoons, perhaps the most relevant is the "Itchy & Scratchy Land" (#107) episode. In this episode, Bart and Lisa beg their parents to take them to Itchy & Scratchy Land, advertised as "the violentest place on earth." This motto is the opposite of Disneyland's "The Happiest Place on Earth!" Among the features at Itchy & Scratchy Land are: Torture Land, Explosion Land, Searing Gas Pain Land, and Unnecessary Surgery Land. Marge does not want the kids to go to such a violent place but reluctantly agrees when Lisa points out another attraction called Parents Island that offers dancing, bowling, fashionable shopping, and over a hundred bars and saloons. Marge also insists that her family must agree to stay out of trouble—a promise that will be all but impossible for Bart and Homer to keep. Upon their arrival to the amusement park, Marge is horrified by all the gratuitous violence. She delivers one of her patented murmurs (the annoyed sound made by many Simpsons characters, but especially by Marge and Lisa).

Park Spokesperson: There's no need to murmur, ma'am. Here at Itchy & Scratchy Land, we're just as concerned about violence as you are. That's why we're always careful to show the consequences of deadly mayhem so that we may educate as well as horrify.

Marge: When do you show the consequences? On TV, that mouse pulled out that cat's lungs and played them like a bagpipe. But in the next scene he was breathing comfortably.

Park Spokesperson: Just like in real life.

Marge's worries are realized as both Bart and Homer are arrested in separate incidents for abusing costumed park employees. After posting bail the Simpson family is attacked by defective Itchy and Scratchy robots. Marge mumbles that the family should have gone to the bird sanctuary instead of the Itchy & Scratchy park. The scene briefly shifts to the bird sanctuary, where the birds have attacked the people similar to Alfred Hitchcock's 1963 movie *The Birds*. Meanwhile, back at Itchy & Scratchy Land, the attack of the robots is thwarted when Lisa realizes that flash photography shorts out the robots' circuits.

The Use of Firearms

"Mistakes were made."
—Bart Simpson

A great deal of violence in the United States involves the use of firearms. Possessing a firearm and aiming it at someone represents power. This is true for military personnel, law enforcement officers, hunters, gangbangers, criminals, businesspersons, and homeowners alike. It is very easy to get a gun legally or illegally in the United States. While the homicide rate among older adults has declined steadily for the past two decades, it has soared among young people, especially in large cities' poor neighborhoods, where many teenagers regularly carry guns. That guns are easy to obtain should surprise no one, as the United States is the world's largest supplier of weapons. The United States is not only the leading exporter of small arms, it is also the area in the world that contains the most small arms (286 million in 2006). Civilians represent the largest percentage (59) of small arms owners, followed by government armed forces (38 percent), the police (2.8 percent), and insurgents/other armed groups (0.2 percent).

Of course firearms don't kill people; however, people with firearms increase the likelihood of violent outcomes. A firearm is a source of power because it provides the possessor of a gun with the sense of being in control. Unfortunately, a great deal of violence and a number of deaths are directly attributed to the use of firearms. For example, according to former California state senator Tom Hayden (2004), more than twenty-five thousand young people have been slain in street wars during the past two decades. The Uniform Crime Reports indicate that about half of all murders and a third of all robberies involve a firearm. Handguns are the cause of death for two-thirds of all police killed in the line of duty. On a daily basis, numerous deaths are attributed to handguns. The breakdown includes: 50 accidents/undetermined, 140 suicides, 250 by war, and 560 criminal homicides. In short, about every fourteen minutes someone in the United States dies from a gunshot wound.

In the "Bart, the Mother" (#206) episode, Bart is forced to deal with the consequences of accidentally shooting and killing a bird. This unfortunate accident occurred after Bart disobeyed his mother's orders to not go over to Nelson's house. Earlier that day, the Simpson family took a trip to the Family Fun Center, where game participants cash in their tickets for prizes. Bart approached the arcade prize counter and asked the attendant what he could get for twelve prize tickets.

> *Attendant*: Two thumbtacks and a mustache comb or five rubber bands and an ice cube.
> (Nelson walks over and puts down a roll of tickets that he had stolen from an arcade machine that he pried open.)
> *Nelson*: What can I get for eight thousand tickets?
> *Attendant*: A BB gun or an Easy-Bake oven.
> *Nelson*: Hmm . . . hot food is tempting, but I just can't say "no" to a weapon.
> (The attendant hands the BB gun to Nelson. Bart looks on and is flabbergasted.)
> *Bart*: Whoa! Can I try that sometime?
> *Nelson*: Yeah, sure. It never hurts to have a second set of prints on a gun.

Nelson's comment on the advantage of having a second set of prints on a gun should serve as a warning to others; if someone invites you to grab ahold of their gun, don't do it!

Overhearing Nelson and Bart's conversation, Marge instructs Bart not to play with Nelson. She is still upset over Nelson's earlier comment to her, "Cram it, ma'am," after she scolded him for ramming Milhouse into the wall at the go-kart track. Bart ignores his mother's warning and goes over to Nelson's house. Eventually Nelson allows Bart to shoot the BB gun. He dares Bart to shoot a robin in a tree. Bart does not want to shoot a bird; he would rather shoot cans or other nonliving objects. Nelson taunts him. Feeling the peer pressure, Bart lines up the bird and takes aim. He moves the bird out of the sight line as he does not want to shoot the bird. Unfortunately, the BB gun had a bad "sight" and when Bart fires he instantly kills the robin. Nelson commends Bart on his excellent shooting and his ability to compensate for a bad sight. He calls Bart "Killer," a nickname that saddens Bart. Looking at the dead bird, Nelson asks Bart, "Should we bury it or chuck it into a car full of girls?" Nelson's nonchalant attitude is the opposite of Bart's growing sense of a conscience. He feels terrible because he has killed a defenseless bird. To make matters worse, Bart discovers that the robin was sitting on top of two eggs. Feeling guilty, Bart talks to the two eggs, "Hi, little eggs. I'm not sure how to tell you this, but your—your mom was involved in an incident. Mistakes were made." All too often, comments such as "Mistakes were made" are uttered to numerous family members on a daily basis as the result of an accidental shooting.

Shortly after Bart kills the robin, Marge arrives at Nelson's house and discovers that Bart not only disobeyed her orders not to go to Nelson's house but also killed a defenseless bird. Marge is so angry at Bart that she drives off without him. Marge eventually forgives Bart when she discovers that he has taken care of the two orphaned eggs, nurturing them until they hatched. In a great bit of *Simpsons* irony, the eggs do not contain baby robins, but instead Bolivian tree lizards. The lizards pose a great threat to the environment but Bart loves them anyway; after all, he has become their mother.

Gun Control

"I don't have to be careful, I got a gun."
—Homer Simpson

There exists a great debate in the United States over the availability of firearms to the general public and whether or not harsher restrictions should be placed on the purchase and possession of firearms. Some people believe that possessing a gun makes them safe from being victimized by a violent crime. The National Rifle Association (NRA) and other proponents of the "right to bear arms" cite the US Constitution as justification of citizens' right to bear arms. Amendment II (ratified December 15, 1791) states, "A well-regulated Militia, being necessary to the security of a free State, the right of the people to keep and bear Arms, shall not be infringed." These people focus on the part of the one-sentence amendment that states, "The right of the people to keep and bear arms shall not be infringed." Opponents to gun control believe that this right to bear arms extends beyond the need to protect the state. They are against nearly all forms of gun control and believe that citizens have the right to possess any number of the vast array of manufactured high-powered firearms.

Other people, however, believe that the crime rate will be reduced if the access to firearms is restricted. Gun control advocates cite the "well-regulated Militia" aspect of the Second Amendment. They believe that the right to bear arms should be restricted (e.g., to military, police, security personnel, and a limited number of private citizens) and they are against the private ownership of military-style firearms, otherwise known as assault weapons. Gun control advocates push for such legislation as that which requires that child safety locks be sold with every handgun and that which bans most people from carrying concealed weapons. Gun control advocates strongly believe in enforcing waiting periods before someone can purchase a handgun. They also want mandatory background checks on people who wish to purchase most types of firearms. The Brady Handgun Violence Prevention Act, or the Brady Law, which went into effect in 1994, requires that background checks be conducted on handgun purchasers in most, but not all, states.

Background checks and a five-day waiting period were the subjects of the *Simpsons* episode "The Cartridge Family" (#183). In this episode, Springfield was experiencing a soccer-related riot and the mayor issues a "Mob Rules" proclamation in response. Homer meets with a home security salesman but decides it is much cheaper to purchase a gun. Homer goes to the Bloodbath & Beyond Gunshop and tells the clerk, "I'd like to buy your deadliest gun, please." Homer reaches for a gun but is halted by the clerk.

> *Clerk*: Sorry, the law requires a five-day waiting period. We've
>   got to run a background check.
> *Homer*: Five days? But I'm mad now! (The clerk takes the gun
>   away from Homer.)
> *Homer*: I'd kill you if I had my gun.
> *Clerk*: Yeah, well, you don't.

Despite the fact that the soccer riot has ended, Homer still wants a gun. He waits impatiently for the five-day waiting period to end. Meanwhile, the clerk at Bloodbath & Beyond reads Homer's background report, which reveals his frequent trouble with alcohol, his stay in a mental institution, and the incident in which he beat up former president George H. W. Bush. (Note: All of these incidents were shown in previous televised episodes.) As a result, the report labels Homer as "potentially dangerous" and he is therefore limited to just three handguns! Homer purchases one gun. He returns home and excitedly shows Marge his new gun.

> *Homer*: It's a handgun! Isn't it great? This is the trigger, and
>   this is the thing you point at whatever you want to die.
> *Marge*: Homer, I don't want guns in my house. Don't you
>   remember when Maggie shot Mr. Burns?
> *Homer*: I thought Smithers did it.
> *Lisa*: That would have made a lot more sense (making refer-
>   ence to a previous *Simpsons* episode—see chapter 1).

Marge cites a number of statistics that reveal homes with guns in them are more likely to wind up with a family member being shot than an intruder. Homer explains his "constitutional right" to have a gun. Lisa suggests that the Second Amendment is irrelevant today and that its original intent—the right of a well-regulated militia (the army) to bear arms—is not applicable to Homer's insistence that he has the right to bear arms. Marge insists that her home be free of firearms. Homer wants Marge to attend an NRA meeting with him and she reluctantly agrees. At the NRA meeting, the "gun nuts" as Marge describes them, defend their right to possess guns and even assault weapons. For example, Lenny states, "Assault weapons have gotten a lot'a bad press lately, but they're manufactured for a reason: to take out today's modern superanimals, such as the flying squirrel and the electric eel." Unimpressed by the NRA membership, Marge tells Homer again, no guns in the house. Homer agrees.

But Homer loves his gun. He feels more powerful and secure—"Like God would feel with a gun." Homer brings his gun into the Kwik-E-Mart. Apu thinks he is going to rob the store. At home, Homer acts reckless and the gun is accidentally discharged a few times at the dinner table. Marge takes the kids and leaves. Homer's irresponsible behavior continues. He shoots the lightbulbs out instead of turning off the light switch and when he cannot find the TV remote control he fires his gun at the channel changer on his television. With Marge and the kids out of the house, Homer decides to host an NRA meeting. Much to his chagrin, even the NRA members find Homer's behavior too excessive and careless and they kick him out of the organization.

At the conclusion of this episode, Marge and Homer make up. The gun is removed from the house but not before Marge has a chance to hold onto it for herself and discovers that she likes the way she looks with a gun in her hand.

SPRINGFIELD: SOMEWHERE, USA

The Simpson family resides in Springfield, a city similar to many other cities across the United States in that it offers its citizens opportunities to enjoy both popular and high culture. We are not really sure what state Springfield is located in; in fact, there are running gags throughout the series about this. Matt Groening wants people to spend time and energy trying to figure out what state Springfield can be found in. Truth be told, there are at least seventy-one nonfictional Springfields in thirty-six states. As explained in chapter 1, Groening has always assumed that Springfield is in Oregon.

The Simpsons's Springfield is a "lovable loser" type of city. While Springfield is large enough to have two universities (Springfield University and Springfield A&M University), it is more infamous for being home to a junkyard where a pile of tires has been burning for twenty-five consecutive years, a toxic waste dump, a federal penitentiary, a pesticide factory, a nuclear plant, and it was voted the "least popular" city in America. Springfield is also home to a number of follies, including an ill-advised monorail that derailed shortly after its grand opening; an escalator to nowhere that results in people falling back to earth; a skyscraper made of Popsicle sticks; and a fifty-foot magnifying glass, which, you guessed it, burned the Popsicle stick skyscraper.

The History of Springfield

"A noble spirit embiggens the smallest man."
—Jebediah Springfield

The history of Springfield is revealed in the 1996 episode "Lisa the Iconoclast" (#144). In this episode, the residents of Springfield are preparing for their bicentennial celebration. The children in elementary school are taught the history of their hometown via the film *Young Jebediah Springfield*. Springfield was founded by Jebediah Springfield in 1796. Springfield led a band of religious pioneers from Maryland to the new "promised land," New Sodom. A young Jebediah is shown breaking a buffalo, similar in manner to breaking a horse. Upon his achievement of greatness, Jebediah proclaims, "A noble spirit embiggens the smallest man." Bart, not impressed by the pioneering spirit displayed in the film of Jebediah Springfield and his followers, states, "I hope they show the time where they traded guns to the Indians for corn, and then the Indians shot them and took the corn."

City officials busily prepare for the bicentennial. On the day of the parade, the leading headline of the *Springfield Shopper* is "Parade to Distract Joyless Citizenry." This newspaper article provides a great social commentary on how politicians use distractions such as parades and fairs to draw the citizens' attention away from real problems.

Lisa, meanwhile, is researching the history of Jebediah Springfield at the Springfield Historical Society and discovers some rather damaging evidence against the mythical man. She learns that the buffalo Springfield "broke" was really a tamed animal that he later killed. Furthermore, his name was really Hans Sprungfeld, a merciless pirate. Lisa tries to inform her family that Jebediah Springfield is a fraud, and therefore the whole bicentennial celebration is a farce, but to no avail. She then writes an essay in school and gets in trouble for trying to reveal the truth.

Miss Hoover: Lisa, for your essay, "Jebediah Springfield: Superfraud," F.
Lisa: But it's all true!

Miss Hoover: This is nothing but dead-white-male-bashing from a P.C. thug. It's women like you who keep the rest of us from landing a good husband.

Lisa is simply trying to reveal the facts about a historical character. However, she quickly learns that most people (including bitter, non-feminist husband-seeking women such as Miss Hoover) do not want their ideal images of heroic figures to be shattered by reason and truth.

Homer comes to believe Lisa, because he reasons, Lisa is always right. Eventually the Springfield Historical Society curator, Hollis Hurlbut, realizes that the evidence Lisa has uncovered is too overwhelming to ignore. He concludes the bicentennial celebration is a sham and decides to stop the proceedings. Hurlbut brings Lisa to the podium so that she can reveal the truth about Jebediah Springfield. As she looks at the crowd, it dawns on her how important it is for people to have something to believe in. She ponders what good it will do to shatter the illusion (or delusion) that the people of her community have for their founder. They eagerly await her words. Lisa shouts, "Jebediah was great!" The community members clap and cheer with great excitement. Further, the statue of Jebediah Springfield—with Jebediah's famous quote ("A noble spirit embiggens the smallest man.") engraved at the base—remains a proud memorial to Springfield's idealistic founding.

Lisa had concluded that a sense of community was more important than revealing a truth that would further tarnish the reputation of her hometown. And, as mentioned previously, Springfield's reputation is bad enough. In the "A Star Is Burns" episode (#121), Kent Brockman announces on his *Eye on Springfield* show that Springfield was voted the least popular city in America and it ranked dead last in science. The scene quickly changes to Principal Skinner, who is tied to a post about to be set ablaze and declares, "I'm telling you people the Earth is round."

A town meeting is called to discuss the poor perception of Springfield across the nation. The citizens share ideas on how to create a more positive image. Selma and Patty offer a suggestion: "The easiest way to be popular is to leach off the popularity of others. So we propose changing our name from Springfield to Seinfeld."

Springfield was not renamed, but it has managed to preserve itself nonetheless.

THE SIMPSONS AND POPULAR CULTURE

The term "popular culture" holds different meanings depending on who is defining it. It is a generic, or conceptual, term that can be defined in a variety of ways (sometimes conflicting) depending on the context of use. Popular culture is generally recognized as the vernacular, or people's culture that dominates any society at a given point in time. As the "culture of the people," popular culture is determined by the daily interactions between people and their everyday activities. Styles of dress, the use of slang, greeting rituals, and the foods that people eat are all examples of the various influences on popular culture. Popular culture is also influenced by such social forces as the news media and the many forms of entertainment, such as television, music, film, and video games. Popular culture serves an inclusionary role in society as it unites the masses on ideals of acceptable forms of behavior. Due to its dynamic nature, popular culture continuously changes. That is, what is "popular" today may not be popular tomorrow.

The Simpsons both reflects and shapes popular culture. As described in chapter 1, *The Simpsons* is a pop culture icon. However, *The Simpsons* characters themselves partake in the vast array of activities that comprise popular culture.

Defining Popular Culture

Popular culture is usually defined in such a way as to distinguish it from folk or high culture (to be discussed later in the chapter). Because popular culture is the "people's culture" it has mass appeal. Mass appeal implies a statistical component. Thus, if large numbers of people enjoy playing sports, sports become a part of popular culture. However, this quantitative approach brings up the question, "How many people must like something in order for it to be labeled "popular"? Another concern with the statistical aspect of popular culture is the realization that some items come to dominate popular culture because profit-driven companies produce and sell items of broad appeal in order to maximize their profits. Advertising these items in such a way that leads consumers to conclude that they must possess these items further fuels the popularity of certain products. For example, in the mid-2000s, iPods were advertised as the "latest" in musical listening devices. Members of the popular culture felt compelled to listen to music this way instead of using their old CD players. Eventually new devices will be produced that will make iPods obsolete. The masses will then be influenced to purchase the replacement product. On the other hand, the majority of items produced by companies are not accepted by the masses. Thus, the people are not simply sheep waiting to be led to the next element of popular culture that they are told to accept. For example, in the 1970s people were told that eight-track players were the new and improved way to listen to music. After a great deal of advertising and promotion, the people did not accept eight-tracks and this product quickly died. *The Simpsons* is popular because people like the show, not simply because the program was created, advertised, and promoted.

There is no universally accepted definition of popular culture. For our purposes, popular culture is defined as the items (products) and forms of expression and identity that are frequently encountered or widely accepted, commonly liked or approved, that are characteristic of a particular society at a given time. Popular culture is a vehicle that allows large heterogeneous masses of people to identify collectively with others. Along with forging a sense of identity that binds individuals to the greater society, consuming the various popular items of culture often enhances an individual's level of prestige as well. Further, popular culture, unlike folk or high culture, provides individuals with a chance to impact, modify, or even change the prevailing sentiments and norms of behavior.

There are numerous sources of popular culture. As implied above, a primary source of popular culture is the mass media, especially television, popular music, film, radio, video games, book publications, and the Internet. In addition, advancements in communication systems allow for the transmission of ideas by word of mouth; especially via cell phones. Many television programs, such as *American Idol* and the *Last Comic Standing*, provide viewers with a phone number so that they can vote for a contestant. The combining of sources (television and communications) of popular culture represents a novel way of increasing public interest and further fuels the mass production of certain commodities.

Popular Culture as Exemplified by the *Simpsons* Characters

The Simpsons characters have participated in numerous popular culture activities in Springfield over the years, including attending movie premieres, the circus, a monster truck event, casino nights, a variety of festivals, beauty pageants, rodeos, sports, relaxing at spas, amusement parks, and air shows. For example, in the "Sideshow Bob's Last Gleaming" episode (#137), the residents of Springfield attend an air show at the Springfield air force base. Air shows are a relatively popular entertainment spectacle enjoyed by people around the world. Krusty the Clown's former sidekick, Sideshow Bob, who is in a minimum-security prison for attempting to murder Bart, learns about the forthcoming air show. Mocking the type of people who attend air shows, and considering himself a member of the social elite (people who prefer high culture functions), Sideshow Bob states, "What kind of country-fried rube is still impressed by that [air shows]?" Meanwhile, the Simpson family is reading an article in the newspaper about the air show coming to Springfield and they all (except for Marge) scream with delight. As this episode indicates, activities that appeal to the masses are a part of popular culture and are generally looked down upon by the so-called social elites who prefer high culture.

In the following pages, a sampling of popular culture activities enjoyed by *The Simpsons* characters will be presented. Discussion begins with television, perhaps the most relevant example of popular culture for a discussion on *The Simpsons*.

Television

Television has been a major part of people's lives for generations. Some shows are (or have been) so popular that their lexicon has found its way strongly ingrained into popular culture. Television programs often reflect elements of popular culture and sometimes stimulate the creation of new ones. *The Simpsons* has done both. As we shall see throughout the remainder of this book, *The Simpsons* is relevant to numerous spheres of social life and has managed to carve its own niche in culture. Not only that, but the Simpson family is regularly shown watching television. In fact, each episode begins with the entire family in front of the TV. Homer loves to drink beer and eat snacks while watching a variety of television programming. Bart and Lisa regularly watch the *Krusty the Clown Show* and have a particular fondness for the cartoon *Itchy & Scratchy* shown on the Krusty program. As previously mentioned, the crude *Itchy & Scratchy* cartoons shown on the *Krusty the Clown Show* are reminiscent of the original crude *Simpsons* shorts shown on the *Tracey Ullman Show*. In this case, television is reflecting real life. Even little Maggie loves television. In the "Moaning Lisa" episode (#6), Lisa and Bart argue over which sibling Maggie loves more. Standing at opposite ends of the couch, Lisa and Bart both call to Maggie, who is sitting in the middle of the couch. As if understanding the question, Maggie looks back and forth at her two siblings. She gets off the couch and both Lisa and Bart wait anxiously. Instead of picking either sibling, Maggie heads directly to the television and hugs it.

Well, most of us do not hug our television sets, but a large number of people watch numerous hours of television every day. For example, American children and adolescents spend twenty-one to twenty-eight hours per week, or three to four hours per day, watching television. Some people watch so much television that they resemble Homer Simpson's "couch potato" persona. With the vast array of television programs available on cable or satellite combined with high-density, large-screen viewing capacity, is it any wonder we watch as much television as we do? Television brings us news, weather, sports, and entertainment. It is such a prevalent aspect of contemporary culture that it is difficult to imagine life without it.

However, there are people who believe that television is responsible for the "dumbing down" of society. Critics are especially concerned that children watch too much television and that the couch potato syndrome has contributed to the growing epidemic rate of childhood obesity. While doing time in prison, Sideshow Bob becomes a critic of television. Although he was once a regular on the *Krusty the Clown Show*, Bob has become obsessed by television's harmful effect on society. In the "Sideshow Bob's Last Gleaming" episode (#137), Bob argues that everyone's life would be much richer if TV were done away with. After escaping from prison, Sideshow Bob hijacks the televised broadcast of the Springfield air show. He apologizes for distracting people away from all the "noise and shiny things" that the air show provides, to rant against television. (Bob also notes that he is aware of the irony of appearing on TV in order to criticize it.) The air show spectators express their displeasure with Sideshow

Bob and Homer states, "Go back to Massachusetts, pinko." Sideshow Bob then informs the crowd that he has stolen a nuclear bomb and will detonate it unless all television broadcasts are abolished in Springfield within two hours. Unable to locate Bob, Springfield's city officials meet to discuss his demands of eliminating television. A panicky Krusty the Clown proclaims, "Would it really be worth living in a world without television? I think the survivors would envy the dead." Although there are people who agree with Sideshow Bob's negative perspective on television, the masses who make up popular culture would more likely agree with Krusty—that living in a world without television is not really living. Eventually, Bart and Lisa find Sideshow Bob hiding inside the blimp. The bomb turns out to be a dud and Sideshow Bob is captured. Television is saved!

The Federal Communications Commission (FCC), established by the Communications Act of 1934, is charged with regulating all non-federal radio and television broadcasts. The FCC has one major regulatory weapon, the ability to revoke licenses and levy fines. Broadcast licenses are routinely renewed if the station meets the "public interest, convenience, or necessity." In the "Girly Edition" episode (#199), the FCC is cracking down on Springfield's Channel 6, home of the *Krusty the Clown Show*. The FCC is especially concerned over the *Itchy & Scratchy* cartoon and informs Krusty that kids are not learning anything of value from the cartoon. In order to meet the FCC's educational programming requirement, Channel 6 proposes a newscast for kids by kids. Principal Skinner informs Lisa Simpson that she will be anchorchild of the news program. Lisa is stoked and eager to present quality educational programming. However, she is quickly overshadowed by Bart's charisma. Channel 6 executives quickly realize the potential of Bart to draw an audience and are willing to compromise the integrity of Lisa's ideal broadcast. They want Bart to be Lisa's coanchor. Lisa is not keen on the idea.

> *Lisa*: I don't need a coanchor! I'm a straight-A student!
> *Channel 6 executive*: Lisa, Bart's got something you can't learn in school—Zazz!
> *Lisa*: What is zazz?
> *Channel 6 executive*: Zing, zork, kapowza. Call it want you want, in any language it spells mazuma in the bank!

Bart conducts a number of fluff human interest pieces for the show and becomes a huge success. The educational programming that the FCC demanded and that Channel 6 promised to deliver is quickly compromised. Before long, the kids' news show is replaced by *The Mattel and Mars Bar Quick Energy Chocobot Hour*—providing more ammunition for those who point to television as the primary culprit of the "dumbing down" of America's children.

In the "Homer Simpson, This Is Your Wife" episode (#371), Lenny throws a big party built around his making a "major announcement." His big surprise is revealed as a huge plasma television. Homer is so entranced by the giant lifelike images on the big screen TV, he camps out on Lenny's couch for three days. Lenny finally throws Homer out of his house. When Homer returns home he expresses his disappointment with his home television, "Stupid nonplasma TV. Picture so blurry I might as well rub dirt in my eyes." As the episode progresses, the Simpson family goes to Hollywood. They won third place in a contest that Marge had entered, hoping to win the first place prize of a plasma TV. Instead, they get a tour of FOX studios. While on the tour, Homer learns that a married couple is needed for a wife swap show. A "wife swap" show is an example of the growing number of "reality shows" that are dominating American prime-time television. The participants are awarded a plasma TV. Homer convinces Marge to participate. Lisa does not want her family flaws exposed on national television, but Homer explains they must be on TV so that they can have a new TV. From Homer's perspective this scenario kind of represents the circle of life!

Music

Popular music, whether it is rock, rap, hip-hop, jazz, or country, is a big part of popular culture. Many people consume music on a daily basis. They wake to it when their alarm clock goes off in the morning, play it on their home and car stereos, listen to it on headphones throughout the day, and occasionally attend live performances of musicians at a bar or concert. The lyrics may stimulate some people while offending others. Music can be inspiring, spiritual, liberating, soothing, or depraved, sexist, immoral, and hideous, depending on one's perception. The billions of dollars spent by consumers each year is one of the strongest indicators of its appeal and influence on popular culture.

Music has always been an integral aspect of *The Simpsons*. There have been enough musical episodes to inspire the "All Singing, All Dancing" episode (#189) that features flashbacks from past shows. In this episode, Homer expresses his disdain toward musicals, especially a Clint Eastwood movie that involves singing. Homer states, "Singing is the lowest form of communication." In other episodes, however, Homer gleefully rocks out with such musical icons as the Rolling Stones and Tom Petty. Homer has also promoted the talents of Grand Funk Railroad, among other bands.

In the "Homer's Barbershop Quartet" episode (#82), Bart and Lisa find an album at a swap meet with Homer on the cover. We learn that Homer was once a member of the Be Sharps, a barbershop quartet. Homer, Skinner, Apu, and Chief Wiggum were the original members of the Be Sharps but their manager, Nigel, convinced them to replace Wiggum with Barney, who has a striking tenor voice. The band was a one-hit wonder with its song "Baby on Board." (Note: "Baby on Board" was a reference to the famous car sign first made popular in 1985.) The band won an award at the twenty-ninth annual Grammy Awards for its first album and Homer met George Harrison. This cleverly written episode draws many comparisons to the Beatles. Barney dated a Japanese woman named Kako (similar to Yoko Ono, John Lennon's girlfriend) who allegedly becomes responsible for the band breaking up. Lisa and Bart are amazed to learn that their dad was once such a big star that his band toured and had its own groupies. They wonder what happened.

> *Lisa*: I can't believe you're not still popular.
> *Bart*: What'd you do? Screw things up like the Beatles and say you were bigger than Jesus?
> *Homer*: All the time. It was the title of our second album.

The Be Sharps ran out of ideas and when *US Magazine* rated them "Not Hot," their summer of fame was over. In a classic ending to this episode, the Be Sharps decide to jam together one last time and meet on the rooftop of Moe's bar. The scene is reminiscent of the famous Beatles rooftop performance decades ago. Homer states, "I'd like to thank you on behalf of the group and I hope we passed the audition."

Homer often attempts to pass down his love for music to Bart. In "The Otto Show" episode (#57), Homer takes Bart to his first concert. Marge expresses concern for how loud heavy metal bands like Spinal Tap play.

> *Marge*: My little guy's first rock concert. I hope the Spinal Taps don't play too loud.
> *Homer*: Oh Marge, I went to thousands of heavy metal concerts and it never hurt me.
> (Marge continues to talk but Homer only hears a ringing in his ears.)
> *Homer* (grabbing Bart and heading out the door): I hear ya. Come on, boy.

As someone who attended numerous heavy metal and rock concerts beginning with his youth in the 1970s, I can attest to the fact that prolonged exposure to loud music can have harmful effects on your hearing, such as ringing in the ears. Will someone answer that damn phone!

Bart was so inspired by the Spinal Tap concert, he declares that he wants to be a heavy metal rocker. Marge and Homer purchase Bart a guitar and encourage him to pursue his dream. Unfortunately, Bart cannot master the guitar.

In the "Jazzy & The Pussy Cats" episode (#380), Marge and Homer once again try to encourage Bart to play an instrument. This time it's the drums. Bart plays the drums all day long and even plays the drums in his sleep. Bart and Lisa decide to attend the "Children's Bee-Bop Brunch" at Jazzy Good Times, a suburban jazz club. Bart plays the drums and Lisa plays the sax with other children. As the "true" musician, Lisa is jealous when two professional jazz players ask Lisa to convince Bart to join their trio as their drummer. Bart is such a great drummer that he makes the cover of both local jazz magazines, *Blowin'* and *The Sugar Sheet*. (Lisa is shown on the cover of *Dream Denied* magazine.) Bart hangs out with the professional jazz musicians in his attic and Marge goes to check on them. Bart tells Marge that they are "not smoking reefer"—a stereotype of early jazz players as "potheads."

As the episode continues, Bart is bitten by a tiger named Buttercup. Buttercup is one of the many animals that Lisa has recently provided shelter to. Bart needs an expensive surgery if he ever hopes to play the drums again. Worried that he may never drum again, Bart says, "I was a great drummer and now I'm nothing, just like Phil Collins." Although the jazz musicians host a fund-raiser for Bart and raise the necessary money for his surgery, Bart gives the money to Lisa so that she can fund a shelter for all the unwanted animals she rescued.

As mentioned above, Lisa is the "true" musician of the family. Lisa is a member of the school band and is shown playing the sax at the start of every episode. Unfortunately, Homer does not encourage Lisa to pursue her musical talents as much as he has tried to help cultivate Bart's interest in music. Homer finds Lisa's saxophone music to be mostly sad and depressing.

As mentioned in chapter 1, Lisa befriended Bleeding Gums Murphy, a highly talented saxophone player. In the "Round Springfield" episode (#125), we are reintroduced to Murphy. Lisa is visiting Bart in the hospital because he had to have his appendix removed. She finds Murphy hospitalized as well. The two start to talk and Murphy reminisces over his career. The two jam together in his hospital room. Lisa mentions that she has a jazz recital that evening and Murphy lends her his prized sax. Lisa rocks the house and runs excitedly to tell her hero how well her recital went. When she arrives at the hospital she is told that Murphy has died. She cries. Maggie offers Lisa her pacifier. Homer tries to comfort Lisa but fails miserably. Lisa is sad for days and becomes really depressed when no one shows up for Murphy's funeral. Lisa tries to organize a special musical tribute to Murphy but the local jazz station does not have his only album, *Sax on the Beach*.

Lisa discovers a copy of Bleeding Gums's album at a store but she cannot afford the $500 asking price. (It was $250 but went up in cost after Lisa informs the clerk that Murphy just died.) Bart, who was awarded $500 after eating a jagged metal Krusty-O (in his bowl of cereal), gives Lisa the money so that she can purchase the album. She is very thankful and rushes to the jazz station, KJAZZ. (Note: The sign on the station reads, "KJAZZ, 152 Americans Can't Be Wrong." This sign is a clever jab at the lack of popularity of jazz music in the United States with an implication that there are only 152 Americans who listen to jazz.) KJAZZ has a very weak signal and Lisa is saddened yet again that no one can hear Murphy's music. Suddenly a storm emerges and a bolt of lightning hits the radio station tower, giving it a huge energy burst. Bleeding Gums's music is blasted throughout Springfield. Lisa jams along. The whole town enjoys the soothing sounds. Lisa has successfully honored her hero, Bleeding Gums Murphy.

Providing sounds of comfort and tribute is just one of the reasons so many people love popular forms of music, even if it is, as *The Simpsons* creators point out, jazz.

Film

Although a small city and far away from the film industry capital of Hollywood, California, Springfield residents have enjoyed glimpses of the film world. Movie stars, such as Alec Baldwin, Kim Basinger, and Ron Howard, have, on occasion, resided in Springfield. In the "When You Dish Upon a Star" episode (#208), Homer befriends the aforementioned celebrities. Ron Howard explains Springfield's appeal: "It's the only town in America that'll let me fish with dynamite." Homer first meets Alec and Kim when he crashes through their skylight while parasailing. Alec and Kim ask Homer to promise to keep their residency in the Springfield countryside a secret. Homer agrees. He also volunteers to do their odd jobs, such as grocery shopping, for them. Soon Homer, Alec, and Kim are acting like best friends. Ron Howard shows up and joins the group.

Before long, Homer is aching to tell someone that he is friends with celebrities. He spills the beans, betraying his Hollywood friends. Homer sells their belongings from his Mobile Museum. Justifying his behavior, Homer states, "If celebrities didn't want people pawing through their garbage and saying they're gay, they shouldn't have tried to express themselves creatively." This quote and Homer's behavior reflect how the masses both adore movie stars and yet love to see them brought back down to earth. Hero worship is a funny thing. (Note: The topic of heroes will be discussed further in chapter 12.) However, this episode concludes with a strike against the integrity of Hollywood as Ron Howard promotes a movie idea first pitched to him by Homer as his own, and it is a go.

On another occasion, Hollywood executives choose Springfield as their site to film the latest installment of *Radioactive Man* starring Rainier Wolfcastle. The executives will spend $30 million while in Springfield, providing a huge economic impact on the community.

(The Springfield business community, in turn, raises all their prices to gouge the Hollywood filmmakers.) Further, they have announced that they will hire a local boy to play Fallout Boy (similar to Batman's Robin). Bart, of course, wants the role as Fallout Boy and considers himself a shoo-in for the part. Bart is disappointed when the executives choose Milhouse instead of him. The director tells Bart he is one inch too short. Bart discusses his displeasure with his sister Lisa.

> *Bart*: George Burns was right. Show business is a hideous bitch goddess.
> *Lisa*: Cheer up, Bart. Milhouse is still going to need a true friend, someone to tell him he's great. Someone to rub lotion on him. Someone he can hurl whiskey bottles at when he's feeling low.
> *Bart*: You're right, Lis. I can suck up to him, like the religious suck up to God.

Ironically, Milhouse does not want to be a star. And when Milhouse fails to show up for a scene, Radioactive Man is seriously injured. The entire movie production is shut down and they head back to Hollywood where, as one movie executive proclaims, "People treat each other right."

Video Games

Bart Simpson has a particular fondness for playing video games. The contemporary craze among young people to have the latest and most popular video game is often reflected on *The Simpsons*. In the "Moaning Lisa" episode (#6), Homer plays an ultraviolent boxing video game with Bart in an attempt to bond with him. Bart easily beats his dad and mocks his futility. Homer is so frustrated by losing that he dreams he is the boxing character in the video game and that Bart continues to beat him mercilessly. Later in the episode, Homer goes to the Noiseland Video Arcade to improve his skills. He wants desperately to beat his son and regain his sense of patriarchy. Homer elicits help from a video whiz kid at the arcade. Homer obtains enough useful tips to challenge Bart. In the father-son rematch, Homer comes out strong. Bart is shocked by this turn of events. Just as Homer was about to deliver the "death" blow on Bart's character,

Marge unplugs the television in an attempt to get his attention. Homer is furious and Bart decides to retire undefeated.

In the "Marge Be Not Proud" episode (#139), Bart craves the ultraviolent video game, *Bonestorm*. Bart is influenced by a television advertisement that encourages kids to "Tell your folks: Buy me *Bonestorm* or go to hell!"

> *Bart*: Buy me *Bonestorm* or go to hell!
> *Marge* (yelling): Bart!
> *Homer*: Young man, in this house, we use a little word called, 'please.'
> *Bart*: But it's the coolest game ever!
> *Marge*: I'm sorry, honey, but those games cost up to and including seventy dollars. And they're violent and they distract you from your schoolwork.
> *Bart*: Those are all good points, but the problem is they don't result in my getting the game.

Marge has pointed out two of the primary concerns of parents about children's desire to play video games: the cost and link between playing video games and poorer school grades. But Bart is so headstrong and determined to have this video game that Marge never anticipates just how far he is willing to go to get this latest fad video game. After being pressured by two of his friends, Bart steals the video game but gets caught red-handed. When his parents eventually discover that he was caught stealing, Bart loses his mother's respect. She acts so different that Bart fears he has lost her love. All she wanted was a family photo from the Try-N-Save store that Bart was banned from after being caught stealing. At the conclusion of this episode, Bart comes home with a framed photo of himself for his mother. As always, Marge forgives Bart. Ideally, video games would not be so costly that kids find it necessary to steal them.

HIGH CULTURE

"I've eaten eight different meats. I am a true 'Renaissance Man.'"
—Homer Simpson

A key characteristic of popular culture is its accessibility to the masses. It is, after all, the culture of the people. High culture, on the other hand, is not mass produced or meant for mass consumption. High culture belongs to the socially elite. (Note: This does not mean that social elites do not participate in popular culture or that members of the masses do not participate in high culture.) High culture (e.g., the arts, opera, theater, and intellectual superiority) is associated with the upper socioeconomic classes. Cultural items of high culture often require extensive experience, training, or reflection to be appreciated. The ideology of high culture entails a belief that certain kinds of objects and behaviors are intrinsically better than others. In this manner, people who are exposed to high culture, such as the arts, come to believe that they are enriched for having partaken in such high pursuits. Karl Marx referred to this process as the fetishism of commodities. The fetishism of commodities takes place when people believe that value arises from natural properties of things. Marx borrowed the term "fetishism" from French anthropologist Charles de Brossess. De Brosses used fetishism to describe certain features of animistic religions, where some cultures created attributions of demons or spirits and then found themselves controlled by their very own mental products (Delaney 2004).

High culture items seldom cross over to the domain of popular culture. Consequently, popular culture is generally looked upon as being superficial, especially when compared to the sophistication of high culture. As a result, many people from the masses attempt to "enrich" their lives by participating in high cultural events. The Simpson family, although firmly entrenched in the pop culture world, is periodically introduced to the world of high culture, generally through Marge's insistence. This is quite a challenge for Marge; after all, Homer once claimed to be a "Renaissance Man." Homer made this boast in the "Lisa's Wedding" episode (#122) while the Simpsons attended a Renaissance fair. Homer proudly says to Lisa, "I've eaten eight different meats. I am a true 'Renaissance Man.'" The term "Renaissance Man" is generally reserved for a person who excels in multiple fields but especially the arts and sciences, speaks multiple languages, and has the ability to write poetry. The ability to eat eight different meats at one single occasion seldom qualifies one to claim such a lofty status.

In the "Scenes from the Class Struggle in Springfield" episode (#142), Marge attempts to climb the "social ladder" via clothing style. While shopping at a discount store, Marge discovers a Chanel suit marked down to $90. With Lisa's encouragement, Marge treats herself and purchases the Chanel. Lisa tells Marge that she looks as sophisticated as Mary Hart (of *Entertainment Tonight*). Marge loves the way she looks in her Chanel. She feels like she is a part of high society and wants to show off her classy suit. Marge asks Homer to take her to the symphony or theater. Tired of waiting for Homer to show her off, Marge wears her Chanel while conducting everyday errands. She meets a former classmate and current socialite, Evelyn Peters, while at the Kwik-E-Mart. Evelyn struggles to pump her own gas, so Marge shows her how to do it. Thinking Marge is both sophisticated and practical (a Renaissance Woman?), Evelyn invites Marge and the family to the country club. Evelyn, by all accounts, is one of those "high-class" people who think they are better than others and try to create a world separate from the masses. Country club living represents one of those methods of social class isolation.

On their way to the country club, Marge warns her family to be on their best behavior. She very much wants to fit into "high society." At one point, her family feels so out of place that Homer tells his children, "Uh, c'mon, kids, let's go sit in the car till your Mom's done fitting in." Marge does relatively well fitting in with the women and becomes increasingly comfortable in her new setting. Later that evening, at home, Marge basks in the afterglow of the country club lifestyle. Bart was not comfortable there and Lisa points out that there was clearly a cultural difference between her family and the country club members.

> *Lisa*: The rich are different from you and me.
> *Marge*: Yes, they're better. (Pause) Socially better. And if we can fit in we will be better too.

Lisa is disappointed by her mother's comments. She notices that Marge is being sucked into the high-society world. The family is invited back to the country club. Marge alters her Chanel suit to make it appear new. She is class conscious about her wardrobe and knows this could be a major obstacle in her becoming accepted by the country club crew. At the club, Lisa is shown the stables and allowed to ride a horse. She is very happy. Homer goes golfing with PGA golfer Tom Kite. He is very happy. And Bart manages to stay out of trouble. Aside from a couple snide remarks from one socialite, Marge has "pulled off" wearing her altered Chanel suit. Marge becomes further entranced with the high society. She begins yelling at Lisa for little things. She is ashamed to ride in the family car. Further, needing a new dress for a big night at the country club (where she is expected to be voted into the club), Marge purchases a second Chanel suit at full retail price, $3,300.

As the family drives up the long driveway to the country club, Marge again warns her family to be on their best behavior. She is so ashamed of the family car that she makes Homer park it a long distance away from the valet parking. She would rather walk than be seen in the car. Her family is very unnerved and uncomfortable. Suddenly it dawns on Marge: she is trying to be someone she is not. She misses her old life. They decide not to go to the country club and have dinner at Krusty Burger instead. They feel more comfortable there. Ironically, the viewing audience is shown a sign that congratulates the Simpsons on being accepted into the club!

Opera, Ballet, Plays, and Film Festivals, Oh, My!

Marge may have missed her opportunity to join the Springfield Country Club, but that never stopped her from trying to introduce high culture to her family. Throughout this long-running series, Marge has always tried to augment the cultural horizons of Homer, Bart, Lisa, and Maggie. In the second *Simpsons* episode, "Bart the Genius," Marge purchases opera tickets for the family in an attempt to nurture Bart's brain. Marge clearly has her work cut out for her as Bart is preoccupied with finding the peanut vendor and Homer becomes upset upon learning there are no beer or opera dogs available.

In the "Marge on the Lam" episode (#87), Homer agrees to go to the ballet with Marge. Homer is new to the world of ballet and envisions a circus-type atmosphere where bears wear fezzes and drive around in electric carts. His buddy Lenny shares this same misconception.

> *Carl*: Hey, Homer, you wanna get a beer on the way home?
> *Homer*: I can't. I gotta take my wife to the ballet.
> *Lenny*: Heh. You're gonna go see the bear in the little car, huh?

Homer never makes it to the ballet. Instead, he gets one arm stuck in a soda machine and his other arm stuck in a candy vending machine. (To make matters more embarrassing, when the rescue people show up, they simply tell Homer to let go of the soda and candy bar, respectively, and he is freed!)

In the "Girls Just Want to Have Sums" episode (#375), the Simpson family attends opening night of the Itchy & Scratchy musical, "Stab-A-Lot." The Itchy and Scratchy characters sing and dance. They substitute red streamers for the blood that would be shown on the cartoon and they sing "The Circle of Life" over and over as the chorus. The high-society crowd cheers wildly in approval of this high-class version of an otherwise lowbrow cartoon.

The city of Springfield plays host to a cultural film festival in the "A Star Is Burns" episode (#121). The residents of Springfield are holding the film festival in an attempt to boost the city's negative national image. They solicit Jay Sherman (played by Jon Lovitz), a film critic from New York City, to judge the competition. (Note: Jon Lovitz played Jay Sherman in the 1994–1995 cartoon *The Critic*.) Sherman stays with the Simpsons in their modest home. Homer quickly becomes jealous of Jay and eventually convinces Marge to let him be a judge as well. Although Homer prefers the lowbrow *Man Getting Hit by Football* film, Barney's artistically dark black-and-white film, *Pukahontas*, a documentary about his alcoholism, wins first place. Although the film festival did not change Springfield's national reputation, this brush with high society made the residents proud of their community.

FINAL THOUGHTS: *THE SIMPSONS* AS A USE VALUE

As demonstrated in this chapter, the Simpsons participate in many cultural aspects, both high and popular. The Simpsons, as with most working- and middle-class families, are more comfortable in the world of popular culture than they are in high society. Marge sees the value of high culture and tries desperately to introduce her family to such activities as the opera, ballet, and plays. Homer is reluctant. He is perfectly comfortable watching television, attending ball games, and drinking beer with his buddies.

The Simpsons reminds us that objects and certain forms of expression have no intrinsic value. Instead, value is found in the way things are used. People who enjoy the opera and ballet are not "better" than people who watch football on television while drinking beer with their buddies. The value of all activities is measured by personal enjoyment. For many of us, *The Simpsons* provides enjoyment and therefore possesses a use value.

Chapter 3

Friendship and Community

"My mom won't let me be your friend anymore."
—Milhouse Van Houten

Friendships play an important role in life. Friends help one another during times of crisis and celebrate with one another after triumphs. Friends welcome one another's company and will exhibit loyalty toward one another. Friends are the individuals you can count on the most and, because of this, they are highly valued.

Of all *The Simpsons* characters, Bart and Milhouse are the two best friends. They have shared many joyous adventures with each other. However, even their close friendship has been tested on several occasions. Generally, it is Bart who tests the bounds of Milhouse's loyalty to him. However, in the "Homer Defined" episode (#40), it was Milhouse who tested Bart. In this episode, Bart and Milhouse are sitting together on the school bus on their way to school. They make small talk as usual. However, Bart soon learns that Milhouse had a birthday party over the weekend without inviting him. Bart is bummed. He wonders how his best friend could have a birthday party without him.

Milhouse (explaining his actions): My mom won't let me be your friend anymore. That's why you couldn't come to my party.
Bart: What's she got against me?
Milhouse: She says you're a bad influence.
Bart: Bad influence, my ass! How many times have I told you? Never listen to your mother!

When people become adults, they can pick their own friends. Children can pick their own friends too, but they run the risk of parental intervention when they believe a bad choice in friends has been made. Milhouse's mother has reason to worry about her son hanging around with the devious Bart Simpson. After all, close associations can lead to behavior modeling. She is willing to ruin her son's primary friendship in order to save him in the long run. In the meantime, the boys are devastated that they can no longer hang out together. As we shall learn later in this chapter, Bart and Milhouse are allowed to be best friends again after Marge intervenes on Bart's behalf.

FRIENDSHIP

"When two best friends work together, not even God himself can stop them."
—Homer Simpson

It has often been said that a truly wealthy person is one who has many friends. If this is true, most Americans are poor. Recent research indicates that Americans, on average, have just two close friends. Further, one in four Americans report that they have no one to discuss important matters with. The only other confidants we have are limited to immediate family members. Longer working hours coupled with less socializing are the primary reasons that Americans have such a low number of close friends. There is good news; many Americans (as with other people around the world) stay close to a large number of friends via the Internet. This type of friendship lacks in intimacy but is generally characterized by regular correspondence. The Internet then, as Lisa explained to Bart in the 1999 episode "Thirty Minutes Over Tokyo" (#226), is much more than pornography. And Homer revealed his ignorance when he quipped, "The Internet? Is that thing still around?" It seems that the Internet has become a means by which to maintain friendships, as superficial as it seems to those who maintain close human contact with others.

One's journey through life is enhanced by the quality of friendships one has nurtured over time. Building friendships is a time-consuming process, but the benefits are well worth it. Just imagine not having any quality friendships.

Friends are much more than mere acquaintances. Friends care for one another. They will be sympathetic and empathetic when the situations require such feelings. Because friends mutually understand one another, they are expected to be honest with one another. This honesty does not come at the expense of being critical; rather, it is viewed as constructive suggestions about what might be in the best interest of the other. In short, friends desire the best for one another. As a result, friendships require cooperative and supportive behavior.

Primary Characteristics of Friendship

The root meaning of the English word "friend" is tied to the concept of "love." The Latin word for friend, *amicus*, reflects *amare* (to love) and the Ancient Greek words *philos* and *philein* reflect a kind of affectionate regard toward others. Inherent with the concept of "friendship" are the ideals of mutual respect and affection. Sharing common experiences (activity) is another vital component of friendship. After all, friends are generally drawn to one another based on specific shared interests. They help to motivate and bring out the best in one another. Thus, the primary characteristics of friendship are mutual respect, affection, and shared activity.

Mutual respect refers to the caring aspect that friends have for one another. Friends genuinely care about each other's feelings and are capable of being both sympathetic and empathetic. Mutual respect also entails promoting the virtues of a friend without any ulterior motive. Friends give each other the benefit of the doubt based on the mutual respect that they have for one another. However, when a friend violates this trust, we feel more betrayed than compared to when a stranger harms us.

The mutual respect that friends share further develops into a type of affection for one another. The affective component of friendship reveals the intimate nature of close relationships. The simple fact that long-lasting friendships exist attests to the reality that such participants are actually fond of each other. Friends tell each other intimate details about their personal lives. Sharing personal details about oneself (self-disclosure) is only possible if trust has been established.

Friendships are in-depth relationships that are usually formed based on activity. Activity allows for ritualistic behavior and celebrations. Ritualistic behaviors that are engaged with others create bonding opportunities. Successfully completing valued activities allow for celebrations. Celebrations reaffirm the importance of certain activities and provide participants (friends) an opportunity to express unity. Georg Simmel referred to such events as examples of "sociability." *Sociability* is the association of people for its own sake and for the pleasure of interacting with others. An example would be friends who get together every Friday night at their favorite restaurant, where each of them orders something different and they share their food with one another. Friends such as these delight in each other's company and use food and drink as an activity to bond. Dining with friends is also a way in which friends celebrate significant events, such as a promotion, an engagement, or a favorite sports team's victory.

FRIENDS OF THE SIMPSONS

The Simpsons has provided us with numerous examples of friendship, including Smithers and Mr. Burns (Note: Their relationship will be discussed in chapter 6), Lenny and Carl, Jimbo and Nelson, and any number of other students at Springfield Elementary. Members of the Simpson family have close friendships as well and they will be the focus of this review on friendship.

Homer Simpson

> **"To Ned Flanders, the richest left-hander in town."**
> —Homer Simpson

Homer has twice the number of close friends as the typical American. His close friends include Lenny and Carl, his coworkers and drinking buddies; Barney, a childhood friend and another drinking buddy; and, even though Homer might disagree, Ned Flanders. Time after time, it is Ned who comes through for Homer when he needs help the most. An argument could be made that Moe is a close friend of Homer's; after all, in the "Dumbbell Indemnity" episode (#194), Homer calls Moe his best friend. But after a car insurance scheme backfires and Homer winds up in jail for stealing Moe's car, we are reminded that Moe seems to barely tolerate people. Instead of telling the police that he let Homer borrow his car, Moe lets Homer stay in jail so that he can pursue a woman. Upset with Moe, Homer breaks out of jail and heads for the bar. The two of them fight in the burning bar and they are overcome by smoke fumes. After being rescued by Barney, Moe asks Homer if he will forgive him. Homer's response reflects the true nature of their relationship, "I could never stay mad at you, Moe. After all, you get me drunk."

As established, one of Homer's favorite activities is drinking beer. "Mmm, beer." Beer drinking is the activity that bonds Homer with his close friends Lenny, Carl, and Barney. They regularly go to Moe's. In the "Fear of Flying" episode (#114), Homer affectionately says about Moe's, "This bar is like a tavern to me." Homer has enjoyed many drunken escapades at Moe's over the years. On some occasions he has been the victim of practical jokes and on others he has been the instigator. In this episode, Lenny, Carl, and Barney all pull pranks on Moe; they put an angry python in his cash register and Barney set his alcohol-stained shirt on fire. They all laugh at these "good-natured" pranks. Moe decides it is important for him to have some coffee before he passes out from the snake bites incurred after opening the register. Homer sees this as an opportunity to pull a lame prank on him by loosening the top of the sugar container. When Moe attempts to slowly pour sugar in his coffee, the lid falls off and sugar spills all over the bar counter. Homer laughs, but oddly, Moe and the gang chastise him. Moe asks Lenny, Carl, and Barney whether or not they agree Homer should be banned from the bar. They all agree. Moe tells Homer he is officially banned.

> *Moe* (reaching behind the bar): I am taking your caricature down from Mt. Lushmore. And I'm pulling your favorite song out of the jukebox.
> *Homer*: "It's Raining Men"?
> *Moe*: Yeah, not no more it ain't.

Homer is in shock. How could his friends do this to him? Homer goes home and complains to his family about being banned from Moe's. Marge suggests that he spend more time with his family. Homer replies, "I'm not going to dignify that with an answer." Homer prefers to spend time drinking with his friends at a bar to spending quality time with his family. So, he goes off to find a new waterhole. The first bar that Homer walks into is way too high class for him. The maitre d' immediately approaches Homer and says, "Good evening sir. Would you please leave without a fuss right now?" Homer complies. His next stop is a bar similar to Cheers but he quickly runs out of there when he discovers they are about to sing karaoke. The next bar he goes to is the lesbian She-She Lounge. He exits there quickly when he discovers there is no fire exit.

Homer goes to the last bar in Springfield, The Little Black Box at the airport. Upon entering this pilots-only bar, Homer is confronted by the bartender.

Homer: I'd like a beer, please.
Bartender: Uh, sorry, you gotta be a pilot to drink in here.
Homer: Uh, but I am a pilot.
Bartender: Where's your uniform?
Homer: Uh, I stowed it safely in the overhead compartment.
Bartender: Well, you talk the talk. (He hands Homer a uniform.) Here's a loaner.

Homer's simple desire to get drunk at a bar is dashed when he is mistaken for a real pilot and told by an official from the Crazy Clown Airline that he is needed to fly a plane to Chicago. Overwhelmed by the instrumentation in the cockpit, Homer attempts to fake being a pilot but promptly damages the plane. (He lifts the tires and the plane collapses to the ground.) Fearing public lawsuits, the Crazy Clown Airline covers up Homer's mistake. An airline official bribes Homer with free tickets for his family to fly anywhere, except Hawaii and Alaska—"the freak states."

Although Homer's banning from Moe's is not resolved in this episode, he does return to the bar he loves so much that he calls it a tavern. (Note: No explanation is given to explain the difference between a bar and a tavern.) He also manages to rekindle his friendships with Lenny, Carl, and Barney.

Homer's search for a replacement bar to his usual hangout was difficult. This is because people who drink at a local bar feel more comfortable with the familiar. They like the people, whereas going to a new bar is like going to a new school. You are the outsider trying to fit in. The regulars already have a history that the new person is not a part of. Consequently, people feel more comfortable doing their normal routine with their best friends than they do being surrounded by strangers in unfamiliar situations.

As stated earlier in this chapter, friends have mutual respect for one another. However, as we all know, even best friends can disappoint us. In some cases, best friends become bitter adversaries. Such was the case with Homer and Barney in the "Mr. Plow" episode (#68). In this episode, Homer drives home drunk from a night of drinking at Moe's. He crashes his car into Marge's car parked in the driveway. They are both totaled. Realizing he will need a new car, Homer takes the family to an auto show. While there, Homer is talked into purchasing a high-end snowplow. He envisions helping President George H. W. Bush get rid of protesters at the White House by plowing through them with his new truck.

Homer sets up his snowplowing business under the name of "Mr. Plow." He creates a logo and places it on his jacket and even crafts a nice little jingle: "Call Mr. Plow, that's my name. That name again, is Mr. Plow!" Homer begins to shamelessly promote his business at such places as the Springfield Church.

> *Reverend Lovejoy*: And now, to read from the Epistles of St. Paul, Homer Simpson.
> *Homer*: Dear Lord, in your infinite wisdom, you know the number to call when you need a plow is KLONDIKE 5-3226.
> *Reverend Lovejoy*: Homer, this is really low.
> *Homer*: Not as low as my low, low prices!

Homer advertises legitimately on the local cable television station. He creates a commercial with his family. Initially no one calls but before long, Homer becomes the regular snowplow man throughout Springfield. His plowing prowess allows him to clear a path for the school bus to keep the school open during a huge snowstorm. (Naturally, the kids at school take it out on Bart!) Because he has managed to keep Springfield open for business, Homer receives the key to the city.

At the bar, Moe gives Homer a free beer. Indeed, a rare event. Despondent by all the attention his friend Homer is receiving, Barney wallows in self-pity. Doing what friends are supposed to do, Homer attempts to cheer Barney up. Homer tells his friend to make something of his life just as he has. Inspired by Homer's pep talk, Barney purchases a super plow that makes Homer's look puny. Barney calls himself the "Plow King." He steals customers from Homer after he misses his scheduled rounds. The reason Homer missed his appointments, though, is because Barney shot out his tires. Barney has not only stolen Homer's idea; he is fighting dirty to bury his friend in a snow pile of betrayal.

Homer cannot believe that his best friend, going back to high school days, could stab him in the back after all he has done for him over the years. Homer has a flashback and we discover that Barney was very intelligent and studious in high school until Homer offered him his first beer. Thus, Homer is, at least in part, responsible for turning Barney into a drunk. Perhaps Barney subconsciously blames Homer for this and is seeking revenge. Issues such as these are not addressed in this episode. Homer decides to retaliate against Barney. He pranks Barney to drive up avalanche-prone Widow's Peak. While Barney climbs the peak, Homer steals back his plowing jobs. As one might have suspected, an avalanche buries Barney. In true *Simpsons* fashion, however, the avalanche is caused by Barney's trademark "burps." Homer learns of Barney's plight. Feeling guilty for setting up his friend, Homer drives up the steep peak to rescue Barney. Homer is successful. He suggests that they form a partnership. Barney agrees.

Homer: When two best friends work together, not even God himself can stop them.
God: Oh no? (God then makes the snow melt.)

Despite the "miraculous" disappearance of all the snow, Barney and Homer remain good friends, and are still close today.

Homer would hate to admit it, but next-door neighbor Ned Flanders might be his best friend. Ned has always been there for an ungrateful Homer. He lets Homer borrow his tools, stay at his beach house, and invites him to barbeques and ball games. And yet, Homer still wishes harm upon Flanders. For example, in the "When Flanders Failed" episode (#38), Ned invites the Simpsons over for a barbeque. Ned announces that he is quitting his pharmaceutical job and investing his money into the opening of his own store, the Leftorium. The Leftorium is a store filled with products for left-handed people, for as Ned reasons, one out of nine people are left-handed. (Note: This is an accurate figure, as it is estimated that 11 percent of the population is left-handed.) As a left-hander, Ned realizes how most products are created for the convenience of right-handed people; just try driving a standard automobile, Ned states. He informs his guests that the store will be located inside the Springfield Mall. Homer, who is always jealous of Ned, becomes upset over Ned's announcement and chokes on a piece of food. Ned promptly saves his life. Still, Homer is not impressed with him.

Homer makes a wish on a wishbone that Flanders's "stupid left-handed store" goes out of business. His attitude toward Ned is summed up in this statement: "I don't care if Ned Flanders is the nicest guy in the world. He's a jerk—end of story." Homer's wish comes true. Ned's store is a complete failure. No one buys his merchandise. Ned fears he will go bankrupt and begins selling all his personal items. Homer takes great delight in Ned's suffering; the audience is introduced to the concept of "schadenfreude."

> *Lisa*: Dad, do you know what schadenfreude is?
> *Homer* (being sarcastic): No, I do not know what schaden-
>   freude is. Please tell me, because I'm dying to know.
> *Lisa*: It's a German word for "shameful joy," taking pleasure
>   in the suffering of others.
> *Homer*: Oh, come on, Lisa. I'm just glad to see him fall flat on
>   his butt!

Schadenfreude is an interesting concept. Wishing ill toward friends you are jealous of violates one of the core principles of friendship, mutual respect. The American version of schadenfreude involves laughing at someone's misfortune. Nelson's regular uttering of "Ha-ha" reflects the pleasure he experiences observing other people suffer. For example, in the "Marge's Son Poisoning" episode (#361), Nelson and Milhouse are in Bart's tree house and observe Marge riding a tandem bike by herself. She is desperately looking for someone to share the bicycle built for two. Noticing Marge's misfortune, Nelson taunts Bart by saying, "Ha-ha, she's lonely."

In the "When Flanders Failed" episode Lisa, like Homer, exhibits her own schadenfreude moment. Lisa's sax is taken from her by thugs just when Bart arrives on the scene. Because Bart has claimed to be taking karate lessons, Lisa asks Bart to kick the thugs' butts. Instead, they kick his butt. Upon looking at Bart's misfortune Lisa states, "It's funny how two wrongs sometimes make a right."

Meanwhile, Homer is beginning to feel guilty about wishing for Ned's demise. Ned has lost his house, and his family is living inside the family car. Just before Ned is officially bankrupt, Homer calls all his left-handed friends to tell them about the Leftorium. Homer convinces Ned to open the store one more day and when he arrives at the Leftorium a crowd is waiting for him. His store is saved. With a *It's a Wonderful Life* backdrop, Ned tells Homer that affordable tract housing made them neighbors but, "you made us friends." Homer replies, "To Ned Flanders, the richest left-hander in town."

Homer came through for Ned in a pinch. Even so, he was still not completely swayed enough to consider Ned his friend. Homer talks with his daughter Lisa about this.

> *Homer*: What's the opposite of that "shameful joy" thing of yours?
> *Lisa*: Sour grapes.
> *Homer*: Boy, those Germans have a word for everything.

Friendships are formed based on shared activities that bring joy and happiness. In the "Homer Loves Flanders" episode (#97) Ned bonds with Homer through two of his favorite passions, beer and football. (Who couldn't bond over beer and football?!) In this episode, Homer wants tickets for the sold-out "Pigskin Classic" football game between the longtime rivals Springfield Atoms and Shelbyville Sharks. But alas, he is unsuccessful. Ned Flanders, however, wins two tickets during a radio contest. He offers to take Homer as his guest. In addition, Ned informs Homer that he will pay for all the food and beer as well. What a deal! We should all have friends as good as Ned Flanders.

Because Homer does not really like Ned and does not want to spend time with him, he is reluctant to go to the game with Ned. As they drive through the stadium parking lot, Homer slides down in his seat so that no one will notice him with Flanders. Inside the stadium, Ned purchases Homer a nacho hat consisting of a wearable, edible tortilla-chip sombrero with nacho cheese in the top. Homer is enjoying his free first-row seats, food, and beer. Ned introduces him to Springfield star quarterback, Stan "The Boy" Taylor, after he leads the Atoms to victory. Because Homer is a friend of Ned's, Taylor gives him the game ball. Flanders is good friends with Taylor because he saved him from a life of partying and sleeping with lingerie models. Homer is now proud to call Ned his friend. He wants everyone to know. Homer hangs out at the Flanders' house and Ned's kids call him "Uncle Homer." Homer even takes Ned to Moe's and introduces him as his best friend. Homer becomes so close to Ned that Ned tries to avoid all contact with him. All those years trying to be Homer's friend have now backfired on Ned. He prays to God for the strength to endure Homer's friendship. Finally, he snaps. With a high-power gun in hand, Ned almost starts shooting people. The townspeople turn on Ned, but it is Homer who convinces them to give Flanders one more chance. A grateful Flanders becomes calm again. By the next episode, Ned is back to being Homer's adversary.

Marge Simpson

"Marge, you're the level-headed friend I never had."
—Ruth Powers

Outside of her immediate family, Marge does not have any close friends. She has contact with some of the other mothers at Springfield Elementary and she socializes with her sisters, Patty and Selma, but rarely does she bond with someone that could be described as a close friend. Of course, it is not really Marge's fault she does not have close friends. Whenever she tries to entertain potential friends, Homer finds a way to embarrass her and they go running off. Such was the case in the "Last of the Red Hat Mamas" episode (#363). In this episode, the Simpsons and other townspeople are at Mayor Quimby's home for the annual Easter egg hunt. Mrs. Quimby gives Marge and a group of other women a tour of the mayor's mansion. She invites them to join her for tea in the parlor. Marge eagerly awaits to be a part of high society when suddenly Homer comes crashing through a window and ruins everything. Marge is very upset with him.

> *Marge*: I don't have many friends and when I finally start to make some you ruin it.
> *Homer*: Oh come on honey, you have lots of friends. There's Lisa, the stove—

Homer tries to find a friend for Marge but is unsuccessful. Depressed, Marge wanders the streets of Springfield aimlessly when suddenly she recovers a wind-blown red hat. The hat's owner, Tammy, thanks Marge and invites her to join a women's group called the Cheery Red

Tomatoes. Marge is happy to join this group. She quickly makes friends with them all. They wear red hats, dine, drink alcohol, and make fun of their husbands. Once Marge is accepted as a full member of the group, they inform her of their plan to rob Mr. Burns. She is an integral part of their plan as she is slim enough to slip through a drainpipe that leads into the Burns mansion. Marge wants no part of the heist. The Cheery Red Tomatoes lay a guilt trip on her by saying, "Friends stick together." Other members threaten to shame Marge by taking her red hat away from her. They repeatedly chant, "Bare hair. Bare hair." Marge goes through with the robbery because of the peer pressure and her desire to have friends. The Tomatoes are caught but let go when Burns refuses to press charges. The episode concludes with Marge realizing she cannot be friends with these women.

In another episode, "Marge on the Lam" (#87), Marge finds a friend named Ruth Powers. In this episode, Marge asks Ruth to accompany her to the ballet. Homer is supposed to go with Marge but he is detained—both of his arms are stuck in vending machines. Marge asks Ruth Powers, her divorced, single mom, next-door neighbor to take Homer's place. The two of them have a grand time. Marge seems to really enjoy her "girl time" with Ruth. At 9:30 p.m. Marge is ready to call it a night. Ruth convinces her to go out for a cup of coffee. At the Jittery Joe's Coffee Shop, Marge and Ruth bond. Ruth mentions how her ex-husband is late on child support payments and makes a confession to Marge.

> *Ruth*: I envy you and Homer.
> *Marge*: Thank you. Why?
> *Ruth*: If you ever met my ex-husband, you'd understand. All
>   he ever did was eat, sleep, and drink beer.
> *Marge*: Your point being?

Marge realizes that Ruth is not that different from her, as she would rather be settled down with a reliable husband.

Ruth and Marge decide to go out again the following evening. Homer becomes jealous over Marge's intention to spend time with a single woman on a Saturday night. He thinks there is something wrong with his wife spending time with a single woman, presumably because Ruth will be on the "prowl." Plus, he wants to watch TV with Marge as they normally do on a Saturday night. Marge ignores Homer's protests and goes out with Ruth.

Ruth pulls up in front of the Simpsons' house in a 1966 T-bird. Ruth looks a little "wild" to Marge; she is wearing blue jeans and a leather jacket, smoking a cigarette, and playing a cassette tape with the song "Welcome to the Jungle" by Guns N' Roses. Marge tells Ruth, "You look . . . nice." Marge, on the other hand, is acting more reserved and wearing a dress, something she nearly always does. Wearing a dress was the trademark of traditional housewives from a bygone era in American society. Marge has adopted this fashion. Thus, while Marge craves excitement at one level, she is really an old-fashioned, conservative housewife at heart. The *Simpsons* writers have created quite an enigma with the Marge character.

Ruth and Marge go to a bar called Sh*t Kickers. The lights on the bar sign of the third letter in the first word are blown out. Marge reads the bar sign as Shot Kickers. Marge's interpretation of the bar sign reflects her naiveté as she does not think of the obvious—Shit Kickers—but instead, conjures an image of a more conservative type of bar—Shot Kickers. During the course of the evening the two friends go to several bars, Ruth teaches Marge how to shoot a gun, and they drive to the Springfield sign (similar to the "Hollywood" sign) that overlooks the city. As Ruth and Marge drive away from the scenic site, Chief Wiggum (with Homer in the car) gives chase after Ruth because of a taillight infraction. Instead of pulling over, Ruth speeds off. She admits to Marge that she has repossessed (stolen) her husband's car because he is late on child support payments. Marge asks why she didn't just call the police (to get the child support checks). Ruth responds, "Marge, you're the level-headed friend I never had." As mentioned in chapter 1, the car chase turns into a parody of *Thelma and Louise* with best friends Marge and Ruth being chased by a slew of police cars toward an open chasm.

Although Ruth stops the car in time and no one is hurt, she does not become a regular character. And with that, Marge's short-lived stint of having a close friend concludes.

Bart Simpson

> **"Really? We can be friends again? Did your mother die?"**
> —Bart Simpson

As described in the beginning of this chapter, Bart and Milhouse are best friends. Friendships require loyalty if they are to survive. In the "Homer Defined" episode (#40), Bart feels betrayed when he learns that Milhouse did not invite him to his birthday party. He still feels this way even after he learns that it was Milhouse's mother who banned Bart from the party and not Milhouse's lack of loyalty. Good friends such as Bart and Milhouse want to find a way to forgive each other so that they can continue their close relationship. As demonstrated by this walkie-talkie conversation between Bart and Milhouse, ten-year-old boys do not always express themselves "properly" in their eagerness to resume their friendship.

> *Milhouse*: Milhouse to Bart, do you want to come over and play?
> *Bart*: Really? We can be friends again? Did your mother die?

Milhouse's mother did not die. Instead, Marge intervened and spoke directly with Mrs. Van Houten on Bart's behalf. Marge was successful despite her rough start.

> *Marge*: Look, I know Bart can be a handful, but I also know what he's like inside. He's got a spark. It's not a bad thing. Of course, it makes him do bad things.
> *Mrs. Van Houten*: Well, Marge, the other day, Milhouse told me my meatloaf sucks. He must have gotten that from your little boy because they certainly don't say that on TV!

Bart and Milhouse did indeed resume their friendship and have continued to have numerous adventures with each other.

Everyone prefers to choose their own friends. Kids, however, are often put together by adults who attempt to forge friendships based on their own needs. For example, it is easier for adult friends to spend time with one another if their respective children are also friends. On other occasions, parents may try to match up their child with another child for other reasons. Such is the case in the "This Little Wiggy" episode (#196). Marge feels sorry for Ralph Wiggum, the socially and mentally underdeveloped son of Chief Wiggum, because he has no friends. Marge and Chief Wiggum watch Ralph run around in circles while barking.

Marge: Is that normal?

Chief Wiggum: Yeah, he's just playing "Wiggle Puppy." That's a dog he made up who flies by wagging his tail. I tell ya, that dog has had some amazing adventures.

Observing this, Marge volunteers her son's friendship with Ralph to Chief Wiggum. The chief is very happy about the offer. So is Ralph.

Upon his arrival at Bart's house, Ralph says, "Hi Bart. We're going to be friends." Bart is aghast. He does not want to be friends with the laughingstock boy of Springfield Elementary. Bart utilizes the classic "let's play hide-and-seek" ploy on Ralph by making him hide without seeking to find him. Marge insists that Bart take Ralph outside and play with him. Bart protests because he does not want to be seen with a "doofus."

The boys head off for Ralph's house. Bart imagines that he might be able to get into all sorts of mischief at the chief of police's house. The chief is so pleased to see Ralph happy and playing with a friend that he lets them play with riot gear (helmets and batons). Bart is especially intrigued when he observes the chief leaving his police passkey around the bedpost. This temptation is too much for Bart, so he asks to spend the night. Later that night Bart steals the passkey against Ralph's wishes. However, hoping to keep a friendship with Bart, Ralph goes along with him. The boys sneak out of the house looking for usage for the passkey. At first, they break into a toy store and have the time of their lives playing with all the games and toys. They go to a bakery next and eat an entire wedding cake and funeral brownies.

After enjoying some relatively harmless fun, Bart and Ralph are confronted by four tough boys: Nelson, Jimbo, Dolph, and Kearney. The tough boys start picking on Bart and Ralph until Bart shows them Ralph's passkey. The other boys are impressed. Bart leads the group to an abandoned prison. Ralph is too afraid to go inside. He wants to go home. Buckling under peer pressure from the tough boys, Bart betrays Ralph and decides to join the others. As he explained to his mother earlier in this episode, it is very important to be popular, especially in school. Bart takes the passkey away from a crying Ralph. He has betrayed his friendship to Ralph. Ralph wants the key back and says to Bart, "I thought we were friends." The other boys tease Ralph. Feeling guilty, Bart changes his mind and decides to honor his friendship with Ralph. The other boys grab the key, though, and throw it through a window in the prison. Bart and Ralph enter the prison and retrieve the key. In so doing, Bart reveals that he is capable of being a good friend even when the person in question is not really his friend.

Bart and Ralph do not become close friends. Throughout most of the *Simpsons* series, Bart picks on Ralph. Bart and Milhouse, however, continue to be best friends. Thus friends are chosen, not compelled.

Lisa Simpson

> **"[Doing] stuff sucks."**
> —Erin

Poor Lisa, she often seems to be on the outside, never quite fitting in. As she states on the last day of school in the "Summer of 4 Ft. 2" episode (#153), "I don't get it. Straight A's, perfect attendance, Bathroom Timer . . . I should be the most popular girl in school." Unfortunately for Lisa, her intellect and organizational skills will not be valued until she reaches college. All too often, children Lisa's age value simpler, superficial things. In other words, children are not as impressed with the intellect of others as they are with other social qualities (e.g., the ability to make others laugh, strength, daring, the possession of material goods, and so on) that their peers possess.

In the "Summer of 4 Ft. 2" episode, the Simpsons go to the beach. Marge tells Bart and Lisa that they can each bring one friend. Bart, of course, invites Milhouse, but Lisa doesn't have anyone to ask. While on vacation, Lisa decides to change her persona. She desperately wants to make friends. Lisa wants to be "cool." She practices to herself a new way of talking, "Like, you know, whatever." (Yes, it is true, people once spoke like this!) Lisa changes her clothing style along with her new attitude. Before long, she finds a group of "cool" kids that includes a girl named Erin. She makes small talk with them and begins to fit in. Bart notices this and becomes jealous of Lisa. Bart has always been the popular one and he is not prepared to be outdone by his younger sister. Bart performs a number of skateboarding stunts in front of the group, hoping to gain their admiration. Instead, they think he is trying too hard.

The cool kids are not really into doing much of anything. Sensing this, Lisa tells Erin that she likes to "hang out."

Erin: Oh, you like hangin' out, too?

Lisa: Well, it beats doin' stuff.

Erin: Yeah. Stuff sucks.

Knowing that the cool kids don't really want to do anything, Lisa decides to take them down to the beach and teach them about nature. When they become overwhelmed by her level of intelligence, they are turned off. In an effort to hide how smart she is, Lisa tells the group she learned all this stuff watching *Baywatch*. They find this explanation very reassuring as *Baywatch*, although relatively entertaining, is not noted for its intellectual content. *Baywatch* also happens to be Erin's favorite show. Lisa has a new friend!

Meanwhile, Bart is still upset that Lisa has a bunch of new friends and he's "stuck" hanging out with just Milhouse. Marge, Bart, and Milhouse observe Lisa and her friends from the front porch of their beach house.

Marge: Let Lisa be alone with her new friends.

Bart: They're my friends rightfully. She only got them by copying me.

Lisa (overhearing Bart): Don't have a cow, man! (Lisa's friends all laugh.)

Bart: See? That's my expression!

Marge: Oh, you haven't said that in four years. Let Lisa have it.

Bart: It's the principle! She's got to learn!

Marge: No! Now park your keister, meester!

Lisa: Ay Carumba! (Lisa's friends laugh again.)

Bart cannot leave it alone. He betrays his sister by informing her new friends that she is really a brainiac. He even shows them a copy of her yearbook, *Retrospecticus*, revealing the "real" Lisa as, among other things, the editor of the yearbook and teacher's pet. Lisa is devastated when she learns what Bart did. She tells Bart that he ruined her life. They fight all day long and with bumper cars at the carnival later that evening. However, when the Simpsons return to the beach house they discover that Lisa's friends have made her a tribute by gluing seashells that spell out "Lisa Rules" on Homer's car. Lisa is pleasantly surprised that the kids still want to be her friends. As

Dean, one of her new friends, explains, "You taught us about cool things like nature and why we shouldn't drink sea water." On their way home the next day, Bart offers Lisa a huge surprise in the family car. He got all of Lisa's friends to sign her yearbook. The outpouring of friendship shown by Lisa's new friends and Bart's sensitivity make Lisa indescribably happy.

BUILDING A COMMUNITY

"Bart, you have roots in this town. You ought to show respect for it."
—Marge Simpson

Close friendships allow for group formations which, in turn, allow for development and a sense of community. Most people are proud of their community no matter how humble it may be. This is easily understood when one realizes that any given community is made up of a number of groups, and groups consist of community members. Thus, if people disrespect their own community they are, in essence, disrespecting themselves. People show pride in their community by joining various groups. The residents of Springfield belong to many groups and exhibit pride in their community despite its many shortcomings.

Group Membership

"Oh, no. I joined the Junior Campers!"
—Bart Simpson

Most species gather in groups. Geese fly in flocks, fish swim in schools, wild dogs and hyenas run in packs, and chimpanzees live in societies made up of groups of affiliated cliques. People also form groups and have done so throughout history. Since the dawn of humanity, individuals have formed groups for safety and basic survival. In contemporary society, social interaction continues to play an important role in an individual's life. Individuals want to feel as though they are a part of a group, community, or the general society and want to experience a sense of unity with their fellows.

Although most people understand what is meant by the term

"social group," it might be worthwhile to define it. A social group consists of two or more people who interact regularly and in a manner that is defined by some common purpose, contains a set of norms and expectations, and possesses a structure of statuses and roles. Displaying loyalty to the group is a fundamental requirement of membership. There are two basic requirements that must be met for a number of persons to qualify as a group. First, they must interact with one another in an organized manner. Second, they identify themselves as group members because of shared common traits, views, circumstances, or goals.

High schools and colleges afford young people plenty of opportunities to join a group. Students can join organized or intramural athletic teams, ethnic clubs, the arts, the band, and the theater, to mention a few. Administrators make all these groups available to students for two primary reasons. The first reason is so that individuals have a chance to join other like-minded people and participate in activities that allow for bonding. Second, group membership allows for community building. Adults who are out of school must find their own groups to join. People who remain in the community they were raised in already know about all the wonderful group associations available to them to join. People who move to a new community and wish to blend in will quickly learn of the numerous community associations available to them. Considering every community has nearly the same associations (e.g., church groups, sports booster teams, political parties, veterans organizations, youth groups, volunteer organizations, and so on) available for people to join, finding a group to be a part of is quite easy.

Springfield provides many of the typical group associations found in most communities for its residents to join. Two such examples, one for youth, and one for adults, are discussed below.

In the "Boy-Scoutz N' the Hood" episode (#89), Bart and Milhouse find twenty dollars and spend it on two "Super-Squishees" at the Kwik-E-Mart despite Apu's warning that they are made entirely of syrup. Bart and Milhouse experience an extreme sugar rush. During his sugar-induced state of mind Bart stumbles upon a Junior Campers meeting and inadvertently joins them. He learns of his "drunken" mistake the next morning.

Lisa: Tsk, tsk. The remorse of the sugar junkie.
Bart: I don't remember anything.
Lisa: Really? Not even this? (Lisa pulls back his bed covers to

reveal that Bart is wearing the khaki uniform of the Junior Campers.)

Bart: Oh, no. I joined the Junior Campers!

Lisa: The few, the proud, the geeky.

Bart shares Lisa's impression of the Junior Campers as geeky and devises a scheme to get out of it. At the breakfast table Bart states, "Okay, look, I made a terrible mistake. I wandered into a Junior Camper recruitment center. But what's done is done. I've made my bed and now I've got to weasel out of it." Marge offers encouragement and points out that the campers are not "uncool" and that they do neat things like participate in sing-alongs and flag ceremonies.

The Junior Campers are based on the Boy Scouts. Most communities have a club similar to, if not the actual, Boy Scouts of America and the Girl Scouts of the USA. According to the Boy Scouts of America's homepage, the scouts were incorporated to provide a program that offers effective character, citizenship, and personal fitness training for youth. Scout leaders oversee the development of scouts. They organize a number of activities, but place a special emphasis on physical fitness and nature outings.

Intent on quitting, Bart arrives at a Junior Campers meeting. (The sign on the door for the Junior Campers states, "Not affiliated with the Boy Scouts of America.") He finds Ned Flanders (dressed as a Junior Camper) is the camp leader. Ned tells Bart he has arrived just in time to partake in the "Sponge-Bath the Old Folks Day." Bart views Jasper, grandpa Abe Simpson's buddy at the retirement home, in the tub and is frightened by the very idea of bathing him. Jasper tells Bart, "Help yourself, but stay above the equator!"

Bart's impression of the Junior Campers changes when he learns that he can carry a pocketknife (if he passes his safety training) and he is excused from taking a test to attend a meeting. He is given an instructor's safety manual for pocketknives titled, "The Ten Do's and Five Hundred Don'ts of Knife Safety." Bart decides to remain a camper. He is actually looking forward to the group activities. When he returns home wearing his uniform, Homer insults him.

Homer: How was jerk practice, boy? Did they teach you how to sing to trees? And make crappy furniture out of useless wooden logs? Huh?

Bart: Actually, we were just planning the father-son rafting
    trip.

As with the Boy Scouts, the Junior Campers have a hierarchical structure with built-in roles and statuses. The first advancement rank for
the Boy Scouts is "Tenderfoot." Bart will reach the Junior Campers'
first rank of "Pussy Willow" when he earns his knife badge. Bart has
a goal to reach and he is determined to accomplish it. The Junior
Campers taught him this. He has also established a sense of loyalty
and commitment to the group, another important feature of group
membership. Loyalty, commitment, and bonding among group
members lead to group cohesiveness. Cohesiveness is the liking, the
sense of belonging, and the bond that creates the sense of being an
integrated unit. Group cohesion, sometimes referred to as group solidarity, is the extent to which the influences on members to remain
in the group are greater than the influences on members to leave the
group. Bart is ignoring the social forces (for example, the teasing
from Homer and the tough kids at school) to quit the Junior
Campers and is concentrating on those forces that lead to cohesiveness within the group.

The father-son rafting trip is something that Bart really wants to
partake in, but he is worried that Homer will embarrass him. Bart
hopes that his father will say "no" to joining him on the rafting trip,
but Homer agrees to go with Bart. Homer and Bart are teamed with
Ned and another boy (not one of Ned's sons). Disaster occurs when
Homer loses the map and they paddle the wrong way, eventually
drifting to sea. In the end, Homer helps to secure their rescue and
Bart is proud of him. All the while, Bart learns the valuable lesson of
participating in a group.

Adults have a number of associations they can join. Some of
them are "secret" organizations. These organizations help create a
strong bond among group members but are not always designed for
the better good of the community. In the "Homer the Great" episode
(#115), Homer discovers that his friends Lenny and Carl belong to a
secret organization called the Stonecutters. (Note: The Stonecutters
are based on the Masons.) Many other members of the Springfield
community also belong to the Stonecutters, including Moe, Chief
Wiggum, Krusty, and Mr. Burns. Homer really wants to be a part of
this group too but he is shut out. Complaining to Marge, Homer

states, "Why don't those stupid idiots let me in their crappy club for jerks?" Homer also recounts a trauma he had in childhood. He wanted to join a group then but they refused his admittance. They even called the club the No Homers Club.

After learning that his father, Abe, is a member of the Stonecutters, Homer informs the secret organization that he has legacy rights. Homer passes the initiation and is greeted by "Number One," the highest-ranking member of this hierarchical organization, "You have joined the sacred order of the Stonecutters, who since the ancient times have split the rocks of ignorance that obscure the light of knowledge and truth. Now let's all get drunk and play Ping-Pong!" While group members are in session, the Stonecutters' hierarchy supersedes that of the outside world. Everyone is identified in rank by number. The lower the number, the higher the rank. For example, Lenny is "12," Carl is "14," and Mr. Burns is "29." As such, both Lenny and Carl can boss Mr. Burns around during club meetings. Membership does have its privileges! (Although, as "908," Homer enjoys fewer privileges than most members.)

As usual, Homer manages to mess things up. He uses a sacred parchment as a table napkin and is stripped (literally) of his membership. As a naked Homer departs, a unique birthmark is revealed that identifies him as the "Chosen One." Homer is now treated like royalty. He is told many secrets including dialing "9-1-2" instead of "9-1-1" during emergencies because "9-1-2" is the real emergency response phone number. He learns of a special road to take to work that is only available to Stonecutter members. Surprisingly, Homer becomes a little tired of all the attention he receives as the Chosen One. Lisa suggests that he use his power with the Stonecutters to help the greater community. He agrees with Lisa and attempts to implement his power for the greater good. At a Stonecutters meeting, Homer greets his "brothers."

> *Homer*: Brothers, I've learned a wonderful lesson. Helping others makes our own lives better, and makes us better people. So instead of just shooting pool and drinking beer, let us Stonecutters use what we have to help the less fortunate.
> (The reaction of the Stonecutters is a stunned puzzlement.)
> *Moe*: He's gone mad with power. Like that Albert Schweitzer guy.

The Stonecutters are so against Homer's idea to use the organization to help all the members of the community that they attempt to vote him out of the group. However, because their own charter recognizes Homer as the Chosen One, they are powerless to do so. Instead, they vote to disband the group and form a new group called the Ancient Mystic Society of No Homers. The decree passes and the group resumes its old tactics, only under a different name. The Stonecutters formed their own community but shunned their obligation to the greater Springfield community. *The Simpsons's* writers are offering us a social commentary regarding the greed of the elite in that the social elite are more concerned with their own needs being fulfilled than they are with the needs of the greater community being met.

Community Formation

Group membership provides opportunity for, and a sense of, community. Community, which has taken many structural forms in the past, may best be defined as a network of social relations marked by mutuality and emotional bonds (Bender 1991). A community implies shared interests and associations among people. A community is the fusion of feeling and thought, of tradition and commitment, of membership, psychological strength, and historically and symbolically regarded as family (Nisbet 1969). When people have formed a bond with the community, it is much more difficult for them to deviate from the established norms. With that in mind, parents typically attempt to instill a sense of community within their children. Such is the case in the "Lemon of Troy" episode (#127).

In this episode, Bart notices a "Wet Cement" sign over an area of a sidewalk. Unable to stop himself, Bart writes his name in the fresh cement as a means of immortalizing himself. Marge witnesses this act of deviance and yells at him, "You graffito-tagged public property." She tells Bart that he should have pride and respect for Springfield because it represents his roots. She asks Bart, what would Jebediah Springfield think? Marge reiterates, "Bart, you have roots in this town. You ought to show respect for it. This town is a part of us all, a part of us all, a part of us all. Sorry to repeat myself, but it'll help you remember." Marge's voice does resonate in Bart's mind. He will soon take to heart his mother's heartfelt words.

Springfield is home to a famous lemon tree. It is located near the border of Springfield and Shelbyville. All the Springfield kids make lemonade from the fresh lemons provided by this landmark tree. Bart and Milhouse make small talk underneath the tree. Bart mentions that Springfield is not so bad; it has good friends and a lemon tree. Suddenly, a bunch of kids from Shelbyville taunt Bart and Milhouse. They put down Springfield. Later, the kids from Springfield discover that the lemon tree has been stolen. The tracks lead to Shelbyville. Bart insists that they get the tree back. Bart says to his friends, "That lemon tree's a part of our town, and as kids, the backbone of our economy. We'll get it back, or choke their rivers with our dead!" Bart and his crew go to Shelbyville to retrieve the very symbol of Springfield, the lemon tree. He has clearly taken to heart his mother's speech about having pride in his hometown. The lemon tree itself is not that special, but it *does* belong to Springfield. The children recognize that the tree, therefore, belongs in Springfield and not in Shelbyville. For Bart and his friends it is a matter of community pride to retrieve something that belongs to them.

Marge realizes that Bart is missing. Other parents realize their children are missing as well. Concerned for their safety, Homer rallies up the Springfield parents to venture into Shelbyville to rescue their kids (and the tree). They use Ned Flanders's RV as a rescue vehicle. Once in Shelbyville they ask for help from the local townspeople. The Shelbyville parents mock the Springfield parents for having a discipline problem with their kids. One Shelbyville parent yells out, "That's why we beat you in football nearly half of the time."

The Springfield parents eventually find their kids. They also discover that the lemon tree is in the impound lot. Homer confronts the owner of the impound lot and demands the safe return of the tree. Homer states, "That tree's been in Springfield since the time of our forefathers. Give it back, or we'll bust in there and take it." The owner mocks Homer, telling him that he'll never be able to break in there and steal the tree back. The Springfield contingent devises a clever plan modeled after the Trojan horse lore. They allow their rescue RV to be impounded by parking illegally at the Shelbyville Hospital. The Springfield citizens are tucked away inside the RV. Once inside the impound lot, they reclaim the lemon tree and drive off. Homer and Bart yell out at the Shelbyville people, "Eat my shorts!" Ned joins in and says, "Yes, eat all of our shirts!"

The affective component of a sense of community had consumed the good folks of Springfield. They saved their kids, the lemon tree, and the reputation of Springfield. As Bart learns, Springfield is not so bad after all.

Chapter 4

Love and Marriage

"Our marriage is like soft serve ice cream and trust is the hard chocolate shell that keeps it from melting onto our carpet."
—Homer Simpson

Marge and Homer Simpson are members of a minority group. Not because of their race or religion but because they are married. Recent research indicates that married couples are now the minority in the United States. In 2005, just 49.7 percent of the nation's households were made up of married couples. There exists a great disparity in marriage rates from one geographic place to another. For example, in Utah County, Utah, 69 percent of households were made up of married couples, compared to just 26 percent in Manhattan County (New York City). The low rate of married couples in Manhattan is not surprising considering this urban metropolis had the nation's highest percentage of single-person households of any county in the United States in 2005.

There are numerous reasons for America's low national rate of married households, including people putting off marriage until an older age, a growing number of couples who cohabitate before marriage, and an increasing number of people who are remaining single. Data from the US Census Bureau indicates that the age at which someone typically marries for the first time rose from 20.8 for women and 23.2 for men in 1970 to 25.4 and 27.2, respectively, in 2005. Cohabitation—unmarried couples who live together—has been on the rise since the 1970s. Some people think of cohabitation as a "trial marriage" while others just prefer this lifestyle choice. Census data reveals that there were 5.2 million unmarried opposite-sex couples living together in 2005. This figure represents a little more than 5 percent of US households. (Note: The census also estimates that there were 413,000 households with unmarried male couples and 363,000 unmarried female couples in 2005.) Interestingly, all three major networks (ABC, CBS, and NBC) passed on the 1977 midseason replacement television show *Three's Company* because of the taboo against unmarried men and women living together. ABC eventually agreed to air the show. Sponsors were boycotted, but the show was a huge success and still airs in syndication today. Compared to most contemporary television shows, *Three's Company* is a very tame show. Despite the expected norm that adults will eventually marry, there is a growing societal acceptance for remaining single. Nearly 10 percent of all US households (accounting for more than 27 million Americans) consist of an adult living alone.

With the odds against them, how is it that Marge and Homer came to be married? Well, they did it the old-fashioned American way. They met while they were in high school, a courtship (dating) followed, they fell romantically in love with each other, and then they married. And, despite the occasional argument, Marge and Homer Simpson have managed to remain successfully married all these years.

LOVE: "I CHOO-CHOO-CHOOSE YOU."

Love is a cherished emotion among humans. Love involves feelings of affection, or attraction, to another person(s). Love may be romantic (to be discussed later in this chapter) or platonic. In either case, love is an expression of positive sentiment that involves deeply caring about another. Love is a stronger version of "like" and is contrasted with "hate." Love may be expressed at any time, but, on certain occasions, it may be expected. Special days such as weddings, anniversaries, and Valentine's Day are characterized by certain expectations of expressions of love.

Valentine's Day

"Everybody's getting some but me!"
—Homer Simpson

Valentine's Day is *the* day associated with love. Every February four-
teenth candy, flowers, gifts, and other signs of affection are
exchanged between people in love. And, as Homer sees it, this is a
day where he can assume love and affection from his wife. Homer's
expectations regarding Valentine's Day are articulated in the "C. E.
D'oh!" episode (#306). In this episode, Homer is anxious to make
love with his wife on this very special day of love. In his haste to do
so, Homer attempts to distract the kids.

> *Homer*: So kids, it's Valentine's Day, and you know what that
>   means! You get to stay downstairs watching TV with the
>   sound turned way up!
> *Lisa*: What about you and Mom?
> *Homer*: Oh, well, we'll be upstairs in the bedroom, making
>   love . . . ly rope ladders, in case there's a fire.

Homer prepares a nice hot bath for Marge and pours champagne for
her to enjoy. He lays out flower petals across the bedroom and sprays
cologne in the air. Despite all of Homer's romantic overtures and
expectations, his hopes for love are threatened when Marge reveals
she is too tired to make love.

> *Homer* (using a sexy voice): Hey there, Little Red Riding Hood!
>   I ate your granny, and now I'm in the mood for love.
> *Marge* (who is very sleepy): Oh, Homie. I'm sorry. You know I
>   usually bring my A-game to the bedroom, but tonight I
>   just can't throw the heat.
> *Homer*: But it's St. Valentine's Day! God wants us to do it!
> *Marge* (kisses Homer): You're so cute when you're begging for sex.

Despite Homer's attempt to instill a religious component and obligation on Marge's part to make love on St. Valentine's Day, she falls
asleep anyway. This leaves a very blue Homer on his own. He walks
aimlessly around Springfield and notices couples everywhere cele-

brating Valentine's Day. Homer assesses his situation and proclaims, "Shot down on Valentine's Day! That's supposed to be a gimme. Everybody's getting some but me!"

Homer reminds us of at least two important points. First, there is no such thing as a "gimme"! Second, Valentine's Day does have roots with religion. Containing vestiges from both Christian and Roman origins, this day of love honors St. Valentine. But who was St. Valentine? The Catholic Church recognizes at least three different saints named Valentine or Valentinus, all of whom were martyred. One tale purports that Valentine was a priest in third-century Rome. The ruler at this time was Emperor Claudius II, who had decided that single men make better soldiers than married men. In an effort to increase the ranks of his army, Claudius II ("Claudius the Cruel") outlawed marriage for young men. Valentine believed that this decree was unfair and performed secret marriages for young lovers. Valentine's actions were reported to Claudius, who ordered the priest's death.

A popular version of the St. Valentine legend involves the origin of the first "Valentine's Day" card. This story entails Valentine being imprisoned. While in jail, Valentine fell in love with the jailor's young daughter, who visited him regularly. Just prior to his execution, Valentine wrote a letter to the girl and signed it, "From your Valentine." Thus Grandpa Simpson, although voicing a popular anti-Valentine's Day and anti-mass-marketed holiday sentiment, is wrong when he claims in the "I Love Lisa" episode (#74) that Valentine's Day is a Hallmark holiday to sell greeting cards. After all, while it may be true that greeting card companies may exploit this popular version of St. Valentine's Day, the origin of giving someone a card as a sign of affection far precedes the development of greeting card companies! Nonetheless, exchanging Valentine's Day cards is now an expectation among lovers.

First Crushes and the Agony of Defeat

> **"Watch this, Lis, you can actually pinpoint the second when his heart rips in half."**
> —Bart Simpson

The exchanging of Valentine's Day cards is not, however, limited to lovers; instead, it is a common practice in most elementary schools across the United States. Teachers like to encourage students to exchange cards with everyone in the class as a sign of friendship toward all. However, as most readers may recall from their own early childhood experiences, not all students receive an equal number of Valentine's Day cards. In fact, some kids are totally left out because their classmates have shunned them. The effects can be highly damaging to the young fragile child. *Peanuts* character Charlie Brown suffered from this indignity.

Springfield Elementary School implements the tradition of having students exchange Valentine's Day cards. In the "I Love Lisa" episode (#74), Lisa is the only kid in school to give Ralph Wiggum a Valentine's Day card. The card has a little train on it and states, "I Choo-Choo-Choose You." Mistaking Lisa's kindness for something more, Ralph develops an immediate crush on Lisa. He waits for Lisa after school to walk her home. Later, Lisa tells her parents that she doesn't want to hurt Ralph, but she is not interested in him romantically.

> *Lisa*: Ralph thinks I like him. But I only got him a Valentine 'cause I felt sorry for him.
>
> *Homer*: Ah, sweet pity; where would my love life have been without it?
>
> *Lisa*: What do you say to a boy to let him know you're not interested?
>
> *Marge*: Well, honey—
>
> *Homer* (interrupts Marge): Let me handle this, Marge. I've heard 'em all. (He counts on his fingers.) "I like you as a friend," "I think we should see other people," "I no speak English," "I'm married to the sea," "I don't want to kill you, but I will. . . ."

Instead of letting Ralph down easy, Lisa takes advantage of him. He has something that she really wants, tickets to Krusty's Anniversary Show gala, an event so big that Bill and Hillary Clinton attend! Lisa agrees to go to the Krusty show with Ralph. Chief Wiggum drives the young couple to the show. During the segment of the show when Krusty talks to members of the audience, he stops to chat with Ralph and Lisa. Krusty asks Ralph about his date, and Ralph proudly and naïvely proclaims that he is going to marry her when they grow up. Lisa does not want the viewers or the members of the audience to think she is Ralph's girlfriend so she blurts out that she only gave Ralph a Valentine's Day card because she felt sorry for him. Ralph is understandably devastated.

The Krusty show was televised and Bart recorded it. He plays it back for Lisa, who watches in horror the knockout punch she delivered to Ralph. Bart acts as a commentator reviewing the tape: "Watch this, Lis, you can actually pinpoint the second when his heart rips in half."

Ralph is so depressed that when he tries to feed the ducks in the pond, they won't go near him. Ralph tells his dad that "she [Lisa] made a fool out of me." Lisa tries to apologize but does not get the chance before the night of the school play. Ralph plays George Washington in the play. Using his pain to motivate himself, Ralph gives a great performance. The audience loves it. Backstage, the girls all ask for his autograph and shower him with attention. Lisa walks over and gives Ralph a card with a bee on it and a caption that states, "Let's Bee Friends."

Ralph has learned the tough lesson that often accompanies first crushes, unrequited love, followed by the "Let's be friends" line.

Ralph is not the only person on *The Simpsons* to experience a failed first crush. Among others are Bart and Lisa. Bart's crush ended as badly as Ralph's did. In the "New Kid on the Block" episode (#67), Bart falls for Laura Powers. Laura is new to Springfield. She has just moved there with her mother, Ruth. (Note: Ruth Powers is the same woman that befriends Marge. See chapter 3.) Laura is a few years older than Bart. One night, Homer and Marge hire Laura to babysit. Bart is very excited that Laura will be at his house. As a result, he pretends to act more mature. For example, he wears a robe and smokes a pipe that makes bubbles, à la Hugh Hefner. Bart and Laura start to hang out together and he quickly develops a major crush on her. Like most people who have a crush on someone, Bart begins to fantasize about a future with Laura. Suddenly, Bart's fantasy world is shaken when Laura happily informs him that she has a boyfriend. Bart shifts back to his fantasy world, but it is now a house of horrors. His dreams have become a horrible nightmare. Laura reaches into Bart's chest and pulls out his heart and proclaims, "You won't be needing this!" To make matters worse, Laura's new boyfriend is Jimbo, an older kid who regularly beats Bart up. Bart had his little heart wounded and the salt was added.

All first crushes do not end as poorly as Ralph's and Bart's. Many of them simply run their course. For example, in the "Lisa's Date with Density" episode (#160), Lisa develops a crush on bad boy Nelson. She tells her friend Milhouse (who has a major crush on Lisa) about her crush on Nelson and he spits up his milk. Lisa knows how Milhouse feels about her so she tries to set things straight. Lisa tells Milhouse, "I like you too, Milhouse, but not in that way. You're more like a big sister." Ouch! Milhouse has his heart destroyed.

Meanwhile, Lisa tells her mom about her crush on Nelson. She hopes to change him. Marge tells Lisa, "Well, most women will tell you that you're a fool to think you can change a man—but those women are quitters!" Ah, women who love the bad boys and then think they can change them! Lisa invites Nelson over to her house to hang out. Nelson agrees but tells Lisa if anyone sees them together at her house, he is going to say that he's just there to steal her bike. Lisa also goes to Nelson's house. She is concerned about his poor living conditions. Lisa works on changing Nelson. She tries to dress him nicely and asks Nelson to share his feelings with her. Of course, these are two things that most boys that age hate to do, and Nelson is no exception. Nelson's buddies give him a hard time for hanging out with a "goody-goody" girl. Before long, no matter how much Nelson and Lisa attempt to compromise, they cannot overcome their drastic differences. Nelson *is* a bad boy and enjoys a life of deviance and criminal behavior with his buddies. Lisa, on the other hand, is a good girl and cannot participate in Nelson's capers. After Nelson lies to Lisa about something, she breaks up with him and says, "Smell ya later." This is the expression that Nelson often used and it rubbed off on Lisa. So, even though Lisa and Nelson go their separate ways, they had a good time while it lasted and no one was devastated when the brief crush concluded.

Dating

> "Why would a Twinkie want to date a Ding-Dong like me?"
> —Ned Flanders

People go on dates for a variety of reasons, ranging from "let's just have fun" to "getting to know you better" as a precursor to something more serious. A great number of the characters on *The Simpsons* have gone on dates. A select few examples are described here.

Abe "Grandpa" Simpson, long separated from his wife, Mona, has not let his old age and residency in a retirement home stop him from dating. Abe is not exactly Hugh Hefner, but even an occasional date is better than none at all. Abe has not ventured far from home to find his dating partners. In the "Old Money" episode (#30), Grandpa Simpson dates a woman named Beatrice Simmons. Bea also lives in the retirement home. The two of them take their medication pills together. They drink water to wash the pills down similar to the way people drink champagne at a wedding, with their drinking arms wrapped around each other. Their dates are simple and yet intimate and meaningful. Homer, Marge, and the kids spend every third Sunday with Grandpa. But this particular family day also happens to be Beatrice's birthday and Abe wants to spend it with her. Despite Grandpa's protests, Homer whisks Abe away from the retirement home as scheduled. After a long day Abe returns to the retirement home only to learn that Bea has died. Abe is devastated and yells at Homer, "I have no son."

Beatrice left a substantial sum of money ($106,000) to Abe. Initially, he spends money foolishly. But this does not ease his pain. Meanwhile, Homer is deeply depressed because his father has disowned him. Beatrice comes to Abe in a dream and tells him to reconcile with Homer. Abe does so. Abe discusses with his family what he should do with the money that Beatrice has left him. Lisa suggests that Grandpa give the money to the less fortunate. Abe agrees. Unfortunately, as he tries to ascertain who is most deserving, Abe finds despair and greed everywhere. Eventually, Abe decides to use the money to help benefit the residents of the retirement home and opens the Beatrice Simmons Memorial Dining Hall equipped with comfortable chairs, a big-screen TV, a pool table, and a number of other recreational devices. As Abe opens the door to the new dining hall he says to the other residents, "C'mon in. Dignity is on me, friends." Beatrice surely would have been proud of Abe.

In the "Principal Charming" episode (#27), Homer tries to find a date for Marge's sister, Selma. Selma is lonely and believes the statistics that indicate it is rare for a woman over forty years old to find her Prince Charming. Selma states, "I'll get right to the point. I'm getting older, fatter, and uglier. . . . Help me find a man before it's too late." Homer agrees to try and find a man for Selma. He meets with Principal Seymour

Skinner to discuss Bart's most recent episode of misbehavior. Upon learning that Skinner is single, he invites Seymour to dinner at his home. Instead of falling for Selma, it is her sister Patty who catches Skinner's eye. Skinner asks Patty out on a date but she refuses—out of respect to her sister. However, when Selma insists that Patty go on the date, she does so.

Patty has not gone on a date in twenty-five years and is understandably rusty on dating protocol. She is especially weak on making romantic small talk. For example, she tells Skinner about her trip to Egypt. Seymour is eager to hear all about it.

> *Skinner*: So Patty, tell me more about your trip to Egypt.
> *Patty*: Nothing more to tell, really. The Nile River smells like cattle rot and they've got horseflies over there the size of your head.

As Patty and Skinner get closer, Selma becomes increasingly depressed. After all, as Marge explains to Homer, Patty chose a life of celibacy, whereas Selma's celibacy was thrust upon her! Homer sets Selma up on a date with Barney. Selma is so desperate that she agrees. Meanwhile, Skinner proposes marriage to Patty. Although Patty is tempted to say "yes," she is more concerned about leaving her sister alone and therefore says "no" to Seymour's proposal. Patty goes to Moe's bar and leads Selma away from her date with Barney. They leave for pancakes and, most likely, a continued life of abstinence.

Patty and Selma represent the dichotomy of single people. Some have freely chosen to live a single lifestyle while others have failed to find the person of their dreams.

There are many people like Moe who have not necessarily chosen to live a single lifestyle, but, instead, have had that choice made for them due to other circumstances—they are a little creepy! Moe, a former boxer who is now permanently "punch drunk," is not only suicidal; he flat out does not know how to talk to women. He solicits Homer's help finding a date. As Moe explains, "It's been four years since my last date with a whatchoo-call-it, uh, woman." Moe is indeed feeling very depressed.

> *Moe*: No girl wants to end up with a Joe Pukepail like me.
> *Homer*: Now, now, I won't hear of it, Moe—you're a fabulous catch!

Moe: Oh yeah? Well, uh, how come I ain't fending off movie
    starlets with a pointy stick?
Homer: Oh, it's probably due to your ugliness, but that doesn't
    mean we can't find you a woman. C'mon! We're going to
    the darkest bar in town!

Homer takes Moe to Stu's Disco in an attempt to meet women. But
Moe strikes out. His opening pickup line does not help: "You look
pretty clean. So, hi there. Uh, don't scream." Outside the disco, Moe
talks to a flower vendor, Renee (voiced by Helen Hunt). He calls her
gorgeous.

Renee: Really? You think I'm gorgeous?
Moe: Yeah, well, the part that's showin'. Guess you could have
    a lotta weird scars or a fake ass or somethin'.
Renee: You don't talk to a lot of women, do you?

Despite Moe's shortcomings, the rather attractive Renee agrees to go
out on a date with him. He is so excited that he tells Renee not to eat
anything for the next three days because he is taking her to a place
where the steak is the "size of a toilet seat." Moe and Renee go out
on numerous dates. He spends all his money on her and quickly
maxes out his Players Club credit card. He calls in bar tabs from all
his regular drinkers at the bar but all the drunks go running off. After
a failed insurance fraud scam backfires, Moe is left penniless. He can
no longer afford to take Renee out on dates. (Note: This episode
never clearly spells out what happens to Renee but we never see her
again.) Moe reluctantly returns to the life of singlehood.

Dating presents many challenges. People are often unsure how
to behave on a date. For instance, do they reveal their true selves
immediately, or do they present the best first impression possible by
keeping many key tidbits of information about themselves private
until a later date? People who were once married and then reenter
the dating pool often feel awkward. Such is the case for Ned Flanders. For many years, Ned was happy married to his wife, Maude.
However, in the "A Star Is Born-Again" episode (#304), widower Ned
finds himself attracted to Sara Sloane, a Hollywood movie star. Ned
meets Sara in his Leftorium store. Sara is in Springfield to film her
new movie, *The Zookeeper's Wife*. Sara finds Ned fascinating and asks

him out on a date. A surprised Ned responds, "A woman asking a man out? Well . . . well, why not? And maybe I'll eat my steak with a spoon!"

Sara is not only gorgeous and famous, she lives a completely different lifestyle from Ned's. It seems that opposites do attract. Still, Ned wonders why a woman like Sara would want to date him. Ned asks Homer, "Why would a Twinkie want to date a Ding-Dong like me?"

Ned invites Sara to his house. Sentimentality quickly overwhelms her as she looks around Ned's home.

> *Sara*: You know, I grew up in a house like this. I didn't know there were people like you left in the world.
> *Ned* (snickers): Yep! We occupy the useless mass of land between Los Angeles and New York called America.

Ned and Sara go on numerous dates and become very close. Ned tries to change nearly all aspects of her life. He convinces Sara to persuade the movie producer to eliminate her nude scene in the movie. Ned encourages her not to move back to Hollywood and to instead move to Springfield. And he tries to get her to dress more conservatively. The entire time Sara and Ned date they do not have sex. Sara wants to, but Ned insists that they wait until after they are married. Ned is a traditionalist. He believes in love, marriage, and then sex. After attending an outdoor concert together, Ned eventually gives in to his biological urges and makes love to Sara under the stars. Ned now assumes that Sara will marry him. He pops the questions but she refuses. She is not ready to be tied down. Sara wants to remain single and enjoy the life of a movie star in Hollywood.

This was one occasion where opposites were attracted to each other but the major differences between Ned and Sara precluded their being together. Shortly after Sara returned to Hollywood, the reality of the extreme differences between Ned and Sara were revealed while Ned watched the television show *Publicity Tonight* (a spoof the TV show *Entertainment Tonight*).

> *Male Host*: Screen siren Sara Sloane shocked Tinseltown last night with a midnight marriage to *Gosford Park* mega hunk Bob Balaban.
> *Ned*: Gasp!

Male Host: This was followed three hours later by a quickie divorce.

Ned: Sigh. I bet we could have lasted twice as long.

After numerous dates, Ned and Sara experienced a short-lived romance. Their relationship ended the way the vast majority of all relationships end—in failure. However, there are times when romances develop into relationships where both partners experience romantic love. In turn, this romantic love may lead to marriage.

Romantic Love

"[We have a] profound, mystical understanding [of one another]."
—Marge Simpson

What is romantic love? Romantic love involves physical and emotional attraction. It is valued in Western societies because it is viewed as an important step toward marriage. Romantic love lasts only a couple years. In order for the relationship to survive, the couple must learn to grow beyond the limits of romantic love. A lasting relationship must be based on shared goals, commitment, and compromise.

Social psychologists Lindersmith, Strauss, and Denzin explain that love alone cannot guarantee a lasting relationship. They describe falling in love as being similar to getting hooked on drugs. The process typically begins as a "weekend habit" and as it continues and becomes more serious—often without the realization of the participants—the two become progressively more psychologically dependent on each other. As they learn more about each other and the relationship becomes more intimate, a mutual trust and dependency develops. The lovers discover that nobody else can provide them with this same "high" that they experience with each other. They are officially "hooked" on each other. When asked why they love each other, lovers usually give varied and unilluminating answers. "Like heroin users who praise the drug in exaggerated terms, lovers often extol the virtues of their partners in extremely unrealistic terms. Both love and drug addiction have their honeymoon periods when the habits are new, before reality intrudes itself and brings the individual back to earth" (Lindersmith, Strauss, and

Denzin 1991, 310). As the joys of their habit lose their novelty, disillusionment sets in with the lovers. They clear their heads of the romantic haze created by blind love and begin to see each other in more realistic terms. The drug has worn off. The question is, will the couple remain happy with each other after the initial romantic haze dissipates? Are they truly in love, or were they in love with the idea of love? As with most aspects in life, time provides the answer.

Falling out of love involves a breaking away process that is generally very emotional and agonizing. Withdrawal has these same effects. Couples that were meant to be will outlive this romantic period and enter the "true love" phase of their relationship. The term "soul mates" is sometimes applied to describe couples who can outlast the limitations of romantic love and commit to the long haul. Homer and Marge Simpson are soul mates.

The story of Homer's and Marge's romance is detailed in "The Way We Was" episode (#25). The Simpson family is watching television together when the TV set breaks. Marge tells the kids the story of how she and Homer first met and fell in love while they were in high school in their senior year, 1974. The young Homer is caught smoking with Barney and is given detention. Marge, interestingly enough, is a women's libber, and is given detention after she burns her bra in protest against male-imposed shackles. Homer falls in love with Marge immediately. Bart and Lisa are impressed.

Lisa: So, it was love at first sight!
Bart: It was a jailhouse romance, man.

Homer seeks advice from his father about how to approach Marge and ask her to the prom.

Grandpa: Now, this girlfriend of yours. Is she a real looker?
Homer: Uh-huh.
Grandpa: A lot on the ball?
Homer: Oh, yeah.
Grandpa: Oh, son, don't overreach. Go for the dented car, the dead-end job, the less attractive girl. Oh, I blame myself. I should have had this talk a long time ago.

Despite Abe's less than stellar advice to Homer, he manages to persevere. In an attempt to win Marge over, he joins the debate team. He also solicits her tutoring skills in French. He begins to flirt with Marge in French and they dance to the "Hustle." Feeling more confident, Homer asks Marge to go with him to the prom. She replies, "Oui." He is as excited as can be—he is high on love! Consistent with his character throughout adulthood, Homer goofs up and admits to Marge that he only asked her to tutor him in French so that he could get close to her. Marge feels deceived by this and tells Homer that she will not go to the prom with him. Instead, she goes with Artie Ziff.

Undaunted by Marge's rejection, Homer shows up at her house on the night of the prom expecting to take her to the big event. Artie shows up shortly afterward and Marge leaves with him. Homer is deeply depressed—he is experiencing withdrawal without her. Homer walks away. At the prom, Marge and Artie are voted king and queen of the prom. Their prom theme song, "Time in the Bottle" (the same prom theme song of this author), plays in the background. At the prom, Homer once again professes his love for Marge, but again she shoots him down. Homer walks home even more dejected than he was earlier. But Homer's fortune soon changes. On their way home, Artie makes unwanted advances on Marge and she has to push him aside. When Marge arrives home she thinks about Homer and how she should have gone to the prom with him instead of Artie. She drives off and finds Homer walking home. Marge invites him into the car, and they have been together ever since.

As previously stated, Homer and Marge have had their marital troubles, but they have indeed reached the "true love" phase of a relationship. Further, in the "El Viaje Misterioso de Nuestro Homer" episode (#162), Homer actually questions whether Marge is his "soul mate" because they don't seem to have anything in common with each other. After an argument with Marge, Homer leaves his home in search of his soul mate. He questions his friends.

Homer: Hey Barney! Soul mate! Let me buy you a beer.
Barney: Okay, but I'm not your soul mate. I'm really more of
    a chum.
Homer: Well, what about you, Lenny?
Lenny: I'm a crony.
Homer: Carl?

Carl: I'd say acquaintance.
Larry: Colleague.
Sam: Sympathizer.
Bumblebee man: Compadre.
Kearney: Associate.
Dr. Hibbert: Contemporary.
Moe: I'm a well-wisher, in that I don't wish you any specific harm.

Homer wanders off aimlessly and winds up at the lighthouse. He contemplates his life and just when he is ready to give up on the idea of having a soul mate, Marge shows up. Homer is amazed that she found him. Marge explains to him a number of clues she used to track him down, including her realization that Homer likes blinking lights. It occurs to Homer that no one understands him like Marge. As Marge explains, they have a "profound, mystical understanding" of each other. Homer replies, "We do! Oh, Marge! We're number one! We're number one!"

MARRIAGE

"We can always get divorced!"
—Manjula Nahasapeemapetilon

The love affair between Marge and Homer has afforded them a happy and relatively long-lasting marriage, especially by today's standards. As Homer explains to Marge in the "Ice Cream of Marge (with the Light Blue Hair)" episode (#385), "I would never let you down. Our marriage is like soft serve ice cream and trust is the hard chocolate shell that keeps it from melting onto our carpet. In conclusion, here's the scoop, I love you." Despite their enduring marriage, Marge and Homer have a long way to go if they hope to break the *Guinness Book of World Records* for the world's longest-lasting marriage, established in June 2005 by Percy and Florence Arrowsmith of England. The Arrowsmiths celebrated their eightieth wedding anniversary (in 2005) and claimed that the key to their long marriage was not to go to sleep on an argument.

What Is Marriage?

Marriage was once regarded as a sacred social institution where the bonds of matrimony were supposed to supersede such "frivolous" concerns as "irreconcilable differences" and temptations to others. Historically, divorce was a taboo in American society and reserved for very special circumstances. None of this is true today. Contemporary definitions of marriage have been forced to deal with certain realities about the changing nature of society. With this in mind, marriage is defined as a relatively enduring socially approved sexual and economic relationship between at least two persons for the purpose of creating and maintaining a family. (Note: The "family" will be discussed in chapter 5.) The high divorce rate accounts for the "relatively enduring" aspect of the definition of the family. Overall, 43 percent of marriages dissolve within fifteen years. Roughly half of all marriages fail. Couples who lived together before getting married do not fair better than those who did not. They have a slightly higher probability of divorcing than couples who did not cohabitate prior to marriage.

As stated at the beginning of this chapter, the US Census estimated that less than half of US households involved married couples in 2005. This was the first time that less than half of American households were made up of married couples. Homer and Marge have a successful marriage. Their marriage is monogamous—one individual married to another individual at a given time—and representative of the legal system of marriage in the United States and most Western nations. Many people participate in serial monogamy—the practice of having more than one spouse during the course of a lifetime, but only one at a time. Glynn (Scotty) Wolfe, who died in June 1997, holds the Guinness World Record for the most marriages, twenty-nine of them. His last wife, Linda Essex-Wolfe, was a veteran of twenty-two marriages herself. This is one record that Homer and Marge Simpson are highly unlikely to break.

With all the problems associated with the institution of marriage, why would anyone want to get married? Beyond the obvious answers of love and companionship, studies have linked marriage to healthier people. According to the National Center for Health Statistics, married people are, overall, more active, less likely to get sick, smoke and drink less, and in general feel better than single, divorced, never married, or cohabitating people. The primary reasons married people have greater health and generally report higher levels of happiness than their unmarried counterparts are increased economic resources, social and psychological support, and encouragement of healthy lifestyles.

Arranged Marriages

> **"I have come to see the woman for whom Apu was willing to disgrace his family and spit on his culture."**
> —Mrs. Nahasapeemapetilon

In societies of the West, romantic love is cherished as an ideal precursor to marriage—"First comes love, then comes marriage . . ." However, in many cultures, it is common for marriages to be arranged by people other than those actually getting married. Arranged marriages are common in the Middle East and parts of Asia and Africa. Social standing (e.g., caste location), economics, and education level are among the key variables considered when arranged marriages are at play. Generally, arranged marriages are set up by immediate family members involving young children promised to marry each other at a later date. Honor, duty, obligation, and tradition keep this system alive and well in contemporary society. Generally, the bride's family will provide the husband's family with a dowry. The better the dowry, the "better" the husband a bride's family could expect her to marry. In all but a few rare cases, the bride gives up control of her dowry once she is married. Although people from the West generally frown upon the idea of arranged marriages, they do have a number of advantages, including lower divorce rates, rational rather than emotional considerations for mating, and an increased probability that the couple are compatible (e.g., same religion, caste, dietary preference, linguistics, education, professional status, and so forth).

The Simpsons provides us with an example of an arranged marriage in "The Two Mrs. Nahasapeemapetilons" episode (#185). In this episode, Apu Nahasapeemapetilon informs Homer that his mother has arranged for his marriage. His mother has just written him a letter that included a lotus—which means it is time to get married to his promised bride. The wedding was arranged when he was eight years old. Apu is torn. He is accustomed to the American lifestyle and yet he feels honor-bound to abide by his cultural heritage and family upbringing. With Homer's prompting, Apu initially decides to lie to his mother by telling her that he is already married. (Homer has Marge pretend she is Apu's wife.) This prompts an immediate visit of Apu's mother from India. Upon her arrival to Springfield, Mrs. Nahasapeemapetilon states, "I have come to see the woman for whom Apu was willing to disgrace his family and spit on his culture."

The scam of having Marge pretend to be Apu's wife quickly backfires as Mrs. Nahasapeemapetilon discovers the truth. Apu's mother becomes very upset with him. The arranged marriage is back on. Attempting to get out of the marriage, Apu warns his mother that one out of every twenty-five arranged marriages ends in divorce. Sensing the inevitable and not wanting to upset his mother, Apu reluctantly agrees to go on with the marriage.

Apu's wife-to-be is named Manjula. Her dowry includes ten goats, an electric fan, and a textile factory. Apu has no idea what Manjula looks like, for as tradition dictates, the bride and groom are not allowed to talk to, or see, each other before the wedding. Apu discusses his reluctance to go ahead with the arranged marriage.

Apu: Has this whole world gone crazy?
Homer: Nah, just your screwy country.

Despite his lack of enthusiasm, Apu's wedding ceremony is scheduled to proceed. It is held in Homer's backyard. During the ceremony Apu sees his bride for the first time. He is extremely happy to find that Manjula is gorgeous. In fact, both Apu and Manjula fall for each other and decide to give the marriage a try. After all, as they reason, what is the worst thing that can happen? As Manjula states, "We can always get divorced!" Apu replies, "Of course! God Bless America!"

Serial Sham Monogamy

> **"Is this a sham marriage?"**
> **—Selma Bouvier**

In the "Black Widower" episode (#56), Selma reflects the cultural sentiment (and advantages of being married described earlier in this chapter) shared by many aging adults; namely, they do not want to die alone. Aunt Patty attempts to explain this to Bart.

> *Aunt Patty*: You see, Aunt Selma has this crazy obsession about not dying alone, so in desperation, she joined this prison pen-pal program. Her new sweetie's a jailbird.
> *Bart*: Cool, he can teach us how to kill a guy with a lunch tray.

Although Bart thinks it's funny to make fun of Aunt Selma dating an inmate and finds the idea of meeting a killer intriguing, he is alarmed to discover that her pen pal is none other than Sideshow Bob. Bart is responsible for Bob's incarceration and immediately distrusts his intentions toward Selma. Sideshow Bob manages to get released from prison and continues his romance with Selma. On an evening that Patty, Selma, and Sideshow Bob are at the Simpsons' home, Bart tries to warn his family not to trust Bob. He knows that there is something fishy about Bob dating Selma. However, no one heeds Bart's warning and Bob's relationship with Selma continues. In fact, on this evening, Bob puts his devious plan in motion by proposing marriage.

> *Sideshow Bob*: Selma, would you mind if I did something bold and shocking in front of your family?
> *Selma*: All right, but no tongues.
> *Sideshow Bob*: Although kissing you would be like kissing some divine ashtray, that's not what I had in mind. Selma, will you marry me?
> *Bart*: Don't be a fool, Aunt Selma. That man is scum.
> *Selma*: Then call me Mrs. Scum.

Before long, Bob and Selma marry and go off on their honeymoon. Selma sends a videotape of their honeymoon to the Simpsons. Selma appears to be blissfully happy. And yet, Bart is still convinced something is amiss. He pays particular attention to a part of the video where Sideshow Bob is shown in the background making a big deal about having a room with a gas fireplace. Realizing that Selma has lost her sense of smell and that she is a chain smoker, Bart believes Bob will try to somehow kill Selma via the combination of an open gas line and a lit cigarette. Bart is able to convince the police to investigate and Bob has indeed set up a plan to kill Selma for her insurance money. The police are able to save her just in the knick of time. Bob is sent back to prison and Selma ends the sham marriage.

Selma becomes a part of another sham marriage in the episode "A Fish Called Selma" (#147). The famous former B-movie actor Troy McClure is at the DMV office, where Selma works, attempting to renew his driver's license. He is in Selma's line. Troy fails the vision test, but a smitten Selma tells him, "Stars like you don't need glasses." Selma agrees to renew his license if he'll go on a date with her. He agrees. Certain that little will amount of their date, Selma relaxes and smokes a cigar at the dinner table. An avid smoker, Selma comments that smoking a cigar is like smoking five cigarettes at once. As Selma had suspected, Troy is "going through the motions" while on the date. However, at the end of the date a group of paparazzi take notice of Troy out on a date—with a woman! They eagerly snap photos of the couple and one of them appears on the front page of the *Springfield Shopper*. Due to the positive publicity generated by Troy's dating Selma, his estranged agent, MacArthur Parker, contacts him. Parker tells Troy to keep dating because he'll be able to find work again.

Although some observers might think that Selma is serving as a "beard" for Troy because he is gay, this is not the case. The reason everyone is shocked to see Troy out on a date with a woman is because of a bizarre past incident where it was revealed that Troy has a very unnatural fish fetish. His deviant sexual desires led to McClure being shunned by Hollywood. That is, until he was seen with Selma. Troy takes his agent's advice and continues to date Selma. On their second date, Selma smokes a cigar at a restaurant and both the patrons and the waiter are disgusted. Selma storms out of the restaurant because she believes that Troy will have nothing more to do with her. Instead, Troy joins her outside and lights up his own cigar. They bond over smoking.

As Troy and Selma continue to date, his popularity soars. Parker informs Troy that if he marries Selma he can get him a part in a big movie. Troy asks Selma to marry him and she says "yes." The night before the wedding Troy joins Homer at Moe's. He admits to Homer that the wedding is a sham and that he is marrying Selma simply for the good publicity. Because he was drunk at the time, Homer forgets all about Troy's confession until after the wedding ceremony. Once he tells Marge, she and her sister Patty inform Selma of the news. Selma confronts Troy directly.

Selma: Is this a sham marriage?
Troy: Sure, baby. Is that a problemo?

Troy and Selma's relationship has nothing to do with romantic love or an arrangement made by the families. It is a relationship of convenience that is economically driven for Troy and companionship-driven for Selma. Although Selma wishes for more than a sham relationship, at this point in her life she is ready to settle for almost anything. Meanwhile, Troy realizes that being married is good for his career. This sham relationship further illustrates the point that people marry for many reasons other than love.

Selma's sham marriage to Troy does not last much longer than her sham marriage to Sideshow Bob did. Troy's agent pushes him to impregnate Selma. After all, if being married "looks good," then becoming a father and family man is all the better. Selma, however, has a different perspective. It is one thing to involve herself in a sham relationship, but it is another issue entirely to purposely bring a child into the world and raise it in a loveless environment. Selma takes her iguana, Jub-Jub, and leaves Troy.

Keeping It Fresh

"Sometimes moms and dads need new ways to express their love."
—Marge Simpson

Just as true love requires growth beyond the limits of romance, marriage must grow beyond the newlywed stage of gleeful joy. The longer any couple is married, the longer the period that something can go wrong. Even marriages relatively free from significant problems risk becoming stagnant if couples ignore ways to keep their relationship fresh.

Homer and Marge attempt to keep their marriage fresh in a variety of fashions. For example, in the "Natural Born Killers" episode (#203), the Simpsons are celebrating their wedding anniversary. Marge and Homer go out to dinner and it turns out to be quite mundane and unromantic. Things get worse later that night when they return home and neither of them is interested in getting intimate. They have become bored with each other. Nothing is new or exciting. The next day Marge and Homer head off to purchase a new refrigerator motor. Marge expresses her concern to Homer that they may be in a rut.

> *Marge*: When we got married, is this how you thought we'd be spending our Saturdays? Driving out to the boondocks to trade in a refrigerator motor?
> *Homer*: Eh, I never thought I'd live this long.

While driving on a back road during a rainstorm, the Simpsons' car gets stuck in mud. They seek shelter in a nearby barn. The farmer who owns the barn investigates. He has a shotgun with a pitchfork tied to it and yells out, "If somebody's in here, you're in for some serious ass-forkin'!" The farmer does not find Homer and Marge hiding in the hay mound and heads back inside his house. Highly stimulated by the excitement of nearly being caught trespassing and facing possible death, Marge and Homer experience a tremendous adrenaline rush and make mad, passionate love.

Marge realizes that the "fear of getting caught is a turn-on." Later in this same episode, Homer and Marge play miniature golf and sneak into the miniature windmill to have sex. Realizing that other patrons are still playing golf, Marge and Homer are highly aroused and turned on. A number of the golfers begin to realize that someone or something is in the windmill and they begin to poke inside. Moe sticks a hose inside filled with carbon monoxide. Homer mutters, "Why are people always trying to kill me?" Marge and Homer manage to sneak away, naked, and run through town trying to find their way safely home. They try to hide inside an auto dealer's promotional hot air balloon but it becomes free and flies directly toward Springfield Stadium. The balloon flies at a low elevation just over the football field. They are so close to the field that Homer blocks a field goal attempt! Adding to their shaming experience is the fact that it is "Camera Day" at the stadium so everyone in attendance takes photos of the naked couple. One of the photos winds up in the local newspaper. When Bart and Lisa question their parents about the incident Marge explains, "Sometimes moms and dads need new ways to express their love."

In the "Milhouse of Sand and Fog" episode (#359), Milhouse's separated parents rekindle their relationship the old-fashioned way, via alcohol. In this episode, Homer is throwing a chicken pox party. Maggie has the pox and other parents want to take advantage of this by purposely exposing their children to an infected child. (It is better to be exposed to the chicken pox as a child than as an adult.) Homer takes advantage of this situation by charging fifteen dollars per child! While Maggie makes contact (she systematically coughs on all the kids) with the other youngsters, the adults drink alcohol in the kitchen.

Ever since their separation, Luann and Kirk Van Houten generally attempt to avoid coming into contact with each other. On this occasion, however, they decide to be civil to each other. They drink heavily, get drunk, and go home together. Basking in the afterglow of make-up sex, the Van Houtens decide on a "trial unseparation." Everything seems to be working out fine initially, Luann and Kirk are getting along with each other and Milhouse is ecstatic that his parents are back together. That is, until Bart informs Milhouse that now his number of presents will be cut in half. They devise a scheme to break up the Van Houtens' reunion bid. Based on an *O.C.* spoof, Milhouse "plants" a woman's bra in his father's side of the bed. The bra belongs to Marge and has her name on it. When Luann finds the bra she not only yells at Kirk, she accuses Marge of sleeping with him. Homer then accuses Marge of cheating based on Luann's accusations. Such a soap opera! Before long, Marge and Homer are able to resolve the misunderstanding but Luann and Kirk's attempt to rekindle their relationship is ephemeral.

Surviving Every Challenge, Even Amnesia

"Do you remember being an enabler?"
—Homer Simpson

Nineteen seasons and counting. That's how long Marge and Homer's marriage has lasted so far. As the sampling of stories told in this chapter would indicate, Homer and Marge have met and survived many challenges. Perhaps they really are "soul mates." After all, in the "Regarding Margie" episode (#376), Homer and Marge manage to find their way back to each other even when Marge suffers from amnesia. As she recovers, Marge slowly recognizes everyone but

Homer. Initially, Marge thinks Homer is her uncle. Undaunted, Homer attempts to win her back anew. But Marge finds it hard to believe that she would love such a brutish man as Homer.

In an attempt to trigger her memory, Homer shows Marge numerous photos, including those where he is fighting former president George H. W. Bush and President George W. Bush. Homer starts courting Marge. He wines and dines her. He takes her miniature golfing and tells her about the times they had sex there. She is offended by the very idea of such a thing and becomes very angry. Marge tells Homer, "The best thing that ever happened to me was forgetting about you." Marge kicks Homer out of his own house. Her sisters, who have never approved of Homer, take Marge on a relaxing car ride. But they have a particular destination in mind and an ulterior motive. They drive to Shelbyville for the "Single Mingle" speed-dating event in an attempt to find Marge a new man. Marge reluctantly goes along with the idea. She meets a nice man and agrees to have a cup of coffee with him. As they make small talk and begin to bond, Lenny and Carl happen to see the two together and call their friend Homer.

Homer rushes over and finds Marge and her date making small talk. Fearing he has lost Marge forever, Homer becomes very sad. However, when Marge tells her date that she has amnesia and three kids, he takes off running! Homer scolds the guy for running away from such a great woman as Marge. She overhears Homer defending her honor and is pleased. She is now willing to give Homer a second try. As he drives her back to Springfield, Homer mentions the word "beer." Like a bell ringing, Marge's memories of her husband come flooding back to her. She remembers how Homer always gets drunk and that she is always there to nurse him back to health. Marge tells Homer that she remembers everything about him and their lives together.

Homer: Do you remember being an enabler?
Marge: Of course, I do. That's why we're such a great team.

It works for them!

Chapter 5

America's Family

The Simpsons

"Everybody in the kitchen! We're having a family meeting."
—Homer Simpson

Despite the fact that former president George H. W. Bush once criticized *The Simpsons* as a bad representation of the American family (preferring *The Waltons* instead), the Simpson family is now the rare example of the traditional American nuclear family that consists of the breadwinner father, the stay-at-home wife, and dependent children all living under the same roof. In fact, only 5 percent of all American families now fit this once ideal type. Thus, the Simpsons are now the barometer by which all other families are measured.

Marge and Homer Simpson not only reflect the old ideal family type because Homer is the breadwinner father and Marge is a stay-at-home wife but also because they abide by the traditional manner in which to form a family. The time-honored mode of starting a family is echoed in the old childhood rhyme, "Susie and Billy sittin' in a tree / K-I-S-S-I-N-G / First comes love, then comes marriage / Then comes baby in the baby carriage." This concept is outdated today as there are many alternative family types that involve such options as the baby coming before either true love or marriage, single-parent families, dual-earner families (both parents work), same-sex partnerships, and couples who have decided not to have children. Perhaps watching *The Simpsons* affords viewers the same nostalgic look at America's past that *The Waltons* once provided its audience.

The Heir Apparent

"He's the perfect one to suckle at my proverbial teat."
—Monty Burns

The family, defined as a social group of two or more persons who are related by blood, marriage, adoption, or who live together and economically cooperate with each other, serves many functions. The family is the major agent of socialization and serves as a primary group for members. As a social group, it has norms, rules, expectations, and a hierarchy. Ideally, the family provides a positive, nurturing environment for its members to thrive and feel safe and secure. The family also serves as a source of identity. One's race, ethnicity, and ancestral heritage are all determined by family. Many people, especially men, view the family as a manner in which to keep their legacy alive. In patriarchical societies lineage is determined primarily from the male side of the family. As a result, it is often important to have a son in order to maintain family heritage.

As the "Margical History Tour" episode (#324) demonstrates, the importance placed upon having a male heir dates to at least the time of King Henry VIII (1491–1547). In this episode, Marge tells her children about Henry VIII, king of England and Ireland, and his desire to have a male heir. Homer serves as Henry in this animated flashback to the times of old England. King Henry VIII longed for a son but his wife, Catherine, had not produced a male heir. Henry became certain she never would. The king was so obsessed with the idea of having a son because he wanted to assure his legacy would continue after his death. He sought a divorce but the Catholic Church denied his request. Henry abolished the papal jurisdiction in England, established the Church of England (separate from the Roman Catholic Church), and went forth with his divorce from Catherine. He married Anne Boleyn in 1533. But she too failed to produce a son and suffered the same deadly fate (beheading) as the priests who attempted to enforce the Church's authority over the king. Shortly after Anne's death, Henry married Jane Seymour. Jane bore Henry a son, Prince Edward, in 1537, but she died a couple weeks later due to childbed fever. King Henry VIII considered Jane to be his only true wife as she was the only one to give him a male heir. The prince, however, was rather sickly and only reigned for a few years.

In the "Margical History Tour" episode, Homer-Henry is shown dreaming about having a son. Of course, the son looks like Bart and is the model prince in the king's dreams. That is, until the prince says something to upset his father, who then chokes the boy in the same manner that Homer constantly chokes Bart. A Ned Flanders–looking character plays the role of a priest denying Henry's request for a divorce. Henry tells the priest he is going to canonize him. The scene shifts to Homer-Henry overseeing the priest being placed inside a cannon and then fired over the castle wall. This is not how the Catholic Church canonizes someone!

Bart Simpson is Homer's heir and legacy. But in the "Burns's Heir" episode (#99), he temporarily becomes Monty Burns's heir. Monty Burns, the millionaire owner of the Springfield nuclear plant, has always been too busy making money to find the time to start a family. After suffering from a near-death experience, Burns takes stock of his life and realizes that he has no heir. This upsets him. Burns tells Smithers, "Do you realize, if I had died there would be no one to carry on my legacy? Due to my hectic schedule and lethargic sperm, I never fathered an heir."

Burns announces that he is seeking an heir. He holds open auditions for the children of Springfield to apply. Lisa is among the children to try out. She points out to Burns that his heir does not have to be a boy. Burns scoffs at the very idea of such a thing and insists that his heir must be a boy. Other children try out but are also unsuccessful.

> *Milhouse*: I have nothing to offer you but my love.
> *Burns*: I specifically said, "No geeks!"
> *Milhouse*: But my mom says I'm cool.
> *Burns*: Next.
> *Nelson*: Gimme your fortune or I'll pound your withered old face in!
> *Burns*: Oh, I like his energy. Put him on the call-back list.
> *Martin* (enters the room singing): Clang, clang, clang, went the trolley / Ring, ring, ring went the bell / Zing, zing, zing went my heartstrings . . . (Nelson returns and smacks Martin) Oooh!
> *Burns*: Thank you. Give the bully an extra point.

Bart also tries out to be Burns's heir but he is turned down and shamed with a "booting." Vowing revenge, Bart returns to the mansion and vandalizes it. Burns catches Bart creating havoc and changes his mind. Burns states, "He's the perfect one to suckle at my proverbial teat." Bart accepts Burns's offer to be his heir. Bart even moves into the Burns mansion so that Monty will not be so lonely. Burns spoils Bart. He gives Bart a new red sports car. Bart drives recklessly and destroys property free from worry that any harm will come to him because Monty Burns is his new legal father.

After a while, the novelty of serving as Burns's son begins to wear thin on Bart. He misses his family and they miss him. Marge and Homer try to legally take Bart back but the judge rules in Burns's favor. There are strong implications of a bribe having been offered to the judge. Still, Burns realizes that if he does not keep Bart happy, he will lose him anyway. In a desperate attempt to convince Bart that his family no longer cares for him, Burns hires actors who resemble Bart's family. Burns sets Bart up to observe "his family" and their uncaring manner toward losing their eldest son. Convinced he has won, Burns tells Bart to fire Homer from the nuclear plant. Instead, Bart gives Burns the "trap door" treatment—he triggers a trap door that sends Burns plunging down a dark shaft in the same manner that Burns has applied to many others. Bart returns to his family. This is clearly one case where blood is thicker than money.

As the above story illustrates, the Simpson family is quite close. They are so close that Bart was willing to turn down a fortune in order to remain with his family.

Chronological Inconsistencies within the Simpson Family

> **"Marge, you're as pretty as Princess Leia and as smart as Yoda."**
> —Homer Simpson

Providing a historical account of the Simpson family is rather challenging considering the creators decided to keep the characters frozen in a one-year timespan (e.g., Bart has always been ten years old). Reminiscing about past events is extremely challenging for the writers of *The Simpsons*. For example, as stated in chapter 4, Marge and Homer's romance was described in "The Way We Was" episode

(#25), having begun when the couple first met and fell in love in 1974, their senior year in high school.

However, in the "I Married Marge" episode (#47), the viewing audience is offered a conflicting story. In this episode, Marge thinks she may be pregnant with her fourth child. This triggers memories from their past; specifically 1980 when Homer and Marge were first dating. Homer and Marge went to the movies to see *The Empire Strikes Back*. Inspired by the film, Homer states, "Marge, you're as pretty as Princess Leia and as smart as Yoda." A few weeks after this date Marge informs Homer that she is pregnant. The two of them go to the hospital for prenatal advice. They pick up a pamphlet titled, "So You've Ruined Your Life." Later that night, Homer proposes to Marge in order to make an "honest" woman of her. Marge says "yes" to his proposal. Homer basks in the glory, yelling out his car window, "Woo hoo! Woo hoo! Yeah! She's gonna marry me! In your face everybody!" They drive to Shotgun Pete's across the state line to get a quickie marriage. Homer finds a job at the nuclear plant and months later his heir, Bartholomew, is born.

Another example of Marge and Homer reminiscing about the past occurs in the 1997 "Lisa's Sax" episode (#181). In this episode, Marge and Homer discuss, among other things, Bart's first day of school as occurring in 1990. Obviously, this cannot be the case as *The Simpsons* was airing before 1990 and Bart, as he remains today, was already in the fourth grade.

In the "Duffless" episode (#75), Homer has his driver's license voided by Chief Wiggum. We can see on Homer's license that he is 6 foot, weighs 240 pounds, with blue eyes, and no hair. His date of birth is listed as May 12, 1956. However, in the "Simpson and Delilah" episode (#15), the viewing audience discovers that Homer was born in 1955. Inconsistencies when describing past events in historic terms will remain inevitable for as long as *The Simpsons* remains frozen in a one-year time frame. Bart will never enter the fifth grade, the year Marge and Homer first met will keep changing, and the years that the children were born will also have to be adjusted.

As viewers of *The Simpsons*, we are not supposed to pay attention to such details as chronological accuracy; after all, if we did, Bart would be nearly thirty years old and his elementary hijinks would not be nearly as funny as they are now while he is ten years old. Instead, *The Simpsons* is more concerned with presenting viewers with numerous family relationships portrayed in a variety of scenarios.

FAMILY RELATIONSHIPS

"Holy moly! Talk about parenting!"
—Homer Simpson

The trials and tribulations experienced by the Simpson family, along with other Springfield characters, are relatable to most viewers. Father-son, Father-daughter, mother-son, mother-daughter, brother-sister, and grandparent-grandchildren relationships are prevalent on *The Simpsons*. The long-running series has provided us with numerous family relationships. A select number of them are described in the following pages.

Mother-Son

Perhaps the most sentimental *Simpsons* episode is "Mother Simpson" (#136). In this episode it is revealed that Homer's long assumed dead mother is actually alive and well. The reunion that the two share is a truly memorable one. In a most peculiar manner, Homer learns that his mother is actually alive.

Homer's boss, Mr. Burns, has become involved in the "Adopt a Highway" program. This program has been in existence for a couple of decades. Typically, the adopting "parent" pays a fee to have his or her name posted on a highway sign while the highway workers actually maintain the adopted stretch of the roadway. The adopting parent gains recognition from the drivers who pass by the sign every day. The benefits also include a favorable image in the local community. Mr. Burns, however, wants all the glory without any of the costs. As a result he takes advantage of the option where instead of paying a fee to the Highway Department, the adopting parent can actually clean the highway instead.

Burns, of course, is not willing to do this work himself and instead makes his employees clean the highway—on a Saturday, no less! Unwilling to work for free for someone else's glory, Homer refuses to partake in the mandatory cleanup session. He decides to fake his own death to get out of the work patrol. Homer purchases a six-hundred-dollar dummy look-alike and has him jump off a cliff. The dummy hits the rocks, is attacked by beavers, and goes through dam turbines. A number of witnesses view this unfortunate mishap. Considering that the average American worker earns less than six hundred dollars a week, this is a costly way to attempt to get out of a couple hours of work; but we are talking about Homer Simpson here.

Believing that Homer is dead, a number of people stop by the Simpson home to pay their condolences to Marge and the children. Upset by Homer's antics, Marge makes him go down to the Hall of Records to be declared legally alive. Generally speaking, when someone is declared dead, as Homer was, it is often very difficult to update computer records indicating that one is still alive. Expecting the worst, Homer greets the county clerk in a confrontational manner.

> *Homer*: Listen here. My name is Homer J. Simpson. You guys think I'm dead, but I'm not. Now I want you to straighten this out without a lot of your bureaucratic red tape and mumbo jumbo.
> *County clerk*: Okay, Mr. Simpson, I'll just make the change here (he taps a few buttons on his keyboard) and you're all set.
> *Homer* (unprepared for such positive service): I don't like your attitude, you water-cooler dictator. What do you have in that secret government file, anyway? I have a right to read it.
> *County clerk*: You sure do.

Homer leans over and takes a peek at the clerk's computer screen and is dumbfounded to discover that his mother is still alive. Baffled by this discovery, Homer goes to the cemetery to visit his mother's burial plot. While he is at the cemetery Homer meets his mother, who was paying her respects because she thought her son was dead.

> *Homer*: I thought you were dead.
> *Mother Simpson*: I thought you were dead.
> *Gravedigger*: Dang blasted! Isn't anybody in this dad-gummed cemetery dead?

Homer is so excited to be reunited with his presumed dead mother he can hardly contain himself. He brings his mother home to meet Marge and the kids. They all share Homer's excitement and are overjoyed to learn that Mother (Mona) Simpson is still alive.

Naturally, the Simpson family wants to know why she has been gone for so long. Mona Simpson details how she was a 1960s anti-germ-warfare protester. She was the only member of the infamous "Springfield Seven" to be identified in part of a break-in of Burns's germ lab. The FBI attempted to arrest her immediately after the break-in but she escaped. The FBI has been looking for her ever since the Springfield Seven blew up Burns's lab. Abe Simpson was ashamed to have a criminal as a wife so he told Homer that his mother died. An overly emotional Homer is simply ecstatic to have his mother back in his life.

Unfortunately, this reunion will be short-lived as the FBI is quickly closing in on the Simpson home to arrest the fugitive Mona Simpson. She escapes with Homer's help after an anonymous caller tips her off. The anonymous caller is Chief Wiggum. Wiggum was a security guard at Burns's germ lab at the time of the break-in, but because Mona Simpson helped to clear up his asthma, he felt that he owed her one (favor). Miles from home, Mother Simpson informs her son that she must leave him for good or risk imprisonment. Tearful good-byes follow. And as Mother Simpson disappears from his sight, Homer is overwhelmed with emotions. As an animated show that often relies heavily on crude jokes and references, viewers cannot help but be overwhelmed by the sentiment displayed at the closing of this brilliantly written episode. Further, any viewers who have lost their own mother cannot help but feel the sadness displayed by Homer.

Mother Simpson has been only a small part of Homer's life, but her impact on her son's life is immeasurable. In contrast, Marge Simpson has nearly always been the model mother, and yet her children often take her presence for granted. Such is the reality of life. We often take for granted the people we cherish the most and only when they are gone (or presumed gone) do we take full stock of their value to us. *The Simpsons* helps to remind us all about the importance of family.

Father-Son

It has often been said that we can tell a lot about people when we learn how they were raised. Homer went most of his life without a mother and his father's parenting skills are certainly questionable; after all, what kind of father tells his own child that their mother is dead when she is really alive? Even in adulthood, Abe has been a less than stellar father figure for Homer to emulate. Adding to Homer's confusion was Abe's admission in the "Homer's Paternity Coot" episode (#366) that he might not be Homer's real father. As part of a different storyline in this episode, mail is delivered to Springfield residents from a recently discovered deceased postal worker who had been buried alive in an ice cap on top of Mt. Springfield. One of these letters was meant for Mona Simpson. It was written by Mason Fairbanks, a lifeguard at the time when Mona first started dating Abe. Mason's professed love for Mona leads Abe to consider that *he* may actually have impregnated Mona.

Homer seeks and finds his potential real biological father. Mason Fairbanks is now a successful treasure hunter. Homer introduces himself to Mason and the two quickly bond. Mason invites Homer and his family to join him on a relaxing ride aboard his boat, "The Son I Never Had." Homer is quite certain that Mason may be his "real" father. After their lovely excursion, Homer invites Mason to the Simpson home for dinner. When they return home, Abe is already there. He feels disrespected, but agrees to a blood test to determine paternity. The test results indicate that Mason is really Homer's biological father. Abe bows out. In an attempt to bond with his new son, Mason invites Homer to join him on a treasure hunt. While off at sea, Homer and Mason go treasure hunting in one-man submarines. The two get separated and Homer finds himself stuck in a rock tunnel. As his oxygen runs out, Homer appears certain to die. He passes out but is rescued. Asleep in a coma for three days, Homer dreams of Abe, the man who raised him, rather than Mason, the man presumed to be his biological father. When Homer awakens from his coma he declares that he wants Abe in his life. At that point, Abe admits that he actually switched the names on the test tubes of the blood test. Abe is Homer's biological father. Abe believed he was making an unselfish gesture by letting it appear that Mason, who was wealthy enough to provide Homer with everything he financially needed, was Homer's biological father. As it turned out, Homer wanted the man who raised him (Abe) in his life, even if he was not his biological father. Such is the power of nurture over nature.

Without much proper parental guidance himself, Homer tries his best with his own children. And Homer certainly has his hands full with his rambunctious son, Bart. In the "Saturdays of Thunder" episode (#44), Homer's ineptness as a father is revealed with his answers to the "National Fatherhood Institute" test on fathering. Marge administers the test.

> *Marge*: Name one of your child's friends.
> *Homer*: Uh, let's see, Bart's friends . . . Well, there's the fat kid with the thing . . . Uh, the little wiener who's always got his hands in his pockets.
> *Marge*: They want a name, Homer, not a vague description.
> *Homer*: Okay . . . Hank.
> *Marge*: Hank? Hank who?
> *Homer*: Hank . . . Jones.
> *Marge*: Homer, you made that up. Question two, who is your son's hero?
> *Homer*: Steve McQueen.
> *Marge*: That's your hero. Name another dad you talk to about parenting.
> *Homer*: Next.
> *Marge*: What are your son's hobbies?
> *Homer*: Kids don't have hobbies.
> *Marge*: Oh really? Well maybe you should go out to the garage and see.

Homer goes out to the garage to discover that Bart is working on a car to enter into the soapbox derby (see chapter 12 for a description of Bart and his participation in a soapbox derby). Homer had no idea that Bart had any hobbies. Furthermore, since he could not correctly answer any of the fatherhood questions, Homer realizes that he doesn't know anything about his own son. Marge, Selma, and Patty join Homer and stand around him as he watches Bart work on his racer. Homer begins to cry.

> *Homer*: I'm a bad father!
> *Selma*: You're also fat!
> *Homer*: I'm also fat!

Poor Homer. Reality has intruded in a very negative fashion into his life. He is not a great father and he is overweight. (Not that one has anything to do with the other!) However, upon closer examination, we see that Homer actually does come through when he is needed the most. In the "Saturdays of Thunder" episode, Homer hangs out with Bart and takes an interest in his new hobby. He also learns the names of Bart's friends and his hero. (Note: Bart's hero is three-time soapbox derby champ Ronnie Beck.)

In the "I, (Annoyed Grunt)–Bot" episode (#322), Homer reveals just how far he is willing to go, and how much pain he is willing to endure, to show his love for his son. In this episode, Bart is trying to build a robot to enter into the "Robot Rumble" contest. Homer offers to help Bart build his robot. Bart declines his father's help and further shames Homer by saying he can't build stuff. In secret, Homer tries to build his own robot for Bart, but he fails. Homer decides to disguise himself as a robot that is also equipped with a remote control for Bart to command. Bart has no idea that Homer is actually inside the shell of this crude robot. Bart loves the robot and enters it into contests versus other destroying robots. His robot merely has a slamming hammer in its arm to fight off the other far more sophisticated robots.

Bart is having a great deal of fun entering his robot in weekly fighting contests against other robots. Bart tells his father that building the robot was the best thing he ever did for him. Still, Bart is disappointed that Homer continues to find excuses not to join him at the Robot Rumble. Week after week the Homer robot takes a beating but keeps on winning. The Homer robot is scheduled to fight a super robot built by the local mad scientist and his son in the championship round. As the Homer robot takes an extreme beating and is about to be destroyed (literally), it is revealed that Bart's robot is really Homer. The super robot, programmed not to harm humans, spares Homer's life. Bart is amazed that his dad was willing to risk his life for him. They look deeply into each other's eyes. Bart says to his father, "I like you, Dad." And Homer replies, "I like you too, son." The episode ends with father and son hugging each other.

Father-Daughter

Whereas Marge and Lisa have a strong mother-daughter relationship, marked by a relatively clear understanding of each other, Homer has an even more difficult time relating to his daughter than he does his son. Homer generally feels intimidated by Lisa because she is so smart. Further, Homer is a slacker who prefers watching TV and drinking beer in his spare time rather than doing something positive with his free time like volunteer work. Lisa, on the other hand, is constantly fighting for what she perceives as the "greater good." She is an activist, a musician, intelligent, and destined for greatness. Homer has already reached his full potential. Thus, it is understandable why this father and daughter often do not see eye-to-eye. Nonetheless, Homer does try his best and occasionally shines.

Lisa is fully aware of her father's shortcomings. She does her best to ignore most of Homer's faults and realizes his limitations as a father. But she is just eight years old, and as with any girl her age, Lisa seeks her father's attention and affection. As demonstrated in the "Bart on the Road" episode (#148), she is happy just to spend time with Homer. In this episode, Lisa joins her dad at work as part of Springfield Elementary's "Go to Work with Your Parents Day." (As a note of interest, Principal Skinner created this day in order to close the school a day early so that he could leave a day early for spring vacation!) Initially Homer is a little uneasy, as he usually is around Lisa, because he never quite knows what to say to her, let alone how to act. But Lisa loves simply spending time with her dad no matter what they are doing. Going to work with him gives her a full day and plenty of time to bond.

On other occasions, Lisa has not been so content to simply hang out with her father. For example, in the "Lisa's Substitute" episode (#32), Lisa has a crush on her substitute teacher, Mr. Bergstrom. Bergstrom suggests to his students that they all visit a display at the History Museum before it closes permanently. Lisa pesters her parents to take her to the museum. Marge tells Homer it would be a good idea for him to take Lisa so that they can bond. Homer reluctantly agrees to take her. He doesn't pay the "suggested" entry fee for admittance, which annoys Lisa. While they are at the museum, they bump into Mr. Bergstrom. The three walk around the museum together and Homer embarrasses Lisa in front of her teacher by making a number of ignorant and insensitive comments.

Things get worse for Lisa the following week when she learns that Mr. Bergstrom has moved on to take a new assignment. Lisa is devastated. She learns that he is taking a train to Capital City and manages to get to the train station just as her substitute teacher's train is pulling out. Lisa begs him to stay. She pleads, "I need you." Mr. Bergstrom is sympathetic to Lisa but he evokes a life lesson to her that she will not forget. Bergstrom states, "That's the problem with being middle class. Anybody who really cares will abandon you for those who need it more."

Devastated, Lisa returns home. When Lisa looks at her father, who is trying his best to comfort her, all she can think of is how he embarrassed her in front of Mr. Bergstrom at the museum. She takes her anger out on Homer by calling him a baboon.

> *Lisa*: Yes, you! Baboon, baboon, baboon, baboon!
> *Homer*: I don't think you realize what you're saying. . . .
> *Bart*: Well, well, somebody was bound to say it one day. I just can't believe it was her.
> *Homer*: Did you hear that, Marge? She called me a baboon! The stupidest, ugliest, smelliest ape of them all.

Lisa storms off to her room crying. Homer follows her up to her room and attempts to console her. Nothing he says is making matters any better. But still, he is trying his best. Deep down, Lisa realizes this. Pulling out all the stops, Homer starts to make baboon sounds in an attempt to lighten the mood. Before too long, Lisa starts to smile and then laugh. She apologizes to her dad. They hug and all is forgiven. This is a very moving episode.

Interestingly, after Homer successfully consoles Lisa, he then gives Bart a great pep talk and he feels better. Homer walks by Maggie's room and notices that she needs her pacifier. Maggie is now content and falls back to sleep. Homer walks out of her room saying to himself, "Three for three!" Realizing he is on his most successful parental ride of his life, Homer exclaims, "Holy moly! Talk about parenting!"

It seems Homer Simpson is not such a bad father after all. In fact, Homer spends more time with his children than many real-life fathers. Further, according to research results published in *USA Today*, college students report that their fathers are a lot less supportive and accepting than TV sitcom dads—including Homer Simpson (Elias 2007).

Sibling Rivalry

Sibling rivalry refers to the antagonism or hostility between brothers, sisters, and/or brother and sister. With children, sibling rivalry generally manifests itself in the form of fighting, pulling a sibling's hair, the unwillingness to share a valued toy, and so on. In some cases, sibling rivalries may lead to permanent enmity between adult siblings. The primary source of sibling rivalry centers on competition for scarce resources, such as parental attention and love.

Bart and Lisa compete with each other for their parents' attention while at the same time, Maggie, as a toddler, commands a great deal of parental attention. It is the relationship of Bart and Lisa that provides viewers of *The Simpsons* with the most examples of sibling rivalry. Bart and Lisa exhibit many classic expressions of sibling rivalry, including arguing with each other, tattling, making fun of each other, and the occasional physical confrontation. Anyone with a sibling, especially as close in age as Bart and Lisa, is likely to see themselves in the behavior exhibited by Bart and Lisa when they were at that age.

However, in a testament to the parenting skills of Marge and Homer, Bart and Lisa always seem to come through for each other when the chips are down. For example, in the "Bart on the Road" episode (#148), Bart finds himself in great peril and turns to Lisa first for help. The person that any of us turns to first in time of trouble is a true manifestation of trust. In this episode, Bart is at the Department of Motor Vehicles (DMV), observing his aunts Patty and Selma at their jobs. This fulfills his school requirement of "Go to Work with Your Parents Day." Patty and Selma teach Bart a lesson about working at the DMV that many licensed motorists already suspect to be true.

Patty: Some days, we don't let the line move at all.
Selma: We call those "weekdays."

Like most boys his age, Bart has a short attention span. Before long, he finds himself immersed in mischief. Bart takes advantage of his new environment by making himself a fake driver's license. He summons his pals, Milhouse, Nelson, and Martin, to join him in some sort of wayward deed. Earlier in the day, Martin earned $600 working with his father trading commodities. With a fake driver's license and cash, the boys are able to rent a car. They make up stories to tell their parents to cover their whereabouts for the next week and head off to Knoxville, Tennessee. They choose Knoxville because of an advertisement they read in an AAA guidebook proclaiming a World's Fair. What the boys do not realize is that the guidebook is fourteen years outdated. As luck would have it, the car gets smashed in Knoxville and the boys run out of money at the same time.

Because no one knows of their whereabouts, the boys do not know who to turn to for help. Bart decides to call Lisa. He does this because he knows, despite any sibling rivalry that exists, Lisa can be depended on. Bart asks for Lisa's help but makes her promise not to tell their parents. Lisa has been working with Homer at the nuclear plant as part of "Go to Work with Your Parents Day." As an eight-year-old girl, Lisa cannot do much on her own. So, she informs her father—on the condition that he not reveal to Bart that she broke her promise to him—about Bart's predicament. Homer promises Lisa that he will keep her secret and not reveal to Bart he knows the truth about him. Lisa and Homer devise a plan to use Bart as a courier to deliver a T-437 Safety Command Console board manufactured in Knoxville to the nuclear plant in Springfield. Nelson, Milhouse, and Martin are secretly tucked inside the box shipped to Springfield.

Throughout the long run of *The Simpsons*, the sibling rivalry between Bart and Lisa has often served as a standard element of the Simpson family. However, the idea that Bart and Lisa are there for each other when needed the most was also established long ago. The "Bart vs. Thanksgiving" (#20) episode best epitomizes the sorrows and joys of having siblings. In this episode, Bart and Lisa are fighting over glue. Lisa needs the glue as she is busy making a Thanksgiving Day centerpiece. The centerpiece is symbolic of Bart and Lisa's relationship. A great deal of time and effort goes into building a relationship and yet it can fall apart in seconds. Such was the case for Lisa's treasured centerpiece—a centerpiece that she describes as "a tribute to trailblazing women who made our country great."

Just as dinner is about to be served, Lisa proudly sets the centerpiece on the Thanksgiving Day table. She is ready to bask in praise from the other family members . . . until Bart arrives. He is equally proud to be the chosen one to carry the hot-out-of-the-oven turkey to the dinner table. To make room for the turkey, Bart haphazardly shoves Lisa's centerpiece out of the way. It lands in the fireplace and is instantly ablaze and obliterated. Lisa is shocked by the quick turn of events. She attacks Bart and then runs off to her room weeping uncontrollably. Bart dismisses Lisa's pain and is ready to eat. Marge and Homer, however, are deeply concerned over how easily Bart was able to hurt Lisa with no regard for her feelings. They send Bart to his room.

Marge and Homer try to convince Lisa to come down to dinner but she refuses and plays the blues on her sax. Marge tries to console

Lisa but she insists on an apology from Bart. The stubborn Bart refuses to offer an apology to Lisa and instead further enflames the anger of the family by claiming to be the victim. Bart sneaks out of the house with his dog, Santa's Little Helper. Bart and his dog wander the streets of Springfield. They end up in "Bumville" (aka, "wrong side of the tracks"). A couple of bums lead Bart into the local shelter where it just so happens that TV news anchor Kent Brockman is doing a feature story on the facility. Brockman proclaims, "Ladies and gentlemen, I've been to Vietnam, Afghanistan, and Iraq, and I can say without hyperbole that this is a million times worse than all of them put together." Kent turns to interview one of the homeless people at the shelter. It is Bart. Bart taunts his family by saying, "Ha-ha, I didn't apologize."

After a while, Bart begins to feel homesick. He heads back home. When he gets there, he still has lingering feelings that he was being treated as the scapegoat for Lisa's hurt feelings. So, instead of going inside the house, Bart climbs to the rooftop where he can hear Lisa crying in her room. Bart calls out to her and she joins him on the roof. Feeling terrible for hurting his sister so much, Bart offers a sincere, heartfelt apology. He explains that he never wanted to hurt her feelings. Lisa accepts Bart's apology and kisses him. They go back into the house together, as loving siblings. Marge and Homer, worried about their missing son and their depressed daughter, are still awake. Happy to be together, the Simpson nuclear family enjoys a late-night Thanksgiving dinner.

There is one other sibling duo that should be noted: Homer and his half brother, Herb Powell. Herb is the son that Abe Simpson put up for adoption shortly after his birth. Homer learns of his half brother for the first time in the "Oh Brother, Where Art Thou?" episode (#28). In this episode, Abe has a heart attack. Fearing his death is near, Abe admits to Homer that he had a son with another woman—a "carnie" (slang for a person who works at a traveling carnival), as Abe described her. They left the baby at the Shelbyville Orphanage shortly after he was born, and Abe never saw him again. Upon hearing this story, Homer initially feels special because he is the one that his father kept. But then it dawns on him to seek out his half brother.

Homer tells his family about this exciting news. They join him in a car ride to the Shelbyville Orphanage, where Homer hopes to find information that will lead him to his half brother.

Lisa: A long-lost half brother. How Dickensian.
Bart: So, any idea where this bastard lives?
Homer (upset): Bart!
Bart: Well, his parents aren't married, are they? It's a correct word, isn't it?
Homer: Well, I guess he's got us there.
Bart: Bastard, bastard, bastard.
Homer and Marge (both are upset): Bart!!
Bart: Bastard, bastard, bastard . . .

Bart's use of the term "bastard" was once a common expression for a child born out of wedlock back in the time when the traditional nuclear family predominated over all other family forms. Bart also likes the idea that he can get away with saying a swear word because he is using it "properly." Today, the term is out of favor as nearly a third of all children are born out of wedlock.

At the orphanage, Homer learns that his half brother's name is Herb Powell and that he lives in Detroit. After going through the Detroit phone book, Homer finds Herb's number, calls him, and the two make small talk. Herb invites Homer to visit him in Detroit. The Simpsons drive to Detroit and arrive at Herb's address at the same time Herb arrives in his limousine. As it turns out, Herb Powell is a self-made millionaire and CEO of Powell Motors. The brothers meet for the first time and marvel at how closely they resemble each other, except for a couple differences that each of them point out. Homer notices that Herb has a full head of hair, and Herb notes that Homer has a bigger belly, but beyond that, they look like brothers. They are both ecstatic to have each other as brothers.

Nearly overcome by the obvious wealth of his half brother, or bastard as Bart had referred to his uncle, Homer states, "Holy moly, the bastard's rich." Homer calls Abe Simpson to tell him that he found his brother and that he is a millionaire. Abe responds, "A millionaire?! I kept the wrong one!" Seeing an opportunity to cash in on this revelation, Abe prepares himself for a trip to Detroit.

Herb, who is single, childless, and unhappy about it, is thrilled to have Homer, Marge, and the kids in his home. He is so happy, he invites them to live there. Herb allows Homer to pick out any car he wants, for free. He then provides Homer with a job—and a salary of two hundred thousand dollars—at the production plant. Herb wants someone he can trust to provide him with insights from the "common man's" perspective about the design for Powell Motors's next new model of automobiles. Herb believes that he should be able to trust his brother with such important decisions. Unfortunately for Herb, he does not realize how incompetent his new brother really is. Homer comes up with a design that is not pragmatic, and worse, leads to a very expensive car. Regardless, Powell Motors goes into production using Homer's design. The car is mocked within the industry. Herb is ruined. He loses everything, his personal possessions, home, and business. Herb disowns Homer, thus ending a potential lasting sibling relationship. Abe Simpson arrives in a cab from Springfield just in time to watch everything fall apart.

Homer's experience with having a sibling ends quickly, but Herb reappears in a later episode.

Adoption

Ideally, people who want to have children will have them, and people who do not want children will not. But life does not always work out as we hope. For example, despite the fact that Selma Bouvier, Marge's sister, has been married a number of times (six), she has not conceived a child. In the "Goo Goo Gai Pan" episode (#347), Selma decides that she wants a baby. As mentioned in chapter 4, Selma is worried about growing old alone. Selma has more or less given up hope of finding lasting companionship via marriage so she decides to try adoption. At first she goes to the Springfield Orphanage only to learn that there are no babies available for adoption. Lisa suggests that Aunt Selma adopt a baby from China. Selma learns, however, that the Chinese government only allows married couples to adopt.

Despite the fact that Homer has never gotten along very well with either of his sisters-in-law, he agrees to allow Selma to write his name down on the adoption form. One more little catch: Homer must go with Selma to China to finalize the deal and pick up the infant assigned to Selma. Marge and the kids join Homer and Selma—with Marge acting as Bart and Lisa's nanny. Although the Chinese government officials are a little doubtful about Homer and Selma's "marriage," they eventually allow the adoption of a little girl. Selma names the girl Ling Bouvier. Ling usually lives with her adopted mother Selma and Aunt Patty. I say usually because in the

"Rome-Old and Juli-Eh" episode (#393), Selma and Abe "Grandpa" Simpson get married and try living as a family with the toddler.

In this episode, Grandpa acknowledges that he is worried about dying alone—a concern he shares with Selma. After a brief courtship, Abe proposes marriage to Selma. She agrees to this unusual—and highly unexpected—marriage. The newlyweds exit the church under a banner that reads: "Congratulations Selma and Bob (crossed out), Lionel (crossed out), Troy (crossed out), Otu (crossed out), Bob (crossed out), Abe." Abe, Selma, and her adopted baby get a house together. Abe is long retired, so the couple is living off of Selma's income from the DMV. Abe stays home and takes care of Ling. Problems quickly surface as Abe is completely unable to operate simple kitchen appliances and causes a fire. At the conclusion of the "Rome-Old and Juli-Eh" episode Selma informs Abe that the marriage will not work. Abe agrees. They share one last dance together.

Violence and Abuse in the Family

"Why, you little—."
—Homer Simpson

Ideally the family, regardless of its structure (e.g., one parent, same-sex parents, or two parents), is a nurturing environment that provides all of its members a sense of safety and well-being. Many families are characterized by varying degrees of violence and abuse, difficult topics to discuss. Determining the true incidence of family violence is difficult due to dramatic underreporting. Evidence indicates that violence is a serious problem in many families. Examples of family violence include: sibling violence, neglect, spousal abuse, marital rape, child abuse, parent abuse, and abuse of the elderly. When I ask my students whether or not they fought with their siblings, they routinely report such incidents as slap fights, hair pulling, pushing, and punching. When I ask the follow-up question as to whether these incidents were reported to the police, the response is an overwhelming "no." Most people with siblings can recall incidents of violence that were never reported to authorities. And, sibling violence is just one type of violence in the family. This reality underscores the fact that violence and neglect in the family is an all-too-common experience for many.

Attempts to find humor in family abuse borders on dangerous terrain. *The Simpsons* precariously walks this tightrope that hovers over what some may find humorous and others may deem insensitive. Child abuse, in the form of Homer physically attacking Bart, is a common occurrence in many *Simpsons* episodes. Whenever Bart does something to upset his father, Homer almost always responds by choking Bart violently while screaming, "Why, you little—." Regular viewers of *The Simpsons* are either immune to this interaction or they still laugh when it occurs. This leads to a great philosophical question, "Is it okay to laugh at a character that is being physically attacked by his father?" Most viewers discount the child abuse aspect of Homer choking Bart by reminding themselves (and others) that Bart and Homer are simply cartoon characters. Contrastly, imagine if TV character Ralph Kramden from *The Honeymooners* actually did punch his wife, Alice, "to the moon." Although it is true that animated characters being physically harmed does not cause the same visceral reaction that observing a full-grown, huge man choking his ten-year-old son would provoke, nonetheless the constant display of child abuse in *The Simpsons* is disconcerting.

The child abuse demonstrated by Homer choking Bart is out of character. As described earlier in this chapter, Homer may not win any "Father of the Year" awards, but he is, for the most part, a good dad. He has even risked his own life on many occasions to protect his family. In short, Homer does not display a pattern of physical abuse against his family. So why does Homer use physical violence against his son? Homer utilizes a form of corporal punishment—choking— that is not commonly used in most American families. However, other types of corporal punishment, such as spankings, are fairly common.

Corporal punishment is a term used to describe the deliberate infliction of pain as a means to correct or punish misbehavior. Spanking is a common form of discipline administered by parents against their children when they misbehave. Parents who spank their children reason that corporal punishment is an effective manner to correct improper behavior. For the past decade, I have asked my students whether or not they were spanked when they were young. The vast majority of them said "yes." Interestingly, nearly half of these same students say that they will not spank their children (if they have children in the future). This reflects the growing movement in the past decade to discourage parents from spanking their children.

There are many reasons promoted against the use of physical violence against children, including: spanking eventually loses its effectiveness; hitting children teaches them that using physical violence is an effective method to solve problems; a focus on punishment rather than teaching children how to behave properly distracts the child from learning; punishment infringes upon the bond between parent and child; anger and frustration builds inside the child; and physical punishment may send the child the message that "might makes right" and that it is permissible to hurt someone.

Although Homer eagerly chokes his son when he misbehaves, he does not believe in spanking Bart. Bart is one of those boys whose behaviors often cause strangers to comment, "Why don't his parents do something about his behavior?" Sentiments such as these often imply the use of corporal punishment in extreme situations. And Bart is often the cause of extreme situations. Even though Homer will not spank Bart, there are others who will. For example, in "The Mook, the Chef, the Wife, and Her Homer" episode (#379), Otto, the stoner school bus driver, becomes so angry at Bart that he spanks him. Otto is certainly provoked by Bart. On their way to school, Otto pulls off to the side of the road to see if he can help another disabled bus. The disabled bus turns out to be the tour bus for the heavy metal rock band Metallica. Otto is a huge fan of Metallica and is unaware that Bart has commandeered the school bus and is driving away with it. Otto runs after the school bus (after being disrespected by Metallica) and eventually catches up to it on school property. As Bart steps off the bus, Otto grabs him, takes him over his knee, and spanks him. Even though Otto is understandably upset, he has no authority to hit a child. Principal Skinner sees the whole incident and promptly fires Otto for "administering corporal punishment" against Bart. (Note: Although it is not shown in this episode, Otto is rehired.)

In one of the most hilarious *Simpsons* episodes, "Two Bad Neighbors" (#141), former president George H. W. Bush moves in across the street from the Simpsons. Bart, in a parody of *Dennis the Menace* (with Bush as Mr. Wilson), gets on the nerves of George Bush, the elder. After a number of incidents, Bush cracks under the pressure and spanks Bart. Bush tells Bart, "I'm going to do something your daddy should have done a long time ago." (Note: There could be a political message here, that the elder Bush should have spanked his son for misbehaving.) The spanking does not really bother Bart, but he goes home and tells his dad. Homer goes ballistic when he learns that Bush spanked his son. Homer states, "First Bush invades my home turf, then he takes my pals, then he makes fun of the way I talk—probably—now he steals my right to raise a disobedient, smart-alecky son! Well, that's it!" Grandpa Simpson disagrees with Homer. Grandpa recalls how in his day it was common to spank children.

> *Marge*: Grandpa, I know in your day spanking was common, but Homer and I just don't believe in that kind of punishment.
> *Grandpa*: And that's why your no-good kids are running wild.

The dialogue between Marge and Grandpa pretty much sums up the spanking debate. Meanwhile, Homer demands an apology from Bush for spanking Bart. Bush refuses to apologize. Homer calls Bush a "wimp"—a reference to his political ineptness—and one of the grandest neighbor disputes ever develops. Eventually, Bush, rather than apologize, sells the home and moves away from Springfield. Gerald Ford moves in right afterwards. When Ford asks Homer if he would like to watch football with him and eat nachos and drink beer, Homer knows he has a new pal! Albeit, no apology from Bush for spanking Bart.

Today, more and more parents are seeking alternatives to physical punishment in order to discipline their children. Some parents use "timeouts"—a method that encourages the child to quietly contemplate what he or she did wrong while sitting in a corner, or some designated area that is relatively free of outside interference and stimuli. Another alternative to spanking involves the parent gripping the child's wrist firmly and using a firm voice to explain to the child why his or her behavior was not proper. Other parents will emphasize gentle instruction and guidance for proper behavior. Establishing a nurturing environment that is characterized by love and respect represents the fundamental task of parents. After all, if children do not feel safe at home, where *will* they feel safe?

Family Pets

Pets are a common feature for many families. Everyone has his or her favorite type of pet. Aunt Selma, for one, has a pet iguana. And although a number of random animals have served as temporary pets for members of the Simpson family (e.g., Bart once had an elephant and Lisa had a pony), they have two of the favorite American family pets, a dog and a cat. Cats and dogs generally provide unconditional love to their masters and, as a result, they may actually assist children to feel safe at home. Parents usually see great value in having a family pet grow with the child as pets are constant companions.

The Simpsons have a family dog, Santa's Little Helper. The history of how he became a part of the family was described in chapter 1. It is worth noting that Santa's Little Helper's story was shared with *The Simpsons* viewers in the first full-length episode ("Simpsons Roasting on an Open Fire"). In this episode, Marge describes Santa's Little Helper as the best gift the family ever received because it is something to "share our love and threaten prowlers!" In a fairly stereotypical manner, Bart identifies and bonds with the dog, while Lisa identifies and bonds with the family cat, Snowball.

Santa's Little Helper, like Bart, often gets into trouble. He digs up the backyard and tears things apart inside the house with regularity. In the "Bart's Dog Gets an 'F'" episode (#29), Santa nearly meets his masters' limit of patience after he shreds the family quilt.

> *Marge*: My quilt! Six generations, ruined!
> *Homer*: Now Marge, honey, honey, honey. Come on. Come on, don't get upset. It's not the end of the world. We all loved the quilt, but you can't get too attached to . . . (He notices crumbs where his full cookie should be). Ahhhh. My cookie! This is not happening! This is not happening! Everybody in the kitchen! We're having a family meeting.

Homer has had it. Homer threatens to give the dog away if he does not start to behave better. Marge agrees. Bart is distraught. As the person in the family who loves the dog the most, Bart realizes it is up to him to save Santa's Little Helper. Bart takes the dog to Emily Winthrop's Canine College. He must pass obedience school or Homer will kick the dog out of their home. Bart tries to train his dog at home so that he will pass the school exam. Unfortunately, the dog has not learned the basic commands (sit, roll over, and bark on cue) necessary to pass. It seems hopeless and Bart cries because his dog is "stupid." Suddenly, and unexplainably, on the night before the final exam, Santa's Little Helper begins to obey all of Bart's commands. Santa's

Little Helper passes the exam easily and the Simpson family is there to bask in the glory. Santa's Little Helper's place in the family is secured. Luckily for Santa's Little Helper, *The Simpsons* is frozen in a one-year time frame or he would be nearly 140 dog years old by now.

A partial history of the Simpson's cat was also provided in the "Simpsons Roasting on an Open Fire" episode and reviewed in chapter 1. However, in the "I, (Annoyed Grunt)–Bot" episode (#322), a more detailed description is provided. In this episode, we see Dr. Hibbert run over Snowball II. The family has a burial for Snowball II in the backyard. (She has a headstone saying "Snowball II" and there is another headstone for "Snowball I" right next to it.) The death of a beloved family pet can be relatively traumatic for some. Typically, the family comes together and has some sort of burial ceremony. This gathering affords the family a golden opportunity to bond with one another. Younger family members may struggle to understand the emotional grief they are experiencing. They are exposed to "death" and begin to contemplate its meaning. This provides a great teaching opportunity for parents.

Some people need a grieving period after their pet dies before they replace it. Other people believe that replacing the pet immediately heals the wounds quicker. Marge thinks that Lisa will benefit from having a new cat right away and takes her to the Springfield Animal Shelter. Lisa finds a cat that she really likes and decides to call it Snowball III. Sadly, Snowball III dies on her very first day in the Simpsons' home. The cat tries to catch a fish in the fishbowl but falls in and drowns instead! Marge tries to reassure Lisa by reminding her that she is a Buddhist and that her cats will come back at a higher level in the next life.

Marge and Lisa return to the shelter and pick out another cat. She names this one Coltrane, in honor of the American legendary jazz saxophonist and composer John William Coltrane. As a budding saxophonist herself, Lisa admires the highly influential Coltrane, who is often credited with reshaping modern jazz. As soon as they get home, Lisa is eager to play some Coltrane on her sax for her new cat. Unfortunately, the cat is so startled when Lisa plays her first note that it leaps up in the air, falls out of Lisa's bedroom window, and dies upon crashing to the ground below. In a bit of comedic irony, the shelter refuses to allow Lisa and Marge to bring another cat home!

Lisa returns home empty-handed and brokenhearted. Suddenly,

the Springfield "Cat Lady" appears. She offers Lisa one of the many cats clinging to her ratty clothes. Lisa tries to say "no" but the Cat Lady throws a cat at Lisa anyway. Lisa quickly realizes that this cat is tough, tough enough to survive the Simpson family. Lisa is not sure what to name this cat. She calls it "Snowball V" at first (Coltrane serves as "Snowball IV"), but then decides to call her cat Snowball II because that way she can save money by not buying a new dish.

As we have learned, to survive in the Simpson family, pets had better be as strong and as durable as the family members. The Simpson family may be relatively dysfunctional, but when it matters the most, they are there for one another. Just as families always should be.

Chapter 6

Gender Roles and Expectations

"Let's buy makeup so the boys will like us."
—Malibu Stacy

Are little girls made of sugar and spice and everything nice? And are boys made of snips and snails and puppy dog tails, as the old nursery rhyme suggests? Although never meant to be taken literally (boys are clearly not made of snails and puppy tails), the basic implication behind this old nursery rhyme is that gender roles and expectations are biologically determined. In this regard, boys are expected to play rough, get dirty, be assertive and aggressive; while girls are expected to be sweet, clean, passive, and act "ladylike."

However, gender roles and expectations are not biologically determined; instead, they reflect cultural norms and values. Regardless of individual personality, every society has expectations of appropriate behavior based on one's sex. In Western societies, men and women are treated equally and have a relatively equal opportunity to secure valued resources. Women are free to dress as they please and are encouraged to compete against men. In Middle Eastern societies women have far fewer rights and must abide by a strict code of behavior that governs such activities as style of dress and lifestyle choices.

The fact that gender expectations vary from society to society clearly reveals that gender roles are socially learned and taught by the agents of socialization (e.g., parents, family, media, religion, schools, and peer groups). The process of learning gender roles begins early in life, typically with children modeling significant others, especially parents. Some parents will teach their children gender equity while others will teach that specific social roles should be applied based on one's gender. Thus, the messages parents send their children regarding gender appropriateness are often critical and can have an effect that lasts a lifetime.

The importance of modeling is discussed in the very first episode of *The Simpsons*, "Simpsons Roasting on an Open Fire." In this episode, aunts Patty and Selma are mocking Homer as the extended Simpson family awaits his return home on Christmas Eve.

> *Aunt Patty*: I'm just trashing your father.
> *Lisa*: Well, I wish you wouldn't. Because, aside from the fact that he has the same frailties as all human beings, he's the only father I have. Therefore, he is my model of manhood and my estimation of him will govern the prospects of my adult relationships. So, I hope you bear in mind that any kind of knock at him is a knock at me and I am far too young to defend myself against such onslaughts.
> *Aunt Patty* (feeling uneasy about Lisa's comments): Mmm, hmm. Go watch your cartoon show, dear.

Lisa is trying to point out the important role of her father in her life while Aunt Patty is being dismissive of Lisa because she is a little girl who does not "know her place" in the adult world. But what is Lisa's place in the social world? The role of women has certainly changed over the past half century. In the 1950s, Lisa would have been socialized to fulfill the expectation of her eventually becoming a wife and mother. Today, she can strive to fill the social role of her choosing.

BEING A MAN

"Dancing is for girls!"
—Bart Simpson

If the role of women has changed dramatically in the West over the past half century, has the role of men also changed? Men's Studies programs surprisingly pale in number to Women's Studies programs on most college campuses, despite the simple logic that if a change has occurred in gender expectations for one sex, then a change has also probably occurred in those for the other sex. And if so, shouldn't this also be examined?

Everyone struggles to find his or her identity. Gender identity is just one aspect of individual personality, but for some people, it is a very critical characteristic. As stated previously, modeling the behavior of significant others is one very important element in learning gender roles. Bart and Lisa have Homer for a primary role model. Consequently, they have relatively conservative and traditional views of what it is to be a boy and what it is to be a girl.

In the "Homer vs. Patty and Selma" episode (#120), Bart is confronted with mixed emotions about the ballet. In this episode, Bart arrives to school late on the day kids have to sign up for physical education courses. Because he is late, all the "good" activities are filled. The only class open is ballet. Bart protests to the school principal.

Bart: Dancing is for girls!
Skinner: Well, you should have gotten here earlier.

Bart believes that any boy who takes ballet is a sissy, and he complains to the ballet teacher. The nameless, Russian-accented ballet teacher informs Bart, "Ballet is for the strong, the fierce, the determined. But for the sissies? Never. Now put on this fuchsiatard. You are a fairy." Bart reluctantly puts on his tights and prepares to perform. He says to himself, "Okay, steady Bart. Taking ballet doesn't make you any less of a man." Much to his and the entire class's surprise, Bart is a natural! He is such a good dancer that Bart loves ballet. He practices at home. He is so good that the ballet teacher casts him in the school recital. However, Bart is also concerned about his image. He worries that the girls will laugh at him and the bully boys will beat him up for dancing ballet.

Quite the gender quandary. Bart, as with most boys his age, is very concerned about his sense of self and the image he portrays to others. He wants girls to like him and boys to respect him. But he also knows the perception of ballet among American males—it is for sissies. On the other hand, he really likes ballet. And that's the point about breaking down gender barriers. If a boy wants to perform in the ballet, shouldn't he be allowed, or encouraged, to do so? Just as girls who want to play baseball should be allowed, or encouraged, to pursue it. Bart finds a compromise. He decides to perform wearing a mask to hide his identity. Bart's performance (in front of an audience consisting mostly of boys on detention) is brilliant. Even two school bullies, Jimbo and Nelson, are impressed with the "Masked Dancer" and search desperately for ways to express appreciation without compromising their masculine identities.

> *Jimbo*: He's graceful yet masculine. So it's okay for me to enjoy this.
>
> *Nelson*: This reminds me of the movie *Fame* and to a lesser extent the TV series, which was also called *Fame*.

Based on the loud applause at the end of his dance routine, Bart has a renewed sense of confidence in his gender identity and decides to reveal himself to the audience by taking his mask off. All the boys immediately yell out, "Sissy!" and run after him. Bart tries to leap to safety, but he does not make it. The boys beat him up. Bart has learned a tough lesson; boys are not as enlightened as he had hoped. Because reinforcement is another critical aspect of learning, a second lesson that Bart has likely learned is to keep to gender "appropriate" behaviors for boys.

In the "New Kid on the Block" episode (#67), school bully Jimbo learns that even tough boys can be "broken" by a bigger threat. In this episode, Jimbo has "stolen" Bart's love interest, Laura Powers. Laura was hired to babysit the Simpson kids. She likes Bart, but tells him that he is too young for her. Instead, Laura is attracted to bad boy Jimbo. She invites Jimbo over to the Simpsons' house while she babysits. Upset by this turn of events, Bart decides to get even with Jimbo. Bart pulls one of his typical phone pranks on Moe, but this time identifies himself as Jimbo and provides Moe with his street address. Moe, who has vowed revenge against the prankster who has tormented him all these years, charges over to the Simpson home to confront Jimbo. The surprised Jimbo is unnerved when Moe threatens him with a knife.

Jimbo immediately breaks down crying and begging for his life (perhaps a pragmatic course of action when a madman with a weapon threatens your life). Moe looks at Jimbo with disgust and tells him, "I wasn't really gonna kill ya; I was just gonna cut ya. Aah, forget it." Moe views Jimbo as such a wimp that he walks away. He is not going to waste his time executing "justice" against someone as unmanly as Jimbo. Laura is also immediately turned off by Jimbo's behavior. Laura tells Jimbo that she has no respect for a wimpy boy. She looks at Bart and acknowledges that she could fall for him, but only if he was older. Laura and Bart then call Moe's and prank him! (Note: See chapter 14 for examples of prank phone calls.)

The historically dominant role held by men in Western patriarchal societies has encouraged the objectification of women. The objectification of women was the central focus in the "Homer's Night Out" episode (#10). In this episode, Homer is at a stag party with his male friends. Marge happens to take the kids out to dinner at the same restaurant where the stag party is being held. Bart, who has just attained a mail-order spy camera, excuses himself from the dinner table to go to the bathroom. He happens to peek into the room where the stag party is being held and snaps a photograph of Princess Kashmir, a hired belly dancer, dancing seductively for Homer.

After Bart develops the film, he gives Milhouse of a copy of the photo of Homer with Princess Kashmir. Milhouse, in turn, makes multiple copies for his classmates, and before long, copies of the photo have spread throughout Springfield as quickly as photos of a cheating or flashing celebrity spread throughout the Internet. Marge is among the citizens of Springfield who acquire a copy of this devious photo. She confronts Homer upon his arrival home from work. Homer proclaims his innocence, saying it was meaningless. Bart walks by his parents while they are arguing and says, "Hey, my photo!" Homer and Marge simultaneously shout, "Your photo?!" This prompts Homer to yell at Bart, "Why you little—," as he starts choking his son.

Marge is so angry at Homer that she kicks him out of the house. She believes that Homer has set a bad example for Bart because he is shown objectifying women in that photo. Princess Kashmir may argue that she is empowering herself because she can make men give her their hard-earned money simply by dancing seductively for them. Most feminists, however, will agree with Marge's take on stag parties.

Homer wants Marge's forgiveness. She will let him back in the house if he shows Bart that women should not be objectified. Marge wants Homer to apologize to Princess Kashmir in front of Bart. So, Homer and Bart set off looking for Kashmir. Naturally, they go to the

Vegas-style burlesque show in town. Meanwhile, true to the double standard that still often exists in society, the highly circulated photo of Homer and the belly-dancer has bestowed a "player" reputation on him. At this club, Homer is introduced to the crowd with this announcement, "It's an honor to have a real swinging cat with us tonight; Homer Simpson, party guy." Homer joins the dancing girls on stage. Smithers turns to Burns (both of whom are at the same club) and says of Homer that he "is a love machine." Such a reputation could go to most men's heads. However, when Homer looks out at the crowd and hears Bart shout out, "Way to go Dad!" he realizes what a negative message he is sending his son.

With the entire club hanging on his every word, Homer states, "You know something folks, as ridiculous as this sounds, I would rather feel the sweet breath of my beautiful wife on the back of my neck as I sleep than stuff dollar bills into some stranger's G-string." Marge, who had gone to the club looking for Homer and Bart, overhears Homer's proclamation and is obviously pleased. Almost instantly, nearly all the men in the club get up and leave to join their wives. Everyone is happy; that is, except for the women who hoped to make money dancing that night.

BEING A WOMAN

"Please note, homemaker is not allowed as it's not real work. That's why you don't get paid for it."
—Springfield Elementary

Marge is a homemaker, an often thankless job. A homemaker is a person whose primary responsibility is to care for family and/or home. The term "homemaker" replaced the term "housewife" or "househusband" because it is an inclusive term that defines a social role in terms of activities and is independent of one's gender. The terms "stay-at-home mom" and "stay-at-home dad" may also be used, especially if childcare is viewed as the central role of that person. The homemaker not only performs daily chores without much recognition, but according to Springfield Elementary it does not even qualify as a job.

In the "Bart on the Road" (#148) episode, Principal Skinner has announced "Go to Work with Your Parents Day." Children are supposed to learn job skills from their parents that they may apply in the future. Having little respect for the work that his mom does, Bart decides to sign up to go to work with his mother. Bart envisions sitting around the house all day relaxing. The next morning, Lisa is upset that Bart gets to stay home. She questions his motives. Bart tells her, "I have always been an advocate of women in the workplace." However, Bart's plans are thwarted when he asks his mother to sign the school form. Under "Parent's Occupation" is written: "Please note homemaker is not allowed as it is not real work. That's why you don't get paid for it." Ouch! Marge's lifestyle has been demeaned. Marge does not expect to be paid for what she does around the house—after all, where would that money come from—but she would like occasional recognition. Interestingly, some people have attempted to place a dollar value on the work that homemakers perform. A study conducted by Salary.com (2006) indicates that female homemakers would earn $134,121 per year. Their male counterparts (which are much fewer in number), would earn $125,340 per year (Salary.com 2006B). Among the job duties that homemakers perform without receiving pay are: computer operator, day-care center teacher, laundry machine operator, facilities manager, psychologist, driver/chauffeur, cook, and groundskeeper.

One might ask, "How are these salaries determined?" Salary.com utilizes a format that involves determining how many hours a week a homemaker spends on the various jobs performed. Next, the annual salaries for the various jobs performed are applied. The "stay-at-home dad" salary is broken down as follows:

Job Performed	Hours per week	Yearly Salary
Day-Care Center Teacher	17	$11,741
Maintenance Worker	14.5	10,753
Cook	13.4	10,726
Computer Operator	12.6	9,926
Driver/Chauffeur	6.3	5,012
Facilities Manager	4.5	8,949
CEO	4.1	31,203
Laundry Operator	4	1,874
Groundskeeper	2.3	1,505
Family Psychologist	2.3	4,334

Under this sampling of job duties performed by the male home-maker, his yearly earning for a forty-hour week would be just under $49,395 and his overtime salary would equal $75,945, totaling $125,340 (Salary.com 2006). A stay-at-home mom performs many of the same duties listed above and her compensation is slightly higher.

Marge Simpson is far less troubled with any calculations of what her salary would be if someone was available to pay for it than she is concerned over Bart's attempt to learn about women in the work-force going unfulfilled. Ever so helpful, Lisa points out that Bart could go watch aunts Patty and Selma, who work at the Department of Motor Vehicles. Bart does not appreciate his sister's "help."

GENDER STEREOTYPES

"Boys are better in math and science—the real subjects."
—Principal Skinner

Bart does learn about women in the workplace by observing his aunts; although, unfortunately, they do not take their jobs too seriously. Nonetheless, they work at a profession that men and women are equally qualified to perform. In fact, nearly all jobs can be equally performed by men or women. Despite this reality, a number of stereotypes about gender and occupations still exist. For example, at most diners if a cus-tomer were to order a cup of coffee, chances are good that the person who brings it will be a woman, and the person who delivered the coffee grounds to the diner was a man. The occupations of firefighter and police officer are disproportionately held by males. Further, women are more likely to hold lower-paying service jobs such as waitress, nurse's aide, childcare worker, and social worker than are men. Sales and office jobs are also likely to be dominated by women. Collectively, these lower-paying, lower-status jobs are referred to as "pink collar" jobs (Vogel 2003). Because women hold a large number of lower-paying jobs, when women's average earnings are compared to men's average earnings, women earn just seventy-six cents for every dollar a man makes.

Despite all the attempts to eliminate gender stereotyping in the workplace, many occupations are still perceived to be gender specific. The construction industry, in particular, is a male-dominant occupa-tion. Marge learns of this veracity in the "Please Homer, Don't Hammer

'Em" episode (#381). In this episode, Marge uses carpentry tools to make numerous repairs around the house. The carpentry self-help books that Homer purchased, but never read, assist Marge in her various projects. Bart and Lisa are both very impressed with Marge's skills.

Bart: It's like you're the Jesus of carpentry!
Marge: Oh, what sweet blasphemy.

Lisa suggests to her mom that she sell her services. Unfortunately for Marge, she learns that potential customers do not like the idea of a woman carpenter. Marge declares, "I guess people just expect their carpenter to be some fat guy with his butt crack showing." Undaunted in her pursuit to crack the male-dominated world of carpentry, Marge decides to use the pragmatic approach of having her husband serve as a "front." Homer meets with the customers and pretends to be the carpenter while Marge does all the actual work. And with this arrangement, "Simpson Carpentry" is established.

Before long, Simpson Carpentry has performed a number of odd jobs around town. Local newsman Kent Brockman hires Simpson Carpentry to build him a gazebo. Brockman is so impressed by the handiwork he refers to Homer as a "master craftsman." Homer feels a little guilty taking credit for Marge's work so he asks Kent how he would react if he learned that a woman actually built the gazebo. Brockman tells Homer, "I'd have this gazebo torn down and built into a coffin for your manhood." Homer is disappointed by Kent's response and, for the good of Simpson Carpentry, he decides to let Brockman believe that he actually did all the work.

Homer begins to let the accolades of "his" handiwork go to his head. Marge becomes increasingly, and understandably, upset with Homer for taking all the credit for her work. Homer reminds Marge that it was all her idea.

Homer: Look, I'm sorry you're upset. But, if we tell the truth now, I'll be humiliated in front of the whole town. Then, you won't be married to a man; you'll be married to some kind of gay jellyfish floating outside the Florida Keys cruising for rich snorkelers. You don't want that.
Marge: I guess I don't.

As a result of this conversation, and stereotypical occupational expectations, Marge continues to do the work while Homer continues to take all the credit. Homer's friends Lenny and Carl, who are used to his otherwise ineptness, wonder if Homer is really doing all this handy carpentry work.

> *Homer*: Who would help me? My wife?!
> (Homer, Lenny, and Carl all laugh.)
> *Lenny*: The only thing women can build is credit card debt!

Finally, Marge reaches her tolerance limit and insists that Homer come clean with the truth, that she is the real carpenter of the family. Homer refuses and Marge quits the team. Homer allows all the praise he has received to go to his head and he naively believes that if Marge can do carpentry work, then so can he. Thinking big, Homer submits a bid—that is accepted—to rebuild "The Zoominator" roller coaster. Because they lack confidence in him, Homer's hired crew quits. Homer proceeds with the repairs without the crew. He even vows to ride the maiden voyage of the roller coaster after his repairs are finished. Lisa, fearing for her father's life, pleads with Homer to put aside his male ego. Homer's male ego is as fragile as they come, so he refuses to admit that Marge was the real carpenter of the family.

Marge may be upset with Homer for taking all her handiwork credit but she still loves him and does not want to see him harmed. She quickly repairs the numerous flaws to Homer's work and saves his life as he takes the first roller coaster ride after restorations. Homer publicly admits to the truth as the roller coaster collapses behind him!

There are many similarities and differences between men and women. Among the commonalities of both men and women are their desire to fulfill such fundamental needs as survival, self-esteem, confidence, intimacy, and personal growth. Both men and women want some sense of control over their lives as well. And despite the joke that men are from Mars and women are from Venus, there are indeed many differences between the sexes that go beyond the obvious biological ones. For example, women live longer than men; men are, on the average, bigger and stronger than women; men are more aggressive than women by almost any measure and regardless of culture or society; men commit more violent crimes than women; women are more relationship-oriented and are more emotional than men; females are better at interpreting nonverbal behavior (such as reading body language, gestures, and "signs"; and males are better at math and science.

In the "Girls Just Want to Have Sums" episode (#375), Principal Skinner is fired for pointing out the differences in test scores between boys and girls in math and science. In this episode, former Springfield Elementary student and current pop-star Julianna returns to Springfield to take part in the festivities surrounding the opening night of the Itchy & Scratchy musical. Skinner introduces Julianna to the audience as a straight-A student. Julianna admits that she received a couple of B grades in math. Skinner laughs and says, "Well of course you did. You're a girl." The audience is aghast at Skinner's comment. He tries to use logic to get himself out of trouble and proclaims, "Boys do better in math and science—the real subjects." Skinner cites the commonly known truth that boys score higher than girls in math and science. He makes no inference beyond this fact and still manages to dig a hole for himself deeper and deeper. (Note: Skinner's dilemma is similar to the trouble former Harvard University president Lawrence H. Summers endured when he publicly speculated that women may lack the same innate abilities as men in math and science. He was citing Massachusetts SAT statistics that reveal girls consistently score lower than boys on the math and science tests.)

The next day, the teachers of Springfield Elementary and a number of women from activist groups protest outside the school against Skinner's comments. They deem such remarks as sexist. Superintendent Chalmers is upset over the negative publicity the school is generating and demands that Skinner deal with these "kooks." Skinner assures Chalmers that he will take care of the problem by pretending to agree with the women. Skinner organizes a diversity forum on sexism. Women's rights advocate Lindsey Naegle and schoolteacher Edna Krabappel are among the attendees at the first forum.

> *Skinner*: Today, we celebrate the first of many, many, many, many diversity forums. Why is it that women "appear" to be worse at math than men? What is the source of this "illusion" or as I call it, the biggest lie ever told?
>
> *Lindsey Naegle*: You're a worse version of Hitler!
>
> *Skinner*: Please believe me. I—I understand the problem of

women. (Skinner moves from behind the podium to reveal that he is wearing a purple dress and purple heels.) See?

Nelson (who is in the audience): Ha, ha! The principal's a tranny!

Skinner (when asked why he is wearing women's clothing): Am I wearing women's clothes? I didn't notice. When I look in my closet, I don't see male clothes or female clothes. They're all the same.

Edna Krabappel: Are you saying that men and women are identical?

Skinner: Oh, no, of course not! Women are unique in every way.

Lindsey Naegle: Now he's saying men and women *aren't* equal!

Skinner: No, no, no! It's the differences of which there are none that makes the sameness exceptional. Just tell me what to say!

Skinner's mind overheats! Whatever he says is taken the wrong way. Chalmers, not at all pleased by the events that have unfolded, fires Skinner as principal and reassigns him as assistant groundskeeper. Skinner is replaced by a woman principal who promptly divides the school based on gender. The idea behind a gender-segregated school is based on the belief that girls are intimidated by boys in school, which is supposed to explain why girls do not do as well as boys in subjects such as math and science.

Lisa, who is very smart and good at math, is eager to learn in her new environment. Her enthusiasm quickly disappears when she discovers that girls' math involves discussing the "emotions" of math This new technique of teaching math is supposed to build confidence and self-esteem. Lisa sees through this farce immediately. She wants to learn "real" math and challenges the teacher. Lisa is told that men merely attack math problems—they try to figure problems out. Lisa exclaims in near disbelief, "That's what math really is!" Lisa worries that she will fall even further behind the boys in math and complains to her mother about her new math class.

Lisa is so driven to learn math that, the next day, she dresses as a "he-she" in order to attend the boys' school. She has developed an androgynous physical look and personality in order to resemble a boy and not look like a girl. Lisa calls herself Jake Boyman. Like most boys new to a school, she is immediately picked on by the bullies.

Lisa is afraid to admit to her mother that she is getting beat up because she really loves her math class. She is especially impressed by the title of her new math book, *Real Math*. Bart figures out that Lisa is Jake Boyman. He decides to teach his sister how to think and act like a boy. These traits, according to Bart, include stuffing French fries in your mouth and making sure only a portion of them actually reach the inside of your mouth, learning to pick on weaker kids, and acting tough by defending yourself.

With Bart's advice, Jake Boyman survives boys' school and receives the highest grade in the math class. Jake reveals herself to be Lisa and remarks, "I'm glad I'm a girl and I'm glad that I am good at math." Bart, being Bart, attempts to undermine Lisa's accomplishments by saying Lisa got her high grade because she thought like a boy.

Interestingly, the gender-segregated Springfield Elementary School is divided by a traditional gender-specific color scheme. The boys' side of the school is painted blue, while the girls' side is painted pink. This color scheme has potential gender stereotypical overtones. Feminists especially argue that perpetuating pink for girls and blue for boys reinforces traditional gender role expectations. The color pink is generally viewed as a passive, soothing color. This was the very image the new (female) principal at Springfield was trying to create as the pink-walled girls' side of the school was also equipped with fountains and paintings. All of this was designed to create a soothing, mellow atmosphere that encouraged girls to tap into their emotions. The boys' side of the school was run-down and clearly victimized by acts of violence—a negative stereotype of boys.

A great deal of research has examined the role of color schemes and gender stereotyping. Pink is generally associated with femininity. And that is why, typically, girls wear pink, and boys do not. Delaney and Madigan (2008) have conducted research on color schemes used in the sports world. Among their findings, there are no men's sports teams that utilize the color pink. This is understandable as the male sports world is filled with "codes of masculinity" that are not to be violated. There are, however, examples of the color pink being used as a weapon in order to gain an edge over an opponent. For example, the football visitors' locker room at the University of Iowa is painted pink in an attempt by the home team to gain a psychological edge. The walls, bathroom stalls, ceiling, urinals, and carpet are all pink. Former Hawkeyes coach (1979–98) Hayden Fry, a psychology major, first had the walls and benches painted pink in 1980, reasoning that the color pink has a calming effect on opponents. Feminists are upset with the University of Iowa for allowing this. They argue that because pink is associated with women (and gay men), when it is used to demean an opponent, it is similar to demeaning women and gays. Thus, painting the visitors' locker room pink as a form of intimidation is viewed as an example of sexism. Interestingly, in the twenty years prior to painting the visitors' locker room pink, the Iowa Hawkeyes had won about 40 percent of their home games. They have won nearly 70 percent of their home games in the twenty-seven years that the visitors' locker room has been painted pink.

FEMINISM

"Is the remarkably sexist drivel spouted by Malibu Stacy intentional, or is it just a horrible mistake?"
—Lisa Simpson

Regular viewers of *The Simpsons* have undoubtedly noticed that Lisa possesses many feminist attributes. She routinely fights for the rights of women and preaches empowerment. Where did this little activist learn such behavior? Believe it or not, from her homemaker mother. Marge has nearly always encouraged Lisa to strive to reach her full human potential. Marge herself participated in a popular form of activism while in high school—she burned her bra during a 1974 protest rally (as revealed in "The Way We Was" episode). In the "Lisa's First Word" episode (#69), Marge reflects back to the year of 1983 when she first learned that she was pregnant with Lisa. (Note: This is another example of the chronological timing problem discussed in chapter 5.) In this episode, Marge describes the spring of 1983 as a wonderful time for women's rights because Ms. Pac-man was created. Marge tells her family, "This story begins in that unforgettable spring of 1983: Ms. Pac-man struck a blow for women's rights . . ." Although feminists seldom reference this achievement among feminists' highlights, it was important to Marge!

Lisa the Lionhearted

The most classic feminist-themed episode of *The Simpsons* is "Lisa vs. Malibu Stacy" (#95). Malibu Stacy is a popular girls' doll similar to Barbie. Lisa lives up to the gender stereotype of girls who have a passive inclination to play with dolls; whereas her brother Bart prefers rough play where possible injury is a very real occurrence.

In the "Malibu Stacy" episode, the Simpson family is shopping at the mall. Lisa is excited to purchase the latest installment of the Malibu Stacy line of accessories—the Summer Fun Set. As she walks through the Valley of Dolls section of the Kidstown USA store, she warns her mother that she may get a little crazy fighting with the other girls over the limited supplies. As Marge starts to say she understands Lisa's eagerness, Lisa has already confronted another little girl. Lisa yells at the would-be competitor, "Hey, horse-face! Get your ugly pie hooks off that Summer Fun Set!" Growing up in the Simpsons' household has taught Lisa to be tough!

As the girls begin to disperse, a stock boy comes out with a big box of unknown contents. One little girl asks, "Hey mister, what's in the box?" The stock boy nervously responds, "Uh, it's the new talking Malibu Stacy." After a brief collective pause of disbelief among all the girls at the Valley of Dolls, the stock boy is suddenly and violently attacked. The new Malibu Stacy becomes an instant rage. Lisa can barely contain her anticipation as she eagerly waits to hear what words of wisdom Malibu Stacy will bestow upon her. In her bedroom, Lisa sets up a mock United Nations meeting for Malibu Stacy's first words. She has her other dolls aligned as audience members. Pretending to be the master of ceremonies, Lisa says, "A hush falls over the General Assembly as Stacy approaches the podium to deliver what will no doubt be a stirring and memorable address." Bart joins Lisa as she pulls the string on the Malibu Stacy doll for the first time.

Malibu Stacy: I wish they taught shopping at school!
Lisa: Ohh.
Malibu Stacy: Let's make some cookies for the boys!
Lisa: Come on, Stacy, I've waited my whole life to hear you
    speak. Don't you have anything relevant to say?
Malibu Stacy: Don't ask me—I'm just a girl. (Stacy giggles.)
Bart (mockingly): Right on! Say it, sister!

> *Lisa*: It's not funny, Bart! Millions of girls will grow up thinking that this is the right way to act—that they can never be more than vacuous ninnies whose only goal is to look pretty, land a rich husband, and spend all day on the phone with their equally vacuous friends talking about how damn terrific it is to look pretty and have a rich husband!
>
> *Bart*: Just what I was gonna say.
>
> *Lisa*: Grrr . . . (While grunting, Lisa throws her new doll out her window—and hits her grandfather who is riding his bicycle.)

Lisa is clearly upset. She realizes the impact that a doll as popular as Malibu Stacy can have on shaping young girls' sense of self and self-worth. (Imagine, a woman talking on the phone all day with other women about trivial issues!) She finds it appalling that a woman would find self-worth as a man's accessory. This is straight out of the feminist "handbook." In fact, Lisa finds all the quotes from Malibu Stacy appalling. Among the other things that Stacy utters:

"Let's buy makeup so the boys will like us."
"Thinking too much gives you wrinkles."
"My name is Stacy, but you can call me—[whistle sound for an attractive woman]."

All these phrases reinforce negative sexist stereotypes of women. Lisa is outraged. She tries to convince her girlfriends that the things Malibu Stacy says are sexist, but to no avail. In fact, some of her friends think that Lisa used a "dirty" word (by saying "sexist") and giggle—like Malibu Stacy has taught them. Lisa and her friends are just eight years old, and although Lisa has a heightened sense of social awareness, the other girls just want to have fun.

Lisa does not want a generation of girls growing up with Malibu Stacy as a role model. Later that evening at the family dinner table, Lisa complains to her mother about the sexist comments coming from Malibu Stacy. "They cannot keep making dolls like this; something has to be done." Marge tries to calm her daughter down, but to no avail. Instead, Lisa becomes increasingly upset and confronts her mother directly.

Lisa: I can't believe that you're just going to stand by as your daughters grow up in a world where this, this (she is holding onto a Malibu Stacy doll), is their role model.

Marge: I had a Malibu Stacy when I was little and I turned out all right. Now let's forget about our troubles with a big bowl of strawberry ice cream.

(Lisa pulls Malibu Stacy's string.)

Malibu Stacy: Let's forget about our troubles with a big bowl of strawberry ice cream.

Marge: Hmm.

Lisa: That's it. I'm calling the company.

It suddenly dawns on Marge that she was brainwashed as a little girl. She offers to take Lisa to the factory where the doll is manufactured so that she can complain in person. Lisa and Marge sign up for a tour of the plant as their pretense to confront the makers of Malibu Stacy. Their tour guide is Claire Harper. On the tour, Lisa and Marge discover that homemaker Stacy Lovell is the inventor of the doll. The first Malibu Stacy was produced in 1959. The stock film footage shown on the tour also identifies Waylon Smithers as the owner of the largest collection of Stacy Malibu dolls. At the conclusion of the film, the narrator asks, "What does Stacy Lovell think of the thirty-five years of global success of the Malibu Stacy doll?" Malibu Stacy responds for Lovell, "Don't ask me. I'm just a girl." She then giggles. The narrator adds, "She sure is!"

Claire: Well, that's the tour, if you have any questions, I'd be happy to—

Lisa (interrupting Claire): I have one.

Claire: Yes?

Lisa: Is the remarkably sexist drivel spouted by Malibu Stacy intentional, or is it just a horrible mistake?

Claire: Believe me, we're very mindful of such concerns.

(At this point, a male executive opens up a door to an adjacent boardroom filled with other male executives.)

Executive (making the type of wolf whistle used in the Malibu Stacy doll): Hey, Jiggles! Grab a pad and back that gorgeous butt in here!

> *Claire* (playing along): Oh, you, get away . . . (She giggles with
> enjoyment).
> *Executive*: Aw, don't act like you don't like it.

As this exchange in dialogue between the male executive and the female subordinate indicates, the Malibu Stacy workplace is itself a sexist place. The males treat the women as objects, and the women go along with it.

Lisa wants to locate and talk to Stacy Lovell. She turns to Smithers for help. Smithers tells Lisa that she has become a recluse and that she has not been in public for twenty years. Smithers provides Lisa with Lovell's last known address (Recluse Ranch Estates). Lisa does find Lovell and she lives in a house similar to the Malibu Stacy Dream House from the catalog. Lisa asks Lovell if she is aware of the things that the new talking Malibu Stacy says. Lisa pulls Stacy's string to demonstrate. Lovell is uncomfortable with such drivel. Lovell (voiced by Kathleen Turner) informs Lisa that she is the inventor of Malibu Stacy, but she is powerless to do anything. Lovell informs Lisa, "I was forced out of my company in 1974. They said my way of thinking wasn't cost-effective. Well, that and I was funneling profits to the Viet Cong." Lovell is herself a questionable role model!

Lisa suggests to Lovell that she make a new doll; one that will serve as a feminist role model. Lisa has a number of specific ideas that should be incorporated with a new talking doll: "She'll have the wisdom of Gertrude Stein and the wit of Cathy Guisewite, the tenacity of Nina Totenberg and the common sense of Elizabeth Cady Stanton. And to top it off, the down-to-earth good looks of Eleanor Roosevelt." Lovell agrees to make the doll. Lisa serves as the voice for the new doll. She offers feminist comments, such as, "If I get married, I will keep my own name." And, "Trust in yourself and you can achieve anything." The last bit of business is to find a name. Lovell suggests "Lisa Lionheart."

The executives at the Malibu Stacy plant view Lovell's new doll as a real threat. They need something to combat the positive prerelease press that Lisa Lionheart is receiving. On the day of the scheduled release of the new Lisa doll, the makers of Malibu Stacy unveil a new Malibu Stacy doll. The only difference with this new Stacy doll is that she has a new hat! And yet the little girls (and Smithers) cannot control themselves. They were set to buy the Lisa doll because their impressionable young minds were directed to do so. But the previous brainwashing efforts of Malibu Stacy prevailed.

The moral of this story reflects the society we live in: social change, especially in regard to gender expectations, is a slow process because changing culture itself is a lengthy process.

THE DEATH OF FEMINISM

"When I grow up, I want to be a sweetie pie!"
—Amber Dempsey

Is feminism dead? The National Organization for Women (NOW) would say "No!" They point to their membership of around five hundred thousand as evidence of the vitality of the feminist movement. NOW took form in the 1960s and was guided by the principles established by Betty Friedan, author of *The Feminine Mystique*. Friedan argued that a woman needs more than a husband and children to attain self-worth. Friedan equated the homemaker to someone who had "sold out" her intellect and ambition. A woman could only find fulfillment outside the home. Ideas such as these were embraced in the 1960s—a period characterized by rapid social change in many social spheres.

However, contemporary feminists are concerned about the growing number of young women who empathetically deny that they are feminists. Women want equality and equal pay, but that does not mean they identify with the feminist movement. Not only are young women rejecting feminist ideals, but they have seemingly embraced the "woman as an object of beauty, worship me" mentality. Among the popular T-shirts being purchased by young women across the United States today are those with sayings like "Future Trophy Wife" and "Who needs brains when you've got these?" scrawled across the front.

Kate O'Beirne, editor of *National Review* and author of *Women Who Make the World Worse*, argues that the feminist movement has led to the breakdown of the traditional family, degraded motherhood, weakened the military, and more. Caitlin Flanagan agrees with O'Beirne that the feminist movement shortchanged a generation of women who could have found self-worth as homemakers. Flanagan, often referred to as an "antifeminist," is the author of *To Hell with It:*

Loving and Loathing Our Inner Housewife. She argues that as women have become increasingly valued in the workplace, they have become less valued in the home. In essence, there exists the "Mommy Wars"—an ongoing argument between working mothers and their homemaker counterparts (Pasko 2006).

The homemaker seems to be in vogue again, as many women are embracing the label. (Maybe Marge Simpson *is* a role model for today's women.) There are many explanations for this, including an antifeminist backlash, a rise in religious conservatism that values traditional family roles, and the increasing celebrity of "professional" homemakers. The two most popular celebrity homemakers are Martha Stewart and Rachael Ray. Stewart, a long-stay in giving homemaking advice, has written numerous books and articles, served as editor of a national homemaking magazine, host of a popular syndicated television show, and has overseen a variety of product lines and signature designs. Her empire has remained secure despite her brief imprisonment. Ray, a relative newcomer to professional homemaking, offers simple recipes and projects a certain aura of sweetness about her. Unlike the relatively uptight Stewart, Ray giggles and flashes a smile that is so big it rivals Batman's archnemesis the Joker.

Feminists are against social institutions that they deem compromise the value of women and perpetuate negative stereotypes. Beauty pageants are among the social traditions that raise the ire of feminists. And certainly a feminist would never enter a beauty pageant, would she? In the appropriately named "Lisa the Beauty Queen" episode (#63), Lisa the feminist-activist enters a beauty pageant, Little Miss Springfield. The name of this pageant is also upsetting to feminists. They prefer the term "Ms." rather than "Miss" or "Mrs.," arguing that one's marital status should not be an identifier of self. Furthermore, if you are a college student, don't ever refer to a female feminist professor as Mrs. So-and-So—it is always Dr. So-and-So. She will point out to you that you have imposed a marital status and ignored her academic achievements.

In the case of Little Miss Springfield, the name of the pageant seems reasonable, considering it is for little girls. Lisa did not sign up for the pageant; her father signed her up. Homer sold his prized Duff blimp ride ticket to cover the $250 entry fee. (Note: Homer had his heart set on taking a ride in the Duff blimp.) He did this because he thinks his daughter is the most beautiful girl in Springfield. Homer was also aware that Lisa was suffering from low self-esteem. Lisa believes that she is ugly and does not want to take part in the beauty pageant. However, after Marge explains to her how Homer came up with the money to pay the entry fee, Lisa decides to participate. As Lisa states, "That ride meant everything to him."

Lisa registers for the Little Miss Springfield contest. She likes her chances against the other girls, but suddenly a beautiful girl arrives, Amber Dempsey. Amber is a professional pageant contestant. She also has fake eyelash implants, illegal everywhere but Paraguay one of the girls tells Lisa.

Interestingly, *The Simpsons* mocks Paraguay again in the "Homer's Triple Bypass" episode (#70). In this episode, Homer shows his disdain for Paraguay's overall poor healthcare system. I am not sure why *The Simpsons* was mocking Paraguay during the 1992–93 season, but there must be a reason! My own personal experience with Paraguay or people from Paraguay is extremely limited. However, I presented a paper in Buenos Aires, Argentina, in 2005, where the opening speaker, Jorge Ramirez of Paraguay, began his talk with this quote: "Being the first speaker is like being married to a duchess!" I am still not sure what this quote means. Maybe the writers at *The Simpsons* can decipher it.

Lisa does not like her chances against Amber, but Marge offers her a complete makeover in an attempt to enhance her self-esteem. Bart even helps out. He offers to teach Lisa the tricks of the trade: "taping your swimsuit to your butt, putting petroleum jelly on your teeth for that frictionless smile, and the ancient art of padding."

The night of the pageant arrives. The girls introduce themselves. Amber starts by saying, "Hi, I'm Amber Dempsey, and when I grow up, I want to be a sweetie pie!" Reflecting the contrasts between herself and Amber, Lisa tells the crowd "My name is Lisa Simpson, and I want to be Little Miss Springfield so that I can make our town a better place." Amber Dempsey wins the pageant and Lisa is the runner-up. Lisa is dejected that she lost. However, some time later, Amber is struck by lightning and Lisa, as the runner-up, takes over as Little Miss Springfield. Suddenly, all the boys at school like Lisa. In the school cafeteria, Lisa walks by a group of boys confidently. One boy says to another, "I love that chewing gum walk." Lisa's self-confidence reaches a new high as a result of winning a beauty pageant. Has Lisa sold out?

Don't fret, fans of Lisa the activist. She is not just another pretty face who has let her beauty and newfound popularity go to her head. She has every intention of making Springfield a better town to live in. However, Lisa quickly realizes she will not be able to fulfill her requirements as Little Miss Springfield. Laramie Cigarettes, a corporate sponsor of the beauty pageant, wants to use Lisa in a campaign to promote cigarettes among young people. The Laramie representative wants Lisa to ride atop a float shaped like a pack of cigarettes in the upcoming parade. Lisa is outraged. She rides on the float just so that she can have a temporary platform to voice her social conscience. The corporate sponsors find a way to disqualify Lisa. But Lisa doesn't care. Her self-esteem is improved and she thanks her father for it.

For a short period of time, Lisa has a platform to voice her feminist and activist concerns. Giving a voice to women is what feminism is about. And, as long as there are little Lisa Simpsons out there, feminism will never die.

THE GAY IDENTITY

"You know me, Marge. I like my beer cold, my TV loud, and my homosexuals flaming."
—Homer Simpson

One other important issue associated with any review of gender roles and expectations is homosexuality. Throughout most of history, gay people have generally kept their sexual orientation private. Around the 1970s and 1980s, gay people started to "come out of the closet" (the private sphere) and openly displayed their gay identity (the public sphere). Despite the fact that a certain amount of discrimination still exists against gays today, most are candid about their identity.

Contemporary television shows such as *The Simpsons* discuss the gay identity in a fairly open manner and touch upon many of the cultural controversies that surround this gender role. One of the primary gay identity themes discussed in *The Simpsons* is Waylon Smithers's refusal to come out of the closet—officially. Everyone *knows* he is gay, and yet, he is a product of the 1970s way of thinking—it is best to keep a gay identity secret. With each passing season of *The Simpsons*, Smithers is seemingly closer to admitting the truth, that he is gay. In fact, as early as the "Homer Defined" episode (#40), Smithers attempts to reveal his true feelings for Mr. Burns. In this episode, a "meltdown crisis" is in effect at the nuclear plant. To no one's surprise, the source of the problem is in Sector 7-G, where Homer works. The situation is so dire that some employees begin to loot, while others pray. Even the rats, perhaps working on some sort of danger instinct, run away from the plant. Smithers and Burns stand their ground. Seizing this perceived moment of doom, Smithers admits his true feelings toward Burns.

> *Smithers*: Sir, there may never be another time to say . . . I love you, sir.
> *Burns*: Oh hot dog. Thank you for making my last few moments on Earth socially awkward.

The crisis is averted and things go back to "normal" at the plant. Even the rats return! Nothing more is said between Smithers and Burns in this episode regarding Smithers's confession. And over the years, Smithers has continued to long for a love that is not returned.

One long-suspected gay character to officially come out of the closet is Patty Bouvier, Marge's sister. In the "There's Something about Marrying" episode (#345), Springfield has legalized gay marriage in an attempt to increase tourism. Gay couples from around the nation show up in Springfield to marry. Reverend Lovejoy, the pastor of the First Church of Springfield, however, refuses to marry gay couples. Lovejoy tells the disappointed gay couples hoping to marry, "While I have no opinion for or against your sinful lifestyles, I cannot marry two people of the same sex no more than I can put a hamburger on a hotdog bun. Now, go back to working behind the scenes at every facet of entertainment!" Like many conservatives, Lovejoy cites the Bible in his opposition to gay marriage. Homer, sensing an opportunity to earn big bucks, becomes an ordained minister after filling out an online application with the ePiscopal Church.

Patty admits to Marge that she is gay and asks Homer to marry her and Veronica. Marge is surprised to learn that her sister is gay. Homer, on the other hand, is not surprised and states: "Hey, Marge. Here's another bomb. I like beer!" Marge invites Patty and Veronica to dinner at the Simpson home. Veronica informs the family that she is a professional golfer. To which Marge comments, "No surprise there." This is an obvious reference to the commonly held (but inaccurate) belief that most professional women golfers are gay. This belief is a carry-over perpetuated by those who do not feel women should be playing sports. It also reflects the perception that most female athletes are not very attractive.

By all appearances, Marge does not seem to approve of Patty's decision to marry Veronica. Patty senses this and confronts Marge. Patty tells her sister that there is nothing wrong with finding "love in her own locker room." Marge becomes especially troubled by Patty's impending nuptials when she learns that Veronica is really a man posing as a woman. (She happened to walk into the restroom and secretly discovered that Veronica was standing up while going to the bathroom.) Marge faces a true dilemma—should she tell Patty the truth about Veronica or let Patty find out the truth for herself?

Meanwhile, the wedding goes on as planned. Marge sits quietly in the audience as Patty and Veronica exchange personalized vows. Patty tells Veronica, "I found the 'yin' to my 'yin.'" Realizing how much Patty loves Veronica, Marge decides to spill the beans before the marriage vows are finalized. Marge believes that Patty deserves to know the truth about her future spouse. Marge stops the wedding by revealing that Veronica actually has an Adam's apple. The audience reacts with shock and Sideshow Mel exclaims, "Look at the size of her Adam's apple!" (Note: An Adam's apple is a chunk of bony cartilage that's wrapped around the larynx. They are far more prevalent in men than in women.) Veronica comes clean and admits that her/his real name is Leslie Robin Swisher—an interesting play on words as the names "Leslie" and "Robin" are names for both males and females. Leslie admits to pulling a scam so that he can dominate the women's golf tour—something he could not do on the men's tour (because of the tougher competition). Leslie is still smitten with Patty and asks her to marry him. But Patty says no and reiterates that she likes girls. The wedding is canceled.

As mentioned earlier, gay people face discrimination. There may be a growing acceptance of gays among the majority of people, but a great deal of discrimination, especially in the form of homophobia, exists in contemporary society. Homophobia is the unreasoning fear of, or antipathy toward, gays and homosexuality. Based on the parameters of this definition, someone may not literally have a fear (phobia) of gays, but if he or she is prejudicial (shows antipathy) toward gays, he or she is still a homophobe. Homophobes generally mock gays as a means of dealing with their own insecurities. In this manner, gays are treated as scapegoats.

Homer Simpson has a number of insecurities, including homophobia. He is portrayed as a homophobe in the "Homer's Phobia" episode (#168). In this episode, the Simpson family befriends the owner/operator of Cockamamie's collectible shop, John. The Simpsons are trying to sell what they think is a family heirloom at Cockamamie's to cover an unexpected nine-hundred-dollar bill from the Springfield Gas Company. (Bart had ignited the gas main while using the laundry dryer in a mock lotto drawing.) Unfortunately, John informs them that the heirloom is nothing more than a decorative liquor bottle. The Simpsons take a liking to John regardless, and invite him to their home for dinner. They also want him to look over their other belongings to determine if there is anything of value.

John takes them up on their offer for dinner and immediately falls in love with the Simpsons and their home. John and Homer bond. They even dance together to an old song. The next morning, Homer tells Marge what a great guy John is and that they should invite him and his wife to do something together. Marge is surprised to discover that Homer is unaware of the fact that John is gay.

> *Marge*: Homer, didn't John seem a little festive to you?
> *Homer*: Couldn't agree more, happy as a clam.
> *Marge*: He prefers the company of men.
> *Homer*: Who doesn't?
> *Marge*: Homer, listen carefully, John is a ho-mo—
> *Homer*: Right.
> *Marge*: —sexual!

Homer screams in disbelief. He becomes worried that someone might think he is gay because he danced with John. In panic, Homer says to Marge and Lisa, "OhmyGod! OhmyGod! OhmyGod! I danced with a gay! Marge, Lisa, promise me you won't tell anyone. Promise me!" Homer is so scared that he blurts out that he is worried his property value will go down just because he danced with a gay man in his house.

Learning that John is gay, Homer wants nothing more to do with him. He refuses to take part in a planned family outing with John.

When John comes over to the house to meet with the Simpson family, Homer calls him a sneak for hiding his gay identity. Marge thinks Homer is making too big a deal about John being gay. Homer says, "You know me, Marge. I like my beer cold, my TV loud, and my homosexuals flaming." Homer shuns John and will not join the rest of the family in a car ride with him.

Later, Homer becomes worried that John may be a bad influence on Bart and "turn" him gay. Homer freaks out when he sees Bart singing while wearing a woman's wig. Homer is also against Bart wearing a Hawaiian shirt. He tells Marge, "There's only two kinds of guys who wear those shirts—gay guys and big fat party animals. And Bart doesn't look like a big fat party animal to me."

John is having coffee with Marge in the Simpson kitchen. Homer confronts John and tells him to stay away from his family.

> *John*: Homer, what have you got against gays?
> *Homer*: You know, it's not—usual. If there was a law it would be against it.
> *Marge*: Oh, Homer please, you're embarrassing yourself.
> *Homer*: No, I'm not Marge. They're embarrassing me. They're embarrassing America. They turned the navy into a floating joke. They ruined all of our best names. Like Bruce, Lance, and Julian. Those were the toughest names we had. Now, they're just, ah—
> *John* (interrupts and offers): Queer?
> *Homer*: Yeah. And that's another thing. I resent that you people use that word. That's our word for making fun of you. We need it. Well, I am taking back our word and I'm taking back my son.

Homer decides he has to make sure Bart turns into a "man." He takes Bart to the side of a highway and leaves him there to stare at a billboard of two women—who happen to be promoting smoking. When Homer returns to pick Bart up, he is dumbfounded that Bart wants to smoke now! Homer takes Bart to a steel factory, to view "real" men doing real "manly" work. However, at closing time, all the men start to dance with one another and "act" gay. Homer is shaken by this unforeseen turn of events and quips, "Oh, my son doesn't stand a chance! The whole world has gone gay!"

Undaunted, Homer proceeds with his attempt to make sure Bart doesn't turn gay. Homer plans a hunting trip with Barney and Moe. He believes that hunting must be a macho thing; after all, it involves men, with guns, killing animals. After this adventure, Bart comments that he thinks there is "something about a bunch of guys alone together in the woods . . . seems kinda gay." The hunters leave the woods, unsuccessful in their attempt to bag a deer. When Homer tells his buddies that his daughter Lisa is a vegetarian, they feel sorry for him. Moe asks if he and Marge are cousins!

The four hunters, Homer, Barney, Moe, and Bart, drive to the Reindeer Park at Santa's Village. Homer is determined to have Bart kill an animal in an attempt to make a man out of him. As we can see, Homer's impression of what it takes and means to be a "real" man is quite archaic. They all tell Bart to shoot a reindeer. But he refuses to shoot a reindeer inside a pen. That would be as unmanly as hunting an animal in a game reserve or a park. Bart is about ready to cry when suddenly the reindeer go into a panic and charge the hunters. Barney and Moe find refuge. Homer and Bart are not so lucky. Homer protects Bart by raising him over his head and allowing the reindeer, with full antlers, to attack him. This is Homer's shining moment of actually demonstrating what it means to be a man because he risks his own life to save his son's.

Just when things appear to be at their bleakest, John arrives with the rest of the Simpson family. He devises a ploy to distract the reindeer away from Homer and Bart by sending a remote-control toy robot Santa into the pen. The deer are startled and run away. John has saved the lives of three "real" men and a boy, despite the fact he is gay. Homer learns the lesson here, being gay does not mean John is not a man. Homer and John re-bond with each other and Moe and Barney are very grateful for John's help—almost a little too grateful. To which Jerry Seinfeld would say, "Not that there's anything wrong with that!"

Chapter 7

Springfield

A Racial Melting Pot
Often Lacking in Tolerance

"From this day forth, I am no longer an Indian living in America. I am an Indian American."
—Apu Nahasapeemapetilon

In the United States, the majority of citizens are white. By the year 2050, however, the US Census Bureau estimates that "minorities" will make up about 49 percent of the total US population. In 1990, just 25 percent of the US population was comprised of minorities. On *The Simpsons*, there are no white characters. Instead, the majority are yellow. Why yellow? Was Matt Groening trying to eliminate race as an issue? No! After all, there are black and Indian characters on *The Simpsons*. Further, in the "Homer Simpson, This Is Your Wife" episode (#371), the animated *Simpsons* characters come to "life"—that is, real-life actors replace the animated ones at the beginning of the episode—and the actors portraying the Simpson family are white—as viewers had assumed the yellow characters to be.

But why yellow? Did Matt Groening make the majority of the *Simpsons* characters yellow because he wanted something offbeat and unworldly? Did he want to make viewers fiddle with their color control, thinking their television set was out of whack? Yellow is certainly different. And it is bright. Further, the color yellow gives *The Simpsons* an instant identity. That is, when you view a show with predominately yellow animated characters, you know you are watching *The Simpsons*. Then again, some people believe there is a more pragmatic reason for yellow characters—yellow ink is inexpensive in

Korea. Matt Groening explains that the *Simpsons* characters were originally black-and-white outlines. However, because of TV, color was necessary. Groening did not want to use the conventional pink color that passes for Caucasian in animated cartoons because he thought the characters would look repulsive. In his *Playboy* (2007) interview, Groening states, "It always bothered me that Walt Disney made Mickey Mouse a Caucasian mouse. It's freakish. So when it came time to give them [the *Simpsons* characters] skin color, the animation colorist, Gyorgyi Peluce, chose yellow skin. She has never gotten proper credit" (p. 58).

Thus, since its inception, Matt Groening was consciously aware of racial overtones built into cartoon characters. Not surprisingly, *The Simpsons* touch upon many racial and ethnic issues, including the use of stereotypes; examples of prejudice, discrimination, and racism; and a presentation of the "we"/"they" nature of intergroup contact.

THE SOCIAL CONSTRUCTS OF RACE AND ETHNICITY

There is great diversity among the cultures and peoples of the world. Each culture is unique with its own set of norms, values, and beliefs. There also exists a tendency among "like-minded" people to view their way of life as "right" or proper. Interethnic and interracial contact between diverse persons often reveals ethnocentric attitudes, beliefs, and behaviors. Ethnocentrism refers to the tendency of people from one cultural group to judge other cultures by the standards of their own. This line of thinking reflects the "we" feeling shared by members of a group. Ethnocentrism promotes group solidarity and group pride (a positive aspect) but it also generally involves viewing the other group(s) as inferior (a negative aspect). When one group deems itself superior it usually displays acts of intolerance toward others. Stereotypes, racism, and prejudice are byproducts of intolerance.

Typically, the greatest level of intolerance displayed by one group against another is the result of racial or ethnic differences. Although the use of such terms as "race" and "ethnicity" are becoming less popular today (some people even deny that there is such a thing as "race"), the fact remains that many people see others based on such categorizations. The US Census Bureau, for example, still asks people to identify their ethnicity/race. The words "race" and "ethnicity" are often used interchangeably. But this would be inaccurate. A racial group can be defined as a category of people who (1) share a socially recognized *physical* characteristic (such as skin color or facial features) that distinguishes them from other such categories, and (2) are recognized by themselves and others as a distinct status group. Skin color is the physical characteristic typically used to determine races. Thus, a racial group is biologically determined through cultural interpretations. An ethnic group, in contrast, is a category of people who are recognized as a distinct group based entirely on social or cultural factors. An ethnic group shares cultural characteristics such as nationality, religion, language, geographic residence, a common set of values, and so on. In short, ancestry determines ethnicity. Traditionally, an ethnic group has been viewed as a subset of a racial category.

Ethnic and racial groups often focus on the differences among people, rather than the similarities. This is problematic. After all, Jews and Arabs are genetically linked and yet they despise one another. Why? The answer is (at least in part) revealed with a discussion on the "we" versus "they" mentality that many people possess.

"WE" VERSUS "THEY"

Racial and ethnic groups are not completely autonomous and self-contained groups. Instead, they are a part of a larger societal system that influences, shapes, and partially determines their life circumstances. Internally, groups often attempt to maintain their distinctive "we-ness" (Shibutani and Kwan 1965). By so doing, external groups come to view the group by their "they-ness" (Rose 1981). Thus, by creating a "we" parameter, it is implied that a "they" label has also been established. Categories of "us" and "them" are similar to "we" and "they" (Delaney 2002A). The "we"/"they" concept reflects ethnocentric thinking.

Social interaction plays an important role in an individual's life. Individuals want to feel that they belong, or "fit" into a group. Individuals like to experience a sense of unity with their fellows. Group participation provides a sense of "we-ness" where using the term "we" is a natural expression. For example, members of specific racial/ethnic groups might say, "We have long been victims of prejudice and discrimination." The creation of the "we" category involves a sense of community. Ethnic communities are deeply rooted in common sentiments, common experience, and a common history. Sharing a common history not only gives an ethnic group a common ancestry and descent but also becomes a significant basis for organizing the present. Often, the historical past is selectively interpreted from the perspective, and from the needs, of the present. Ethnic groups often share special purpose associations to further their political and/or economic needs (e.g., the American Jewish Committee, National Association for the Advancement of Colored People, the Anti-Defamation League, and the Urban League).

The "we" group begins to view outsiders as "they." Interestingly, the "they" is made up of other "we" groups, but is generally viewed or recognized as the larger society itself. Even more ironic is the fact that the outside society, or "they," come to view the "we" group as a "they." Thus, the determination of "we" and "they" groups is simply influenced by perspective. Historically, society's designation of an ethnic group as a "they" has frequently led to discriminatory treatment and creates a sense of shared fate and identity among them.

The "we"/"they" relationship extends beyond racial and ethnic distinctions. Street gangs identify one another on the basis of affiliation. Athletes and sports fans have long drawn distinctions between "us" and "them." Budgetary concerns between different departments within the same organization often create adversarial rivalries expressed in such ways as, "If that other department receives their requested funds, there will not be enough left for us to make our budgetary requests." Charities compete with one another when requesting funds from the government and public donations. And, as demonstrated in "The Bart of War" episode (#312), volunteer youth groups can transform into adversarial "we"/"they" groups.

As explained in chapter 3, Bart and Milhouse are best friends. As typical ten-year-old boys, they often get into trouble together. In "The Bart of War" episode, their respective parents separate the two boys after they ransack the Flanders house. Marge decides that Bart needs additional adult supervision in his life. That is, she wants to keep him too busy to find time to get into trouble. Marge and Homer look over a brochure for the Pre-Teen Braves, a community youth group. They learn that among the group activities of the Braves— designed to teach the Native American way of life—are hayrides, bowling, and cookouts. Marge states, "Just like real Indians." Marge and Homer agree that Bart should join this group. Homer volunteers to be the "chief" of the Braves. Homer's troop includes Bart, Ralph Wiggum, Nelson Muntz, and another boy named Database.

At their first group meeting, Homer reads over the manual looking for Native American activities to do: "Let's see . . . Making wallets . . . faking crop circles . . . respecting nature . . . Geez, no wonder these guys lost the Civil War." Homer decides that the best activity for his young Braves is to learn a little Native American culture by watching an NFL game between the Chiefs and the Cowboys! Homer says things like "the receiver's moccasins were out-of-bounds." And when a play was being reviewed in the official's box, far from the playing field, Homer says, "The Great Father in the sky has ruled that . . ." The Braves were learning about "we" and "they" groups, albeit from a football rivalry standpoint, but they were not learning true Native American cultural history.

Marge is upset with Homer's lack of leadership skills and decides to take matters into her own hands. With Lisa's help, Marge makes smoke signals in the backyard to get the attention of the boys inside watching football. The Braves are impressed with Marge and she becomes the new chief. Marge takes the Braves on a hike and they meet Jim Proud-foot, a Mohican Indian. He describes the past history of his tribe. He likes to emphasize the myth that the Mohican tribe is extinct because, as he says, "Chicks really dig you when you're the last of something."

Proudfoot points out the field and lake in front of him to Marge and the Braves. He describes how beautiful it once was, but now it is polluted. Just then, Homer is shown in the background dumping a treadmill into the lake. The Braves decide to clean the lake and field in honor of Native Americans. They go home for supplies. Marge has thought of every detail including instructing the boys to use Pine-Sol on the pine trees for that "pine fresh smell." As they head back to the cleanup site, Marge psyches the Braves for the work ahead of them.

Marge: What are we gonna do to that field?
Braves: Clean it.
Bart: And why are we gonna do it?!
Braves: Liberal guilt!
Marge: Yaaay!

Proudfoot's earlier historical account of how the European and American settlers treated the Native Americans has clearly made an impression on the Pre-Teen Braves, as they feel guilty for the sins of people who came before them.

Meanwhile, Milhouse has also joined a community youth group called the Cavalry Kids. The Cavalry Kids include Milhouse, Jimbo Jones, Martin Prince, and Cosine. They are led by Milhouse's father, Kirk Van Houten. Unbeknownst to the Braves, the Kids have also made plans to clean up the polluted field. To the surprise of the Braves, the Kids accomplish the cleanup task before they have a chance to do it.

> *Bart*: Hey! Some jerks cleaned our field!
> *Nelson*: It's awful! It looks like Wisconsin.

The Calvary Kids think pretty highly of themselves for besting the Pre-Teen Braves. Milhouse proclaims, "We're the bad boys of nondenominational community youth groups." The Calvary Kids do a number of good deeds throughout the community—and their impact has not gone unnoticed. As illustrated by the conversation between Marge and Apu, a nasty rivalry develops between the two juvenile youth groups.

> *Marge*: Those Cavalry Kids are bigger credit hogs than the Red Cross.
> *Apu*: I must disagree, Mrs. Bart. They've painted this town a fresh coat of "give a hoot."
> *Marge*: Well, you ain't seen nothing 'til you've seen the Pre-Teen Braves.
> *Apu*: Pre-Teen Braves? Is this another of those youth groups that apes the culture of those indigenous people you invaded and destroyed?
> *Marge*: Exactly! The Pre-Teen Braves!

The Pre-Teen Braves view themselves as the violated "we" group and the Cavalry Kids as the "they" out-group. On the other hand, reflecting the nature of the "we"/"they" group relationship, the Kids view themselves as the "we" group and the Braves as the "they" group. The two groups become more concerned with outdoing each other in a variety of contests than learning about cultural history and cleaning the environment. They challenge each other in the Springfield Isotopes candy sale contest. The winning team members get to serve as batboys for the baseball team. The Cavalry Kids win the candy sale. Milhouse taunts the Pre-Teen Braves by misinterpreting history and saying, "Looks like this is one time the Indians didn't win."

"The Bart of War" episode reveals how even friends as close as Bart and Milhouse can become enemies when they take on the mentality of the group they belong to. In the past, their friendship was all that mattered. However, we can learn a lesson from Bart and Milhouse, as they will resume their friendship despite their temporary adversarial roles in this episode. If we look at people as individuals, rather than through their group memberships, it may be easier to peacefully coexist.

The Use of Stereotypes

> **"Well, Edna, for a school with no Asian kids I think we put on a pretty darn good science fair."**
> —Principal Skinner

In chapter 6, we learned about gender stereotypes. In this chapter, we learn about racial stereotypes. A stereotype is an overexaggerated belief and rigid form of thinking about a group of people based on little information. Negative stereotypes often lead to people being victimized because of prejudice and discrimination. (Note: Prejudice refers to negative beliefs one person has toward others without adequate basis; while discrimination refers to actual behavior where a distinction is made in favor of or against one person or group [or thing] compared with others.) The use of stereotypes is common by large numbers of people in every society of the world. People who use stereotypes are generally ignorant as they are relying on limited information regarding an individual or specific group of people. A statement such as "You know how *those* people are" reflects a generalized belief concerning an entire population of people based on limited information, or the actions of a few members from within that group. For example, if someone were to say "All New Yorkers are rude" or "All Southerners are rednecks," he or she is clearly making such a statement based on limited information, as no single person has ever met *all* New Yorkers or *all* Southerners. Are some New York rude? Of course! But then again, there are rude people around the world. Are some Southerners rednecks? Yes, but then again, there are poorly educated bigots found in all regions of the world. (Note: Jeff Foxworthy has never included in his "You might be a redneck" jokes, "a poorly educated bigot" as a definition of a redneck as some people actually embrace this label, even though others use it as a derogatory term.)

In most cases, people use stereotypes to label others as a means of self-esteem enhancement via putting someone else down. Such people generally lack integrity. There are other times when people use stereotypes and may not be aware of the fact that they are being offensive. For example, in December 2006, Rosie O'Donnell made an offensive comment on-air while she served as host of *The View*. Danny DeVito had recently made an appearance on this TV gab fest show while he was allegedly intoxicated. It made quite a stir on gossipy talk shows and Rosie was still talking about it after the fact. O'Donnell said, "You know, you can imagine in China it's like 'ching chong, ching chong chong, Danny DeVito, ching, chong chong chong, drunk, *The View*, ching chong." A number of people in the Asian community expressed outrage with O'Donnell's use of "ching, chong," deeming it highly offensive. Rosie was surprised by this reaction. She later said, "To say 'ching chong' to someone is very offensive, and some Asian people have told me it's as bad as the N-word. Which I was like, 'Really? I didn't know that.'" Not only was O'Donnell surprised by this, so too were *The View*'s studio audience that day, as no one reacted in shock or dismay. This incident reveals how easy it is for people to be ignorant to the fact that they are guilty of negative stereotyping.

Furthermore, some people use stereotypes that they deem as "positive" or "neutral" and, therefore, harmless. *The Simpsons* provides a number of examples of both. For instance, in the "Brush with Greatness" episode (#31), we learn that Marge was once an aspiring artist. She had painted a portrait of Ringo Starr—whom she had a crush on—when she was a schoolgirl. She mailed the painting to Starr along with a personal note, but never heard back from him. Decades later, Ringo has finally found the time to answer his fan mail. He sends Marge a note:

Dear Marge. Thanks for the fab painting of yours truly. I hung it on me wall. You're quite an artist. In answer to your question, yes, we do have hamburgers and fries in England, but we call French fries "chips." Luv, Ringo. P. S. Forgive the lateness of my reply.

Clearly, Marge was under the impression (a stereotypical viewpoint) that the English must not eat hamburgers because they are known to eat fish (and chips). This is not an offensive stereotype of the English; rather, it reflects how relying on stereotypical perspectives may lead to a misinterpretation of a group of people.

In the "Cape Feare" episode (#83), Sideshow Bob is up for parole. (Note: This episode provides a parody of the film *Cape Fear*.) A number of people give testimony to prevent his release. To the surprise of the Simpson family, Bob is granted parole. One of the jurists states, "No one who speaks German can be an evil man." In this case, being stereotyped as "not evil" because of ethnic heritage would be construed as positive. However, it is also clearly inaccurate. While the vast majority of Germans are not evil, history has provided examples of Germans who *were* evil.

Another example of a seemingly positive stereotype is provided in the "Duffless" episode (#75). In this episode, Springfield Elementary is putting on a science fair. At the conclusion of the science fair, Principal Skinner is beaming in delight with the perceived success of the academic event. He tells teacher Edna Krabappel, "Well, Edna, for a school with no Asian kids I think we put on a pretty darn good science fair." It is true, that, in general, Asian American schoolchildren score well in science and math, but it is unfair to kids of other cultures to assume that they are not capable of performing well in a science fair. Further, not all Asian children have the same level of intelligence in math and science, and those who do not earn high academic grades face greater stigma (than non-Asians) because they did not live up to a stereotype. As with many other people, Asians are capable of excelling in areas other than academics. To deny them these opportunities is akin to prejudice and discrimination.

It is, however, the negative stereotypes that are of the greatest concern. Negative stereotypes cause undue harm to innocent victims. A number of negative stereotypes are displayed in *The Simpsons*, especially against such European ethnic groups as the Irish and the Italians. Clearly, the writers of *The Simpsons* are aware (not ignorant) of how offensive some of their sketches are, but they present them nonetheless. Assumingly, the writers and creator of *The Simpsons* are not racists, but rather, have chosen to reflect sentiments expressed by past and present Americans. One group that is shown in a very stereotypical manner is Italian Americans.

Italian Americans

> **"Try-a the cheese-a pizza. It's greasy like-a you."**
> —Milhouse Van Houten

For many years, Italian Americans have been negatively stereotyped as organized crime gangsters. And while it is true that the Italian Mafia was once a dominant force of organized crime in many cities, especially in the Northeast and Las Vegas, the fact remains that the vast majority of Italians are law-abiding citizens. And yet, countless movies and television shows rely on the stereotype of the Italian gangster who speaks broken English. *The Simpsons* often perpetuate this stereotype. For example, in the "Last of the Red Hat Mamas" episode (#363), Lisa is intent on learning to speak Italian. She purchases an "Italian–Italian American" conversion tape. The first lesson involves translating "common" expressions, including:

"I want to rent a small boat."
"I plan to bury this body in the ocean."
"This is what you get for asking questions" (gunshots are heard on the tape).

Lisa is very uncomfortable with this translation tape and seeks educational alternatives to learning Italian. She is eventually assigned a tutor, Milhouse. Milhouse speaks Italian because he has a grandmother from Tuscany who taught him. Interestingly, we hear Milhouse's full name used in this episode—Milhouse Mussolini Van Houten. Let's not draw any stereotypical conclusions from Milhouse's middle name!

In the "'Scuse Me While I Miss the Sky" episode (#307), Bart and Milhouse become involved with the Springfield Italian Mafia headed by Fat Tony. Bart wants to steal Fat Tony's car hood ornament. All the other "cool" kids have stolen a hood ornament so, in an attempt to top them all and reclaim his "cool" status, Bart eyes the golden trophy atop Fat Tony's automobile hood. The risk for tampering with a Mafia boss's car is grave, but the status that would be bestowed upon Bart is what motivates him. Eliciting Milhouse's help, Bart reasons the best way to steal the hood ornament is by setting up a valet scam. With that in mind, "Luigi's New Valet Service" is established. Bart and Milhouse don fake thick mustaches and wait outside Fat Tony's favorite restaurant. Fat Tony arrives.

> *Bart*: Buona sera, Fat Tony. I park-a your car, the way mama used to do.
> *Fat Tony*: Why, thank you. And may I say, your mustache looks thick and hearty. Fully Italian. (While Milhouse holds the door open, Fat Tony gives his keys to Bart.)
> *Milhouse*: Try-a the cheese-a pizza. It's greasy like-a you.

Inside, Fat Tony is informed that there is no valet service available at this restaurant. He runs outside to find Bart trying to saw off the hood ornament. Bart and Milhouse run off.

The wearing of thick fake mustaches represents a stereotypical image of Italian Americans. In addition, the use of fractured Italian-English language, in a stereotypical fashion, is not representative of most Italian Americans. The stereotypical employment of fractured Italian-English is used by another Italian mobster in the "Moe Baby Blues" episode (#313). Don Castellaneta, who speaks with a raspy voice and wears an overcoat draped over his shoulders, states, "I no speak any language so good." Castellaneta is trying to move in on Fat Tony's Springfield territory. Fat Tony gathers his gang and plans his strategy to neutralize Castellaneta.

> *Fat Tony*: Tonight, I want you to take out the Castellaneta family.
> *Louie*: Ah, I dunno boss. My passion for whacking is waning.
> *Fat Tony*: Perhaps this will cheer you up. (Fat Tony does a Marlon Brando impression from *The Godfather*. All the mobsters break out laughing.)
> *Louie*: Oh, that's better! I could whack my own mother now.
> *Fat Tony*: I'm glad you brought that up.
> *Louie*: Kill my mother? She makes such good pasta sauce!

Johnny Tightlips: It comes from a can.
Louie: She's a corpse!

The image of Italians in *The Simpsons* is straight out of the "Stereotypical Portrayal of Italian Americans" handbook. They are criminals who are willing to whack their own mothers, have difficulty speaking English, and value good food—so long as it is homemade.

Despite the many negative portrayals of Italians, it is the Irish that *The Simpsons* displays the greatest negative stereotypical disdain toward. In fact, many of the negative references to the Irish help to illustrate how stereotypical viewpoints can lead to blatant racism.

THE IRISH: ILLUSTRATING RACISM THROUGH *THE SIMPSONS*

"Their drunken singing is ruining St. Patrick's Day."
—Homer Simpson

In *The Simpsons*, the Irish are blamed for nearly every wrongdoing imaginable, from setting the sky on fire to ruining St. Patrick's Day because of their drunken escapades. Racist attitudes against a group of people begin with subtle comments. For example, in the "Please Homer, Don't Hammer 'Em" episode (#381), Marge glances at a book titled *Smiles of Ireland*. She turns to a page with a topic headline, "Red-headed Twins" and comments to herself, "Their mother must have her hands full." The insinuation here is that red-haired people, especially the Irish, are troublemakers; and twins imply twice the difficulty. This negative stereotype, which dates back to the arrival of the Irish in the United States, is still rather common in contemporary society. In fact, in the morning newspaper, on the day I originally wrote about this topic, was the statement, "And then there was Drexel. The city's red-headed stepchild" (Waters 2006). The reference to Drexel University as a "red-headed stepchild" relates to its lower basketball status in the city of Philadelphia. Unofficially, the city of Philadelphia plays host to the "Big Five" conference. No such conference actually exists, but the five tradition-rich basketball schools of Villanova, Penn, St. Joseph's, LaSalle, and Temple have dubbed their intracity rivalries as the "Big Five." Missing from this collection of Philadelphia basketball schools is

Drexel University, an institution of higher learning lacking the traditional pedigree of its neighboring universities. Thus, the reference to Drexel as a "red-headed stepchild" because it does not receive equal status, attention, and love. As a point of interest, Drexel beat Villanova in basketball for the first time in eighteen meetings in 2006. So let's hear it for Philadelphia's redhead!

Marge's comment about redheads is relatively innocent; and by itself would not be considered racist. However, when subtle comments are combined with other general negative beliefs and attitudes (e.g., redheads being equated to second-class citizens), their totality can escalate to discrimination and racism against the targeted group. Racism refers to any attitude, belief, behavior, or social arrangement that has the intent or ultimate effect of favoring one racial or ethnic group over another. It involves denying someone equal access to goods and services because of his/her race or ethnicity.

So, why does *The Simpsons* pick on the Irish? Aren't they as assimilated as any group can be into mainstream American culture? Well, today Irish Americans are known as the "flag-wavers" of the "American way" of life, but this was not always the case. (Note: If *The Simpsons* targeted nearly any other group in such a manner as they attack the Irish they would most likely be confronted by all sorts of lawsuits. Luckily for *The Simpsons* the Irish do not have an antidefamation league watching out for racist comments.) What the creators and writers of *The Simpsons* provide for us is a glimpse to the negative treatment the Irish once endured. The history of the Irish American is a history of nearly every immigrant group to voluntarily come to the United States. That is, typically, a large immigrant group will be blamed by the dominant majority for the social problems of society until they assimilate themselves and some other group of immigrants arrives in large numbers and become the new scapegoat. This pattern began with the Irish.

America's First Urban Ethnic Group: The Irish

In the early 1800s, the majority of American citizens were Anglo-Saxons. In New York City, most citizens were of English and Dutch ancestry, and were Protestants. There were approximately 123,000 inhabitants of New York City in 1820 and, by most accounts, the city was relatively peaceful. There were no police forces at that time either. However, the opening of the Erie Canal in 1825 would change the fate of New York City forever. The canal connected the Hudson River to the Great Lakes, revolutionizing transportation in this rapidly growing young country. Cheap labor was necessary to build the Erie Canal and work the docks. Many of the newly formed labor-intensive jobs were filled by the numerous immigrants entering the United States through New York. The largest number of immigrants entering New York in the 1820s were Irish. These Irish immigrants were poor, spoke a foreign language (Gaelic), were inadequately educated, and of a different religion (Catholic) than the dominant majority. (Notice how this description applies to every other large immigrant group since the Irish.) The Irish became America's first urban ethnic group.

The Irish lived in a ghetto area of New York known as the Five Points (an area where five streets—Cross, Anthony, Little Water, Orange, and Mulberry—once converged). The Five Points was a dismal place characterized by high-density living, a lack of sanitation, and high crime rates. In fact, the first American street gangs were comprised of the Irish from these impoverished neighborhoods (Delaney 2006). (Note: The Irish "Forty Thieves" is commonly given credit as the first street gang of the United States. Further, the film *Gangs of New York* [2002] is based on this and other Irish gangs and their rivals of the 1820s.)

By 1840, the population of New York had risen to 300,000. It was a city being terrorized by a wide variety of street toughs and an estimated 30,000 gang members. The criminal activities besieging New York were being documented by the coinciding rise of the "penny press." The penny press gave access to news events to the rising number of literate people in the city. A moral panic ensued. New York's elite demanded "something" be done about the rising crime rate. The citizens needed someone to blame; they needed a scapegoat. The Irish served as this scapegoat—the source of all social problems.

Despite the dismal life the Irish faced in New York, conditions were even worse in Ireland. During the mid-1840s, a dramatic event occurred called the Irish "potato famine," or the *Gorta Mor* (the "Great Hunger") as it is known in Ireland. The potato famine was not really a famine but an attempt at genocide against the Irish perpetrated by the English. There was, in fact, enough food to feed the Irish during the "famine" but the Irish were forced to pay food as "rent" to England. Most of the more than one million Irish who starved to death could have survived if not for this "rent." And so, facing near certain death in Ireland, the Irish moved to the United States in droves. More than 2.5 million people left Ireland in the 1840s and most of them went to America via New York.

The dominant majority of the United States at that time consisted of a large number of Americans with English ancestry. They despised the Irish and treated them worse than second-class citizens. Other than the black slaves, no group faced the discrimination and prejudice that the Irish did during this era. (Note: It should be pointed out that a number of Native American tribes were still being eradicated in the West at this time, however.) The Irish found it nearly impossible to find jobs. Signs such as "No Irish Need Apply" were common; and not just in New York, but throughout the United States. They were dying a slower death in America than they would have in Ireland.

A number of Irish youth were involved in criminal activity, especially gang behavior. The socially elite citizens of New York demanded law and order. They viewed immigrants as a real threat to their cozy lifestyles. With roots firmly entrenched in protecting the interests of the wealthy, the nation's first formal modern police force, the Metropolitan Police, was formed in New York City. The Metropolitan Police were modeled after the London Metropolitan Police Force. The early Metro police department was quite inept. The Irish gangs regularly attacked them. The Irish held particular disdain toward the police because they dressed in uniforms that attempted to imitate the English Bobbies. The Old World cultural baggage (anti-English sentiment) that the Irish brought with them from their homeland was evident in the New World. The same tormentors that haunted them in Ireland appeared to exist in America.

As the 1800s continued, the Irish slowly became assimilated into mainstream society. Each succeeding generation of Irish Americans became less concerned with the "old ways" and embraced the customs from their adopted land. The Irish found jobs on the docks and building the Erie Canal. They formed many of the early New York fire departments and eventually joined the ranks of the police force. Because of their large numbers, they became a force in New York politics. They could no longer be ignored. The Irish had learned the formula for acceptance into American society: learn and speak English, embrace the prevailing culture, value education, vote and take part in the political system, and work hard to make a better life for succeeding generations. Every European immigrant group that followed the Irish, such as the Italians, the Swedes, the Jews, and the Poles, adopted this blueprint.

The Simpsons provide us with a number of examples of how the Irish were once treated. The fictional city of Springfield often serves as the location for palpable acts of racism carried out against the Irish.

Grandpa Simpson often speaks with disrespect toward the Irish. This is somewhat understandable when one realizes that older people are more likely to hold conservative viewpoints. Many people Abe's age use terms and terminology for groups of people that are deemed unacceptable in contemporary society. They are sometimes surprised that saying things like "colored" people for blacks is considered wrong. In the "'Scuse Me While I Miss the Sky" episode (#307), Abe expresses a belief that is more fitting for the Salem witchcraft trials era than the early twentieth century. In this episode, Springfield's townspeople are enjoying a meteor shower. Abe recalls the last time this rare event occurred: "The last time those meteors came, we thought the sky was on fire. Naturally, we blamed it on the Irish. We hanged more than a few." This statement reveals a number of significant points. First, that the Irish were used as a scapegoat for a number of "problems" they had no control over. Second, that Abe lived in a time where people actually could not explain a meteor shower scientifically so they blamed an innocent victim instead. Third, that hanging was deemed an appropriate sanction. Fourth, there is no sense of justice when a mob takes the law into its own hands.

In "The Day the Violence Died" episode (#146), the history of Itchy & Scratchy is described. In the 1919 original cartoon, Itchy (the mouse) tormented an Irishman instead of a cat (Scratchy). The first episode is titled, "Itchy Runs Afoul of an Irishman." As Bart and Milhouse watch this recently discovered forgotten film, Milhouse gets caught up in the action and yells, "Look out Itchy! He's Irish." As Itchy maims the Irishman, Milhouse screams in delight, "C'mon Itchy, kill him! Kill that guy!" The writers of *The Simpsons* are reminding viewers, via this Itchy cartoon, that many racial groups have been negatively stereotyped in cartoons over the years. For example, Bugs Bunny and Popeye cartoons made use of racist portrayals of the Japanese, and Disney's *Song of the South* (1946) employed racial stereotypes about blacks. In 1919, it would have still been fairly fashionable to pick on an Irishman in a cartoon. In addition, it is clear that Milhouse was raised in an environment that puts down the Irish.

The city of Springfield has an odd annual tradition that most of its citizens take part in, "Whacking Day." Once a year, the residents of Springfield get together to exterminate snakes. As local news anchor Kent Brockman explains, "Whacking Day" is "A tradition that dates back to founding father Jebediah Springfield, every May tenth. Residents gather to drive snakes to the center of town and whack them to snake heaven." Community traditions like "Whacking Day" illustrate two important sociological concepts: manifest and latent functions. These two concepts were first introduced by sociologist Robert Merton. Manifest functions are the obvious, or planned. Thus, with "Whacking Day" the intended function is to kill snakes. Latent functions, on the other hand, refer to the unplanned aspects of communal gatherings. In other words, the fact that the community gathers together for such an event as "Whacking Day" reaffirms group solidarity and common sentiments. The concepts of manifest and latent functions are staples of introductory sociology courses.

Among the townspeople who look forward to "Whacking Day" the most is Homer Simpson. Homer has even purchased a new "whacking stick" for this year's event. He shows it off to Marge, who is a little turned on by it! Homer practices his whacking skills with his new stick similar to the fashion of a martial artist putting on a performance. Often serving as the sole voice of reason, Lisa pleads with her dad not to participate in this group event that she deems highly unethical.

> *Lisa*: Dad, please for the last time, I beg you, don't lower yourself to the level of the mob!
> *Homer*: Lisa, maybe if I'm part of that mob, I can help steer it in wise directions. Now, where's my giant foam cowboy hat and airhorn?

Lisa cannot stop her father from participating in "Whacking Day." However, she is surprised to learn that Bart reads a book (that in itself is surprising!) called *The Truth about Whacking Day* while he is supposed to be cleaning the Simpsons' garage. He reveals to the "Whacking" mob that "Whacking Day" is a sham that dates to 1924 for an excuse to beat up the Irish. Now that is an example of racism! In fact, it is an example of institutional racism (structural discrimination based on one's race or ethnicity) as setting aside a specific day of the year just to beat up members of a racial or ethnic group is overt racism at its worse.

The Springfield mob does not want to believe Bart, but then, a stereotypically dressed and sounding Irishman in the crowd proclaims, "It's true. I took many a lump. But it was all in good fun." The residents of Springfield, to their credit, examine their consciences and realize that a tradition based on beating up an ethnic group is not one to be continued.

Perhaps the most negative stereotype of the Irish involves the belief that they drink too much, cannot hold their liquor, and then get into fights. The stereotype that the Irish often get into fights is illustrated in the "She Used to Be My Girl" episode (#339). In this episode, Marge gets into a fistfight with an old friend of hers from high school, Chloe Talbot, a newswoman for the Global News Network. At the conclusion of the fight, Marge ends up with a black eye. She goes to her medicine cabinet and takes out an aerosol spray can of "Shiner-Be-Gone." The aerosol can has an illustration of an Irish leprechaun similar to the Notre Dame mascot underneath the "Shiner-Be-Gone" label and above the words "Irish Strength." Marge sprays the contents directly onto her black eye. The tune "Irish Lullaby" emanates from the can while she uses the spray. About fifteen seconds later, the shiner is gone. Now why would such a spray can utilize an image of a fighting Irishman unless it was meant as a negative stereotype?

Saint Patrick's Day, a Day When Everyone Is Irish

"Except, of course, for the gays and the Italians."
—Kent Brockman

Saint Patrick is the patron saint of Ireland (and of Nigeria). He was born in Scotland in 387 CE as Maewyn Succat. When he was about sixteen years old he was captured by pirates and sold into slavery in then-pagan Ireland. He learned the Celtic language and customs and later escaped captivity. He later became a priest and took the name Patricius. He claimed to have visions that called him back to Ireland.

His prayers were answered when, in 430 CE, Pope Celestine I sent him to Ireland as a missionary. A number of miracles were attributed to Patrick. On Easter Sunday, March 26, 433 CE, Patrick used the shamrock to illustrate the concept of the Holy Trinity—three leaves, yet still one leaf. Ireland's national symbol was born. Patrick worked for forty years in Ireland and converted pagans into Roman Catholics.

The Irish have celebrated St. Patrick's memory every March 17, but it took Irish Americans to establish a parade in his honor. The early Irish Americans celebrated St. Patrick's Day to show their ethnic pride in their heritage. How things have changed! What was once an example of positive ethnocentrism among a specific group of people is now a "commercial holiday" celebrated by all peoples. And nearly all St. Patrick's Day celebrations involve wearing green and adults getting drunk.

It is unfortunate that St. Patrick's Day is associated with such unofficial nicknames as "Let's get drunk day," especially in light of the fact that among the most negative stereotypes of the Irish is that they drink too much, cannot hold their liquor, lose their tempers, and then get into fights. The "Homer vs. the Eighteenth Amendment" episode (#171) has these and other negative elements often associated with contemporary St. Patrick's Day celebrations. This episode begins on St. Patrick's Day. People are lined up outside Moe's Tavern early in the morning hoping for him to open up for business. This is one day of the year that even Moe is happy to be alive, for it's a great day for bar business.

> *Moe*: Yeah, all right, listen up. This is the busiest drinkin' day
> of the year. Where are the designated drivers?
> (A few men acknowledge Moe by raising their hands.)
> *Moe*: Beat it! I got no room for cheapskates.

Moe wants drinkers in his bar, not responsible adults. And, on this St. Patrick's Day, there will be few responsible adults in Springfield.

While some people with drinking problems are at bars first thing in the morning, most of the residents of Springfield have gathered to watch the annual St. Patrick's Day Parade. News Anchor Kent Brockman reports, "Top o' the mornin' to ye on this gray, drizzly afternoon. Kent Brockman live on Main Street, where today, everyone is a little bit Irish! Ha-ha, except, of course, for the gays and the Italians." Brockman's comment about gays is in reference to their attempts to be allowed to march in St. Patrick's Day parades while the traditional Irish Catholics oppose it. As for the Italians, they and the Irish have a long history of animosity in this country. Some Italians will wear orange on St. Patrick's Day as a sign of disrespect against the Irish.

The parade includes a Duff Beer float equipped with a cannon that sprays streams of beer into the crowd. Included in any crowd assembled to watch a parade are children. Spraying alcohol into a crowd where children are in reach is clearly not a good idea. As the Duff Beer float drives along the parade route, it comes upon Bart, who is in the crowd and blowing a novelty horn. A huge amount of beer sprays into Bart's horn as if it is a funnel or he is a college student doing a beer bong. Bart is instantly intoxicated. He begins to stumble as he tries to walk down the street. Other spectators are alarmed that a young boy is drunk on St. Patrick's Day. People in the crowd begin yelling at one another. A float carrying a banner "The Drunken Irish Novelists of Springfield" and sporting a book with an Irish whiskey bottle coming out of the pages falls victim to a spectator throwing a bottle at the book. The Irish novelists jump off the float and randomly start fighting people. Someone (presumably an Irishman) firebombs a restaurant—John Bull's Fish and Chips—because it has the English flag personified in its name. This starts an even bigger fight.

All of this is caught on TV. Once again Kent Brockman details the events: "Ladies and gentlemen, what you are seeing is a total disregard for the things St. Patrick's Day stands for. All this drinking, violence, and destruction of property—are these the things we think of when we think of the Irish?"

Meanwhile, Homer, who has been drinking at Moe's all morning, is drunk. He puts an empty wooden beer barrel on his head and says to the bar patrons, "Look at me. I'm the prime minister of Ireland!" Everyone laughs. At this time, Kent Brockman's report is being aired on Channel 6 news. His report starts a moral panic, an outrage against drunken behavior. Women's suffragist groups demand a prohibition of alcohol. (Note: It was the women's suffragist groups that first spearheaded the movement for the disastrous Eighteenth Amendment, or Volstead Act, ratified January 16, 1919. See chapter 10 for a further discussion of this attempted prohibition in Springfield and its political implications.)

Interestingly, I remember watching the Detroit Tigers celebrate their 2006 playoff victory over the New York Yankees (October 7) by drinking from large bottles of champagne on the playing field. They wanted to share this celebration with the fans. Some players, including Kenny Rogers, a pitcher for Detroit, went on top of the dugouts with champagne bottles. Rogers poured some over the head of a police officer. The police officer politely "took it." Rogers then took another bottle, shook it up, and sprayed the champagne into the crowd. He walked the length of the dugout while continually spraying the crowd. Some people opened their mouths hoping to get some free champagne. I saw one kid get a mouthful and immediately thought of Bart Simpson! The TV announcers were not from the same school of journalism as Kent Brockman and did not cause a moral panic based on Rogers's spraying alcohol into the crowd!

Does drunken behavior discredit St. Patrick's Day? Or, the Irish for that matter? In the "Kill Gil Volumes 1 & 2" episode (#387), the Simpsons allow a former homeless man, Gil, to live with them. On St. Patrick's Day, Gil has some of his friends over. They drink and sing songs all night long while Gil plays the piano. Upstairs in their bedroom, Homer tells Marge, "Their drunken singing is ruining St. Patrick's Day." Singing songs, hanging out with friends, and having a few drinks *is* what St. Patrick's Day has become. Most people know how to handle all these activities in moderation. Moral panic averted!

THE UNITED STATES: LAND OF IMMIGRANTS

"Yes, I am a citizen. Now, which way to the welfare office?"
—Apu Nahasapeemapetilon

Irish Americans, for the most part, no longer suffer from overt racism. They became assimilated into mainstream society long ago. And although most Americans' ancestors were once immigrants, there remains a great deal of anti-immigrant sentiment in the United States. The outrage expressed by some citizens of the United States over the number of Mexicans and Central Americans entering the country across the Mexican-American border has led to 2006 legislation approving the building of a seven-hundred-mile wall to keep immigrants out. In my lifetime, I have seen the Berlin Wall come down and the "Iron Curtain" collapse due to its own weight; it would be difficult to see such a wall built on US soil.

The Simpsons addresses many of the key issues of immigration in the "Much Apu About Nothing" episode (#151). In this episode, the townspeople are concerned about a potential overrun of wild bears after a solitary bear wanders into Springfield. Kent Brockman provides a news update while flying overhead in the Channel 6 news helicopter. Brockman warns, "A large bearlike animal, most likely a bear, has wandered down from the hills, in search of food or perhaps employment. Please remain calm. Stay in your homes." Brockman creates a moral panic. Just imagine, foreigners (bears) coming into Springfield trying to take away jobs from the citizens! The irrational citizens are outraged and march to City Hall to demand that "something" be done about the bear problem. (Note the parallel between this line of thinking and that which was described earlier regarding the Irish.) Homer leads the townspeople in a chant: "We're here! We're queer! We don't want any more bears! We're here! We're queer! We don't want any more bears!"

Ned Flanders tries to convince people that there is not a bear problem, as this was the first and only bear he has seen in Springfield in thirty years. And yet, the citizens demand that Mayor Quimby establish a special "bear patrol" to keep other bears outside the Springfield border. (This is similar to the US Border Patrol designed to keep illegal aliens out of the country.) In order to pay for the bear patrol, Mayor Quimby must raise taxes. (Imagine the tax increase to build a seven-hundred-mile wall.) The residents are initially happy about the bear patrol because there have not been any other reported bear sightings. However, when they discover the increase in their tax bill they become angry and once again demand that "something" be done. They march on City Hall once more.

> *Taxpayers* (outside Quimby's office chant): Down with taxes! Down with taxes!
>
> *Quimby* (closes his door and says to his aide): Are these morons getting dumber or just louder?
>
> *Aide*: Dumber, sir. They won't give up the Bear Patrol, but they won't pay taxes for it either.

The mayor's aide points out how dumb it is to expect social services, including those which protect citizens from possible attack, without expecting to pay higher taxes.

In an attempt to sidetrack the townsfolk, Mayor Quimby blames the high taxes on immigration. He initiates Proposition 24, an initiative that calls for the immediate deportation of illegal immigrants from Springfield. The proposition will be voted on in one week's time. The people rally behind the mayor.

Once again, Lisa is the voice of reason. She tries to explain to her father that immigrants built this country and urges him to vote "No" on Proposition 24. Homer will have nothing to do with her lesson in history. He tells Lisa that immigrants are overrunning the schools and that's why some American children, like Bart, have lost their interest in schoolwork. Bart says, "There's no denying it, sis." Trying to make a relevant point that even Homer can understand, Lisa reminds him that even the Simpsons were once immigrants to the United States.

Homer goes to the Kwik-E-Mart and discusses Proposition 24 with Apu. Apu informs Homer that he is an immigrant and that if Proposition 24 passes he will have to leave the country. Homer is somehow shocked that Apu is an immigrant. He says to Apu, "Oh, my God! I got so swept up in the scapegoating and fun of Proposition 24, I never stopped to think it might affect someone I cared about. You know what, Apu, I am really, really gonna miss you."

Apu pleads his case to Marge. Apu entered the United States on a student visa, but it has long since expired. He had planned on going home to India but he wants to pay off his student loans first. (Don't all college students have as their top priority to pay off student loans?!) Marge states the obvious by telling Apu, "Really, your only crime was violating US law." Marge tells Apu that she will vote "No" on Proposition 24.

As his next course of action, Apu decides to purchase fake documents from mobster Fat Tony. Interestingly, Fat Tony only changed the first names of the parents on the fake documents he gave to Apu, making him Apu Nahasapeemapetilon, son of Herb and Judy Nahasapeemapetilon. Fat Tony informs Apu to "act American." Apu changes his ways to try to blend in. He wears a Mets jersey and discusses baseball. He changes his voice. But it does not work. He cannot deny who he is. Apu tells Homer, "I cannot deny my roots and I cannot keep up this charade. I only did it because I love this land, where I have the freedom to say, and to think, and to charge whatever I want." Suddenly Homer realizes how much Apu really loves America and decides to vote against Proposition 24.

Bart suggests that Apu get married so that he does not get deported. However, Lisa informs Apu, because he has lived in America for as long as he has, he is eligible to take the citizenship test. Apu studies hard for the test. The test is scheduled for the day before the vote on Proposition 24. On test day, Apu and other immigrants (including Moe in disguise—apparently so no one knows he is an illegal immigrant) take the test. The test reviewer informs Apu that he has passed and that he is now an American citizen.

Apu: Yes, I am a citizen. Now, which way to the welfare office?
Test Reviewer: What?!
Apu: I'm kidding, I'm kidding. I work, I work.

Apu celebrates his citizenship status with the Simpsons and other well-wishers at a picnic. Apu says, "From this day forth, I am no longer an Indian living in America. I am an Indian American." Homer, feeling a bit patriotic, gives a speech to the crowd of Apu's supporters:

Hi everyone! If I could just say a few words—I'd be a better public speaker! [Bart cracks up laughing.] Now that you're all relaxed. Most of us here were born in America. We take this country for granted. But not immigrants like Apu. While the rest of us are drinking ourselves stupid, they're driving the cabs that get us home safely. They're writing the operas that entertain us every day. They're training our tigers and kicking our extra points. These people are the glue that holds together the gears of our society. If we pass Proposition 24 we're losing some of the truest Americans of us all. When you go to the polls tomorrow, please, vote "No" on Proposition 24. [Homer leads a chant.] "No" on 24! "No" on 24! "No" on 24! . . .

Although Homer is not an elegant speaker, he speaks from the heart. He correctly points out that immigrants are an asset to America. And what effect did his speech have on Proposition 24? Well, it passes in a landslide vote: 95 to 5 percent in favor.

The Simpson family hears the news while at Apu's Kwik-E-Mart. Homer utters, "When are people going to learn? Democracy doesn't work." Apu replies, "Please don't knock the land that I love." Apu opens a letter while making his patriotic defense of America. It is a jury duty notice. Excited, Apu states, "Today, I am truly an American citizen." Proving that he really is an American citizen, Apu throws away the jury duty notice. Like most Americans, he is more concerned about his rights than he is about his duties!

Springfield is clearly a melting pot of different races of people. Mirroring many other US cities, Springfield has a history of intolerance toward minorities and immigrants. And yet, most of the residents of Springfield descended from immigrants themselves. *The Simpsons* have clearly touched upon some of the many ethnic and racial issues that comprise contemporary society. Issues such as immigration will continue to be controversial for years to come.

Chapter 8

Religion and Other Things We Believe In

"To think, I turned to a cult for mindless happiness when I had beer all along."
—Homer Simpson

A bullet-shaped hunk of granite that served as a traffic barrier in a past life has been reincarnated as a Hindu shrine in San Francisco, drawing worshipers to an out-of-the-way clearing in Golden Gate Park. Some devotees want permission to build a permanent shrine around the former traffic barrier. Angry mobs in the Ivory Coast burn and beat to death alleged sorcerers after a penis-shrinking scare spread from neighboring Ghana. Because of the spiritual importance of a white buffalo, the birth of a white buffalo calf in Wisconsin leads a Sioux medicine man to compare its significance to the "second coming of Christ" and a sure sign that the nations of the world will unify. A ten-year-old grilled cheese sandwich—it was in a freezer for ten years—is perceived to have been emblazed with the face of the Virgin Mary and sells on eBay for $28,000. (A "ghost" in a jar was also once auctioned on eBay.) The perceived images of Jesus, Mary, and other religious deities are believed to occasionally appear on frozen food cooler doors in American grocery stores, tortillas in Mexico, fish sticks in Ontario, Canada, and eggplants in India.

As these brief stories illustrate, some people are capable of believing almost anything. But why are people willing to believe in something despite the lack of objective factual evidence? Welcome to the fascinating and irrational world of religion!

SCIENCE AND RELIGION: CAN THEY COEXIST IN A RATIONAL WORLD?

"Well, it appears science has faltered once again in the face of religious evidence."
—Reverend Lovejoy

Religion is one of the oldest social institutions of human society. Defining religion presents a few problems. One could begin with a definition that has a concept of God as its core, but many religions do not have a clear concept of God and some religions are polytheistic (believe in multiple gods). One could also define religion in terms of the emotions of spirituality, oneness with nature, mystery, and many other feelings, but that does not provide a very helpful definition. Sociologists define religion as a set of answers to the dilemmas of human existence that makes the world meaningful, a system of beliefs and rituals that serves to bind like-minded people together into a social group.

Historically, one of religion's most primary functions has been to provide explanations for life's uncertainties and perplexing array of social challenges. Throughout the ages, mankind has struggled to grasp the knowledge necessary to explain such basic phenomena as solar and lunar eclipses—often blaming them on angry gods. During those "dark ages," people turned to religion because religious leaders provided simple answers to complex problems. Unfortunately, religious answers to life's mysteries were and are often very irrational, and are seldom based on fact or empirical knowledge.

As humankind evolved a new social force emerged—science. Science is knowledge gained through the scientific method. The scientific method itself is defined as the pursuit of knowledge involving the stating of a problem, the collection of facts through observation and experiment, and the testing of ideas to determine their validity. Science coherently answers the once unexplainable (e.g., natural occurrences such as eclipses). Because science relies on fact and is objective, it instantly became a threat to religion—which relies on the faith of its adherents to accept unverified beliefs. As people began to accept scientific explanations of reality, religion slowly began to lose its power in society. This process is known as secularization.

Most sociologists view secularization as a natural extension of modernization, urbanization, and industrialization. Although some sociologists might point to the fundamentalist revival in the United States as evidence of religion's continued importance in society, we must all accept certain logical, scientific conclusions. Lunar and solar eclipses are not the result of angry gods, but merely the result of celestial body alignments. Creationists' theories of the birth of humanity, once believed by many, have been discounted not only because they lack any sort of rationality and logic but because evolutionary theories and the "big bang" theory have been scientifically proven to be accurate.

In fact, in 2006 two Americans, George Smoot and John Mather, won the Nobel Prize in physics for their measurement of light that is credited for cementing the big bang theory as the cause of the creation of the universe. The big bang theory states that the whole universe started out at a uniform temperature before expanding into the much less homogeneous state we now observe. Smoot and Mather were the chief architects of a NASA satellite observatory named COBE (acronym for cosmic background explorer). Launched in 2006, the COBE spacecraft measured feeble remnants of light that originated early in the history of the universe, about 380,000 years after the big bang. Until then, the universe was opaque to light, making it impossible to directly observe anything older (Crenson, 2006). Per Carlson, chairman of the Nobel physics committee, calls the Smoot and Mather discovery "the greatest discovery" of the century.

Today, science not only answers many of life's complicated questions, it seemingly makes religion obsolete. And, although there are attempts to fuse scientific knowledge and fact with religious beliefs, these two social forces often confront each other as adversaries. *The Simpsons* provides numerous examples of the battle between science and religion as well as pointing out many of the irrationalities of religion. The clever interpretation of religion presented in *Simpsons* episodes often borders on the sacrilegious for adherents of religion, while at the same time, provides great moments of laughter for those who have seen "the light" of scientific reason.

Visions of Angels

"Look, you can either accept science and face reality or you can believe in angels and live in a children's dream world."
—Lisa Simpson

The "Lisa the Skeptic" episode (#186) provides us with a clear example of the role of perception in both reality and religion. In this episode, developers are constructing a mall on a site (Sabertooth Meadow) where several fossils have previously been found. Lisa complains to the developers that archeological work should be allowed on the site before the mall is completed. Lisa hires a lawyer and calls in a favor owed to her by Principal Skinner and a dig is eventually ordered.

During the dig, Lisa unearths fossilized remains. Bystanders immediately believe the remains to be that of an angel. (Like looking at a grilled cheese sandwich and seeing the face of the Virgin Mary.)

> *Lisa*: But it can't be an angel!
> *Moe*: Oh no? Well, if you're so sure what it ain't, how about tellin' us what it am!
> *Lisa*: Well, maybe it's a . . . a Neanderthal who got bitten by some angry fish.
> *Ned*: Well, I gotta say, Lisa, it sounds like you're strainin' to do some explainin'!
> *Wiggum*: Yeah, everyone's heard of angels. But who's ever heard of a "Neanderthal"?

Lisa's attempt to discount the plausibility of finding an angel has left her temporarily stumped. This reveals a great deal about the science–religion continuum. Religious people will rely on faith and belief alone that the fossil is an angel because they *want* it to be an angel. (They may even *need* it to be an angel.) Lisa, on the other hand, realizes it is not logical that the fossil is that of an angel, but she cannot provide the true identity of the fossil at this point. Scientists want to collect evidence and analyze data before offering a logical explanation for events. During this time, religious people dig in deeper and remain true to their convictions.

Until scientific analysis can be conducted, Lisa continues to offer possible explanations, including that it could be a mutant as a result of the nuclear plant. Not buying any of her explanations, newsman Kent Brockman asks Lisa, "Miss Simpson, how can you maintain your skepticism in spite of the fact that thing really looks like an angel?" Brockman, like the other townsfolk, is relying on a perception of an angel based on religious teachings. For all we know, even if angels did exist, they may not look at all similar to the popular religious images of angels that have been presented to adherents.

Dr. Hibbert leads a discussion as to who owns the rights to the "angel." He believes the discovery to be a priceless scientific find. Ned Flanders insists that the remains are sacred and should be treated as such. While everyone argues, Homer has tied the angel bones to the roof of his car. As he drives off, he says, "So long, suckers!" He takes the angel home and sets up a "viewing" of the angel in his garage. He does not really care what the remains are, but he realizes there is an opportunity to profit from it. He charges "believers" fifty cents to view the angel. Interestingly, Homer has placed a fig leaf over the groin area of the angel! Lisa takes a sample piece from the angel to have it tested by Dr. Stephen Jay Gould.

Meanwhile, people continue to pay homage to the angel in the Simpsons' garage. Lisa warns that soon she will have the facts about the angel from Dr. Gould. Homer responds to Lisa by saying, "Facts are meaningless. You can use facts to prove anything that is even remotely true." Dr. Gould appears and tells Lisa that the test results were inconclusive. (Note: We learn later in the episode that he never actually ran the test.) Reverend Lovejoy takes this opportunity to mock Lisa and her reliance on science. Reverend Lovejoy states: "Well, it appears science has faltered once again in the face of religious evidence." Lisa remains undaunted.

> *Lisa*: Look, you can either accept science and face reality or you can believe in angels and live in a children's dream world.
> *Moe*: Go home, science girl.
> *Lisa*: I am home.

Angrily, Lisa heads inside her house and slams the door. She walks into the kitchen complaining to her mother, "Ah, those morons make me so angry." Much to Lisa's surprise, Marge does not take her side on the science versus religion debate.

> *Marge*: Maybe so, but I'd appreciate it if you didn't call them "morons."
> *Lisa*: But they are morons. What grown person could believe in angels?

Marge tells Lisa that she does. Lisa is shocked and says to her mom, "But you're so smart." Marge attempts to explain herself. She tells Lisa that there has to be more to life than what we can see. "Everyone needs something to believe in," she tells Lisa. Marge suggests to Lisa that she take a leap of faith (and believe in angels). She also tells Lisa that she feels sorry for her if she cannot believe in angels. Dejected, Lisa walks away and tells her mother that she feels sorry for *her*. This interaction between mother and daughter is symbolic of the science versus religion debate. Lisa, as a person of science, makes her judgments based solely on reason and scientific rationality. Marge, as a religious person, is willing to accept things on blind faith. Marge and Lisa have reached an impasse and head toward their respective corners.

Undaunted, Lisa continues to fight. She takes her argument to Springfield's TV show, *Smartline*. Lisa tells Kent Brockman and the audience that if you believe in angels you must also believe in unicorns, leprechauns, and sea monsters. The viewing audience is upset with Lisa's comments and turns against science. Ned comments, "Science is like a blabbermouth that ruins the movie by telling you how it ends. Well, I say there are some things we don't want to know—important things." Other viewers are so incensed that they form a mob and attack Springfield's science buildings, including the Museum of Natural History, Springfield Robotics Laboratory, the planetarium, and even the Christian Science Room. Kent Brockman reports, "Technocrats are learning a lesson of humility tonight as angel supporters lay waste to Springfield's scientific institutions."

Aware of the violence directed toward science buildings, Lisa decides to use the same tactic and heads off to destroy the angel. However, she discovers that someone has stolen the angel. The townspeople also want the angel and blame Lisa for its disappearance. Chief Wiggum arrests Lisa. She appears before the judge, who is eager to settle the science versus religion debate. However, the angel is discovered again on a hillside near the original dig site. There is a message carved into the angel: "The End Will Come at Sundown." The judge has no choice but to free Lisa. He also orders religion to stay five hundred feet away from science!

The Springfield residents surround the angel and fear the worst. They assume that the world is coming to an end simply because of the message carved into the angel. Patty and Selma have one last cigarette and mockingly proclaim, "We did it! We beat cancer!" They are pleased to have cheated a cancer-caused death for an apocalyptic death. Smithers kisses Burns. And everyone counts down the seconds to sundown. At sundown, nothing happens. No apocalypse. No damnation. How could the angel of death be wrong? What other possible explanation could exist for the angel's apparent doomsday prediction? And what other possible explanation could there be for the existence of the angel?

Suddenly, the angel rises and begins to float over the heads of the townsfolk. A "heavenly" voice accompanies the rising angel: "Prepare for the end. The end of high prices. . . . Please follow the angel for all your shopping needs." As it turns out, the angel was merely a publicity stunt perpetrated by the Heavenly Hills Mall developers. The developers exploited the people's belief in an angel in order to sell merchandise. Quickly forgetting their religious devotion to a heavenly entity, the people rush to follow the angel to the grand opening of the mall. Ah, the religion of capitalism!

At least in this case, Lisa and science triumphed. The angel was not heavenly but secular. It found its ultimate resting place atop the main entrance to the Heavenly Hills Mall. As for the "followers" of the angel, they too entered the secular world of the mall in an attempt to find heavenly deals.

Praise Be to Miracles

"It was incredible! I saw heaven!"
—Principal Skinner

Miracles have a direct relationship with science. Typically, anything that science cannot explain is interpreted by some as a "miracle." For example, when a person survives a medical disorder for which doctors gave no hope of a recovery, it is likely to be labeled as a "miraculous" recovery by some people. When seeking "divine intervention" for some specific problem, which seems to have no chance of occurring, people hope for a miracle. Thus, miracles comprise two elements. First, the word "miracle" is often applied as an explanation to anything science cannot explain; that is, when no logical, rational explanation presents itself, the religious sector will claim responsibility via a "miraculous" occurrence. Science clearly admits to not having the answers to everything—yet. It is likely just a matter of time before science will be able to explain everything. For now, the religious sector claims responsibility for every positive accomplishment not easily explained by science. (Note: This is sometimes called "The God of the Gaps.")

The second element of miracles deals with statistics. That is, a miracle is really nothing more than an explanation for any event or phenomenon that is statistically rare, or unlikely to occur. The reason many Native American tribes view the birth of a white buffalo calf as "miraculous" is because of the statistically rare occurrence of such an albino birth. It is estimated that one in ten million buffaloes is born white. The white color results from a rare recessive gene that both parents must possess. Thus, while science can explain why and how a white calf is born, the statistical rarity of the event warrants such "miraculous" attributes as an omen of good fortune and peace. Clearly, there is no correlation between the birth of a white buffalo calf and peace for humanity. Now, if the birth of a white buffalo calf *could* be attributed to, say, ending a war, that would be a miracle. That is, until science could prove otherwise!

In the "I'm Goin' to Praiseland" episode (#267), Ned Flanders has established a religious-based theme park in honor of his late wife, Maude. The park is too tame for the visitors' tastes and they start to leave the big grand opening event when, suddenly, a "miracle" occurs. One of the souvenir items is a mask with a replica face of Maude. One of the patrons of the park throws a mask toward the ground in front of the statue honoring Maude and it floats into the air. Immediately, witnesses label the event as a "miracle"—after all, what other explanation could there be?!

The statue becomes known as "Miracle Maude" and people begin to flock to Praiseland to pray. More miracles occur as the people praying at the Miracle Maude statue report having visions. (Note: Drug users sometimes report having visions after taking psychedelic drugs but these visions are not labeled "miracles"; instead they are called "trips" or delusions.) The highly religious Ned is convinced of the authenticity of the pilgrim's visions. Ned explains this to his son Rod.

> *Rod*: How come everybody's having visions, Daddy?
> *Ned*: Oh, there's no explaining God's will, Roddy. That's like explaining how an airplane flies.

Clearly, science *can* explain how an airplane flies. And, as stated earlier, when given enough time, science will most likely be able to explain the "heavenly" visions at the Miracle Maude site. In the meantime, however, the patrons' visions continue. Principal Skinner explains his vision to Bart.

> *Skinner*: It was incredible! I saw heaven! But it wasn't clouds and angels playing harps like at the end of so many *Three Stooges* shorts. It was a golden elementary school with a teacher's lounge that stretched as far as the eye could see. And no one was ever tardy.
> *Bart*: Was I there?
> *Skinner*: No! It was heaven! My vision of heaven.

As Skinner points out, his vision of heaven is specific to his needs. Skinner's vision reflects the nature of selective perception that leads people to see things as they want them to be, rather than as they may really be. Certainly Bart would have a different idea of heaven that did not involve an elementary school.

As it turns out, there was no miracle at Maude's statue. Instead, there was a simple logical explanation for the hovering Maude mask as well as the "visions" people reported to have. There was a leaky gas line at the site of the statue. No miracles, just toxic fumes causing people to hallucinate.

In the "Faith Off" episode (#237), Bart believes that he has acquired faith-healing powers. This "revelation" occurs while the Simpsons attend a preacher's ("Brother Faith") revival in Springfield. Homer has a bucket stuck on his head and he cannot remove it. He asks Brother Faith for assistance. The preacher turns to Bart and suggests that he give it a try. Acting as if he possesses God's power to heal, Bart makes some gestures and he somehow manages to loosen the bucket from his father's head. Amazed by this, Bart later asks Brother Faith how the bucket really came off Homer's head.

> *Bart*: I've gotta know, how did you really get the bucket off my dad's head?
> *Brother Faith*: Well, I didn't, son. You did. God gave you the power.
> *Bart*: Really? Hmm. I would think that he would want to limit my power.

Bart now believes he is a faith healer capable of creating miracles. He decides to start his own revival under the name "Brother Bart." Lisa, always the skeptic when supernatural powers are credited for miraculous events, attempts to introduce rational, scientific reality to Bart's miracles.

> *Lisa*: Bart, I hope you don't believe your own hype.
> *Bart*: Number of miracles performed by Bart: two. Number performed by Lisa: zero.
> *Lisa*: How can you believe all this mumbo jumbo? The bucket came off Dad's head because the bright lights heated it, causing the metal to expand.
> *Bart*: Heat makes metal expand. Now who's talking mumbo jumbo?

Lisa has applied elementary science to explain what others had labeled as a miracle. With the limited scientific knowledge level of past human beings, it is not hard to imagine why people once so easily believed in miracles. However, as science unravels more and more of life's mysteries, the realm of miracles is shrinking quickly.

Angels, visions, and miracles are important elements of religion because they reflect an adherent's willingness to "believe" in something that cannot be proven to be true. Faith and beliefs remain essential elements of any religion.

You Gotta Have Faith and Belief

"Is a little blind faith too much to ask?"
—Sunday School Teacher

Faith and belief go hand-in-hand. Religious people possess both of these rudiments. (Note: It could be argued that secular people have faith and belief in the validity of science.) It is especially common for religious people to rely on faith and belief in times of stress, hope, and need. In this regard, adherents are appealing to a higher authority, typically expressed as "God." Often, the phrase "You gotta have faith" is used as a cop-out by religious people when they are confronted by questions they cannot answer (or do not want to answer because such information threatens the foundation of religious thought). For example, ask a religious person to provide concrete proof of the existence of heaven—they cannot do so. They will tell you, instead, to have faith in its existence.

In "The Telltale Head" episode (#8), Bart and Lisa join other Springfield children at Sunday school at their local church (The First Church of Springfield). The lesson of the day is "Heaven." Naturally, young children are fascinated by the topic of heaven. However, it seems the more questions they ask, the more frustrated the teacher becomes trying to answer their concerns. Lisa wants to know if her cat Snowball will be in heaven. Bart wants to know if a person's amputated leg will be in heaven. The teacher assures Bart that it will. The kids bombard the teacher with questions about specifics to heaven's existence. She cannot answer their questions and instead inquires, "Is a little blind faith too much to ask?"

Faith in the existence of heaven, God, and a soul; a belief in the validity of prayer and the need to attend religious services, are among the fundamental aspects of religion and principles adhered to by many religious persons (e.g., those who follow the Judeo, Christian, and Islamic traditions).

Prayer

> **"Homer, God isn't some sort of holy concierge! You can't keep bugging him for every little thing."**
> —Marge Simpson

Within the religious realm, prayer fosters the contemplative attitudes of listening and receptivity; it brings adherents closer to God (Keating, 1994). In its truest meaning, religious prayer involves a discussion with God, or some other high-ranking figure (e.g., patron saints). Religious people turn to prayer because they believe in an all-powerful God who is willing to and capable of helping them. To move into the realm of prayer is to be open to infinite possibilities. Thus, resorting to prayer in times of need or trouble may be viewed as a pragmatic path toward a favorable outcome.

Typically, when people pray to God for help, they make promises, such as to be a better person, in return for immediate gratification. Marge Simpson provides us with such an example in the "Homer Defined" episode (#40). In this episode, the residents of

Springfield are faced with possible annihilation due to a "meltdown crisis" at the nuclear plant. Marge prays to God for help:

> Dear Lord, if you spare this town from becoming a smoking hole in the ground, I'll try to be a better Christian. I don't know what I can do . . . um, oh, the next time there's a canned food drive I'll give the poor something they'd actually like instead of old lima beans and pumpkin mix.

With this prayer, Marge is promising to be a better Christian if God will spare Springfield from a seemingly deadly fate. Her promise to give "better" food to a canned food drive most likely hits home with many viewers as people typically donate the canned goods they don't really want anyway.

In the "Bart Gets an 'F'" episode (#14), Bart prays to God for help the night before a big test: "Well, old-timer, I guess this is the end of the road. I know I haven't always been a good kid, but, if I have to go to school tomorrow, I'll fail the test and be held back. I just need one more day to study, Lord. I need your help!" Lisa overhears Bart's prayer and mutters to herself, "Prayer, the last refuge of a scoundrel." Bart continues his prayer to God (without offering anything in return), "A teachers' strike, a power failure, a blizzard . . . Anything that'll cancel school tomorrow. I know it's asking a lot, but if anyone can do it, you can! Thanking you in advance, your pal, Bart Simpson."

The next morning Bart awakes to discover a huge snowstorm has hit Springfield and causes the closing of school. Upon learning of the school closing, Bart yells out "Cowabunga!" as he runs toward the front door with his snow sled. However, there is an obstacle confronting him: his sister Lisa. Lisa informs her brother: "I heard you last night, Bart. You prayed for this. Now your prayers have been answered. I'm no theologian. I don't know who or what God is exactly. All I know is he's a force more powerful than Mom and Dad put together and you owe him big." Bart admits to Lisa that she is right and he heads back upstairs to his room to study. Studying is always hard for Bart, but today it is especially difficult as he can hear all the kids joyfully playing outside. Bart is trying to learn about the First Continental Congress for his test the next day but drifts away in thought by envisioning himself seated among the delegates.

The next day, Bart takes his history exam. At the conclusion of the test, Bart's teacher, Mrs. Krabappel, grades his exam immediately. Bart earns a 59 percent grade—an F. He stares at his exam and cries. Mrs. Krabappel, confused by Bart's reaction, states, "I figure you'd be used to failing by now." Bart explains that he really did try to study this time and that is why he is so upset: "Now I know how George Washington felt when he surrendered Fort Necessity to the French in 1754." Mrs. Krabappel is shocked to hear Bart actually apply historical fact to his current situation. She rewards him with a bonus extra credit point on his exam, which raises his grade to a D–. Bart is stoked that he passed the exam. His father is also happy and posts Bart's test on the refrigerator door. Homer tells Bart he is proud of him. Bart responds, "Part of this D-minus belongs to God."

Thus, even though Bart did not promise to do anything for God in return for his help, he did give credit to God for his help in earning a passing grade.

For a nonreligious person, Homer prays often. In fact, he prays not only to God, but also to such otherworldly figures as Superman! In the "Lost Our Lisa" episode (#202), Homer looks for Lisa, who has left the house on her own in an attempt to visit the Springsonian Museum. Homer is having a difficult time locating Lisa, so he appropriates a "cherry picker" truck with an extended ladder in the hopes of spotting her in the crowded streets more easily. He does indeed locate Lisa but the cherry picker rolls down a hill out of control. Homer decides to pray for help: "I'm not normally a praying man, but if you're up there, please save me, Superman." Although Superman does not fly to his rescue, Homer is eventually saved—by Lisa—and lives to tell the tale.

Two episodes after "Lost Our Lisa," Homer prays to God instead of Superman. In the "Lard of the Dance" episode (#204), Homer has gone into the grease business with his son, Bart. Homer has learned that recycling grease can be a profitable business; he just underestimated how much grease it takes to actually make a significant profit. His first visit to the recycling center netted him sixty-three cents for four pounds of grease. Homer decides to steal grease from commercial businesses and starts at Springfield Elementary. Homer leads his son in prayer for a successful mission.

Homer: All right, son, we're about to embark on our most difficult mission. Let's bow our heads in prayer. (Homer and

Bart bow their heads, close their eyes, and clasp their hands in classic prayer ritualistic behavior.)

Homer: Dear Lord, I know you're busy, seeing as how you can watch women changing clothes and all that, but if you help us steal this grease tonight, I promise we'll donate half the profits to charity.

Bart (looking at his Dad in mocking disbelief): Dad, he's not stupid.

Homer: All right, screw it! Let's roll!

Homer has an atypical view of God. First, he assumes God is willing to break one of his own commandments ("Thou shalt not steal") so that Homer can make a profit selling grease. Second, Homer believes that God uses his power to watch women undress. Homer has made the double assumption that God is a man and that God is voyeuristic. Then again, religious people also believe that God "sees" everything we do, which includes changing our clothes! Further, Bart has called Homer on his pitiful attempt to promise God something in return for his favor. All in all, praying to God for help stealing is not a very religious thing to do.

It is often said that God "works in mysterious ways" and that is certainly the case in the "Pray Anything" episode (#301). In this episode, Homer, who has always been jealous of Ned, sees that the grass really *is* greener on the other side of the fence—in Ned's yard. Ned tells Homer that the secret to his successful life is the result of prayer. As a result of this advice, Homer decides to give prayer a chance in making his life better. Initially, Homer prays for some things, such as help finding his lost TV remote and a good TV show to watch. Homer finds the remote and is pleased to find the Monkey Olympics on TV. Homer decides to pray to God for a new snack to munch on: "Dear Lord, as I think of you, dressed in white with your splendid beard, I am reminded of Colonel Sanders, who is seated at your right hand, shoveling popcorn chicken into thy mouth. Lord, could you come up with a delicious new tasty treat like he did?"

Homer's vision of God as an old white man is common within patriarchal societies. This all-powerful being dressed in white is also consistent with the belief that the color white is tied to purity—something God surely must be. However, Homer's belief that Colonel Sanders is seated next to God and shoveling Him with popcorn chicken is the result of his own projection of a perfect being. Then again, all images of God reflect the reality that God is a projection of humans, and not necessarily a fixed reality.

Noticing that Bart is having trouble with his homework, Homer decides to pray for God's divine intervention.

> *Homer*: Oh, heavenly God, my son is plagued with homework. With your vast knowledge of (Homer looks at Bart's book) *The Shore Birds of Maryland*, I know you can help him.
>
> *Homer*: Can and will! Now, to unstop this sink. Lord, please use your space-age clog-busting powers on this stubborn drain. Then, take some time off for yourself. Fly to France. Have a nice dinner.

Homer's prayers are again answered. He is on a holy roll! But still, there are bigger problems to be dealt with. The Simpsons receive word that their house is falling apart due to bad plumbing. Homer is unsure where he will find the money to make the necessary repairs. He is still worried about his financial problems when he and his family attend services at the First Church of Springfield. Homer prays for help. Outside the church, Homer falls into a big hole and breaks his leg. A personal injury lawyer convinces Homer to sue the church for damages. They go to court, and the jury awards Homer one million dollars. Reverend Lovejoy protests the decision, "Your Honor, we don't have that kind of money! We're not a synagogue!" To which, Judge Snyder responds, "In that case, I award Homer Simpson the deed to the church." (Note: Reverend Lovejoy is using a stereotype of Jews—that they are all rich.)

Despite Marge's protest, the Simpson family moves into the church while the contractors repair their home. Beyond treating the church as their private home, the secular intrusion of the Simpsons into the sacred world of the church is demonstrated in a variety of ways. Homer places a television on the altar. He sings and dances on the altar to "I Was Made for Loving You" by KISS. He sacrilegiously uses the holy cross as a mock guitar.

Homer's blasphemous behavior continues. He decides to throw a housewarming party in the church. The party goes on for two days and the partygoers become increasingly hedonistic.

> *Lenny*: Look at all this—the great food, the party, the sunshine
> —it's hard to believe one god came up with all this.
> *Carl*: Oh, there's probably a lot of gods.
> *Lenny*: Yeah, and some of them's gotta be chicks.
> *Carl*: Yeah, with like a thousand boobs.
> *Lenny*: Hoo-hoo! That's the god I'm gonna worship!

The drunken attitude and behavior of Lenny and Carl mirrors the rest of the partygoers. Reverend Lovejoy and Ned Flanders both sense great evil is about to plague Springfield. Lovejoy takes his family and leaves the city. Flanders has built an ark: "Okay, I've got two of every animal. But only males! I don't want any hanky-panky!" Ned is so concerned that God will punish Homer and his followers that he believes himself to be the next Noah. Of course, with just male animals, he will not be able to repopulate the earth as the story of Noah is generally written.

As Lovejoy and Flanders predicted, God becomes angry with Homer's blasphemy. The sky turns dark. Marge warns Homer to repent immediately: "In the Bible, he is always smiting and turning people into salt." Homer tempts God. Suddenly torrential rain pours down on Springfield. Flanders's ark is set to sail. The end appears at hand. What can save Springfield now, against a vengeful God? Homer is stricken by a bolt of lightning. It seems hopeless for him. However, Reverend Lovejoy returns triumphantly on a helicopter and leads the hedonists in prayer. The rain stops and the sky turns blue.

Homer proclaims that he has learned a lesson: "I guess I learned something here. God is capable of great anger and great mercy. But mostly great anger."

At the end of this episode, God is shown again as an old white man with a beard. He also has Colonel Sanders sitting on one side of him and Buddha on the other!

The All-Powerful God

"Whoa, cool! God is so in-your-face!"
—Bart Simpson

Since no one has met God, his/her/its real appearance (if God exists at all) is based on human projections and is subject to interpretation.

For example, most people attempt to attach a gender identity to God—he or she—even though it is highly unlikely that God would have a human form. Famous nonbelievers in God such as Ludwig Feuerbach and Karl Marx have explained God as an example of false consciousness (the inability to clearly see where one's own best interests lie). Feuerbach claimed, "Man makes religion; religion does not make man." Marx viewed religion and God as abstract creations that had become reified throughout time. In short, skeptics argue that God exists only because humans will "his" existence. Skeptics, however, are relatively small in number, as the majority of Americans believe in one, all-powerful God.

The Simpsons provides us with a wide array of conceptions of God ranging from the viewpoint of God as a fictional character to that of an all-powerful, vengeful tease. It is noteworthy, however, that the creators of *The Simpsons*, despite numerous attacks on the validity of God and religion, show him the ultimate animated respect as, unlike all the other *Simpsons* characters, God always has four fingers and a thumb.

In the "Das Bus" episode (#192), Homer and Bart are watching a television show about Noah's ark. Troy McClure plays the role of Noah. God appears to Noah as the sky darkens above him.

God: Noah, thou shalt build thyself an ark measuring three hundred cubits in length.

Noah (as he writes God's commands down on a tablet): Three hundred cubits, give or take . . . (Thunder erupts in the sky above Noah.)

God: Exactly three hundred! And thou shalt takest two of every creature. . . .

Noah: Two creatures . . . (Once again thunder erupts above Noah.)

God: Two of *every* creature!

Noah: Even stinkbeetles?

God: Especially stinkbeetles!

(Bart and Homer are impressed with the portrayal of God in this film.)

Bart: Whoa, cool! God is so in-your-face!

Homer: Yeah. He's my favorite fictional character.

Homer, who has a hard time believing in God and the validity of religion, takes the view of such skeptics as Feuerbach and Marx and views God as a fictional character. Homer shares his thoughts of God in a variety of ways throughout the long-running *Simpsons* series.

In the "Two Bad Neighbors" episode (#141), Homer is in conflict with former president George H. W. Bush. Homer is particularly upset with Bush because he spanked Bart (see chapter 5 for a discussion on this incident). Homer is on a rampage and seeks to even the score with Bush. Homer and Bart are in the sewer that connects their house to the Bush home. Unsure how exactly to accomplish his revenge against the former president, Homer decides to turn to God for help.

> *Homer*: So, I thought to myself. "What would God do in this situation?"
> *Bart* (laughs): Locusts! It will drive him [Bush] nuts!
> (Bart is holding onto a box of locusts.)
> *Homer* (clutching a Holy Bible): It's all in the Bible, son. It's the prankster's bible.

As Martin Luther encouraged nearly five hundred years ago, Homer has (apparently) read the Bible and interpreted its meaning to fit his own needs. In the sixteenth century, Luther nailed his ninety-five theses to the door of the cathedral in Wittenberg, Germany, lighting the fires of the Reformation and Protestantism. Beyond establishing his own religion (Lutheranism) Luther was a strong proponent of mass education. He argued that all people have a right to an education so that they can read the Bible for themselves. It is highly doubtful that Luther had envisioned that people may actually read the Bible to justify harming others as Homer Simpson has.

Homer's usage of the Bible to justify revenge against his enemy makes an even bigger social commentary on the current state of global affairs, as many world leaders use religion and passages from "holy" books to justify such extreme acts as terrorism and war. Are people really interpreting these religious words of wisdom properly?

Of course, Homer is not the only *Simpsons* character to view God as vengeful. In the "Home Sweet Homediddly-Dum-Doodily" episode (#131), Maude and Ned Flanders have taken in the Simpson children while Homer and Marge are under investigation for child neglect (Lisa had head lice and the house was a mess when county welfare officers went to investigate her home life). The Flanders couple greets the Simpson kids: "Welcome to your new home, neglectorinos." Maude comments, "I don't judge Homer and Marge. That's for a vengeful God to do." Ned agrees, "Mmm-hmm. All we want to do is give you kids a good home until they get their act together." Marge and Homer were found to be good parents and the kids were returned to them.

In a less serious misinterpretation of the Bible, Homer views the story of God and Moses in the desert as that of God teasing Moses. He relates the story of Moses to his current sad state of affairs in the "Homer vs. Patty and Selma" episode (#120), where one misfortune after another has beset him.

> *Homer*: Sometimes, I think God is teasing me. Like he teased
>   Moses in the desert.
> *Marge*: Tested, Homer. God tested Moses.

Homer wants life to be simple, good, and rewarding. He, along with most of us, wonders why he must constantly struggle to gain any level of success and/or happiness in life. Most people want things to come easily. They do not want to work hard toward attaining desired goals. This helps to explain why people sometimes resort to prayer—they would rather remove the burden of responsibility from themselves and place it in the hands of an all-powerful being that is capable of granting instant miracles. In turn, this explains why people find the idea of the existence of a god as soothing. After all, if praying to an all-mighty being can bring instant gratification, that *would* be a wonderful thing.

Thus, while the concept of god(s) was important to people in primitive times because it provided easy, albeit illogical and irrational explanations to life's dilemmas, people still find the idea of god appealing today because of a spiritual sense of well-being.

To Go to Church or Not to Go to Church, That Is the Question

"I just had the best day of my life and I owe it all to skipping church."
—Homer Simpson

The nonreligious Homer Simpson shares in common a trait held by other nonreligious persons, and even some people who identify themselves as religious: the desire to skip attending church.

In the "In Marge We Trust" episode (#175), Homer is complaining to Marge once again on a Sunday that he does not want to go to church. Marge explains to Homer, "The Lord only asks for an hour a week." To which Homer replies, "In that case, he should have made the week an hour longer. Lousy God." When the family returns home, Lisa shares her father's relief that the weekly religious service commitment is over.

> *Homer*: This is the best part of the week.
> *Lisa*: It's the longest time before more church.
> *Marge*: Church shouldn't be a chore. It should help you in your daily life.
> *Homer*: It should, but it doesn't.

Marge is expressing the religious belief that it is good to attend church services regularly. The teachings presented at church should inspire adherents throughout the week in their daily lives. The coming together of like-minded people helps to solidify the community as a "we" group. Which, as we learned in chapter 7, automatically creates "they" groups of nonbelievers and adherents to other religions.

In an earlier episode of *The Simpsons*, "Homer the Heretic" (#62), Homer's reluctance to attend organized church services leads to his talking to God and forming his own religion. In this episode, Marge is trying to wake Homer up on a Sunday morning to go to church. Homer tells Marge he is sick of church and refuses to get out of bed. Upset with Homer, Marge takes the kids with her to church. It's freezing cold outside and the heat does not work inside the church. Meanwhile, Homer is warm and toasty at home. He cranks up the heat and dances around in his underwear like Tom Cruise in the film *Risky Business*. From there, things only get better for Homer. He is having the time of his life; after all, he has the house to himself. Homer watches the Three Stooges and football on TV, prepares his favorite breakfast—"Moon Waffles" (waffle batter with caramels) and wins a radio call-in contest.

Back at the First Church of Springfield, the Simpson family, along with the other parishioners, are stuck inside. A huge snowstorm has frozen the doors shut. When they are eventually freed, Marge has trouble starting the car. The dichotomy of the respective days between Marge and Homer could not be much larger. Marge and the kids finally get home and she is boiling mad. Homer's attitude will not help matters.

> *Homer*: I just had the best day of my life and I owe it all to skipping church.
> *Marge*: That's a terrible thing to say. (She looks at the kids.) Your father doesn't really mean that.
> *Homer*: Like fun I don't. Marge, I'm never going back to church again.
> *Marge*: Homer, are you actually giving up on your faith?
> *Homer*: No, no, no, no, well . . . yes.

Marge continues to badger Homer about his decision to stop going to church. Marge, a person who strongly believes that going to weekly religious services is the "right" thing to do, is extremely disappointed with Homer's decision to skip church. Homer uses the Church's own double-talk as a means to justify his decision.

> *Marge*: I can't believe you're giving up church, Homer.
> *Homer*: Hey, what's the big deal about going to some building every Sunday? I mean, isn't God everywhere?
> *Bart*: Amen, brother!

Homer's religion has taught him that God is everywhere. He applies logic to this belief to rationalize his decision that it is not necessary to visit a specific building to acknowledge God. Many religious people agree with this idea; that is, they believe that they can still be good (and "religious") people even if they do not attend scheduled religious services.

Later that night, Marge prays to God for Homer. She wants God to intervene in such a manner as to stimulate Homer to return to the church. Instead, Homer dreams about meeting and talking to God. Homer attempts to explain to God his aversion to going to church.

> *Homer*: I'm not a bad guy. I work hard and I love my kids. So why should I spend half my Sunday hearing about how I'm going to hell?

> *God*: Hmm, you've got a point there. You know, sometimes even I'd rather be watching football. Does St. Louis still have a team?
>
> *Homer*: No. They moved to Phoenix.

Note, perhaps as a sign that God does work in miraculous ways, since this episode first aired, the NFL did allow a franchise—the Rams—to move to St. Louis from Anaheim, California. And while the St. Louis Rams have won a Super Bowl, the Arizona Cardinals (the former St. Louis team) has rarely enjoyed a winning season. Did *The Simpsons* draw something to the attention of God that was later answered?!

At the conclusion of their talk together, God tells Homer, "Now, if you'll excuse me, I have to appear on a tortilla in Mexico."

After his talk with God, Homer feels he has an understanding with the "Big Guy" upstairs and no longer feels any guilty obligation to attend Sunday services. Further, Homer now believes he is some sort of divine messenger of God and he starts wearing a robe and acting "religious." Bart asks Homer to describe God to him. Homer tells Bart that God had good teeth, smelled nice, and was a "class act" all the way around. Homer starts his own religion and compares himself to a Jesus-type character.

Having started his own religion, Homer feels no need to attend church with his wife and kids. The message board on the First Church of Springfield reads: "When Homer Met Satan." They pray for Homer's salvation. The Flanders family wants to "save" Homer from his evil ways. Marge threatens Homer: "Don't make me choose between my man and my God, because you just can't win." It seems everyone is turning on Homer. Even though they are allowed to have their beliefs, he is not allowed to have his own. Then again, Homer mocks other "they" religious groups himself. After discussing the Hindu religion with Apu, Homer states, "No offense, Apu, but when they were handing out religions, you musta been out taking a whiz."

Homer eventually finds his way back to the First Church of Springfield after his hedonistic and solitary Sunday lifestyle leads him to accidentally set the house on fire. Ned Flanders fights the flames and saves Homer's life. Homer believes he is being punished by a spiteful God and denounces the religion he created. Later, God appears to Homer in a dream again. Homer learns that God is also vengeful as he tells Homer that nine out of ten religions fail in their first year. Let that be a lesson to would-be hedonists!

It seems that Homer finally learns the true reason it is important to go to a specific building to pray and worship in the "Bart Has Two Mommies" episode (#370). In this episode, Bart asks Homer why God always needs money as the collection plate is passed. Homer explains that God has lots of bills and planets to take care of and adds: "Did you see the ring he gave Saturn?" Thus, it is important for religious adherents to attend church, if not for enlightenment, then to maintain the infrastructure designed to establish and maintain religious beliefs. After all, running any organization costs a great deal of money. Furthermore, the church is not a nonprofit organization!

The Soul

"It's the symbol of everything that is fine inside us."
—Lisa Simpson

Another interesting concept that many have faith and belief in is the "soul." Most religious people, and even some nonreligious people, believe that each of us has a soul. The soul, apparently, is some sort of energy force; it is the essence that remains even after one's earthly body dies. It is the soul that will travel to heaven or hell (can there possibly be one without the other?).

In the appropriately named "Bart Sells His Soul" episode (#132), Bart argues with Milhouse regarding the validity of the concept of a soul. Bart taunts Milhouse and asks him, where is the soul located?

> *Milhouse*: It's kinda in here (he points to his chest). And when you sneeze, that's your soul trying to escape. Saying "God bless you" crams it back in. And when you die it squirms out and flies away.
> *Bart*: Uh-huh, what if you die in a submarine at the bottom of the ocean?
> *Milhouse*: Oh, it can swim. It's even got wheels in case you die in the desert and it has to drive to the cemetery.
> *Bart*: How can someone with glasses so thick be so stupid? Listen. You don't have a soul, I don't have a soul, there's no such thing as a soul!

> *Milhouse*: Fine. If you're so sure about that, why don't you sell
>   your soul to me?
> *Bart*: How much you got?
> *Milhouse*: Five bucks.
> *Bart*: Deal.

While Milhouse's explanation of the soul reflects his age and limited knowledge level, he has managed to purchase Bart's soul for a measly five dollars. That is, if one believes such a transaction can actually occur. Similar to voodoo, if people believe strongly in some sort of religious practice, they will begin to "find" supporting evidence for their convictions. (Note: this is how the reification process takes place that allows for the prominence of religion. In other words, when people say something is "real" or "true," it becomes real or true to them.)

Bart tells his sister that he sold his soul to Milhouse. Lisa, the voice of reason, questions the validity of the existence of a soul but informs Bart, "Whether or not the soul is real, Bart, it's the symbol of everything that is fine inside us." Lisa's interpretation of the soul leaves open a possible nonreligious explanation of the existence of an energy force of some sort that could be described by others as a soul. In other words, human beings have energy, and energy cannot be destroyed. Thus, even when the human body dies, the energy from that person survives. Is that energy a soul? Or is it part of "the force" as described in *Star Wars* movies?!

Regardless, Bart begins to find evidence that his life is doomed without his soul. The Simpson family's pet animals no longer like Bart, as if they sense he is soulless. Automatic doors do not open for Bart. Bart no longer laughs. Lisa worries that Bart really has lost his soul. She tells Bart, "Laughter is the language of the soul." Bart is freaking out. He wants his soul back. Bart asks Milhouse for his soul back, but he wants $50 for it. Bart does not have that kind of money.

Things only get worse for Bart. He tracks Milhouse down at his grandmother's house. At Nana Van Houten's, Milhouse admits that he sold Bart's soul to the comic book guy for some pogs. The comic book guy tells Bart he sold his soul to some unknown customer. Bart goes home and prays to God for his soul's return. Just then, his soul ownership paper (the original document that Bart used to transfer his soul ownership to Milhouse) appears on his bed. Lisa tracked the document and paid for it with money she had in a hidden piggy bank. Lisa gives the paper to her brother and a truly grateful Bart thanks her.

Bart never quite learned what the soul is, but he did learn that he should keep a better hold of his own.

Cults, the Brainwashing Alternative

> **"A new and better life awaits you on our distant home planet, Blisstonia."**
> —Jane

Although the greatest number of religious people are tied to some major world religion, there are a number of alternative forms of worship to choose from. Generally, these less-established groups are led by charismatic leaders who possess a near hypnotic power to attract followers. This is especially true with cults.

In "The Joy of Sect" episode (#191), Homer and Bart join other football fans at the Springfield International Airport to jeer the returning hometown team after they lost a game. A number of religious fanatics are at the airport as well. Homer and Bart attempt to avoid them all. The first person they blow off is a Hare Krishna member.

Hare Krishna Member (attempting to offer literature): Have you heard of Krishna consciousness?

Homer (as he and Bart are approached next by a man with a Holy Bible): This, Bart, is a crazy man.

Man with Bible: Do unto others as you would have them do unto you.

Homer (sarcastically): Right, that'll work.

(A man and woman, Glen and Jane, hand Homer some literature.)

Jane: A new and better life awaits you on our distant home planet, Blisstonia.

Homer (looking at the pamphlet titled "The Movementarians" with a picture of a man on it with a caption under it that reads "The Leader"): Hmm. Makes sense.

Homer and Bart have just met members of a religious sect, or cult, the Movementarians. Generally speaking, a cult can be defined as a religious movement that has little or nothing in common with other more established types of religious organizations that are found in the same society. Cults are generally regarded as unconventional or unusual from the standpoint of prevailing churches and sects. For example, when Reverend Lovejoy learns of the Movementarians he complains to his parishioners, "This so-called new religion is nothing but a pack of weird rituals and chants designed to take away the money of fools. Let us pray the Lord's Prayer forty times, but first, let's pass the collection plate." The irony of this statement should not be lost on anyone as conventional religions are consumed with ritualistic behaviors (a form of brainwashing), rites of ceremonies, and expectations of donations to maintain the church's hierarchy.

Homer decides to attend the Movementarians "get acquainted session" to learn more about them. But why would Homer, or anyone else for that matter, possibly be interested in joining a cult? Individuals may turn to cults because they lack a connection to the greater society, or because they have not found the answers they are looking for with traditional, more established religions. Those who suffer from chronic distress and unhappiness may find a cult to be an attractive alternative. Some people (especially the vulnerable or weak-minded) are drawn to cults because of the charisma of the leader who attempts to inspire them to new levels of personal achievement. Some become cult members simply because they are lonely (e.g., Moe). Others are born to cult members and are socialized into the cult. In Homer's case, he is weak-minded, unhappy with traditional religions, and possesses a personality that is highly susceptible to suggestion.

At the "meet and greet" gathering, Glen and Jane invite Homer to the Orientation Center to learn more about the "Leader."

> *Glen*: Why don't you chat with us about the Leader at the Welcome Center?
> *Homer*: Will there be beer?
> *Glen*: Beer is not allowed.
> *Homer*: Homer no function beer well without.

Given that Homer loves beer, it is shocking that he actually proceeds with Glen and Jane. Jane proposes a very serious philosophical question that some people may have trouble answering: "Would you rather have beer or complete and utter contentment?" A different philosopher, however, may ask, "Is it possible to have complete and utter contentment without beer?!"

The Welcome Center, of course, is where the cult members attempt to brainwash new recruits. The Movementarians use the "Li'l Bastard Brainwashing Kit" as their preferred method of brainwashing. Brainwashing is designed to strip down the individual's previous thought processes and beliefs and replace them with the cult's idealism. Military personnel are exposed to brainwashing techniques when they go through basic training. They are expected to blindly follow orders and not to question authority. Their entire sense of self is altered. The same process occurs with religious cults, who brainwash new members into believing the validity of the power of the new leader. Homer proves to be a tough nut to crack, but eventually he buys into the Movementarians' way of thinking. Other townsfolk, such as Apu, Moe, Skinner, and Carl, are also at the Welcome Center.

Typically, brainwashing activities involve the converts giving up their freedom, rationality, possessions, friends, relatives, birth names, and ultimately, their lives. The Movementarians, desperate for a larger membership, allow the new converts the opportunity to try to indoctrinate their family members into the cult. Homer broaches the subject with Marge.

> *Marge*: I've never heard of these Movementarians. Are they some kind of church?
> *Homer*: Who cares what it is? The point is these are some decent, generous people that I can take advantage of!

Cultists are not nice people and they are not easy to take advantage of. Further, Lisa reminds Homer, "Watch yourself, Dad. You're the highly suggestible type." Homer is disappointed with his family's reluctance to join him at the Movementarians' "Farm." Homer tells his wife, "Marge, when I join an underground cult I expect a little support from my family."

The family agrees to give Homer's cult a chance and they do move to the Movementarians' compound. Joining a cult entails experiences of intense emotion and a great number of behavioral changes in the convert's life. In some instances, joining a cult may provide a sense of relief and feelings of well-being. At the very least, membership in a cult generally causes the individual to demonstrate a high degree of conformity in response to group pressure and to give up past lifestyles and financial resources. During this conversion period, the Movementarians take control of Homer's personal assets.

Homer's children are brainwashed but Marge remains strong. She is not happy with the new lifestyle Homer has introduced to her and the kids. Marge wants to escape the compound, which is surrounded by an assortment of obstacles, including land mines and wild dogs, to find help getting her family away from the influence of the cult. Marge is displaying the common behavior of family members (and friends) on the "outside" (of the cult) who are not willing to give up on their brainwashed loved ones and who fight to get them out of the cult. At times, legal authorities are called in to settle disputes, handle complaints, or make arrests. At other times, family members may hire vigilantes to "bust" their loved ones out of the cult's compound. In Marge's case (after she does escape the compound), she solicits help from Reverend Lovejoy, who involves Ned Flanders and Willie the groundskeeper in the plan to rescue Marge's family.

The rescue is a success. The rescue team rushes the Simpson family to Ned's home in an attempt to de-brainwash them. The kids are easily won over, but Homer proves to be tougher. Willie works on Homer as the Movementarians' lawyers pound on Flanders's door. They demand Homer's release. Flanders pours a beer and Homer cannot resist the temptation—of a false god!

Much to the surprise of the Simpson family and the rescue team, Homer agrees to return to the Movementarians' compound with their lawyers. Was Homer's de-brainwashing unsuccessful? Had he truly converted to their strange movement?

As it turns out, Homer has a plan to reveal the Leader's dark secret. The Leader has promised to take the Movementarians to a distant planet, Blisstonia, on his spaceship; but his true intention was merely to rip off the members' finances. The reader may note the similarity between this episode and that of the Heaven's Gate cult, formed in the 1970s by Marshall Herff Applewhite, a music teacher who needed psychiatric help in an asylum. By the late 1990s, Applewhite had brainwashed thirty-eight people into giving up their freedom, finances, and lives, leaving a video behind explaining they were shedding their "earthly containers" to join a spaceship trailing the Hale-Bopp comet. On March 26, 1997, the thirty-eight members of the Heaven's Gate cult were found dead after taking a mixture of applesauce, vodka, and barbiturates. It was the worst mass suicide on US soil (Delaney 2002A).

Thanks to Homer and beer, the members of the Movementarians did not face such a dreadful fate. Homer credits beer for making him "Born Again!" He opens the forbidden barn at the Movementarians' compound to reveal an apparent spaceship. However, the spaceship is nothing more than a paper charade surrounding a self-power-generated flying device filled with moneybags. The Leader attempts to fly away with the money but crashes on Cletus's property. (Cletus is a semiregular hick character.) Cletus robs the Leader of the money.

Finally realizing that they have been duped, the other members of the Movementarians start to wake from their brainwashed stupor. Moe mumbles, "Damn it! It fell apart like everything else I've ever believed in. Oh, I guess it's back to good old-fashioned voodoo." Poor Moe; like so many other people, he seeks help in a belief system rather than simply helping himself.

Homer too decides to return to the basics—good old-fashioned beer. He comments on the lesson of the day: "To think, I turned to a cult for mindless happiness when I had beer all along."

Amen, Homer, Amen!

Chapter 9

Beware the Enviromare

"This planet needs every friend it can get."
—Jesse Grass

The earth has a limited capacity ("carrying capacity") to support life. This "carrying capacity" refers to the maximum feasible load, just short of the level that would end the environment's ability to support life (Catton 1980). Among the greatest threats to the earth's carrying capacity are the spread of deserts, the destruction of forests by acid rain, deforestation, the stripping of large tracts of land for fuel, radiation fallout, and the many areas where the population is exceeding the carrying capacity of local agriculture. In short, we are placing high demands on our planet. This is especially true in light of the fact that much of humanity is still primarily dependent on the conversion of fossil fuels (e.g., heating oil and gasoline) to meet its energy needs. Among the chief potential undesirable side effects of a continued dependence on fossil fuels are global warming, many forms of pollution, and a host of environmental nightmares—or, what I call *enviromares*.

Many environmental issues are discussed in *The Simpsons*, including the ever-growing threat of global warming. For example, in the "Homer's Paternity Coot" episode (#366), we learn that the ice cap atop Mt. Springfield is melting due to the pollution caused by the infamous and continuously burning Springfield tire fire. The timely discussion of Mt. Springfield's ice cap melting reflects *The Simpsons'* writers' efforts to remind us of real ice caps melting around the world (note: examples will be provided later in this chapter) due to global warming and the "greenhouse effect."

The overwhelming evidence of global warming has scientists

around the world deeply concerned about the future of humanity on this planet. No longer does science argue over the reality of the existence of global warming (as it is an irrefutable fact). The prevailing evidence of global warming has led to the introduction of the slang terms "fossil fools" and "greenhouse asses." Fossil fools are people who fail to recognize the negative impact of driving Hummers and other fuel-inefficient vehicles. Greenhouse asses are people who insist the environment is in fine shape as it is.

The biggest debate over global warming remains whether it is caused primarily by nature or by human-made conditions. If it is human made, it can be corrected. If global warming is mostly the result of natural conditions (e.g., volcanic eruptions), that will result in far greater challenges. Perhaps the only reason to doubt the validity of global warming, according to former vice president Al Gore, is, "If you accept the truth of what the scientific community is saying, it gives you a moral imperative to start to rein in the 70 million tons of global warming pollution that human civilization is putting into the atmosphere every day" (Borenstein 2006, E-3). (Note: Gore's documentary, *An Inconvenient Truth*, which has been universally hailed as accurate by scientists around the world, points out many of the environmental problems confronting humanity.) The debate then leads to which methods should be employed in an attempt to curtail the negative effects of global warming and other environmental horrors. Furthermore, since we cannot control nature's impact on global warming, we must concentrate on the only aspect we can control—human-made conditions that lead to global warming. After all, even the slightest warming can cause deadly consequences.

THE FIVE HORRORISTS: THE DESTROYERS OF LIFE

The idea that the earth has a limited carrying capacity has been expressed in a variety of fashions for centuries. A number of social thinkers, for example, have long pondered the effects of the growing human population and its impact on the environment. Thomas Malthus, in his *An Essay on the Principles of Population* (1798), presented a pessimistic view of human society. He argued that the world's population was growing too quickly in proportion to the amount of food available. Imagine how Malthus would react to the number of people in the world today! In 2008, there are nearly 7 billion people world-wide. The United States hit the 300 million mark in 2006. It's estimated that we'll reach 400 million in 2040. According to the Census Bureau's Population Clock (in 2006), there is a birth in the United States every seven seconds, a death every thirteen seconds, and a net migrant (the number of immigrants minus the number of emigrants) every thirty seconds. That equals a net gain of one person every ten seconds (Tilove 2006). By 2050, the world's population is likely to reach 12 billion, up from 3 billion in 1960. Today, any person forty years old or older has been alive long enough to have seen the earth's population double. Are there enough natural (let alone social) resources for all these people?

In an alarmist fashion, Malthus already warned us that human need and greed would eventually lead to the depletion of natural resources. Nature will be pushed to its limits and, in an attempt to survive, it will provide "forces" of relief from the strain created by human abuse in the form of the "Four Horsemen." These Four Horsemen (war, famine, pestilence, and disease)—which have bibli-cal roots—would provide the function of human population control. In short, they are the destroyers of human life. Thus, Malthus was stating that nature will find a way to protect itself from the threat posed by humanity. On the other hand, how can humanity survive without nature? In other words, don't worry about the earth; the earth will be just fine. Worry about humanity!

Herbert Spencer, a sociologist, argued that the fight for scarce resources would lead to the "survival of the fittest" doctrine whereby the strong survive and the weak die off. Unlike Malthus, Spencer rec-ognized that the forces (destroyers of life) were not simply from nature, but also from humankind. In other words, it is a combination of natural and human-made forces that may doom humanity. With that in mind, in 2005 I coined the term the "Five Horrorists." The Five Horrorists represent an advanced evolutionary interpretation and development of the Four Horsemen concept. "Breaking com-pletely from the religious roots and deemphasizing the natural com-ponent of the four horsemen, the Five Horrorists emphasize the social forces that will lead to the destruction of humanity, if left unchecked by global powers" (Delaney 2005, 351).

In reality, famine, pestilence (plagues caused by locusts and other swarms of insects), and disease are as much the result of human con-ditions as they are natural ones. War, of course, is completely human-made and not caused by nature. In the conception of the Horrorists, war, famine, pestilence, and disease are described in a more accurate fashion than previously employed by Malthus. (See my *Contemporary Social Theory* for a complete description of the Horrorists.)

It is the fifth Horrorist that is of greatest concern for humanity. I call this fifth Horrorist the "enviromare." As stated earlier in this chapter, an enviromare is an environmental nightmare that causes great harm to humanity and/or the ecosystem. The enviromare is the new destroyer of life separate from Malthus's conception of the Four Horsemen. In Malthus's era, it would appear that there was little concern about protecting the environment. After all, the environment was in fairly good condition and had been barely exposed to the harmful effects of industrialization. Today, however, industrialization, the extreme use of fossil fuels, and a lack of good common sense have led to great harm to the earth's physical environment—the biosphere.

Humans have come perilously close to altering the earth's fragile ecosystem (mechanisms, such as plants, animals, and microorganisms, that supply people with the essentials of life) in a potentially dangerous and irreversible manner. Although enviromares are directly associated with forces of nature (the ecosystem, the biosphere, and so on) they are also influenced by a number of social forces, such as overpopulation, the increased use of fossil fuels, and the "throwaway" mentality that is associated with conspicuous consumption and conspicuous leisure.

The Enviromares

There exists a great variety of enviromares, but they are all associated with some type of pollution that causes a problem for the environment. Among the enviromares are water pollution and the corresponding shortages of drinkable water (generally the result of toxins being dumped into drinkable bodies of water); land pollution (especially as the result of overgrazing by domesticated animals, deforestation, agricultural mismanagement, the increased use of chemical fertilizers and pesticides, erosion, urban sprawl, and strip mining); solid waste pollution (Americans produce nearly 4.5 pounds of garbage per person, per day); noise pollution (mostly an urban problem as the result of high-density living); celestial pollution (space is already littered with trash such as rocket fragments, used-up boosters, Soviet nuclear reactors, and so forth); air pollution (caused by both nature and humanity); and chemical and nuclear pollution (dangerous chemicals, radiation, and radioactive fallout top these concerns).

Although the term "enviromare" has not been used on *The Simpsons*, the writers have examined many aspects relevant to it. For example, if we reexamine the ice cap melting on top of Mt. Springfield, we can see the potentially devastating effect of air pollution. The problems associated with air pollution are numerous. The importance of clean, breathable air should be obvious to all as it is the most essential ingredient of life. And yet, the atmosphere is bombarded by toxins, natural and human made, on a regular basis. Among the ways nature compromises the quality of air are volcanic eruptions (which spill a variety of toxins into the air) and lightning (which compromises the ecosystem by emitting nitrogen dioxide and igniting wildfires). Humans destroy the quality of air primarily via the burning of fossil fuels. The dependence on burning fossil fuels continues to contribute to conditions that cause smog and thermal inversion. In some regions of the world, living with smog (a thick haze) is a daily reality.

The burning of fossil fuels is a primary culprit for the depleting ozone layer. The ozone layer is the earth's upper atmosphere, which screens out a great deal of the sun's harmful ultraviolet rays. Acid rain, the greenhouse effect, and global warming are among the other agents associated with this enviromare (Delaney 2005). Rising global temperatures lead to more melting glaciers, rising sea levels, lower crop yields, drinking water shortages, increased health problems (especially for poorer nations), and a strain on power grids.

As for global melting, there is indisputable evidence of Arctic melting. Scientists have detailed that the Arctic perennial sea ice has been decreasing at a rate of 9 percent per decade since a first satellite sensor image began its tracking in 1979. Animation data presented by the Defense Meteorological Satellite Program's Special Sensor Microwave Imager shows that the greatest amount of melting has taken place in the most recent years. (Visit the NASA Web site for more information.)

Greenland's glaciers are also thawing. Huge chunks of ice have been breaking off the Sermeq Kujalleq glacier for years. "The frequency and size of the icefalls are a powerful reminder that the frozen sheet covering the world's largest island is thinning—a glaring sign of global warming, scientists say" (Olsen 2005). When glaciers melt, they raise sea levels, which in turn may cause further problems to humans (as well as the entire ecosystem).

In the Netherlands, a country with much of its mainland below sea level, there is overwhelming evidence of rising seas. A significant sea surge could cause far more damage there than in New Orleans following Hurricane Katrina. The Dutch have long utilized a system of dikes and dams to control water flow in their country. But draining water in the Netherlands can cause other problems; specifically the ground in the Netherlands is sinking. A large amount of the country sits on alluvial peat soils. When drained of water, the soil compresses and oxidizes. Realistic fears of a devastating storm and/or a continued rise in the sea level have people (not just scientists) treating global warming as a given (Melvin 2005).

The melting of the Siberian permafrost—which contains pools of water—could expel hundreds of billions of tons of extra greenhouse gases into the atmosphere over the next hundred years. The Siberian permafrost is a layer of soil at varying depths below the surface of the earth in which the temperature has remained below freezing continuously for thousands of years (Davidson 2006). The melting of the Siberian permafrost could eject about five hundred billion tons of carbon dioxide into the atmosphere, scientists from Russia and the United States warn.

Somehow, there are still a few people utilizing the "mighty" ostrich approach to the global warming problem—they have their heads buried in the sand! They are assuming the problem will go away; or they are discounting the problem altogether. Such naive and dangerous thinking is illustrated by newsman Kent Brockman in the "Mr. Plow" episode (#68):

> Could this record-breaking heat wave be the result of the dreaded "Greenhouse Effect"? Well, if seventy-degree days in the middle of winter are the "price" of car pollution, you'll forgive me if I keep my old Pontiac.

In actuality, the question is no longer whether or not the greenhouse effect or global warming is real and presents potential dire consequences, but rather, "Is it too late to do something about it?" Some scientists warn that it is already too late to stop the greenhouse effects. Certainly, we cannot stop the forces of nature. That is, we can no more bottle up volcanoes to stop them from spewing toxins into the air than we can stop lightning. However, we can control human-made pollutants. Therefore, with the help of science and the cooperation of all humans, we can end our dependency on burning fossil fuels and try to save this planet. People need to stop driving their fuel-gouging automobiles and start driving more eco-friendly vehicles. If we do not change our harmful behaviors, the negative effects of global warming (and all related forms of air pollution) will be felt in our lifetime, not the distant future.

In the case of Mt. Springfield, the ice cap was melting due to the long-lasting tire fire. The landfill that houses the Springfield tire fire has a sign out front that proclaims: "Now smelled in 46 states." That proclamation underscores the reality of air pollution—it is often transitory. It may be the residents of nearby Shelbyville that suffer the most from the tire burning, but the harmful toxins have spread to influence 46 states.

A real-life scenario involving tire burning took place between the International Paper Company (IP) and the state of Vermont in late 2006. An IP plant on Lake Champlain in New York announced its intention to conduct a two-week trial period of burning tires as an alternative form of fuel to power its boiler. In this regard, IP hoped to reduce its dependency on oil. During this two-week period IP would measure the specific toxins released into the air so that it could determine what types of emissions controls would be most effective if the tire-burning alternative went on permanently. Hoping to protect its citizens from an unknown number and variety of toxic heavy metals and other pollutants, neighboring Vermont officials sought, in federal court, to stop IP from its planned tire burning. Vermont officials complained in federal court that the emissions from the mill would blow eastward over Lake Champlain and into Vermont. The court ruled in favor of IP. IP officials first performed baseline tests in November (2006). The state of Vermont set up its own monitoring stations near the eastern shore of Lake Champlain to measure emissions. Environmentalist demonstrators held signs with such slogans as "Burning Tires Stinks." Just ask anyone living near a tire-burning mill or landfill what it's like to breathe such polluted air and they will agree—it stinks!

Clearly, air pollution is a real problem. Heed this warning: Beware this enviromare!

NUCLEAR ENERGY AND THE
SPRINGFIELD NUCLEAR POWER PLANT

> **"We're especially thankful for nuclear power, the cleanest, safest energy source there is, except for solar, which is just a pipe dream."**
> —Homer Simpson

Air pollution is just one of the environmental problems that threaten Springfield. Of all the enviromares, it is nuclear pollution that is the most relevant to *The Simpsons*.

As we all know, Homer Simpson is employed at the Springfield Nuclear Power Plant. For someone without any qualifications whatsoever, he is lucky to be gainfully employed there. And, generally speaking, Homer remains loyal to his employer. For example, in the "Bart vs. Thanksgiving" episode (#20), Homer offers a prayer of gratitude to the Springfield Nuclear Power Plant just prior to eating Thanksgiving dinner:

> And, Lord, we're especially thankful for nuclear power, the cleanest, safest energy source there is, except for solar, which is just a pipe dream. . . .

Homer gives thanks for nuclear power during grace before dinner in "Oh Brother, Where Art Thou?" (#28) as well. In this episode, Homer says, "And thank you most of all for nuclear power, which is yet to cause a single proven fatality, at least in this country." Is Homer correct in his assessment of nuclear power? Is it the cleanest, safest source there is for energy?

Nuclear Energy: One Nuclear Bomb Can Ruin Your Whole Day

Humanity is dependant upon harnessing energy in order to sustain its evolutionary progressive growth. As described earlier in this chapter, the current largest source of energy involves the burning of fossil fuels (e.g., oil, coal, and natural gas). Although there is still a relatively sufficient amount of this type of energy source available to tap into, the potential negative effects of a continued reliance on this energy source may have dire consequences for the environment, and thus, humanity. Because burning fossil fuels is so dangerous to the ecosystem, scientists have been developing alternative energy sources for generations. The top two energy alternatives are solar and nuclear. (Note: Other alternatives, such as harnessing wind power, are less feasible at this time.) However, as Homer Simpson points out, developing solar energy, a far better alternative than fossil fuels or nuclear energy, is mostly a pipe dream. The biggest drawback with solar energy is its high cost of development. As a result, nuclear energy has been promoted as the most viable alternative to fossil fuels. Nuclear energy has one big advantage over fossil fuels; that is, it doesn't put carbon dioxide (CO_2) into the atmosphere. The question remains however, "Does the development of nuclear energy create greater risks than CO_2?" In other words, what drawbacks are involved with the development and reliance on nuclear energy?

A brief explanation about how nuclear energy is developed is warranted. Nuclear energy is harnessed from the atomic nucleus. Nuclear energy comes about in one of three ways: fusion (the fusing together of atomic nuclei); fission (the breaking of the binding forces of an atom's nucleus); or decay (the slower, natural fission process of a nucleus breaking down into a more stable form). Typically, nuclear energy comes from the fission of uranium, plutonium, or thorium; or the fusion of hydrogen into helium. Currently, nuclear energy is produced almost entirely from uranium. The energy created by the fission of an atom of uranium produces ten million times the energy produced by the combustion of an atom of carbon from coal. Natural uranium is almost completely a mixture of two isotopes, U-235 and U-238. U-235 can fission in a reactor, and most power plants today use enriched uranium in which the concentration of U-235 has been increased from 0.7 percent to about 4–5 percent.

There are hundreds of licensed power reactors in the world, including one fictional power plant in Springfield. A power reactor contains a core with a large number of fuel rods. Each rod is full of pellets of uranium oxide. An atom of U-235 fissions when it absorbs a neutron. The fission produces fragments and other particles that fly off at high speeds. When they stop (become stable) the kinetic energy is converted to heat (energy). The heat is too high to be useful; consequently, the heat from the fuel rods is absorbed by water, which is used to generate steam to drive the turbines that generate electricity. During operation a large nuclear power plant generates about one million kilowatts of electricity. According to John McCarthy, professor emeritus of computer science at Stanford University, a kilowatt is a rate of generation of energy, specifically one thousand joules per second. A million-kilowatt plant will generate a million kilowatt-hours per hour. Kilowatt-hours are what you pay for.

So, what's the bad news? Unfortunately, there are numerous potential negative aspects of nuclear energy. Most immediately, the fuel rods must be replaced regularly (about every two years). What to do with these spent fuel rods is what causes the greatest concern over nuclear power. The unresolved challenges in long-term management of nuclear wastes represent the tip of the iceberg of concern that surrounds nuclear energy. Other problems include the relative high costs of producing nuclear energy (compared to fossil fuels); environmental and health concerns (via meltdowns, radioactive fallout, and nuclear contamination of soil and water supplies); and potential security risks. In this era of terrorism, nuclear power plants represent a viable target for any terrorist intent on harming as many people as possible in an easy fashion. People living near a nuclear power plant should be very concerned about their overall safety. Nuclear weapons and radioactive fallout represent other important potential problems associated with nuclear energy. As the old adage warns: "One nuclear bomb can ruin your whole day."

Industrial Accidents and Nuclear Meltdowns

"There, there, Homer. You've caused plenty of industrial accidents and you've always bounced back."
—Marge Simpson

With all the things that can go wrong at a nuclear power plant, it is essential that employees are highly trained and responsible. Homer Simpson hardly fits this prototype. Homer's ineptness as a nuclear power plant employee is described early on in *The Simpsons* series. For example, in "Homer's Odyssey" (#3), Bart's fourth grade class takes a field trip to the Springfield Nuclear Power Plant. The bus ride from Springfield Elementary to the power plant includes passing a toxic waste dump and the burning pile of tires (previously described).

At the power plant, the children are introduced to the world of nuclear energy via the plant's animated mascot, Smilin' Joe Fission.

During the infomercial, Smilin' Joe Fission downplays the problem of nuclear waste: "I'll just put it where nobody'll find it for a million years." Next, the children are taken on a tour of the plant. They notice that the water used to cool the nuclear reactor dumps directly into the nearby river. A three-eyed fish is shown swimming in the river. (Note: The three-eyed fish will be discussed later in this chapter.) Meanwhile, Homer is riding an electric cart through the plant in an effort to find his son's tour group. Waving at Bart, Homer becomes distracted and crashes the cart into a radioactive pipe. This mishap results in the plant being shut down and Homer being fired.

At home, Homer feels like a complete failure and feels as though he has let the entire family down due to his incompetence. The family tries to hearten Homer and offers words of encouragement.

Marge: There, there, Homer. You've caused plenty of industrial accidents and you've always bounced back.
Lisa: Yeah, Dad. You can do it.
Bart: Yeah, go for it, Dad.

Homer searches for work, but he is unsuccessful. Disappointed, Homer goes to Moe's bar. Short of cash, Homer asks Moe for an extension on his bar tab. Moe says no, explaining, "I don't think you're ever going to get another job and be able to pay me back."

Things get so bad for Homer that he contemplates suicide. He leaves a suicide note at home and heads off to Springfield Bridge to commit the deed. Lisa finds the note and warns Marge. The Simpsons rush to the Springfield Bridge in an attempt to save Homer. As they rush across the street, they are almost run over by a speeding truck. It is Homer who saves his family instead of the reverse. Homer curses the dangerous intersection that almost led to his family's death. He feels someone should do something about it. This insight leads Homer to embark on a safety campaign. A speed bump here, a warning sign there, and before long, safety signs *everywhere* for *everything*. Among the more obscure safety signs: "Please Drive Friendly" and "Sign Ahead."

With traffic safety under control, Homer decides to take on the nuke plant. Homer rallies people to protest the unsafe conditions of the Springfield Nuclear Power Plant. A large crowd gathers outside the plant. Homer warns, "Our lives are in the hands of men no smarter than you or I. Many of them incompetent boobs. I know this because I've worked alongside them, gone bowling with them, watched them pass me over for promotion time and again." A group called "People against People for Nuclear Energy" assembles alongside Homer. They are sure Homer will make good on their demands that the nuclear power plant clean up its near-disastrous safety record.

Observing all this from his office window, Mr. Burns, the owner of the power plant, worries about Homer's growing power. Burns summons Homer to his office. Burns offers him a position as safety supervisor with a large raise. All he has to do is tell the crowd that everything is okay at the plant. Homer looks out at the crowd and cannot compromise his convictions. He returns to Burns's office.

Homer: I can't do it, Mr. Burns.
Mr. Burns: You mean you're willing to give up a good job and a raise just for your principles?
Homer: Mmm. When you put it that way it does sound a little far-fetched.

Proving the old adage that "everyone has a price," Homer concedes to Burns's demands and tells the crowd that he has taken the job as safety supervisor in order to secure their safety.

Is Homer Simpson really the type of person we want safeguarding our welfare from possible nuclear disaster? Certainly not. And the US government (along with other respective governments around the world) agrees. There is a guardian for the people designed to save humanity and the environment from nuclear accidents and melt-downs—the US Nuclear Regulatory Commission (NRC). The NRC is an independent agency established by the Energy Reorganization Act of 1974 to regulate civilian use of nuclear materials. According to its Web site: "The NRC's mission is to regulate the Nation's civilian use of by-product, source, and special nuclear materials to ensure adequate protection of public health and safety, to promote the common defense and security, and to protect the environment." The NRC's regulatory mission covers three main areas: reactors (commercial reactors for generating electric power, and research and test reactors used for research, testing, and training); materials (uses of nuclear materials in medical, industrial, and academic settings and facilities that produce nuclear fuel); and waste (transportation, storage, and disposal of nuclear materials and waste, and decommissioning of nuclear facilities from service) (Nuclear Regulatory Commission 2007A, 2007B). Before the NRC was created, nuclear regulation was the responsibility of the Atomic Energy Commission (AEC), which Congress first established in the Atomic Energy Act of 1946.

Perhaps the best weapon of the NRC is the unannounced inspection. Inspections are an important element of the NRC's oversight of nuclear facilities. NRC inspectors investigate nuclear facilities to make sure that all licenses are up to date, examine the physical buildings, check for any safety risks (e.g., maintenance, fuel handling, environmental and radiation protection programs complying with NRC safety requirements), confirm the security of nuclear materials, and review the qualifications and training of personnel. The NRC conducts about two thousand inspections of nuclear licenses and facilities per year (Nuclear Regulatory Commission 2007A).

The NRC conducts a surprise inspection of the Springfield Nuclear facility in the "Homer Goes to College" episode (#84). Burns is not happy to see the NRC as he commits numerous violations at his plant. Initially, Burns tries to keep the inspectors at bay by telling them his plant makes cookies. Naturally, the inspectors do not believe him. So Burns then attempts to insult the inspectors: "The watchdog of public safety. Is there any lower form of life?"

The inspectors order a test in a simulation van. As safety inspector, Homer is the one who has to run the test. Homer does so poorly; he accidentally causes a meltdown and the van dissolves into the ground. Burns and the inspectors look at one another in disbelief.

> *NRC Inspector*: I'm still not sure how he caused the meltdown. There wasn't any nuclear material in the truck.
> *Burns*: Oh, very well, it's time for your bribe. Now, you can either have the washer and dryer where the lovely Mr. Smithers is standing, or you can trade it for what's in the box.
> *NRC Inspector*: The box! The box!

Parodying the game show classic *Let's Make a Deal*, Mr. Burns is still working on the assumption that everyone has his or her price. Burns realizes that government agencies are drastically underfunded and most government employees are underpaid. The idea that nuclear test inspectors are susceptible to bribes should alarm all citizens. After all, if these "watchdogs of public safety" can be bought, our safety is compromised.

Shortly afterward, Homer—who is glowing in a bright radiation haze color—climbs from the abyss. He mutters, "Must destroy mankind." Then his watch alarm goes off and the green radiation glow disappears. The alarm triggers Homer back to reality as he proclaims, "Ooh, lunchtime." The inspectors are, understandably, alarmed. As they learn more about Homer Simpson, they become even more concerned. They tell Burns that Homer's position requires university training in nuclear physics. Homer has not even attended college, let alone received formal training in nuclear physics.

With Mr. Burns's help, Homer is accepted into Springfield University. Homer acts like someone who does not belong in college by sitting in the back row and laughing at his physics professor when he drops his notes to the floor. Homer thinks he knows more than the professor and attempts to demonstrate how the proton accelerator works. Instead, he causes an accident that requires a hazard crew to come to class and clean up the radioactive mess. The professor assigns Homer three nerdy tutors, Gary, Doug, and Benjamin. Instead of the bright, young, and impressionable tutors influencing Homer in a positive manner, Homer teaches them how to conduct college pranks. The four of them steal the rival university's (Springfield A & M University) pig mascot, Sir Oinks-a-Lot.

The tutors keep the pig with them but eventually get caught by school officials. They are expelled from school. Because Homer was not with the tutors when they got caught, he is not expelled. Feeling guilty, Homer devises a plan that eventually leads to their reacceptance into school. Because he has skipped all his classes, Homer must pass the final exam in order to pass the course (and retain his job at the nuclear plant). The tutors help him study, but he still receives an F grade. Dejected, Homer pouts, "I'm going to lose my job because I'm dangerously unqualified." Although all unqualified people should lose their jobs, it is especially important that nuclear safety inspectors be qualified to do their jobs. As it turns out, the tutors are computer hackers and change Homer's grade to an A+. Because of this, Burns gives Homer his job back. In real life, this would be a scary conclusion. And most likely, the start of a real nuclear meltdown about to happen.

Nuclear Waste

"I wouldn't mind having a third eye, would you?"
—Charles Darwin

As mentioned earlier in this chapter, among the potential problems of nuclear energy is the nuclear by-product—radioactive waste. The safe disposal of nuclear waste is a very real concern. Just what do we do with it? Can we bury it? If so, where? Will the containers be able to keep the nuclear waste safely intact until the radioactive material no longer poses a threat to the ecosystem? And, just how long must nuclear waste be buried before it is "safe"? Many nuclear power plants are approaching the end of the operational time periods allowed in their licenses. Further, the close of the cold war left us with radioactive waste from decommissioned nuclear missiles throughout Eastern Europe and parts of Asia.

Radioactive waste contains chemical elements that do not have a practical purpose. It is generally the by-product of a nuclear process, such as nuclear fission. Disposing of radioactive waste is determined by its classification level. Generally speaking, nuclear waste can be either "low-level" or "high-level" radioactive waste. Low-level nuclear waste (the majority of radioactive waste) usually includes material used in nuclear reactors (e.g., cooling pipes and radiation suits) and waste from medical procedures involving radioactive treatments or x-rays. For safety purposes, storing these materials for a ten- to fifty-year period is usually sufficient. High-level radioactive waste is generally material from the core of the nuclear reactor or nuclear weapon. This waste includes plutonium, uranium, and other highly radioactive materials made during fission. Most of these highly active elements possess a danger to the ecosystem for tens of thousands of years. Imagine burying high-level materials underground, say, in the Yucca Mountain, Nevada (the long-proposed burial site for nuclear waste), only to have them unearthed in some unknown time in the future due to erosion, an earthquake, or some other natural or humanmade condition. The safe disposal of nuclear waste remains the top concern of a reliance on nuclear energy as a primary power source. This is why politicians and scientists debate about which energy source is "safer" or "less harmful" than the others. Burning fossil fuels that emit CO_2 into the air and continue the progression of global warming, or turn to nuclear energy and die of radiation poisoning. Decisions, decisions!

The Simpsons provides us with a glimpse of the potential damage nuclear waste can cause to the ecosystem in the "Two Cars in Every Garage and Three Eyes on Every Fish" episode (#17). In this episode, the previously mentioned topic of illegal nuclear waste dumping comes to light. The earlier concerns over how to best store nuclear waste involved the assumption that those handling the waste *want* to protect the public. Unfortunately, there are many rogue operators, such as the Mr. Burns–type, who are looking only at the bottom line (profits) and will take shortcuts wherever possible, even when it comes to dumping nuclear waste.

In the "Two Cars . . ." episode, Bart and Lisa are fishing at the "Old Fishing Hole" located near the Springfield Nuclear Reactor and, much to their surprise, Bart catches a three-eyed fish. An investigative reporter, Dave Shutton, who just happened to be driving by and pulled his car over to make small talk with Bart and Lisa, turns the three-eyed mutant fish into a worthy news story. Among the headlines appearing in the *Springfield Shopper*: "Fishin' Hole, or Fission Hole?" At the Simpson breakfast table, Marge reads an article in the newspaper that the state governor has called for an investigation of the Springfield Power Plant. Upset by this news, Homer heads off to work; but not before he is taunted by his kids.

> *Lisa*: Try not to spill anything, Dad.
> *Bart*: Keep those mutants coming, Homer.
> *Homer*: I'll mutant you.

Later that morning, a government inspection team arrives to tour the plant and check for safety violations. Among the immediate violations the inspection team finds are gum used to seal a crack in a coolant tower; a plutonium rod used as a paperweight; monitoring station unmanned (Homer was asleep at his station); nuclear waste glowing throughout the hallways; and radioactive waste dripping on the clipboard of the inspector writing up the report. In an attempt to pass the inspection, Burns offers the inspectors a suitcase full of money. The inspector informs Burns that he will overlook the felony Burns just committed (for attempting to bribe a government official) but the 342 safety violations will not be overlooked. Further, Burns is told that if he does not bring the plant up to safety code, it will be shut down. Smithers estimates it will cost $56 million to make the necessary repairs.

In despair, Burns drinks alcohol for the rest of day. At 9:30 PM Homer finds Burns, drunk, in his car. (Homer had fallen asleep for the entire day at his workstation.) Burns tells Homer that the plant has been deemed unsafe and that he will have to close it down. Homer tells Burns that if he was governor, he could determine what is safe and what is not. Burns loves the idea and decides to run for office. He hires a team of lawyers and high-priced advisers. However, one big obstacle remains—the three-eyed fish. Burns must find a way to turn this mutation into a positive story. With that in mind, Burns decides to run a campaign ad on television. He hopes to gain the public's trust, and thus, their votes.

Mr. Burns begins his public address by holding a fishbowl with the mutant three-eyed fish inside of it. In this manner, Burns is attempting to convince the public that the fish is not a scary mutant, but rather, a lovable petlike creature. He even gives the fish, his "little friend," a name: Blinky. His next ploy involves the implication that Blinky represents an evolutionary advancement over other fish. To accomplish this, Burns holds a mock interview with naturalist Charles Darwin.

> *Burns*: I'm here to talk to you about my little friend here, Blinky. Many of you consider him to be a hideous genetic mutation. Well, nothing could be further from the truth. But don't take my word for it; let's ask an actor portraying Charles Darwin what he thinks. . . .
>
> *Darwin*: Hello, Mr. Burns.
>
> *Burns*: Oh, hello Charles. Be a good fellow and tell our viewers about your theory of natural selection.
>
> *Darwin*: Glad to, Mr. Burns. You see, every so often Mother Nature changes her animals, giving them bigger teeth, sharper claws, longer legs, or in this case, a third eye. And if these variations turn out to be an improvement, the new animals thrive and multiply and spread across the face of the earth.
>
> *Burns*: So, you're saying this fish might have an advantage over other fish, that it may in fact be a kind of super-fish.
>
> *Darwin*: I wouldn't mind having a third eye, would you?

Burns continues his speech by emphasizing that Blinky is simply a product of natural selection—a "miracle of nature" and a "taste that can't be beat." Burns is implying that Blinky should be embraced and loved like all other creatures found in nature. He condemns the antinuclear people as being antinature. Burns concludes his speech by saying he can take the heat but asks people to "stop slandering poor defenseless Blinky." (Note: This is a parody of President Franklin Roosevelt who said once that he could take the criticism but his little dog Fala resented it!) The townspeople rally behind his call for the government to stop picking on Blinky. Burns is climbing in the polls as a result of this television appearance.

His campaign advisers believe Burns needs just one final push to win the election. (Note: See chapter 10 for a further discussion of Burns's political campaign.) They arrange for Burns to have dinner with one of his employees to show that he is in touch with the workingman. The employee's family chosen is, of course, the Simpsons. Lisa and Marge are staunch opponents of Mr. Burns. But, as the dedicated wife, Marge realizes how important this meal is for Homer's career and agrees to cook dinner for Burns. A media circus accompanies the dinner.

But Marge has a clever idea of her own. If this fish is really safe to eat and not a dangerous mutant, it should make for a wonderful meal. She serves Blinky to Burns. With the media watching, he has no choice but to eat it. The taste is obviously very foul, and Burns immediately spits it out in front of the media. His campaign is ruined. Furthermore, we now know that mutant radioactive fish do not taste good.

Nonetheless, Burns leaves us with interesting food for thought: Does nuclear radiation speed up the evolutionary process? And, if so, does this provide any sort of comfort to a public worried about the dangerous effects of nuclear waste and warfare? Or, does it heighten the concern?

Either way, Burns is certainly doing his share to speed the evolutionary process via nuclear waste. In the "Marge vs. the Monorail" episode (#71), Smithers and Burns are caught by agents of the Environmental Protection Agency (EPA) hiding barrels of nuclear waste inside tree trunks. The EPA is a government agency designed to protect human health and the environment. The EPA, in existence since 1970, develops and enforces regulations of environmental law enacted by Congress (US Environmental Protection Agency 2007). The EPA has the right to levy sanctions (punishments) to violators of environmental law. In the case involving Mr. Burns, the EPA takes him to court and the judge fines him $3 million. (Note: In a spoof of Hannibal Lecter in the film *Silence of the Lambs*, Burns is wheeled into court bound and caged.) While laughing, Burns instructs Smithers to reach into his pocket for the money. Burns is so rich that he carries that kind of money around with him. Burns's attitude and great wealth make a mockery out of our system of justice and illustrate once again the tough battle facing the "watchdogs of public safety."

It was also revealed in this episode that Burns and Smithers have been illegally dumping nuclear waste at a playground and inside other tree trunks as well. In one tree, the radioactive side effects are drastic. The tree limbs appear to act like an octopus's tentacles. A squirrel has become mutated and developed mutated "skills." For example, it has the ability to emit dangerous rays of radiation with its eyes. This power was demonstrated as the squirrel zapped an acorn before it dropped to the ground, then the squirrel extended its tongue (like a frog) to catch it. We can now add radioactive squirrels to the list of mutant creatures that lurk in Springfield. Nuclear waste has indeed altered the environment there.

Nuclear energy involves many risks, including threats to the environment, safety concerns to workers and the general public, health concerns, potential national safety concerns (especially regarding terrorists), and unresolved challenges in long-term management of nuclear wastes. On the other hand, because of global warming due to the burning of fossil fuels, nuclear energy may be a viable alternative. However, it is not the only non-carbon-based form of energy. The development of solar energy and other options, such as the use of renewable energy sources, should be pursued as well. One thing is certain. If we continue to mutate the environment, drastic change will occur. This change will be accelerated, and it will most certainly come in the form of an enviromare.

SAVING THE ECOSYSTEM

"Oh, so Mother Nature needs a favor?"
—Monty Burns

Thankfully, we still have science and the will of humanity to survive as beacons of hope that our environment can be saved in time. There are measures that can be implemented to help save the ecosystem. As individuals, we can do the little things, such as recycling and driving energy-efficient automobiles. We can support organizations that are attempting to save the earth. At the macro level, we must demand that our political leaders make drastic decisions designed to protect the environment. For example, solar, wind, and other alternative energy sources must be pursued; and the continued deforestation of the Amazon must be stopped.

Electric Cars

"Electricity—the fuel of the future."
—Television Announcer for the Elec-Taurus

Nearly a decade ago, *The Simpsons* aired the episode, "Beyond Blunderdome" (#227). In this episode, electric cars were promoted. Well, they weren't promoted so much as they were mocked as a serious alternative to gasoline-fueled automobiles. Ten years later, and we are still nowhere near accepting electric cars as a serious alternative.

Homer learned about electric cars while watching a TV commercial promoting the Elec-Taurus. A dismal scene is presented in the commercial. Cars are stuck in gridlock traffic and smog surrounds the highways and nearby neighborhoods. The scene shifts to schoolchildren playing in a playground but being overcome by the foul stench and pollutants in the air. One boy falls down the ladder to the slide. In a somber voice, the announcer asks, "Is this the kind of air we want to leave for our children? Don't they deserve better? Electricity—the fuel of the future. . . . Test drive the Elec-Taurus today and get a free gift." The word "free" hits Homer like Pavlov ringing a bell for his dogs.

The Simpson family heads to the dealership. Lisa tells her father that she is proud of him for trying to do his part to save the environment when it finally dawns on her that Homer is only participating in a test drive for the free gift. As the Simpsons enter the dealership lot a salesperson approaches them.

Saleswoman: Thinking about saying good-bye to gas?
Bart: You betcha. (Bart burps.)

Marge: Bart! (Marge makes her own flatulent noise.)
Marge: Well, that shut me up.

Bart has crudely pointed out that there is more than one kind of gas! The saleswoman turns her attention to Homer.

Homer: Hello, I, uh, love your planet deeply and am interested in purchasing one of your electronic autos. (Homer can barely stop himself from laughing.)
Saleswoman (as she hands Homer the keys): Well, it's always nice to meet people concerned with the environment.
Homer: What kind of mint?

Clearly, Homer is not testing the car with the intent of saving the environment. His comment to the salesperson, "I love your planet," is reflective of Homer's ignorance of how to even properly mock someone.

The family drives off in the new car. Marge is happy with how quietly it runs. Homer drives the car into the harbor and "drives" underwater. Every creature the car comes in contact with is electrocuted. Homer manages to get the car back to the dealership. He rushes inside to the saleswoman's office and says, "I'm sorry, the car did not meet my eco-concerns. Can I have my prize now?" The saleswoman responds, "certainly" and immediately after she hands Homer the prize he runs off. She then notices the damaged car in the lot and says, "What the—." The car, which apparently has a "speaking" option, pleads with the saleswoman, "Help . . . help . . . it burns." The car is in flames.

Homer destroyed an electric car for a free prize (movie tickets) and did not help save the environment. It seems like the vast majority of people have followed Homer's lead as electric cars may, or may not, be part of an eco-friendly future, but they are certainly not part of the solution in the present.

Recycling

> **"Aw, recycling is useless. . . ."**
> —Bart Simpson

There are several *Simpsons* episodes that discuss ways to help save the ecosystem. For example, in "The Old Man and the Lisa" episode (#174), the value of recycling is examined from a number of angles. First, the Junior Achievers Club at Springfield Elementary has put together a paper drive in order to go on a field trip. They bring one-half ton of paper to the Uriah's Heap recycling center run by a guy known simply as "Hippie." All the Junior Achievers receive is seventy-five cents. Everyone is disappointed because they cannot afford the field trip. Trying to look on the bright side of things, Lisa points out that at least they saved one tree (with their newspapers to be recycled). But then Principal Skinner backs his car into the tree, knocking it down.

Lisa continues to promote recycling. Recycling is an easy way that every human being can help to maintain the "carrying capacity" of the ecosystem. Despite the logic behind recycling, Lisa runs into a number of obstacles while trying to convince others of the value of recycling. For example, her brother suggests that it is pointless to recycle. Bart tells Lisa, "Aw, recycling is useless, Lis. Once the sun burns out, this planet is doomed. You're just making sure we spend our last days using inferior products." Bart has introduced a problem we are completely helpless to correct—the sun burning out! Clearly, we would all be doomed if that occurred. However, the likelihood of the sun burning out before humans destroy the planet is slim.

Lisa tries to convince Mr. Burns that it is a good idea to recycle in order to save Mother Nature. Burns quips, "Oh, so Mother Nature needs a favor? Well, maybe she should have thought of that when she was besetting us with droughts and floods and poison monkeys. Nature started the fight for survival and now she wants to quit because she's losing? Well, I say, 'Hard cheese!'" Burns is so out of touch with reality that he thinks humanity can win a battle against nature! This is not, and will never be, the case. Burns will change his mind about recycling when he learns that he is nearing financial bankruptcy. Lisa convinces Burns that he can regain his wealth by opening up a recycling plant. Burns agrees. He builds his recycling plant in honor of Lisa—the "Li'l Lisa Recycling Plant." Upon its completion, Burns gives Lisa a tour of the new plant.

Learning from a previous lesson that Lisa had taught him—that a plastic six-pack holder is large enough to entangle and kill a fish—Burns has sewn together a giant net of six-pack holders.

Burns: I figured if one six-pack holder will catch one fish, a million sewn together will catch a million fish. Watch—

>(Burns pushes a lever and the net pulls in a variety of fish, squid, seaweed, dolphins, and a whale.)
>
>*Lisa* (aghast): What's going on?
>
>*Burns*: I call it the Burns Omni-net. It sweeps the sea clean!
>
>(The netted haul is moved to a mashing area where all the sea life is reduced to a reddish-color goo that continues down a trough into industrial drums.)
>
>*Lisa* (even more horrified): Oh, dear God.
>
>*Burns*: I call our product: Li'l Lisa's Patented Animal Slurry! It's a high-protein feed for farm animals, insulation for low-income housing, a powerful explosive, and a top-notch engine coolant. And best of all, it's made from 100 percent recycled animals!

This is clearly not what Lisa had in mind when she encouraged Mr. Burns to recycle. She is outraged. She runs through the town warning people about Mr. Burns's Li'l Lisa Slurry and urges everyone to stop recycling. (Note: This scene is a parody of Charlton Heston in the movie *Soylent Green*.)

Regardless of the troubles Lisa has encountered with recycling, it remains a simple and relatively efficient way for all humans to do something positive toward saving the ecosystem. Most humans do their small part by separating paper, plastics, and glass from their trash. We feel better about ourselves when the recycling trucks come and haul our dutifully separated refuse away. This is because we assume that this material will be recycled. But what if all these recycling trucks end up at the same landfill?! Certainly that is not happening, is it?

Hug a Tree, But Save a Forest

>**"And whether you love or hate her politics, you've gotta go gawk at this crazy idiot."**
>—Kent Brockman

Lisa Simpson, of course, is the most visible environmental activist of all the characters found on *The Simpsons*. In fact, the 2007 *Simpsons Movie* centers on Lisa's campaign to save Lake Springfield. Numerous *Simpsons* episodes deal with Lisa's attempt to bring environmental awareness to the inhabitants of Springfield.

Lisa's attempt to educate people on the value of recycling, for example, is commendable as recycling represents a modest attempt on behalf of humanity to save the planet. Lisa also tries to educate us on the value of saving trees. In the "Lisa the Tree Hugger" episode (#252), Lisa's crusade to save the environment receives a boost when she meets and becomes attracted to a teenage boy activist named Jesse Grass (Joshua Jackson provides the guest voice). Jesse is an idealistic, dreadlocked, fifth-level vegan, who leads a group of protestors known as "Dirt First." In an attempt to both help save the environment and impress Jesse, Lisa joins the Dirt First group to strike up a conversation with her new crush. (Note: "Dirt First" is a parody of the radical environmentalist group "Earth First!" whose motto, according to its Web site, is "No Compromise in Defense of Mother Earth.")

Jesse: This planet needs every friend it can get.
Lisa: Oh, the Earth is the best. That's why I'm a vegetarian.
Jesse: Heh-heh . . . well, that's a start.
Lisa: Uh, well, um, I was thinking of going vegan.
Jesse: I'm a level-five vegan. I won't eat anything that casts a shadow.

Regular viewers of *The Simpsons* have long been aware of Lisa as a vegetarian. But after learning about the existence of fifth-level veganism, it hardly seems appropriate to make a big deal of her being a vegetarian. Although, when you think about it, Jesse must have a hard time finding a food supply that does not cast a shadow.

The Dirt First group has a goal to save a giant redwood tree in the Springfield Forest that is about to be cut down. Lisa volunteers to live in the tree in order to save it. (Note: This story mirrors the many examples of activists who have lived in giant redwood trees over the years in an attempt to save them.) She also hopes to impress Jesse. Lisa's parents are understandably concerned about their eight-year-old daughter living in a tree by herself. After a few days in the tree, Lisa becomes increasingly lonely. She reads a letter that Bart has sent to her: "Dear Lisa, you rock! Mom is calling rescue agencies. Dad is building a giant ladder, but it is of poor quality. We miss you, Bart." Lisa is happy to read a supportive letter from her brother.

The media have also been following Lisa's tree-living escapade.

Newsman Kent Brockman reports: "It's Day 4 for Springfield's li'lest tree hugger. Hee-hee. Excuse me, that's littlest tree hugger. And whether you love or hate her politics, you've gotta go gawk at this crazy idiot." Brockman has introduced us to a reality about environmentalism. Namely, that politics are often involved. This is surprising considering all people, regardless of their political beliefs, must live in the same environment. And, if saving the environment cannot unite people of all political affiliations, what will?

As the days go on, Lisa becomes increasingly sad and lonely without her family. So, one night, she sneaks down from the tree and goes home. Lisa plans on sleeping at home for a few hours and then returning to the tree before sunrise. But Lisa oversleeps. She runs back to the forest and is horrified to see the tree lying on its side. She fears that loggers noticed her out of the tree and chopped it down. As it turns out, the tree was hit by lightning—damn nature! Everyone assumes Lisa to be dead, but thankfully she is not.

Lisa's effort to save a tree (as with all other tree huggers) is praiseworthy but it pales in comparison to our *true* need—saving the Amazon rain forest. The Amazon is a critical producer of oxygen. Because its vegetation continuously recycles carbon dioxide into oxygen, it has been described as the "Lungs of our Planet." It produces about 20 percent of the Earth's oxygen. The Amazon rain forest is also the most efficient ecosystem in nature. Whenever a tree or creature dies, it decomposes and its nutrients turn into a food source and mulch for the rest of the rain forest. The Amazon River, which flows through the rain forest, is the world's largest river system.

That was the good news. The bad news is that, today, more than 20 percent of the Amazon rain forest has been destroyed and is gone forever. The rain forest is being cleared for cattle ranching, mining operations, logging, and subsistence agriculture, and some forests are destroyed to make charcoal to power industrial plants. More than half of the planet's rain forests have been destroyed in the past half century. Over 200,000 acres of rainforest are burned every day around the world. This translates to over 150 acres every minute (Lakshmanan 2006). There is a very simple explanation as to why the rain forest is so critical. The greatest number of trees are found in a rain forest. Trees that live in the rain forest emit oxygen. Conversely, whenever a tree dies, it emits carbon dioxide. Common sense alone should allow people to deduce that if we continue to destroy the rain forest and rely on burning fossil fuels at the present rate of consumption, the high level of carbon dioxide in the atmosphere will accelerate the greenhouse effect which, in turn, will hasten global warming. We all know what comes next. What is humanity thinking?

Thus, as noble as it may be to save a tree, it is the forest that represents our salvation, or our doom.

OUR FINAL HOPE

"Ah, there's nothing more exciting than science."
—Principal Skinner

The material in this chapter presents a fairly pessimistic view of the future. The Five Horrorists are riding roughshod across the globe and the growing threat from the enviromares have all but doomed humanity. And yet, there is hope. We can believe in the power of science and will of humanity to find solutions that allow the ecosystem to survive.

In the "Bart's Comet" episode (#117), Principal Skinner is punishing Bart for his misbehavior by making Bart assist him with his astronomy project—at 4:30 AM. Skinner is tracking the sky for comets, as he has always wanted to have one named after himself. Skinner had once discovered a comet but someone beat him to a phone to call it in. Skinner keeps a cell phone with him now. Skinner is also hoping that maybe Bart will learn to love science and its value to humanity. He tells Bart, "Ah, there's nothing more exciting than science. You get all the fun of sitting still, being quiet, writing down numbers, and paying attention. Yeah, science has it all."

Skinner steps away from his project for a few minutes and as one might predict (especially based on the title of this episode!), Bart notices something unusual in the dark sky. Using Skinner's phone, Bart reports his findings to an observatory. The astronomers confirm that Bart has discovered a comet. They congratulate Bart and inform him that the comet will be called "Bart's comet." Skinner is understandably perturbed. Bart is treated like a hero. However, astronomers ascertain that the comet is headed directly toward earth and will hit, you guessed it, Springfield! The community begins to panic, but scientific technology provides the solution—send a rocket directly at the comet to blow it up. Unfortunately, the rocket misfires and blows up the only bridge out of Springfield.

While everyone else is panicking, Homer oddly remains calm. He states, "What's everyone so worked up about? So there's a comet. Big deal. It'll burn up in our atmosphere, and whatever's left will be no bigger than a Chihuahua's head." Homer believes that our polluted atmosphere will protect us from harmful elements. And much to everyone's surprise, the comet does break apart once it hits a thick layer of pollution in the earth's atmosphere. The very thing Lisa and environmentalists protest against—pollution—turns out to be the earth's salvation. But this would never happen in real life, would it?

Well, the seemingly far-fetched idea that pollution may actually be our salvation has actually been discussed in scientific circles. A former Nobel Prize winner (1995), Paul J. Crutzen, best known for his research on ozone depletion, believes that politics have interfered with humanity's attempt to limit human-made greenhouse gases that cause global warming. In an attempt to get people's attention, Crutzen has suggested that pollution may actually provide "shade" to help keep the planet cool. (Note: The "Bart's Comet" episode first aired on February 5, 1995, and Crutzen was awarded the Nobel Prize on October 11, 1995. Perhaps *The Simpsons* should have shared the award with Crutzen!) While discounted as lunacy by most scientists, there are some who are so concerned that the negative effects of global warming are irreversible that such drastic measures as purposely producing certain types of pollution (via releasing particles of sulphur in the upper atmosphere, which would reflect sunlight and heat back into space) to save the earth from dangerous levels of radiation may represent our best means of salvation.

As Homer Simpson might say, "Mmm . . . purposely producing pollution to save the ecosystem from global warming, you say?" It makes one wonder whether science really does have all the answers. One thing is for certain, at this current pace of destroying the ecosystem, we will soon learn what does, or what does not, save this planet.

Chapter 10

The Political World of Springfield

"Ah, just one thing. Are you guys any good at covering up youthful and middle-aged indiscretions?"
—Krusty the Clown

Politics is often a nasty business. Many involved with politics seem to be corrupted by the temptation that power brings. Power may even breed corruption and that is why absolute power corrupts absolutely. Springfield Mayor "Diamond Joe" Quimby is often involved in some sort of shady or flat-out illegal behavior. (Note: The Quimby character serves as a parody of Massachusetts Senator Ted Kennedy, speaking with a Boston accent, throwing money at political problems, and taking vacations in a costal resort called the "Quimby Compound.") And, as discussed in chapter 9, some people, such as Mr. Burns, enter politics for their own selfish reasons. In the "Two Cars in Every Garage and Three Eyes on Every Fish" episode (#10), the Springfield Nuclear Power Plant is found guilty of 342 violations by a Washington regulatory investigative team. Rather than assure public safety and bring the plant up to code, Burns decides to run for governor. Burns believes that he will have the power to change safety codes in his state with the power entrusted upon him as the state's highest government official. Thus, as Burns demonstrates, when the law works against you, if you are powerful enough you can attempt to change the law.

Politics is about power, running for office, holding a political position, lobbying, campaign contributions, corruption, interest groups, and, believe it or not, taking a stand on issues of morality, decency, and the public good. All of these political issues (and more) are discussed in a variety of *Simpsons* episodes. Discussion begins with a brief explanation of politics itself.

POLITICS: POWER AND AUTHORITY

In any given society, someone or some groups make decisions about how to use resources and how to allocate goods and services. Such power and authority rests in the domain of politics. Politics involves any activity in which people and groups fight for control over resources, such as wealth, status, power, rewards, and punishments. People involved with politics are able to dictate the way social life is arranged, maintained, and ordered. In short, as political scientist Harold Lasswell (1936) articulated long ago, politics determines "who gets what, when, and how."

Power and Authority

Power and authority are key elements within the political system as social interactions between individuals and groups are often predicated by power relationships. Sociologist Max Weber argues that the distribution of power and authority in society is the basis of social conflict. Karl Marx points out that people with power will want to keep it, whereas those without power will want some. Those with power ultimately determine the allocation and distribution of scarce resources. Naturally, the people with power receive a larger portion of desired resources. Because there is a clear power differential among individuals, groups, and social classes, resentment and hostility are constant elements of society. Thus, from this standpoint, conflict is inevitable because of the universal unequal distribution of power.

Although everyone understands that power relationships exist in society, defining the word "power" is relatively difficult. The term "power" is quite abstract and difficult to measure. But again, it is easy to recognize that some people have more power than others. Dictionaries define "power" with such descriptions as: "a position of ascendancy over others," "the ability to act or produce an effect," "force," and "control." Sociologist George Homans defines power as the ability to provide rewards for, and levy punishments against, others. Those in a position to distribute rewards (e.g., wealth, income, fame, praise, promotions, and so forth) can influence the behavior of others and, therefore, have power. Similarly, when one is in the position to punish others, either by levying punishments (e.g., suspension) or withholding rewards (e.g., denial of a promotion that was promised and/or deserved), he or she has power. A college professor, for example, is in a position to distribute rewards (an A grade) and to levy punishments (an F grade, or a grader lower than an A when an A is deserved). The teacher, boss, police officer, parking lot attendant, and so on, are people in a position to exercise potential power over others. In short, all social relationships in life are subject to power relationships.

Weber states that power is the ability of individuals and groups to exert their will over other individuals and groups despite their desire not to comply. In other words, if one person can control another person's behavior, he or she has power over the other. A parent generally has control over a child much in the same manner as a teacher has over a student, a coach over an athlete, an employer over an employee, and so on. Weber also points out, however, that power can be exercised in illegitimate means. That is, people outside of typically accepted power relationships may be able to exert their will over others. For example, an armed robber can intimidate a cash register clerk into handing over money. People exercising power outside the letter of the law do not have the legal authority to do so. With that in mind, authority can be viewed as legitimate power.

The term "authority" refers to institutionalized power that is recognized and accepted by the people over whom it is implemented. Authority still involves individuals and groups having influence over others, but this power is explicitly legitimate through elected or publicly acknowledged positions. Under the limitations of authority is the realization that power is limited to specific circumstances. For example, Nuclear Regulatory Commission (NRC) investigators have the authority to investigate nuclear plants whose licenses are believed to be out of code, but these investigators do not have the power to commandeer the personal belongings of the employees working there.

However, legal authority that has been extended to the government, vis-à-vis "the state," becomes transformed into the "final" authority. The state—the political institution—refers to the public organizations that create and enforce decisions that are binding upon every member of a society. The state includes the branches of government; appointed and elected officials, the police, military, and judicial courts. The state has the legal authority to exercise power through force, if and when necessary, within a given territory. Holding a position within the state certainly places individuals (and groups) in an advantageous position over others.

Although a number of people enter politics with such great intentions as "helping others," it is the thirst for power and authority over others that attracts many people to politics. Thus, because politics represents power, it becomes an attractive profession to a variety of people for a diversity of reasons.

Running for Political Office

"My worthy opponent seems to think that the voters of this state are gullible fools."
—Mary Bailey

The first step in becoming an elected official involves running for office in some type of election. Elections occur fairly regularly throughout the United States, nationally, statewide, and locally, so there seems to be someone always running for something. Campaign ads are designed to draw voters' attention to specific candidates and issues. Seemingly, these campaign ads are becoming increasingly negative. Negative ads are often the last resort of a candidate who realizes he or she cannot win on his or her own merit. Such was the case with Mr. Burns when he challenged Governor Mary Bailey.

As stated in the introduction to this chapter, rather than spend a large amount of money to assure public safety (by making the necessary repairs to his nuclear power plant), Montgomery Burns opts to run for state governor with the hopes of winning the election so that he can change the state's safety codes. Burns has quite a challenge in store for himself in this election as the incumbent governor is well respected and admired. In his attempt to beat Bailey in the election, Burns hires a political team that consists of a speech writer, a joke writer, a spin doctor, a personal trainer, a character assassin, a mudslinger, a muckraker, a makeup man, and a garbologist. (Note: It is never explained why Burns would need a garbologist, but for those unaware of what garbologists do, they study garbage; specifically, what people throw away as garbage. Garbology is designed to help save the environment.)

While Burns has resorted to a number of dirty political tactics in his campaign, such as attempted character assassination, Governor Bailey continues to take the "high road" in her campaign. Members of the press ask Bailey about Burns's negative campaign and whether or not she plans to match her opponent's approach. Bailey responds, "My worthy opponent seems to think that the voters of this state are gullible fools. I prefer to rely on their intelligence and good judgment." A media person in the crowd mumbles, "Interesting strategy." Others in the crowd, almost mockingly, say, "Good luck with that!" Interesting strategy indeed. And for most of us, refreshing. Bailey is relying on her record of public service, her good name, and has confidence in the voters.

As is often the case, Burns's negative campaign strategy has served its purpose and he climbs in the poll until he draws even with Bailey on the night before the election. (Note: the reason many candidates use negative ads is because they have been proven to be effective.) Only when he spits the infamous piece of three-eyed fish out of his mouth at the Simpsons' home during a media circus does Burns lose the election to Bailey.

Along with negative campaign ads, many voters complain that they don't care for any of the candidates running for a particular office. As a result, people often say they vote for the "lesser of two evils." In the "See Homer Run" episode (#362), Homer runs for Springfield mayor (in a special recall election) with a campaign of "the lesser of two evils." The events leading to Homer's decision to run for mayor start with his insensitive disregard of Lisa's homemade Father's Day gift. Lisa's feelings are hurt. She is angry at her father and becomes angry at men in general. Lisa begins to misbehave at school. She sasses back to a teacher and breaks a window. Principal Skinner calls Homer and Marge to his office to discuss Lisa's sudden negative behavior. A school psychologist joins them. The psychologist blames Homer, claiming him to be a negative role model for Lisa. The psychologist also warns that if Homer doesn't straighten out soon, Lisa may hate men forever.

In an attempt to regain Lisa's love and respect for him, Homer dons a "Salamander Safety" suit designed to teach safety to kids. While wearing the suit, Homer comes across a huge pileup of automobiles. Kent Brockman reports, "Springfield needs a hero and it needs one now." With total disregard for his own safety, Salamander Homer pulls numerous people out of burning cars to their safety. Salamander Homer becomes the toast of the town. He is awarded the "keycard" to the city (instead of the customary "key" to the city).

Meanwhile, the citizens of Springfield have become fed up with Mayor Quimby. A special election is held, giving the voters a chance to elect a new mayor. This special election is a nod to the special election that led to the recall of then governor Gray Davis of California—who was replaced by Arnold Schwarzenegger in 2003. Davis had become so unpopular that activists were able to gather a sufficient number of citizen signatures for a recall election. The recall was successful and became the first gubernatorial recall in California history, and only the second in US history.

Just as was the case in California, a number of oddballs run for mayor of Springfield. Among the candidates are the cat lady and Kent Brockman. Springfield chef Luigi, an overly stereotypical Italian, also runs for office and proclaims (in fractured English), "Vote Luigi. I make a gooda government, just the way you like it." Actor Rainier Wolfcastle (an Arnold Schwarzenegger–type character) is another candidate to run. Wolfcastle tells a gathering of people, "Vote for me . . . a pot smoking, woman groping, son of a Nazi, washed up has-been movie star." The crowd shouts their support for this actor with no political experience. However, when Wolfcastle adds, "Oh also, I think we should keep an open mind on stem cell research," the crowd turns on him. Jimbo Jones, one of the worst kids in school and associate of such other delinquents as Dolph and Kearny, runs for office. He has somehow managed to finance a TV ad where he speaks to the public similar to a seasoned politician. Jimbo says, "If you're lame enough to vote. Vote for me." The voice-over announcer adds: "Jimbo. Tough on nerds. Tougher on dorks."

Lisa encourages Homer to run because he is so popular as the Safety Salamander. Lisa also wants to be his campaign manager. Marge is in favor of Homer running for office but prefers that he not wear the suit. She tells Homer that he looks like a mascot for some "terrible Southern college." Beyond looking like a mascot for a Southern college, Homer's suit smells. He has worn it so long without washing it that—well, you can imagine. Marge makes him wash the suit, but it does not hold up too well. Just prior to the recall election, Homer makes an appearance and his suit falls apart. And despite the fact he is still the same person with ideas that the public had previously respected, without his Salamander Safety suit Homer is doomed to lose the election. In fact, no candidate receives more than 5 percent of the vote and, as a result, Quimby remains as mayor of Springfield.

It should be noted that, despite the fact Homer lost in his campaign bid to become mayor, he did regain the respect of his daughter. Lisa admires her father because at least he tried to help make Springfield a better place. Ideally, that is why all people run for office, to make society a better place.

In the "Mr. Spritz Goes to Washington" episode (#305), Krusty the Clown runs for Congress. Krusty's running for office was spurred by good intentions, to help out residents such as the Simpson family who have had their quality of life greatly compromised as a result of the newly enacted flight path of airplanes in and out of the Springfield International Airport. The planes now fly directly over residents' homes in the Simpsons' neighborhood. The residents have trouble sleeping at night and household items are falling apart due to the deafening noise and vibrations caused by the planes flying directly overhead. The Simpsons, like many of their neighbors, consider selling their home, but no one is interested in buying a house with planes flying so closely overhead.

The Simpson family complains to the Airport Authority, but they are unwilling to do anything about the problem. Next, they decide to visit their congressman, Horace Wilcox. Unfortunately, the elderly politician becomes so upset with the quandary of the Simpsons that he dies from a heart attack. With the congressional seat open, an election will have to be held. The Simpsons convince Krusty to run for office. They believe that with his popularity, Krusty will be a shoo-in to get elected. Bart points out to Krusty that many entertainers who run for office become elected. For example, Jesse "the Body" Ventura, Sonny Bono, and Mary Bono. (Of course, Bart could have mentioned Ronald Reagan and Arnold Schwarzenegger, among others, as well.)

It takes some convincing, but eventually Krusty decides to run for Congress. He can help his fellow residents of Springfield—an altruistic motive—while pursuing his own ulterior motive—changing the

Federal Communications Commission (FCC) code of conduct. Krusty wants the right to use certain words on the air that the FCC has deemed inappropriate. This storyline reflects the many highly publicized challenges against the FCC during this time. Howard Stern, for one, had such a long-standing battle with the FCC that he ultimately left the public airwaves in favor of satellite radio. Satellite radio, like paid movie channels, is beyond the control and jurisdiction of the FCC because it is not broadcast on free, public stations.

Unlike many popular entertainers, Krusty is a Republican. (Although it should be noted that most former entertainers who run for office run as Republicans.) This will help his cause, as the Republican Party held a firm grip over the American political landscape when the "Mr. Spritz Goes to Washington" episode was first aired (2003). Krusty is concerned, however, about the "skeletons" in his closet. Whenever someone runs for office, it is all but inevitable that his or her past will be dredged up by political opponents hoping to defeat their rivals because of past indiscretions. As the scene shifts to the Springfield Republican Party headquarters it becomes clear that Krusty has the full support of the party and that his indiscretions can be minimized.

> *Republicans* (chanting): We want Krusty! We want Krusty!
> *Krusty*: Ah, just one thing. Are you guys any good at covering up youthful and middle-aged indiscretions?
> *Mr. Burns*: Are these indiscretions romantic, financial, or . . . treasonous?
> *Krusty*: Russian hooker. You tell me.
> *Burns*: Oh, no problem! We'll say you were on a fact-finding mission.
> *Krusty*: I did find out one fact . . . she was a guy!

It is often fascinating how certain indiscretions are easily accepted and pushed aside while others destroy a politician's career. President George W. Bush used cocaine in his younger days and yet was still elected president. Along with his outstanding socioeconomic achievements, Bill Clinton's two-term presidency was also marked by controversy due to his extramarital affairs. Despite his questionable behavior, Clinton's 67 percent approval rating is the highest for an exiting president (Newman 2003). George Washington, one of many presidents alleged to have had extramarital affairs while in office, is still highly regarded and is considered the "father" of our country. Jerry Springer paid for a prostitute with a check, was caught, and was still elected as mayor of Cincinnati. Conversely, former president Richard Nixon's involvement with the Watergate scandal forced his early resignation from office. Although Watergate is actually a hotel, the word "Watergate" has become synonymous with political scandal and corruption. Nixon's approval rating was a dismal 24 percent when he left office.

Krusty hits the campaign trail. He is certainly not a seasoned veteran at playing the "politically correct" game. In fact, he manages to offend a number of groups. For example, Krusty makes a number of insensitive comments during his speech to the League of Women Voters.

> *Krusty* (addressing the League of Women Voters): Let me say, I was the first clown to get a woman in sketches. Miss Bada-Boom-Boom-Boom! She had more acting talent in one boob than most women have in their entire rack!
> (A number of women raise their hands to ask Krusty a question.)
> *Krusty*: Yeah? You, with the million-dollar gams.
> (Many women are shocked by Krusty's comment and one woman can be heard walking out of the rally.)
> *Marge* (trying to save Krusty): Don't you see? He's pointing out how sexist men can be.
> *Krusty*: Yeah. Listen to the tomato with the melons.

John Armstrong is running against Krusty. His campaign involves the use of negative stereotypes against Krusty. Of course, in this case, Armstrong's pointing out Krusty's shortcomings is well deserved. Lisa convinces Krusty to focus on a real issue, specifically, how he will help regular families, like the Simpsons, once he is elected into office. Krusty's campaign turns around and he begins to receive positive news coverage, especially in the dominant conservative media. In a classic spoof of FOX News, the highly biased Republican brand of news, Krusty is deemed a hero while his Democratic challenger is shown with television-imposed devil horns over his head. The communist hammer and sickle emblem is also shown in the background when Krusty's Democratic rival is shown on the screen. Despite his shortcomings, Krusty is elected to Congress.

Krusty goes to Washington expecting to make quick changes. He is clearly clueless about how politics really operates. Krusty tries to get his airplane rerouting bill passed, but as a newly elected congressperson, no one will listen to him. Krusty has not learned how to "play" politics. We learn a lot about how politics is done in this episode. Everyone expects something and no one votes for free. Every politician expects something in return. For example, "I'll vote for your bill, but I need you to add this rider," or, "I'll vote for you, but what will you do for me?" types of scenarios are common in the world of politics. Krusty becomes so frustrated that he is ready to give up and move back to Springfield—without completing his primary goal of rerouting the airplanes. The Simpsons visit Krusty in Washington only to see how despondent Krusty has become. They offer him a pep talk and it works. Krusty heads back to the hallowed halls of Congress determined to get his bill passed.

> *Krusty*: I came here for a reason! And, I will not be silent until . . . Hey, where is everybody?
> *Congressperson*: No one usually shows up unless there's a vote.
> *Krusty*: Well, then why are you here?
> *Congressperson*: I steal stuff when everyone's gone. (He takes a number of lamps.) My Christmas shopping is done!

Once again, Krusty shows how out-of-place he is in the world of politics. Not only is he clueless as to how to get a bill introduced, let alone passed, he does not even know when Congress convenes.

Disappointed yet again, Krusty and the Simpsons contemplate their next move when they receive a great tip from an unlikely source—the janitor. The janitor has been around a long time and he knows how things are really done. The janitor claims that the key to getting Krusty's bill passed is to distract a prominent Southern congressperson by getting him drunk. The congressperson arrives.

> *Janitor*: Now, Homer, that Southern congressperson is your biggest obstacle. Your job is to drink him under the table so he misses the vote. Do you think you can do it?
> *Homer*: Sir, I studied under Ed McMahon! (Homer approaches the congressperson.)
> *Southern congressperson* (to Homer): How 'bout a drinkin' contest, boy? Right after I vote on the latest bill.

Homer: How 'bout before?

Southern congressperson: Hah! You remind me of my high
    school drinking coach. Now enough talkin'. Let's drink!

With the prominent Southern congressperson distracted, Lisa employs
the second aspect of their plan. Lisa paperclips the rerouting bill to the
most popular bill up for vote—free American flags for orphans! Naturally, no one is going to vote against a bill designed to help orphans,
especially when it involves distributing American flags. When the free
flags for orphans bill is passed, the rerouting of Springfield's airplanes is
also passed. Krusty has learned the *game* of politics and is pleased: "The
system works! I've become enchanted and illusioned with Washington." (Note: Krusty retires from politics shortly after his bill is passed
and returns to civilian life in Springfield. It is never explained why.)

The Simpsons return home and are pleased to discover that the
planes have indeed been rerouted. Politics have worked for the bet-
terment of the community. Or have they? The planes have to incorporate some sort of flight pattern, so whose homes are they flying
over now, the rich? Certainly not! The rich and powerful do not want
their lives disturbed by such inconveniences as noisy airplanes flying
overhead. So, what other option is there? What group of people are
the most politically powerless? You guessed it, the poor. As Bart and
Homer contemplate this, Bart states, "At last those planes are flying
where they belong." Homer replies, "That's right—over the homes of
poor people." "American the Beautiful" plays in the background over
this final verbal exchange as the episode ends. It is a fitting commentary on politics. If you know how to play the game, you can change
the rules for your benefit. However, if you are poor, you are without
power. And those without power are generally found on the short
end of the political spectrum.

IT'S A POLITICIAN'S LIFE

"Well, let me put it this way, Jerry, timber!"
—Congressman Bob Arnold

As Krusty learned, once a candidate is elected, he or she must learn
to play the political game. It seems inevitable that all politicians, no

matter how pure their original political intent, learn that they must make compromises in order to get things done. While some politicians work hard to maintain their credibility and take noble stands on issues they believe in, other politicians are being corrupted by special interest groups.

Corruption and Special Interest Groups

"The fetid stench of corruption . . . hangs in the air."
—Lisa Simpson

Earlier in this chapter it was explained that Marx and Weber believed that conflict between social groups (especially social classes) is inevitable due to their conflicting interests. Those in power will, naturally, want to maintain their advantageous position and cannot be expected to voluntarily relinquish their power. Logic alone dictates this premise. It is in the interests of the ruling group to maintain the status quo. Conversely, it is in the best interests of the subjected groups to seek change. Thus, it becomes a universal occurrence for people to act in their own best interests. In addition, if we take this one step further, every corporation and big business in existence will seek laws that favor their best interests. Whenever possible, lobbyists for these special interest groups will seek the favor of politicians who are in a position to help fulfill their needs and goals.

Special interest groups have become increasingly powerful and prevalent in American politics since the inception of the US Constitution. An interest group can be defined as an organized collection of people who attempt to influence politicians and/or government policies. Nearly every group has a special interest group working for them. For example, gun advocates have the National Rifle Association (NRA), college professors have the American Association of University Professors (AAUP), laborers have the American Federation of Labor–Congress of International Organizations (AFL-CIO), and so on. All special interest groups attempt to influence public opinion via advertisement, ground-level petitions, letter-writing campaigns, and so on. They also attempt to influence sympathetic candidates by supporting their campaigns. Special interest groups also hire lobbyists who deal directly with government officials and attempt to influence them on behalf of the groups. On the surface, there is nothing wrong with special interest groups; after all, they do represent the needs and concerns of people. They also provide information to candidates and politicians on topics they might otherwise be ignorant of.

It is when special interest groups cross over to corrupting (or attempting to corrupt) politicians and government officials that the political system becomes compromised. Some people believe that lobbyists own both Republicans and Democrats because most people cannot win an election without special interest money. Further, many of these lobbyists work for the same corporations that also own the large media outlets. Ultimately, the United States political system is one that is dominated by corporate-sponsored politicians and government. Keeping an eye on powerful lobbyists is critical in a democracy.

Lisa Simpson learns about corruption in American politics in the "Mr. Lisa Goes to Washington" episode (#37). In this episode, Lisa wins a regional *Reading Digest* essay contest with her paper, "Patriots of Tomorrow." As a semifinalist, Lisa earns an all-expenses paid trip for herself and family to Washington, DC, where she can compete in the national essay finals as well as view American politics first-hand. Our little overachiever is stoked. Upon their arrival, the Simpsons are given VIP badges that allow them access to areas that other visitors are not granted. For example, while on tour of the White House, the Simpsons enter a bathroom while First Lady Barbara Bush is taking a bath.

Meanwhile, the Simpsons' congressperson, Bob Arnold, is meeting with Jerry, a lobbyist from a logging special interest group. The lobbyist is attempting to sway Arnold to vote against what is in the best interests of his constituents by voting in favor of destroying the Springfield Forest.

> *Jerry*: Congressman, this is Springfield Forest. Now, basically what we want to do is cut 'er down. (The lobbyist shows Arnold a drawing of a decaying, dying forest.)
>
> *Jerry*: As you can see in our artist's rendition, it's full of old growth just aging and festering away . . . (The lobbyist shows Arnold a second drawing of animals having a tea party among tree stumps.)
>
> *Jerry*: In comes our logging company to thin out the clutter. It's all part of nature's, you know, cycle.

Congressperson Arnold: Well, Jerry, you're a whale of a lobbyist and I'd like to give you a logging permit, I would, but uh, this isn't like burying toxic waste. People are gonna notice those trees are gone.

Bob Arnold alerts us to a number of major areas of concern. For example, we see how quickly Arnold asks for a bribe; Arnold is willing to sell out the very people he represents, and assumingly, people from his own community; he has apparently allowed the burying of toxic waste in Springfield (something discussed in chapter 9); and, his biggest concern regarding destroying the forest is explaining where the trees disappeared to, instead of being worried about the compromise to the environment.

Before Congressperson Bob Arnold can finalize his deal with Jerry the lobbyist, the Simpsons appear at Arnold's office for a scheduled photo op. Arnold discretely tells Jerry to meet him at the "usual place." Photo ops, although tiresome at times, are a politician's delight. When politicians have their photos taken with a member of the community they represent, they establish a great deal of good will. Citizens are pleased when their elected officials take time from busy schedules to acknowledge their existence. These citizens are likely to go out of their way to inform people "back home" about their positive experience. And positive experiences generally equate to votes in the future. Further, the photos taken of politicians and citizens generally appear in the local media and local people generally view such photos in a positive manner. In short, it is a win–win scenario for politicians to have their photos taken with constituents.

The next morning, Lisa is too excited to sleep. She can hardly wait to present her paper at the *Reading Digest* finals. Lisa walks into her parents' room while they are still sleeping.

Lisa: Mom?

Marge: Lisa, the contest isn't for three hours.

Lisa: I'm too excited to sleep. Anyone up for the Winifred Beecher Howe Memorial?

Homer: Who's that?

Lisa: An earlier crusader for women's rights. She led the Floor Mop Rebellion of 1910. Later, she appeared on the highly unpopular seventy-five-cent piece.

(Note: the highly unpopular seventy-five-cent piece is a reference to the unpopular Susan B. Anthony dollar coin.)

As her parents go back to sleep, Lisa heads off for the (fictional)
Winifred Beecher Howe Memorial. She hopes to find further inspiration at the memorial of one of her feminist heroes. The quote at the
base of the Howe Memorial should inspire Lisa: "I will iron your
sheets when you iron out the inequalities in your labor laws."
      Unfortunately, it is not inspiration that Lisa finds at the Howe
Memorial this early morning; instead, she discovers political corruption. The "usual place" Congressperson Arnold meets with his lobbyist cronies is the seldom-visited Howe Memorial. Lisa overhears
the conversation between Bob Arnold and Jerry the lumber lobbyist.

> *Congressperson Arnold*: I told you no one ever comes here.
> *Jerry* (snickering): So, Bob, where do we stand on the Spring-
>   field Forest? Do I get my logging permits? (Jerry opens up
>   a briefcase filled with a huge sum of cash.)
> *Congressperson Arnold*: Well, let me put it this way, Jerry,
>   timber!

The congressperson and the lobbyist laugh and then make a crack
about the unattractiveness of Winifred Beecher Howe. Lisa is completely disenchanted. She no longer believes in democracy. As the
moral conscience of *The Simpsons*, Lisa's discontent with democracy
reflects the feelings of many Americans toward politics. We realize
that many politicians are corrupt, or corruptible, and yet, most of us
do little about it. In a daze, Lisa wanders to the Lincoln Memorial
seeking some sort of politically divine insight. A number of other
folks are already there seeking answers to problems. Lisa heads off to
the Jefferson Memorial but (in her mind) she is mocked by it. Lisa is
so upset now that she views all politicians as corrupt. In a tiff, Lisa
rewrites her essay for the *Reading Digest* essay final. Unbeknownst to
her family and the audience, Lisa begins her altered speech:

> The city of Washington was built on a stagnant swamp some two
> hundred years ago and very little has changed; it stank then and it
> stinks now. Only today, it is the fetid stench of corruption that
> hangs in the air.

Everyone in the audience is in shock. (Except Bart, who is happy to witness Lisa's radicalism.) Lisa continues her speech and names "names." She specifically mentions seeing Congressperson Arnold take a bribe from a lobbyist. Lisa concludes her speech with a powerful ending: "One nation under the dollar with liberty and justice for none."

This was one of the top episodes in which the writers of *The Simpsons* clearly presented sociopolitical commentary. Most of the events presented so far in this episode are fairly believable. That is, a young person becomes disenchanted with politics, a lobbyist offers a bribe, a politician takes a bribe, and a politician sells out his own community. However, this episode concludes quite unbelievably. After Lisa completes her speech and runs off the stage, a judge from the essay contest notifies a senator, who informs the FBI of two things: one, there is a corrupt representative in Congress; and two, a young citizen has become disillusioned with politics and lost her faith in democracy. The FBI quickly sets up a sting and arrests Arnold for corruption. (Fairly predictably, Arnold repents and announces that he has become a "born-again Christian"!) Lisa's faith in the democratic system is restored. And, although she did not win the essay contest, she is happy that corrupt politicians are quickly removed from office. Now, if only that were true!

The secret deals between most politicians and lobbyists are just that, secret. Even with instances in which corruption is revealed, justice is often fleeting. As described earlier in this chapter, Springfield Mayor Quimby is so corrupt that a special election is held to kick him out of office. But even then, Quimby holds onto his position. Quimby's corruption is described in a number of episodes, but perhaps the funniest one is "Mayored to the Mob" (#212). In this episode, the Simpsons go to a science fiction convention attended by Mayor Quimby and starring actor Mark Hamill of *Star Wars* fame. Quimby introduces Hamill on stage. Hamill appears in his Luke Skywalker costume to the delight of the attendees. Hamill announces that he needs a volunteer from the audience to assist him in a skit. The audience members argue with one another over who is more deserving of such an honor. Before long, a melee develops. The mob turns toward the stage. Quimby looks around for his bodyguards, but they are nowhere to be found (they are outside sitting atop the mayor's car, admiring clouds). Quimby and Hamill feel threatened.

Fearing for their safety, Homer rushes to their aid. He securely escorts the two dignitaries to safety. The mayor sees his bodyguards and yells at them.

> *Quimby*: You call yourselves bodyguards? You're fired!
> *Ernie*: Fired, huh? Who else you gonna find to take a bullet for ya?
> *Big Tom*: Or have his genitals hooked up to a car battery?
> *Quimby*: I'll tell ya who! Him! (Quimby points to Homer.)
> *Homer*: Woo-hoo!
> *Marge*: Homer, I don't think you were listening to what he just—
> *Homer* (with a firm voice): I said, woo-hoo.

And so, Homer becomes Mayor Quimby's bodyguard. Quimby sends Homer to Leavelle's Bodyguard Academy where he learns a wide variety of self-defense techniques. Homer utilizes one of his new talents—the "sleeper pinch" on his kids and wife whenever they start to bother him! The "sleeper pinch" is applied to specific pressure points on the neck to temporarily incapacitate someone. Spock used this technique in *Star Trek*.

Homer's primary job, of course, is to protect the mayor. Homer also drives the mayor's limo and accompanies him as he makes his rounds. Homer turns his back to Quimby's corrupt tactics because he is receiving his own benefits. At Moe's Homer is allowed all the premium beer he can drink while the mayor promises Moe he will pass the health inspection for a sum of money. Moe hands Quimby a pile of cash. Homer escorts the mayor out while carrying a number of beer bottles with him. At the Krusty Burger Homer receives free burgers while the mayor gets his kickback money from Krusty. Apu also pays off the mayor. We are led to believe this is just the tip of the iceberg of the mayor's corruption.

To this point, Homer has kept his mouth shut about Quimby's dirty dealings. This changes when Homer discovers that Mayor Quimby is involved with Fat Tony's criminal organization. The mayor has worked out a deal with Fat Tony to supply the milk to Springfield Elementary. The milk Fat Tony provides for the schoolchildren is rat's milk! Upon learning this, Homer rushes to the school and tells his kids never to drink milk again. Homer then confronts the mayor in his office. Quimby is running on his treadmill while Homer yells at him and pounds on the treadmill. Homer hits the speed control button and the mayor cannot run fast enough to keep up. The momentum pushes him backward and out a window.

Mayor Quimby does not fall to his death, but instead, he is hanging onto the window ledge. Homer promises to save the mayor but only if he promises to break his deal with Fat Tony. Quimby agrees. The police raid the rat-milking facility and drain the milk down the sewer. Fat Tony is arrested but vows revenge against the mayor.

Quimby is afraid for his life. But Homer convinces him that he needs to go and have fun. Homer escorts Quimby to the theater to see a production of *Guys and Dolls* staring Mark Hamill, who again plays Luke Skywalker in the production. As if this scenario is not odd enough, the finale of this episode is even odder. Fat Tony is also at the theater with his henchmen (presumably he made bail). Fat Tony orders one of his flunkies to kill Quimby. But the flunky ends up on stage and fights Hamill. Eventually, the henchman attacks the mayor, but Homer rushes to his defense. While Homer fights off the would-be assassin, Fat Tony himself is beating up the mayor in the background.

The mayor recovers and corruption in Springfield continues. Only now, it will have a new bodyguard.

TAKING A STAND

"That's right. A *girl* wants to play football. How about that?"
—Lisa Simpson

There comes a time in everyone's life that they must take a stand on an issue they deem important. Regular citizens and politicians alike possess this virtue. Lisa, for example, has taken a stand on many political issues. Some of the issues that Lisa believes in strongly have been discussed throughout this book. For example, in chapter 9, Lisa took a stand on environmental issues and, in chapter 8, she took a stand on gender equality. In fact, Lisa seems to take a stand on numerous issues. In the "Bart Star" episode (#184), Lisa attempts to make a political statement against Bart's peewee football involvement. (See chapter 11 for a further discussion of this episode.) Lisa shows up at Bart's first practice, intent on making a scene. She plans to demand to be allowed to play football and assumes she will be told "no" because she is a girl. Geared up for one of her typical confrontations, Lisa addresses the coach, Ned Flanders.

> *Lisa*: What position do you got for me? (The crowd gasps.)
> *Lisa*: That's right. A *girl* wants to play football. How about that?
> *Ned*: Well, that's super-duper, Lisa. We've already got four girls on the team.
> *Lisa* (disappointed): You do?
> *Ned*: Ah, huh. But we'd love to have you on board!

Instead of being happy that four girls are already on the team, Lisa is upset that she does not have a platform to take a political stand on. She goes to plan "B."

> *Lisa*: Well . . . football's not really my thing. After all, what kind of civilized person would play a game with the skin of an innocent pig?!
> *Ned*: Well, actually, Lisa, these balls are synthetic!
> *Janey*: And, for every ball you buy, a dollar goes to Amnesty International!
> *Lisa* (crying): I gotta go!

Lisa runs off. She picked a bad day to take a stand on issues ("political correctness") that are no longer subject to debate. She humiliates herself by admitting she does not even want to play football. Why would anyone take a stand on an issue that she has no actual interest in?! Ideally, Lisa will leave football alone and concentrate on taking a stand on things that are far more urgent, such as the environment.

Unfortunately, when taking a stand on an urgent political issue such as the environment, Lisa learns that even the best of intentions can sometimes backfire. In "The Wife Aquatic" episode (#388), the Simpson family visits Barnacle Bay, the childhood summer vacation spot for Marge and her family. (Note: The episode title is a reference to the film *The Life Aquatic with Steve Zissou*, starring Bill Murray.) A very important environmental message is presented in this episode.

The local fishermen have depleted the fish supply of Barnacle Bay and the community has suffered a tremendous financial burden due to the loss of tourists. This once-thriving seaport town now resembles a dump. Bart and Lisa comment on how bad the town looks.

> *Lisa*: This is the most disgusting place we've ever gone.
> *Bart*: What about Brazil?
> *Lisa*: After Brazil.

The Simpsons talk to the captain/owner of *The Rotting Pelican* fishing boat. He explains that the disappearance of the delicious-to-eat "yum-yum" fish is the reason the economics changed at Barnacle Bay. Lisa quips that the yum-yum fish probably disappeared due to overfishing. Taken aback by this little girl's comment, the captain blames the lack of fish on underspawning!

Marge is so disappointed that her childhood dreams of Barnacle Bay have been shattered by the reality of a brutal environmental nightmare (an enviromare!) that Homer decides to join the captain of *The Rotting Pelican* in search of the yum-yum fish. (Bart, by the way, has hidden aboard the fishing ship rather than spend time with his mother and sisters.) They are hoping for one great supercatch. As a result of Homer accidentally pouring beer batter over the fishing net hooks, the yum-yum fish reappear in record numbers. The crew of *The Rotting Pelican* enjoys a record haul. They will all be rich and treated as heroes upon their safe return to Barnacle Bay. However, Mother Nature has a different idea. A huge—no, a "perfect"—storm suddenly confronts the brave fishermen. (Note: This storm scene is similar to that of the film *The Perfect Storm*.) The crew and, of course, the fish are dumped overboard.

Back at Barnacle Bay, a funeral service is held for the brave (or stupid!) fishermen who dared to confront the seas in search of the yum-yum fish. The grief-ridden ceremony is interrupted when the crew members arrive. A large Japanese fishing vessel (the kind accused by environmentalists for overfishing the seas) had scooped the fishermen up in one of their giant nets. Lisa attempts to take another political stand by warning the fishermen not to rely on fishing to revitalize their town. What she really hopes for is a conservative form of fishing that involves allowing time for the fish to spawn and placing limits on the number of fish caught. Instead, the townspeople note all the giant trees in their bay. The scene shifts to rapid deforestation. A truck driver states that the trees are being used for Larry Flint's magazines, *Hustler* and *Barely Legal*. Lisa is aghast. She took a stand on one political issue (overfishing), but was taken aback when another important issue she believes in was disregarded.

In chapter 7, the topic of Prohibition in Springfield was discussed. A St. Patrick's Day parade celebration was marred by drunken misbehavior and the local suffragist groups argued that the best way to curtail negative behavior was to put a prohibition on alcohol. This movement mirrors the Prohibition movement of the early twentieth century spearheaded by pietistic religious denominations and the women's temperance movement (suffragists). These organizations argued that alcohol was responsible for many of the evils of society, especially violent and criminal behavior perpetrated by drunks. Eventually, the proponents of Prohibition were successful in spearheading the "noble experiment" via the ratification of the Eighteenth Amendment to the US Constitution in January 1919.

This "noble experiment" was supposed to reduce crime and other social problems by reducing the quantity of alcohol available to consume. Thus, Prohibition outlawed the production, sale, transportation, import, and export of alcohol, while allowing the purchase, possession, and consumption of small amounts of alcohol. A small quantity of homemade wine for personal use was okay. This is commonly referred to as the "Dry Law" aspect of Prohibition. Initially, the consumption of alcohol in the United States did decrease. After all, people had few options for obtaining alcohol. After this early drop, however, consumption rates of alcohol increased steadily. This did not come as a surprise to criminologists, economists, sociologists, and other people who are aware of the well-established reality: When people want a good or service, and the government does not provide legal means for consumers to purchase this product, a "black market" will arise.

Sure enough, Prohibition, which was designed to reduce crime, actually increased it—especially organized crime. The black market consists of individuals and criminal groups who create and maintain traffic flow and distribution of illicit goods and services. Speakeasies sprang up to provide "watering holes" for people who wanted to drink. Bootleggers assured the safe arrival of alcohol to the speakeasies. Politicians and beat police officers were "on the take" and took bribes from bootleggers, moonshiners, crime bosses, and the owners of speakeasies. (Note: I was informed by the host of McSorley's Pub, the oldest bar in Manhattan [NY], that the US infantry delivered beer to that pub during Prohibition.) All of these occurrences were depicted in the "Homer vs. the Eighteenth Amendment" episode (#171).

Prohibition was not "passed" as legislation in Springfield in this episode. Rather, a city clerk discovers an old prohibition law that was still "on the books." The St. Patrick's Day drunken melee leads to the discovery of this old law and the suffragists compel its enforcement. Just as all Americans experienced during national Prohibition, the residents of Springfield suddenly find themselves to be criminals for engaging in a behavior that was legal just the day before. Springfield is now a "dry" town. After the initial shock and dramatic decrease in alcohol consumption in Springfield, a black market emerges. A number of bootleggers run booze into Springfield from nearby Shelbyville. Moe's bar becomes a speakeasy. All the regulars, including Homer, return to Moe's.

In criminal law detective fashion, a narrator (superimposed in this episode) retells the story.

> *Narrator*: Dateline: Springfield. With prohibition back in force, sobriety's peaceful slumber was shattered by its noisy neighbor, the speakeasy.
> *Homer*: Glad you're finally back in business, Moe.
> *Moe*: Yeah, that was a scary coupla hours.
> *Narrator*: The suppliers of the illegal booze? Gangsters, running truckloads of smuggled hooch all the way from Shelbyville. And John Law was helpless!

Chief Wiggum is "Johnny Law" in Springfield. He is indeed incapable (or unwilling) of curtailing the smuggling of booze into Springfield. Suffragists storm into Moe's one night and are outraged by patrons openly drinking booze. The suffragists complain to Mayor Quimby to replace Wiggum with a federal agent. The mayor crumples under their political pressure and sends for Rex Banner, a lawman from Washington. Wiggum is removed from duty and Banner takes his place. Banner (voiced by comedian Dave Thomas), dressed in 1920s Chicago-style attire, quickly and competently cleans up the town.

Once again, there is no booze in Springfield. That is, until a "Beer Baron" arrives on the scene. The mysterious Beer Baron has found a new supply of beer and has cleverly found a way to deliver it to Moe's. Who is this beer baron? Why, none other than Homer Simpson.

Homer discovers barrels of Duff beer at the local landfill. The beer was part of the alcohol gathered up and supposedly destroyed/dumped by law officials. Homer takes Bart with him in a rented U-Haul to retrieve the barrels of beer. He is chased by the police through a graveyard but manages to elude them. Homer hides the barrels of beer in his basement. He conceals the beer inside bowling balls and delivers them to Moe's through a series of complicated underground tunnels. (Note: Their origin and construction are not explained to the audience.) When the bowling balls arrive at Moe's, Moe serves them to customers and returns the empty bowling balls to Homer by rolling a gutter ball. Throughout the first night, Homer and Bart roll bowling balls filled with beer to Moe's. As Homer explains to Bart, "The real money is in bootlegging."

Marge ascertains quite quickly what Homer is up to. But surprisingly, her actions are not those of a curmudgeon. Quite the contrary, Marge is actually proud of Homer because it's the cleverest idea he has ever come up with. She also believes that Prohibition is silly and an outdated concept.

Moe and Homer are making a killing in the black market. But Homer's beer supply is limited. Addicted to the rush of being a bootlegger, Homer decides to make his own hooch. His homemade stills routinely explode. Marge advises Homer to quit while he is ahead—financially speaking. Marge also convinces him it is just a matter of time before "Johnny Law" catches up with Homer's illegal doings. As a result, Homer devises a plan to help Chief Wiggum and chase Banner out of town. Homer, as the "Beer Baron," gives himself up to Chief Wiggum. The townspeople are pleased and Wiggum gets his job back. However, instead of upholding his end of the bargain by letting him off with a warning, Wiggum pushes for the punishment as stipulated by the old Springfield Prohibition law—Homer must be catapulted! Prior to this unusual form of punishment, the city clerk discovers a more recent version of Springfield law and discovers that Prohibition had officially been repealed. Thus, Homer was not guilty of any wrongdoing and did not have to face catapulsion.

Utopian dreamers and naïve believers were the people who supported Prohibition. But to their credit, pro-Prohibitionists took a political stand—albeit, an ill-advised one. Their well-meaning attempts at reform failed to acknowledge basic human behavior (e.g., when people really want something, they will use whatever means necessary to attain it) and, in the end, Prohibition was such a huge failure that the Eighteenth Amendment was repealed by the Twenty-first Amendment. The Eighteenth Amendment remains as the only amendment to the US Constitution to be repealed. The lesson to be learned here is, "We the People" are capable of making political stands of our own. Undoubtedly, there exists many Homer Simpson/Beer Barons in waiting throughout the United States, and the world. As Homer Simpson himself exclaims, "To alcohol! The cause of—and solution to—all of life's problems."

INTERNATIONAL POLITICS

> **"We had to invade. They were working on weapons of mass destruction."**
> —Kodos

The Simpsons has managed to offend a number of groups of people within the United States. At times, it has taken shots at a number of other nations and their cultures. For example, earlier in this chapter Brazil was labeled as the "most disgusting place" the Simpson family had ever visited. In chapter 6, Paraguay was mocked. But it is, perhaps, the *Simpsons's* attack on Australia (the native country of Rupert Murdoch, owner of FOX, which airs *The Simpsons*) in the "Bart vs. Australia" episode (#119) that stands out the most.

An International Incident

> **"You're just some punk kid, aren't you? Ooh, you picked the wrong guy to tangle with here, mate."**
> —Bruno

In the "Bart vs. Australia" episode, Bart is fascinated by Lisa's claim that the water drains in the opposite direction of the United States (the northern hemisphere) in Australia (the southern hemisphere). Bart does not believe Lisa. So, he randomly calls a number of people in the southern hemisphere to find out which way (clockwise or counter clockwise) the water flushes in a toilet. Bart makes a long-distance collect call to a random number in Australia as well. When Bart asks the naïve Australian boy to confirm with his neighbor, it takes six hours for the boy to return. All this time, the Australian family has rung up a huge long-distance bill. By the time the boy returns, Bart has gone to bed and left the phone off the hook—which runs up the long bill. The Australian boy's father, Bruno, calls Bart's number to complain.

> *Bruno*: You're just some punk kid, aren't you? Ooh, you picked the wrong guy to tangle with here, mate.
> *Bart* (laughs): I don't think so. You're all the way in Australia. Hey, I think I hear a dingo eatin' your baby.

According to Hugo Dobson (2006), Bart's comment about the dingo eating a baby is an insensitive reference to the disappearance of a nine-week-old Australian baby, Azaria Chamberlain, in 1980. It should be noted that the Elaine character on *Seinfeld* uttered the phrase "Maybe the dingo ate your baby" in "The Stranded" episode (#27), which first aired November 27, 1991—nearly three and half years prior to *The Simpsons* first airing of "Bart vs. Australia."

Bruno makes a federal case out of the nine-hundred-dollar long-distance collect phone call that Bart refuses to pay for and has not informed his parents about. Bruno hires the Hopping Mad Collection Agency to collect the money. The case reaches the US State Department and Undersecretary of State for International Protocol, Brat and Punk Division, and Evan Conover (voiced by Phil Hartman) shows up at the Simpsons' home. Bart's parents don't understand why Bart's prank call is such a big deal. Conover explains that Bart's escapade could not have happened at a worse time because, "Americo–Australian relations are at an all-time low. As I'm sure you remember, in the late 1980s the US experienced a short-lived infatuation with Australian culture. For some bizarre reason, the Aussies thought this would be a permanent thing. Of course it wasn't."

Conover also explains to the Simpsons that Australia wants Bart imprisoned for five years. The Aussies want to make an example out of Bart. Although Homer agrees with the decision, Marge protests. Conover explains that there is a second option that entails Bart going to Australia and apologizing in person to the Australian government. And with that, the Simpson family is off to Australia with all expenses paid by the US government just so that Bart can diffuse an international incident via a personal apology. When the Simpsons arrive at the Australian airport, a sign on the wall states that foreign animals and plants are not allowed into the country. Bart has his frog with him. He places it in a nearby pool of water with the intention of picking it back up on his way home. Of course the frog hops off.

The Simpsons go to the US embassy. The toilets there flush the American way! The government has actually devised an expensive device that forces the water to flush as it would in the United States. The government did this to combat homesickness! (Note: There is also a sign at the US embassy that states: "Restroom for Citizens Only.") Bart is advised by US officials on how to behave. Surprisingly, Bart later offers a very sincere apology in front of the Australian Parliament. Bart proclaims, "I'm sorry. I'm sorry for what I did to your country." Homer is proud of his son for taking responsibility for his actions. However, Homer soon becomes outraged when he learns that Conover has sold Bart out to the Aussies. The Australian government also demands a "booting" punishment be administered against Bart. (A "booting" is a form of Australian corporal punishment that involves a man wearing an oversized boot kicking the offender in the butt.) Homer yells at Conover, "You sold us out, Conover!" The Aussie officials head toward Bart, but Homer steals the boot and threatens the prime minister, Andy. Homer and Bart run out of the Parliament and back to the US embassy. The embassy guards try to close the gates on the Simpsons but they move too slowly. (Note: This scene is most likely a reference to the young American who was caned in Singapore for littering.)

Now there is a real political incident. Both countries need to find a way to save face. Political officials from both countries try to work out a deal. Conover explains to the Simpsons the proposed deal. Bart will accept a booting from the prime minister through the gate. In that manner, Bart remains on US soil, but the Aussies get their justice. They also agree to a "wing-tip" shoe instead of an oversized boot. Once again, Bart is prepared for his punishment. He solely walks to the gate and bends over for his booting. However, this time Bart has a surprise. While bent over, he pulls his pants down to moon the Aussies. He has written on his butt: "Don't Tread on Me." The

Aussies are not amused. An angry mob attacks the embassy. And in a scene reminiscent of the US departure from Vietnam in 1975, the Simpson family is whisked away from the embassy via helicopter. From the helicopter, the Simpsons view millions of frogs eating away at crops.

The single frog that Bart brought with him to Australia led to this infestation. Lisa comments, "Well, that's what happens when you introduce a foreign species into an ecosystem that can't handle them." In a bit of irony, there is an Australian creature riding along on the helicopter with the Simpsons. Will it find its way to America and ruin our environment as an enviromare?

The Simpsons vs. President Bush—the Second One!

> **"I don't know, I am starting to think Operation 'Enduring Occupation' was a bad idea."**
> —Kang

The Simpsons has long been known to make commentary about American politics. In the early years, many comments were made about the first President Bush. During the middle years, Bill Clinton bore the brunt of many jokes. In recent years, President George W. Bush's politics, especially those regarding the war in Iraq, have received attention in a variety of episodes.

In the "Simple Simpson" episode (#332), the Simpsons attend the Springfield County Fair. There is a stereotypical male country singer performing on stage (for example, Toby Keith). Between songs, he insults liberals for their antiwar political stand. For example, he insinuates that Barbra Streisand has spit on the American flag by challenging the politics of Bush and the legitimacy of the Iraq War. The country singer begins one of his songs by saying, "This song is about a country I love; you may have heard of it . . . America!" The Simpsons is mirroring what has occurred throughout the years that the Iraq War has been waged. A number of singers and musical groups have written and performed songs that either support or condemn the war. Country music, in particular (with a glaring exception from the Dixie Chicks), has taken the pro-Bush and pro-war stand. Typically, those who are against Bush and/or the war are portrayed as anti-American by those who support Bush and/or the war.

The first two episodes of the eighteenth season of *The Simpsons* addressed specific aspects of the Iraq War. First, in the "Treehouse of Horror XVII" episode (#382), a spoof of Orson Welles's *War of the Worlds* is used to draw a comparison to the current conflict in Iraq. In this episode, the recurring Halloween space monsters, Kang and Kodos, invade Earth. Much of Springfield lies in ruin. Social services are nonexistent. Death lurks for everyone. Three years later . . . and nothing has changed. Springfield still lies mostly in ruin. The residents that lived through years of war are growing increasingly upset with the space invaders who destroyed their homeland. Kang and Kodos wonder why the residents still resist their presence and perceive them as invaders, rather than liberators.

> *Kang*: The Earthlings continue to resent our presence.
> *Kodos*: Don't worry, we still have the people's hearts and minds.
> *Kang*: I don't know, I am starting to think Operation "Enduring Occupation" was a bad idea.
> *Kodos*: We had to invade. They were working on weapons of mass destruction.
> *Kang*: Sure they were.

The scene shifts to reveal a bombed wasteland that was once Springfield. *The Simpsons* is making a clear political statement. No matter how one tries to disguise it, a foreign army that causes devastation to a people's homeland will not be perceived positively by the local people.

By the end of 2006, President Bush made it very clear that he believed more troops were needed to fight terrorism in the Middle East. Many service personnel have served multiple tours of duty and it was clear (to President Bush) that many fresh troops must be sent to war. This issue was addressed in the "G. I. (Annoyed Grunt) D'oh!" episode (#383). "Join the Army" booths are set up in the Springfield Mall. Army recruiters approach ten-year-olds Bart and Milhouse. One recruiter animatedly proclaims, "Because of exciting current events, the army needs new members." The second recruiter adds that enlistees will earn money for college and see a part of the world that tourists never go to. Of course, there is generally a reason tourists do not go to these places—war! Recruitment is so poor in Springfield that the army recruiter's office has a sign that says: "Suicidal Teens Wanted."

A series of mishaps occur throughout this episode. For example, Homer is temporarily enlisted into the US Army and a $50 million simulation war game is conducted in Springfield. The army wreaks havoc in Springfield. Among the mishaps of this simulated war is Lenny's car being run over by an army tank. Eventually, the townspeople get the army drunk and capture the renegade colonel leading the operation. Rather than admit guilt or that a mistake had been made, the colonel stands firm to his officer's training. He states: "US government policy is very clear. Never back down. Never admit a mistake. That's why we've won over one-half of the wars we fought." "Staying the course," as this army colonel is implying, reflects the commander-in-chief's stance regarding the war at this time. Lisa, like many Americans, has a different perspective and says to the colonel: "Colonel, I hope you learned that an occupying foreign force can never defeat a determined local populace."

In the "Revenge Is a Dish Best Served Three Times" episode (#389), *The Simpsons* takes another swipe at America's involvement in the Iraq War. In this episode, the family is out for a drive when suddenly an erratic driver nearly cuts them off. Homer chases after the driver waving a baseball bat out the window. He is trying to hit the other car with his bat. Marge warns Homer not to seek out revenge.

Marge: Revenge never solves anything.
Homer: Then what's America doing in Iraq?

The Simpsons has regularly delved into the world of politics. This chapter has provided a glimpse. However, because *The Simpsons* often presents both liberal and conservative viewpoints on a variety of political topics, the show has managed to maintain audiences from the left, right, and center.

Chapter 11

The Wide Diversity of Sports in Springfield

"Mom, I never won before, and I may never win again."
—Bart Simpson

From late December to early January, football fans are presented with an opportunity to watch college bowl games and NFL playoff games on a nearly daily basis. In particular, January 1 represents a football junkie's paradise, as televised football coverage lasts nearly fifteen consecutive hours. Even die-hard fans have a difficult time sitting on their couches all day watching every game available. But make no mistake: there are millions of these American football junkies out there.

Being labeled a "couch potato" was once viewed as a stigma, but for many it now serves as a badge of honor. This is especially true when it comes to competing in ESPN's annual "Ultimate Couch Potato Contest." In this not-so-physically demanding challenge, contestants are seated—strangely in reclining chairs rather than couches—in a restaurant in front of a number of large-screen televisions broadcasting sports events. As one contestant explained, "I couldn't think of anything better than to sit and watch a bunch of games and get served food and drink all day" (Syracuse *Post-Standard*, January 3, 2007). The toughest part of the challenge occurs at night when the restaurant closes and ESPN repeats *SportsCenter* over and over. In 2007, Jason Pisarik successfully defended his "couch potato crown" after watching sports consecutively for thirty-nine hours and fifty-five minutes. Pisarik was awarded a forty-two-inch high-definition television, gift certificates, and a trophy. Any contestant lasting longer than twelve consecutive hours of sports programming received a leather recliner. (Note: Bathroom breaks are allowed.) There are millions of people, including this author, who have watched twelve consecutive hours of football (on numerous occasions) and no one has ever given them a free recliner! I guess we all now know an easy way to earn one: enter ESPN's annual "Ultimate Couch Potato Contest." And wouldn't it be interesting if the millions of sports fans who have watched a minimum of twelve consecutive hours of sports programming all entered this challenge?!

It should be noted that sports fans are not necessarily the biggest couch potatoes. The world record (as of January 2007) for consecutive TV watching (of any kind) is sixty-nine hours and forty-eight minutes set in 2005 by Canadian Suresh Joachim (Syracuse *Post-Standard*, January 4, 2007).

BIRGing on Sports

"We won! We won, Flanders, we won!"
—Homer Simpson

In chapter 1, Homer Simpson is described as a couch potato. Among the television programming Homer finds most appealing is sports coverage. And, like many sports junkies, Homer will watch just about anything that is sports-related. In the "Pray Anything" episode (#301), Homer watches the "Monkey Olympics." He is not the only one of his cohorts to watch this "sports" program, as the next day at work Homer discusses the Monkey Olympics with Carl. Visibly upset by the poor quality of judging, Carl asks Homer, "Ooh, by the way, did you see the judging in the monkey figure skating? Whose banana you gotta peel to get a five point nine?"

Monkey Olympics!? Why would anyone watch such programming? Further, why would any network broadcast such an event? There are many and diverse answers to these questions. The simplest explanation is the expansion of cable networking and twenty-four-hour programming. ESPN, the leading twenty-four-hour sports network, for example, recognizes that it takes a great deal of sports coverage to fill 264 hours of airtime per week. Beyond its reliance on broadcasting *SportsCenter* for nearly a third of a typical day, ESPN has aired a wide variety of sports and entertainment programs in an attempt to fill this time void. Its coverage of Australian Rules Football in the 1980s created a cult following among many Americans (oddly, this programming was halted). And since that time, ESPN has shown a variety of traditional sports (e.g., baseball, football, basketball, bowling, and so on) and nontraditional sports (e.g., snowboarding). (Note: ESPN created the Summer and Winter "X" Games, which consist of many nontraditional sports.) ESPN also broadcasts a variety of quasi-sports that can most generously be described as forms of entertainment (e.g., poker and competitive eating). As ESPN president George Bodenheimer (2006) explains, we can expect to see even more sports coverage on television in the future, especially paid sports, as 80 to 85 percent of Americans pay for television (e.g., cable, pay-per-view), the largest percentage in the world.

Sport as a Microcosm of Society

> **"What began as a traditional soccer riot has escalated into a citywide orgy of destruction."**
> —Kent Brockman

Americans, like billions of other people around the world, love sports. In fact, beyond religion, no other social institution is participated in, discussed, and commands the energies, passions, and emotions of individuals and groups of people more than sports. Sports reflect the mores, values, norms, and general idealistic beliefs of a culture. Sport sociologists argue that sports serve as a mirror of society. That is, the elements of society are reflected in sports. This is true with regard to both positive and negative aspects of culture. For example, the "win-at-all-costs" philosophy often leads to elitism, sexism, racism, nationalism, extreme competitiveness, abuse of drugs (including steroids), gambling, violence, cheating, corporate greed, and disregard for the people (e.g., via sports franchise relocation), and a number of other deviant behaviors.

However, sports also reflect many of the positive attributes of society, including notions of cooperation and teamwork, fair play, hard work, dedication, striving for personal excellence, obedience to rules, commitment and loyalty, and so forth. In short, one would be hard-pressed to find any element of the general society that cannot be found in sports.

Although football reigns as the unchallenged most popular sport in the United States, Americans love to play and watch numerous other sports. Over the past couple decades many school-age children have grown up playing soccer, but interest in that sport does not extend to the professional level or watching it on television as a spectator sport. Since the rise of soccer participation in the United States, a cliché has become vogue: "Kids play soccer and grow up watching football."

Cultural differences help to explain America's lack of interest in soccer (or "futbol" as it is known everywhere else)—the worldwide favorite sport. In sports, as in life, Americans enjoy opportunities that lead to rewards (the mirror effect). In other words, we like to score! Popular American sports, for the most part, are designed with scoring in mind. Soccer, or futbol, is a low-scoring sport. Where soccer fans find beauty in a 0–0 or 1–1 score, Americans find boredom. "The Cartridge Family" episode (#183) illustrates this reality.

In this episode, the residents of Springfield attend a Continental Soccer Association match between Mexico and Portugal held at Springfield Stadium. International soccer games fuel machismo nationalism among players and fans. The stadium PA announcer mirrors this sentiment when he states, "This match will determine, once and for all, which nation is the greatest on Earth. Mexico. Or Portugal." Homer states, "I'll kill myself if Portugal doesn't win." Now remember, Homer is not from Portugal, but the point of his comment is to reflect how passionate fans of sporting teams can become. They may "kill" themselves in pity or "kill" rivals out of anger.

The fans are expecting an exciting match, but, as Americans, they will be disappointed. The players, in a monotonous fashion, kick the ball back and forth, back and forth, and yet no progress is made going downfield. The PA announcer describes the game, "Fast kicking, low scoring, and ties? You bet!" Soccer has it all! Before long, the residents of Springfield grow weary of the "nonaction" and their restlessness leads to a number of people getting up at the same time to head toward the exits.

Sideshow Mel: I can't bear this any longer. I'm leaving.
Moe: Yeah, not before me you ain't.
Ned: Now, now. There's plenty of exits for everyone.

Moe (upset with Ned's comment, places him in a headlock):
Oh, that's it! You're dead, pal!
Skinner: Hey now, that's uncalled for!
Lenny: Shut your hole, Skinner!

Lenny punches Skinner in the stomach, causing a chain reaction of people bumping into one another and beers being spilled. Within minutes, the stadium melee turns into an out-of-control riot. Kent Brockman reports: "What began as a traditional soccer riot has escalated into a citywide orgy of destruction." The term "traditional soccer riot" reflects the preponderance of violence associated with many soccer matches between soccer-loving, passionate, rival fans. In the Springfield case, the "nontraditional" riot was caused by bored Americans trying to beat one another to the exits.

As a sport sociologist, I have conducted research on sports fans and their peculiar behaviors. Among the diverse areas of sport that I find interesting is the occurrence of BIRGing and CORFing.

BIRGing, CORFing, and Joining the Bandwagon

"The Isotopes are winning? To the bandwagon!"
—Homer Simpson

Sport sociologists have found that many sports fans have a greater tendency to wear their favorite team's apparel (e.g., hats, T-shirts, sweatshirts) following a victory and a decreased likelihood following a favorite team's defeat. Further, many sports fans are more likely to use "we" in discussing wins, but use "they" when describing losses. In this regard, "we" won and "they" lost are common expressions used by sports fans to describe the same team (one's favorite team).

In other words, when our favorite team wins, we are naturally happy and bask in the glory of "our" victory. Thus, the expression "Basking in Reflective Glory," or BIRG, is used to describe the phenomenon of individuals purposely manipulating the visibility of their connections with winners in order to make themselves look good to others. Individuals, then, are showcasing their positive associations in an attempt to encourage observers to think more highly of them and to like them more. Homer Simpson displays the BIRG behavior in the "Homer Loves Flanders" episode (#97).

In this episode, Homer wants to attend the "big game" between Springfield and archrival Shelbyville. The problem is, he cannot get a ticket. He feels so poorly about himself for not being able to get a ticket that he asks Bart what is wrong with him.

> *Homer*: Why am I such a loser? Why?
> *Bart*: Well, your father was a loser, and his father, and his father . . . it's genetic, man. (At this point, Bart does not see the connection of this genetic argument to his own future.)
> *Bart* (after he realizes): D'oh!

Feeling like a loser just because he cannot find a ticket for a football game tells us a great deal about the fragility of Homer's self-esteem. People with low self-esteem often search for ways to improve how they feel about themselves. Homer is a perfect candidate for BIRGing as a result of a team victory. But, will he find a ticket?

As it turns out, Ned Flanders has an extra ticket and offers to take Homer as his "guest" (this includes paying for all of Homer's snacks, including a clever "nacho hat" that has nacho cheese in the center). Unlike the soccer game, this football game is exciting to the finish. With mere seconds remaining in the game and the Atoms trailing 27–21, star quarterback Stan "the boy" Taylor throws a long pass to his wide receiver, who catches the ball in the end zone. After the extra point is made, Springfield is the winner. Homer immediately shifts into BIRG mode by yelling, "We won. We won, Flanders, we won!" He then kisses Ned several times. Ned laughs uncomfortably. Homer taunts the Shelbyville fans: "Losers! Losers! Kiss my big Springfield behind, Shelbyville."

Homer and Ned wait outside the stadium. Homer is hoping to get an autograph from any one of his football heroes. The players ignore Homer's pleas for an autograph. But then, Stan Taylor notices Ned.

> *Stan*: Ned? Is that—Ned Flanders?
> *Ned*: Heidely-ho, Stanster.
> *Homer*: You know Stan Taylor?
> *Stan*: Know me? Ned Flanders saved me. I used to party all night and sleep with lingerie models until Ned and his Bible group showed me that I could have more.
> *Homer*: Professional athletes, always wantin' more.

Stan: Ned, they gave me the game ball, but I want you to have it.

Homer: (Gasps.)

Ned: Tell you what—Homer Simpson here's just about the biggest Atoms fan that's ever graced God's green Earth. I bet he'd enjoy it even more than me!

Stan: Sure, anything for Neddy. Here you go! (Stan tosses the ball to Homer.)

Homer: Wow. Now I have four children. (Looking at the ball.) You will be called "Stitchface."

Homer is living the life he dreamed of. He not only saw his team play and win, he also met his favorite player who happened to give him the game ball. This is a BIRGing experience that few fans have a chance to enjoy.

Of course, sports, like life itself, are not always fair. There are times when we do not receive anticipated rewards, just as there are times when our favorite teams no longer win. This point leads us to another interesting occurrence, people who attempt to distance themselves from perceived losers—CORFing. CORFing is short for "cutting off reflective failure" and is another self-esteem enhancement technique. CORFing is akin to guilt by association. In other words, some sports fans will stop wearing their favorite team's apparel when the team loses because they worry others will see them as losers.

Research (including my own) indicates that highly identified fans are less likely to BIRG than moderate or lowly identified fans. Thus, a true fan sticks by his or her favorite team (e.g., wears their apparel and shows outward allegiance) despite the team's win-loss record. The highly identified fan, or "true" fan, may BIRG as the moderate and lowly identified fan (or "fair-weather" fan) does, but his or her victory celebration will be all the sweeter because of the long-term investment into the team. Homer qualifies as a fair-weather fan. When his teams are losing, he loses interest in them. However, when the favorite team begins to win again, Homer, like other fair-weather fans, participates in the "bandwagon" effect.

The "bandwagon" effect refers to the incidence of fans who had lost interest in a losing team beginning to grow a corresponding interest in the team as it starts, and then continues, to win. Naturally, the "true" fan tends to dislike the "fair-weather" fan, but since "everyone loves a parade," sports teams are happy to have the fair-weather fans back to support them as they push through the remainder of the season. The "Marge and Homer Turn a Couple Play" episode (#378) provides us with an example of the bandwagon effect. In this episode, the Simpsons are watching television and Kent Brockman provides a report on the Springfield Isotopes baseball team.

> *Kent*: The 'Topes are in first place since the acquisition of homerun king Buck Mitchell. Thanks to him, Springfield is once again overrun with fair-weather fans.
> *Homer*: The Isotopes are winning? To the bandwagon!

And with that, Homer and his family are off to support the Isotopes. It is fashionable once again to attend Springfield baseball games because the home team is winning. And when a team is winning, even the scalpers are happy!

YOUTH SPORTS

"I've got to quit smoking."
—Nelson Muntz

Similar to towns and cities, small and large, across the country, the residents of Springfield are more than mere spectators (and consumers) of sports; they are active participants in sports as well. Interest in sports and games generally begins at youth, and this is understandable, as it is only natural for children to participate in some sort of play. Young children generally engage in unstructured and informal forms of play with their peers (e.g., skipping rope, hopscotch, tag, and hide-and-seek). Some prefer individual sports (e.g., skateboarding) while others prefer organized team sports (e.g., peewee football).

Whether children play informal or formal sports should be a decision left to the youths themselves. For as long as we have known Bart Simpson he has enjoyed skateboarding—an unstructured activity for ten-year-olds. (Note: Bart's skateboarding will be discussed later in this chapter.) But Bart, as well as Lisa, has also participated in organized youth sport leagues. The vast majority of youth sport participants will benefit from the experience and most parents have the best intentions when they encourage their children to play sports. However, it is important that the decision whether to participate in sports or not should rest with the individual's desire to play sports. A child's desire to play a sport should be encouraged by the parents in the same manner as any other productive, nondeviant behavior would be. Determining what sport a child should play is initially addressed by the child's own interests. That is, if a child expresses a desire to play football, joining a children's football league should be encouraged. Not surprisingly, the most motivated youths to play sports are those who receive encouragement from their parents. Peer support is another important source of encouragement. Perhaps most important, the early participation in sports for children should be *fun*. Too much emphasis on rigorous practices, drudgery, analysis of plays, and overbearing parents can discourage children and make them no longer wish to take part in the game that once gave them pleasure.

Origins and Development of Youth Sports

Midway through the nineteenth century, people in Europe, the United States, and Canada began to develop efforts to organize children's lives through a combination of sports and education. In 1861, the English Parliament's Clarendon Commission proclaimed that playing cricket and football promoted such social values as team spirit and group loyalty. Furthermore, it has often been reported that the Duke of Wellington stated, "The Battle of Waterloo was won on the playing fields of Eton"—implying that sports helped to prepare soldiers for battle. Toward the end of the nineteenth century, advocates of youth sports were proclaiming the moral value of participation. "Muscular Christianity" is the term used to describe the philosophy of teaching values via sports. The idealism of Muscular Christianity had a great impact on the development of sports in English and American society, especially for boys in American schools. Team sports were supposed to teach boys how to cooperate and work productively together for others. It was believed that sport participation would help boys become strong, assertive, competitive men when they grew up. (Promoting sports for girls is a fairly recent phenomenon.) The idealism of Muscular Christianity led to the establishment of the Young Men's Christian Association (YMCA), and later the Young Women's Christian Association (YWCA).

The development of organized youth sports was not limited to the schools or a religious realm. A "play movement" developed outside the schools and gained momentum toward the end of the nineteenth century. Building playgrounds for children to play in was considered an important step in keeping kids off the streets. This mentality has continued to the present day; that is, if children are kept busy in such conventional activities as sports, they have less time and energy to engage in deviant and criminal activities. Thus, sport participation is often viewed as a positive alternative. Throughout the twentieth century, a number of organized, formal youth sports leagues developed, with baseball as one of the most popular. Today, youth soccer programs are very popular. And for good reason, as soccer is a much cheaper sport to operate and equipment is minimal when compared to such sports as football, baseball, and hockey.

In brief, it has become idealized that sport participation helps to develop positive character traits (e.g., sportsmanship, leadership skills, competition, physical fitness, cooperation, motoric competencies, and so forth).

Living Vicariously through One's Children

> **"Well, if you know a better way for me to live through my son, I'd like to hear it."**
> —Homer Simpson

As stated above, youth sport participation has many potential benefits; chief among them is physical fitness. The physical well-being of the youth of Springfield comes to the forefront in the "Bart Star" episode (#184). The Simpson family attends a "Free Health Fair" where the kids' fitness is measured and labeled as either "fit" or "fat." The Springfield boys are in bad shape and many are stigmatized with "fat" stickers placed on their oversized bellies. (Note: The topic of obesity is discussed in chapter 13.) To combat their children's obesity problem, the parents of Springfield field a peewee football team.

Playing football requires a great deal of equipment, including wearing a protective cup. Marge endures a problem often experienced by single mothers: going to the sporting goods store with her son to get the cup. Marge is uncomfortable asking the salesclerk for assistance, and Bart, as a young boy, has no experience with this either. Eventually, the purchase is made. Bart is anxious to test the efficiency of his new protective cup and challenges Milhouse to kick him in the groin in an attempt to injure him. Milhouse repeatedly kicks him in the groin and Bart laughs it off. The device works. Bart is now ready for football practice.

Ned Flanders has volunteered to coach the Springfield Wildcats. It is common for a parent of one of the players to serve as coach in youth sport leagues. Ned's two sons, Rod and Todd, are on the team. (Interestingly, Rod's jersey number is "66" and Todd's is "6," so when the two brothers stand next to each other on the sideline their combined numbers look like a "666"—the sign of the devil.) As mentioned in chapter 10, the team is co-ed. The star player is clearly Nelson and, as a result, Ned makes him the team's quarterback. The team is set. Flanders leads the team to victory after victory. However, Homer is acting like a typical overzealous parent who often detracts from the true meaning of youth sports. Homer shouts insults at Ned. He tells Ned that he is a bad coach. Ned finally reaches his boiling point and quits as coach while challenging Homer to do a better job.

Unlike Ned, Homer is an overbearing, "old-school" type of coach. He works his players too hard and makes "cuts" on a whim. Homer is now acting like the type of coach who has no business in youth sports. This reflects a problem that often arises in a variety of organized youth programs—coaches who ignore the primary reasons why youths play sports. Youth sports are supposed to provide pleasurable experiences for youths. The sports environment should be a place where youths have fun, reaffirm friendships, burn off excess energy, and receive positive reinforcement from their parents and family members. Instead of following this mantra, Homer pressures Bart to do well. Marge tells Homer to lay off Bart and accuses him of living vicariously through Bart's sport participation. Homer replies, "Well, if you know a better way for me to live through my son, I'd like to hear it." Once again, Homer has missed the point. So too, unfortunately, do many parents. Some parents actually want to relive memories of their own sporting days gone by. Other parents want to live vicariously through their children's sporting lives.

Marge reminds Homer that his father, Abe, once pushed him as hard as he is pushing Bart. But Homer is relentless in his quest to make Bart a star. Homer replaces Nelson with Bart as quarterback. This turns out to be a very unpopular decision among the Wildcats. Even Bart tells Homer that he does not want to be quarterback. This reflects the reality that most kids are aware of their own talent levels and the talent levels of others. Bart wants to be a team player and realizes the team's best chance to win is with Nelson as the QB. Homer remains firm. Bart is the quarterback and the team loses 59–0. Nelson threatens Bart after the game (he wants Bart to relinquish his QB position).

Bart is experiencing great stress—another disturbing but growing trend in youth sports. Youth sports are supposed to provide pleasurable experiences for children. Stressful situations are the result of demands that test or exceed the resources of an individual. To combat this stress, Bart fakes an injury so that Nelson can play quarterback. Although Homer wants to forfeit the game rather than play without his son, the game goes on. Nelson single-handedly (literally) leads Springfield to a 28–3 victory over visiting Arlen, Texas. After catching his own long-bomb pass for a touchdown, the out-of-breath Nelson proclaims, "I've got to quit smoking." Visiting Arlen fans are disappointed with the outcome. One Arlen supporter, Hank Hill (of the animated cartoon *King of the Hill*), comments, "We drove two thousand miles for this?" (Note: If Hank's statement is accurate, we now know that Springfield is two thousand miles from Arlen, Texas. Further, we know Springfield is a costal town as the characters have sailed out to sea from the local port.)

Homer feels really bad about pressuring his son. He invites Bart to return to the team as an offensive lineman for the last game of the season—the championship game pitting the Wildcats against Capitol City. (Note: Capitol City is not spelled consistently in *The Simpsons* series; sometimes it is spelled Capital City.) Bart is pleased. Other team members rejoin the team. They are poised to win the championship with Nelson as their quarterback and a full contingent of players. However, a rather unusual problem emerges. Chief Wiggum shows up at the game with an arrest warrant for Nelson Muntz. Bart, who has clearly learned the concept of "taking one for the team," pretends to be Nelson and allows the police to take him away. Nelson leads the team to victory. Springfield wins the championship. What a season!

Dealing with the Pressure

> **"Mercy is for the weak, Todd."**
> —Ned Flanders

Children enjoy playing with others. They like competition and they like to win; but ultimately, they want to have fun. They do not enjoy being pressured by their parents and other adults. Stress may have such a negative effect on youths that they abandon the formal sports environment. On other occasions, children may actually teach adults a lesson on true sportsmanship by developing unique coping behaviors when presented with stressful situations. Two examples are described below.

In an early episode of *The Simpsons*, "Dead Putting Society" (#19), the rivalry between Homer and Ned is passed onto their reluctant sons, Bart and Todd, respectively. Homer has always been envious of Ned, but the jealousy escalates after Ned invites Homer to his rumpus room for a beer. Not being one to turn down a free beer, Homer accepts the invitation. The rumpus room is magnificent and includes a keg of imported beer. Homer notices how well Ned gets along with his boys and becomes even more covetous. Ned's wife, Maude, serves snacks. Despite the hospitality shown to him by Ned and Maude, Homer complains to Ned: "You've been rubbing my nose in it since I got here! Your family is better than my family, your beer comes from farther away than my beer, you and your son like each other, your wife's butt is higher than my wife's butt! You make me sick!" After finishing another beer and sandwich, Homer returns to his home complaining about Ned.

Marge suggests that Homer spend some time with Bart, and off they go to play miniature golf. As it turns out, Bart is very good at putt-putt golf. Homer's golfing outing is ruined when he notices Ned and Todd are also playing miniature golf. The negative competitiveness that Homer often displays rears its ugly head yet again. Homer brags to Ned that Bart is better than Todd at miniature golf. Ned proclaims that Todd is quite a good golfer himself. Homer counters by saying Bart is going to sign up for the youth miniature golf tournament and that he will win it. Flanders warns Homer about putting too much pressure on Bart but changes his attitude after one too many insults from Homer. As a result, Ned enters Todd in the contest as well.

Homer is flat-out teaching his son to view Todd as the enemy. He makes Bart glare at a photo of Todd for fifteen minutes a day so that he will build a hateful competitive attitude. Marge confronts Homer about how hard he is pushing Bart.

Marge: Homer, I couldn't help overhearing you warp Bart's mind.

Homer: And?

Marge: Well, I'm worried that you're making too big a deal over this silly little kiddy golf tournament.

Homer: But, Marge, this is our big chance to show up the Flanderses.

Marge: I am sure it is, but why would you want to do that?

Homer: Because, sometimes the only way you can feel good about yourself is by making someone else look bad.

Homer is utilizing the self-esteem enhancement technique of "blasting." Blasting, as explained by Homer, involves the peculiar method utilized by many insecure people; specifically, making themselves feel better by putting down (or defeating) others. The idea is, if "I can beat my rival, I am better than my rival." Thus, blasting is a strategy used to reestablish or reinstate lost self-esteem. That is, when an individual has suffered a blow to his (or her) social identity, he will try to regain his positive social identity by blasting a member of an "out-group" (a rival).

Although Bart and Todd are not close friends, they do not view each other as adversaries. Bart feels like a pawn in his father's rivalry with Ned. Bart is stressing as a result of the pressure his father has placed upon the importance of his winning the miniature golf tournament. Lisa tries to help Bart. She finds books in the library on putting and Zen philosophy (*Tao Te Ching* by Lao Tzu) so that Bart can block out distractions. Lisa later applies geometry to figure out specifically where Bart should bank the ball so that it rolls into the cup. She even offers words of encouragement (something Homer should be doing): "Bart, having never received any words of encouragement myself, I'm not sure how they're supposed to sound. But here goes: I believe in you."

As the day of the tournament arrives, Homer and Ned make a bet: the father of the "nonwinning" (rather than losing) son must wear a dress and mow the other's lawn while wearing it. The wording of the bet will become critical at the conclusion of the contest! The boys are anxious and each performs admirably. Ned and Homer, however, are still living vicariously through their sons. Ned yells to his son, "Mercy is for the weak, Todd." Homer counters, "Come on Bart, remember what Vince Lombardi said, 'If you lose you're out of the family.'"

Marge slaps her husband and disgustedly says, "Homer!" (Note: There is no evidence of Lombardi ever having made this statement!)

The boys, who would rather simply have fun than compete against each other, have figured out a way to end the competitive madness. With the score tied heading to the final hole, Bart and Todd both quit and call the game a draw. Because neither boy "won," both Ned and Homer have to wear a dress while mowing the lawn. Upon viewing this sight, Marge moans, "Oh, my best dress." Lisa adds, "Why do I get the feeling that someday I'll be describing this to a psychiatrist?" Despite his own embarrassment, Homer tries to take some small comfort in realizing that Ned is also humiliated. Instead, Ned causes Homer further distress.

> *Ned*: Y'know Simpson, I feel kinda silly but, uh, you know, what the hay, you know . . . kinda reminds me of my good ole' fraternity days.
> *Homer*: D'oh! Oh my God! He's enjoying it!

Playing for a tie, although discouraged in nearly all sporting circles, Bart and Todd found a way to have fun and make their fathers' rivalry look silly—even if Ned did enjoy wearing a dress!

The playing for a tie philosophy in order to end a sports rivalry was also applied in the "Lisa on Ice" episode (#111). In this episode, Bart is on a youth hockey team—the Mighty Pigs—coached by Chief Wiggum. Homer is proud of Bart because of his hockey-playing ability. Lisa attends one of Bart's hockey practices and, at the end, Bart flings garbage at Lisa with his hockey stick. But Lisa is able to block his every attempt at hitting her. Seeing this, Apu, the coach of the Kwik-E-Mart Gougers, signs her up to be his team's goalie. Suddenly, Bart and Lisa are on opposite sides. Lisa leads her team to consecutive victories. Perceiving Lisa as a better hockey player than Bart, Homer now views her as his "number one" child. Because Homer turned on Bart, Marge cheers for Bart and his team so that he will not feel abandoned. Bart and Lisa, who have often gotten on each other's nerves, are uncomfortable being pitted against each other. Their mother tries to reassure them at the dinner table.

> *Marge*: We love you both! You're not in competition with each other! Repeat: You are not in competition with one another.

Homer: Hey! Apu just called. This Friday Lisa's team is playing Bart's team. You're in direct competition. And don't go easy on each other just because you're brother and sister. I want to see you both fighting for your parents' love.

During the week leading up to the big hockey game, the siblings act tough toward each other. The sibling rivalry has also piqued the curiosity of the townspeople. A great deal of money has been gambled on the game. In fact, Moe, who owes gamblers sixty-four thousand dollars, visits the Simpsons' home looking for any inside information (e.g., whether or not Bart or Lisa has any injuries unknown to the public).

Hockey night in Springfield arrives. Krusty sings the national anthem. He forgets some of the words and, overall, does a poor job, although not as bad as Roseanne Barr's infamous rendition in 1990 before a "Working Women's Night" crowd of more than thirty thousand people in San Diego for a Padres–Reds game. Barr's effort was highlighted by her spitting and then grabbing her crotch. Roseanne claimed that she was merely attempting to demonstrate baseball humor. Most observers and commentators were offended.

As for the game, Bart manages to score one goal and Lisa blocks another one of his attempts. Ultimately, regulation ends with the score tied 3–3. The game comes down to penalty shots. It is Bart versus Lisa for the game. Homer and Marge are divided. Homer tells his wife, "Oh, my God, Marge. A penalty shot, with only four seconds left. It's your child versus mine! The winner will be showered with praise; the loser will be taunted and booed until my throat is sore." As Bart and Lisa intensely stare at each other, each flashes back to moments in their lives when they were there for each other. They both drop their gloves and sticks—not to brawl but to cause a draw. They would rather have the game end in a tie where neither one of them is the winner at the other's expense. Marge says she has never been so proud of Bart and Lisa. Homer counters that they are both losers!

The audience members are, at first, impressed by this display of sibling love. Snake, who has escaped from prison, thinks the kids are sweet and wishes there had been peewee hockey when he was a kid. Who knows, maybe he would not have been a criminal if he had played youth sports. The euphoria and happiness of the children's innocent gesture of playing for a tie as a coping device for dealing with overbearing parents, adults, and stressful environments are no match for the growing realization among the many gamblers in the hockey arena that all bets are off. A riot ensues. Snake, the criminal who was raised without benefit of youth sports participation, joins in.

The Soapbox Derby

> **"I might remind you both, I did design that racer, the driver is essentially ballast."**
> —Martin Prince

Another popular organized youth sport activity is the well-known Soapbox derby. The original derby started in 1933 in Dayton, Ohio, and later moved to Akron. Derbies are now held throughout the United States. The original idea behind establishing soapbox derbies is that such an activity provides a valuable bonding experience for fathers and sons to work together to create various self-powered vehicles. Despite past scandals, the derby has become an international event that includes female participants. A great emphasis has been placed on catching cheaters (some people, for example, use weights and magnets to increase speed).

Bart and Homer become involved with the Soapbox derby in the "Saturdays of Thunder" episode (#44). As described in chapter 5, Homer has failed a "fatherhood" test. He is so out-of-touch with what his son is up to that he has no idea Bart is building a soapbox racer in the garage. Homer asks Bart how his racer, "Li'l Lightning," is coming along. Bart responds, "It's slow, it's ugly, it handles like a shopping cart." Homer offers his assistance and Bart reluctantly accepts. With help from an instructional book written by Bill Cosby, Bart and Homer manage to build a mediocre racer. Proud of their achievement, Homer says, "Thank you, Bill Cosby, you saved the Simpsons!"

Among the other Springfield boys to build racers are Martin—who has his racer tested in a wind tunnel—and Nelson—who has a racer with gladiator-type weaponry attached to its wheels. At the qualifying race, Bart has false hope that his racer will do well. He quotes his hero, three-time Soapbox derby champ Ronnie Beck, "Gravity is my copilot." If this is truly the case, the laws of gravity have been altered, as Bart's racer does so poorly it fails to cross the finish line. Martin's racer is easily the fastest. However, he loses control, crashes, and breaks his arm. He will be unable to compete in the championship event. However, Martin wants anyone to win except for his nemesis, Nelson. As a result, Martin offers Bart the opportunity to race his car against Nelson in the finals. Bart happily accepts.

At first, Homer is upset and feels betrayed that Bart would rather race someone else's car than the one they helped to build together. (Note: There is a gap in this storyline because the audience was led to believe that "Li'l Lightning" never crossed the finish line and, therefore, Bart never would have qualified to race his own car in the championship event.) Bart feels confident that with Martin's car he will easily win the race against Nelson. But his victory will be shallow if his father is not there to share in the celebration. As the race looms and Bart looks around the stands for his father, Homer is home retaking the "fatherhood" test. After all the time he has spent recently with his son, he passes the test easily. Suddenly it dawns on Homer that he needs to be at the soapbox race to support his son no matter what car he races. Homer arrives in time. And when Bart sees his father cheering for him, he is stoked. The race proceeds and Bart wins. Displaying unsportsmanlike behavior, Bart taunts Nelson. Marge scolds her son, "Bart, you know, there is such a thing as being a bad winner." To which Bart replies, "Mom, I never won before, and I may never win again!" A fairly plausible explanation!

Bart is given one more opportunity to BIRG at the medal ceremony. His hero Ronnie Beck hands him the championship trophy. Bart takes this opportunity to thank his father for his support.

> *Bart*: I was alone out there, but someone was riding with me in spirit. This is for you, Dad!
> *Homer*: No, son, you earned it.
> *Martin*: I might remind you both, I did design that racer, the driver is essentially ballast.

In the Simpson family, like many American families, any kind of victory is one to be cherished!

ALTERNATIVE AND EXTREME SPORTS

> **"Hmm. I'm afraid the bone's broken. Well, that's all of them."**
> —Dr. Hibbert

The development of sports' increasing popularity throughout the twentieth and twenty-first centuries has had some interesting consequences. Many youths have become frustrated with the stressful, overly specialized, highly competitive, and selective character of organized sports. Many sports have become so rule-oriented that people have sought alternatives to "traditional" sports. Further, many of these "alternative" sports involve a relatively high-risk scenario that has led them to be called "extreme" sports.

Skateboarding

> **"It's always good to see young people taking an interest in danger."**
> —Captain Lance Murdock

When *The Simpsons* first began, Bart was the primary focus. Bart's persona has generally been that of a rebel and an individualist. Thus, despite the organized team sports (previously described) that Bart has periodically participated in, he is most accurately identified as a skateboarder and a daredevil.

The original skateboarders of the 1930s and 1940s used nothing more than a two-by-four on roller-skate wheels. Their single focus was to start at the top of a hill and successfully avoid colliding with something, or someone. Skateboarding was modestly popular in California during the 1950s. The sport grew in popularity along with surfing. In fact, these skateboarders were known as "sidewalk surfers." Water surfing and sidewalk surfing were sports for nontraditional, rebel, sport enthusiasts. Skateboarding took a huge step forward in the late 1970s when Alan "Ollie" Gelfand invented the "Ollie"—a now fundamental skateboarding jumping technique that allows skaters to hop over obstacles and onto curbs, guardrails, and so on. When properly executed, the skateboard appears to stick to the skater's feet in midair. By the time *The Simpsons* first aired in the late 1980s, skateboarders were the rad pack of daredevils who would take on any jump or height challenge. Their individualistic flair for drama and daring made skateboarders the envy of all would-be daredevils.

Today, skateboarding, as with most extreme sports (to be discussed later in this chapter), is relatively popular with the younger generation. Sports such as inline skating and skateboarding continue to gain in popularity due in part to increased media exposure, such as ESPN's "X Games." For many youths, it is skateboarder Danny Way who is their favorite athlete, not basketballer Kobe Bryant, tennis player Roger Federer, or pro football player LaDainian Tomlinson. In late 2002, Way built the first Megaramp, which allowed him to set skateboarding records for the farthest "ramp to ramp" distance skated (sixty-five feet) and "highest air" (eighteen feet, three inches). He has built a number of ramps since then to increase his record in both categories. In July 2005, Way jumped the Great Wall of China on a skateboard, becoming the first person to clear the wall without motorized assistance.

Perhaps Way's skateboarding prowess was inspired by the "Bart the Daredevil" episode (#21), which first aired in 1990. In this episode, the Simpson family attends an event at the Springfield Speedway featuring "Truckasaurus"—a giant, fire-breathing mechanical dinosaur made out of trucks. Running late for the event, Homer mistakenly drives onto the field of the Speedway and gets the car stuck in the muddy terrain. Truckasaurus attacks the Simpsons' car and nearly crushes it with the family still inside. (Fearing a lawsuit, the Simpsons receive a minor-sum check from the Truckasaurus owners for damages.)

A special treat that evening includes a surprise guest appearance from Captain Lance Murdock—the "World's Greatest Daredevil." (Murdock's character is based on real-life daredevil Evil Knievel.) Murdock attempts to jump (with his motorcycle) over a water-filled tank of sharks, electric eels, and even a lion! He successfully makes the jump. However, while celebrating, Murdock falls backward into the tank and has to be rescued and sent to the hospital. Highly impressed with the nature of daredevilry, Bart believes he has found his purpose in life. Bart tells Homer he wants to be a daredevil. Homer discounts Bart's determination and says, "He-he. Kids say such stupid things."

Bart begins to perform skateboarding stunts for the kids in the neighborhood. One stunt backfires and he gets injured. His friends are afraid and run away, leaving Bart quivering in pain. Eventually, Bart is discovered lying on the ground and is taken to the hospital. Dr. Hibbert is concerned by Bart's daredevil exploits and he warns Bart of the "Three Stooges Ward"—a ward of the hospital reserved to give care to children who have injured themselves imitating stunts they saw "on television, films, and the legitimate stage." Bart is undeterred by Dr. Hibbert's attempt at aversion therapy. Furthermore, Bart's desire to become a daredevil is only fueled all the more when he meets the recuperating Lance Murdock.

> *Bart*: It's an honor, Lance. How are you feeling?
> (Lance is in so much pain that it hurts as he gives Bart the "thumbs up.")
> (A loud crack is heard.)
> *Lance*: Ow! Doc, I heard a snap.
> *Dr. Hibbert*: Hmm. I'm afraid the bone's broken. Well, that's all of them.

Murdock's dangerous stunts have led to literally every bone in his body having been broken at least once. Murdock is impressed with Bart's skateboarding stunts and tells him, "It's always good to see young people taking an interest in danger." Lisa is outraged by Murdock's comment to her brother. She realizes that the last thing Bart needs is someone to actually encourage him to engage in dangerous stunts. Before they leave his hospital room, Bart receives an autograph from Murdock. (He signed his autograph by putting the pen in his mouth.)

Bart continues his skateboarding stunts. But the thrill is gone for both the kids in the neighborhood, who have seen all his tricks by now, and for Bart, who has just learned the lesson all adrenaline junkies face: once the thrill is gone, a more dangerous stunt is needed to maintain the "rush." As a result, Bart announces that he is going to jump the Springfield Gorge.

The scene is set. Bart has climbed the top of the gorge and after looking down below he becomes a little apprehensive about the jump. But he is willing to go on with his stunt nonetheless. As he prepares himself, Bart is confronted by his father, who has climbed the gorge after him. Homer pleads with Bart not to attempt this dangerous stunt. He takes Bart's skateboard away from him and stands on it. Bart (perhaps a bit relieved) promises his father that he will not attempt any dangerous stunts again. Homer is pleased. The two hug when, suddenly, Homer starts rolling down the hill. Terrified at first and then thinking he might actually successfully sail over the gorge, Homer proclaims, "This is the greatest thrill of my life! I'm king of the world! Wooo, wooo! Wooo, wooo!"

Unfortunately, Homer does not make it over the gorge. Instead, he is seriously injured and must be airlifted out. He is then transported to an ambulance, which crashes. Homer and the gurney strapped to him wheel out the back of the ambulance, and you guessed it, Homer falls all the way down into the gorge again.

Extreme Sports

> **"I'm getting aggro on this kicker."**
> **—Nelson Muntz**

Before his crash into the gorge, Homer experienced such an extreme rush that he shouted out he was enjoying the thrill of his life. Such is the appeal of extreme sports. The term "extreme sports" is a collective idiom used to describe a number of sporting activities that involve risky, adrenaline-inducing action. Features of extreme sports may include speed, height, danger, peril, stunts, and illegality. Participating in extreme sports involves a willingness to experience extreme results (e.g., death or euphoria). Extreme sports include (but are not limited to) base jumping, bouldering, bungee jumping, inline skating, elevator surfing, skateboarding, surfing, snowboarding, parasailing, ultimate fighting, whitewater kayaking, and windsurfing. Extreme sports are most often engaged in by young adults who bring with them their own subcultural behaviors (e.g., slang language, clothing style). Marketing, rather than any inherent danger, often has a great influence on which sports are labeled extreme and which ones are not. For example, snowboarding is labeled an extreme sport and skiing is not, even though skiing down a mountain is at least as fast and dangerous as snowboarding. Furthermore, sports such as football and rugby are as adrenaline-inducing as any extreme sport, and yet, they would not be considered as such.

Beyond Bart's skateboarding, examples of extreme sport participation are far more limited than those of more traditional sports (e.g., football and baseball). In the "When You Dish upon a Star" episode (#208), Homer is parasailing with his family. Parasailing is a relatively popular sport in which the rider is hitched to a parachute-like canopy, known as a parasail, and is set aloft in the air. The parasail is attached to a long towrope, which is pulled by a speeding form of transportation (e.g., a speedboat). When the speed exceeds the stalling speed, the parasail rises, hoisting the rider into the air. Homer insists on going first. However, because of his weight, he has a hard time getting airborne. He keeps yelling at Marge to make the boat go faster and eventually he is off the ground. Homer is having such a great time sailing in the air—admit it, it sounds like fun to fly like a bird—that he yells at Marge to go even faster so that he can climb ever higher. Marge tries to abide by Homer's wishes, but the strain on the boat's engine causes it to overheat, spark a fire, and burn off the rope tied to the boat and Homer. Without the safety rope, Homer is adrift on his own. He heads inland through a thick area of trees and crashes through the skylight of Alec Baldwin and Kim Basinger's secluded house. Although injured, Homer survives the ordeal and for a short period of time befriends Alec and Kim (see chapter 2).

In the "Little Big Mom" episode (#236), Homer takes his family snow skiing at Mount Embolism. Many of the dangers associated with skiing are cleverly presented, starting with that tricky "jumping on the chairlift while it is moving" requirement. As the family awaits their turn to board the chairlift, Bart distracts Homer, who then gets his ski stuck in the chair and ends up riding up the hill upside down beneath the chair. Marge, Bart, and Lisa have successfully boarded the chairlift together. As they climb increasingly higher, Marge becomes more apprehensive about skiing. They finally reach the top; Bart and Lisa execute the tricky dismount out of the chair, while Marge stays in it. She yells back to the kids that she will meet them at the lodge.

Lisa decides to cross-country ski. She thinks that it's fun and safer. However, she is attacked by very menacing deer. A park ranger has to rescue her, but he yells at Lisa to leave the deer alone. The park ranger does not believe her story about the deer attacking her. Meanwhile, Homer has made it to the top of the mountain. The trail names he has to choose from are less than reassuring (for the fainthearted skier): "The Widowmaker," "The Spinebuster," and "The Colostomizer." While looking over his options of trails to ski, Homer is greeted by

Ned Flanders. Ned is wearing a very tight, formfitting ski outfit that leaves nothing to the imagination. This outfit represents the role of technology in a sport that has been around for centuries. Tight-fitting outfits are more aerodynamic and allow for faster speeds. And as Ned explains to Homer, "It allows for maximum mobility. Feels like I'm wearing nothing at all!" Ned then shakes his body. The image disturbs Homer so much that he leans backward and starts tumbling down the mountain. (Note: This scene is similar to the classic footage of ABC's *Wide World of Sports* example of the agony of defeat.)

Bart has found a snowboarding class being taught by Otto the bus driver. Snowboarding would seem to be a perfect fit for Bart. Surprisingly, snowboarding is a very small aspect of this episode and is primarily limited to the dialogue between Otto and his students. The lesson of the day: teaching subcultural, or slang, language.

> *Dolph* (commenting on Nelson's trick stunt): Whoa! Phat 540!
> *Nelson*: I'm getting aggro on this kicker!
> *Bart*: Stomp that pickle revert!
> *Otto*: Excellent! Your lingo is progressing nicely.
> *Bart*: Can I go to the bathroom?
> *Otto*: Uh, uh! Say it in "Snowboard."
> *Bart*: Um . . . I gotta blast a dookie?
> *Otto*: Dook on!

As stated previously, participants of extreme sports (as with any subculture) often establish their own subcultural behaviors, such as slang language. It is important for subcultures to create their own unique jargon as it distinguishes them from the wider society. As a snowboard instructor, Otto teaches not only the techniques of snowboarding but also the lingo (supposedly) spoken by participants. As Bart might say, "Here's hoping you stomp your pickle, reverts!"

Meanwhile, as Homer, Bart, and Lisa were all having their adventures on the slopes, Marge is relaxing in the ski lodge. (Note: It is never quite clear where Maggie is during this ski trip.) She is stretched out on a comfy lounge chair drinking hot chocolate near a blazing fire. Marge is so relaxed that she is unaware of Disco Stu's attempts to "hit" on her. Before long, her family arrives and Marge attempts to explain why she is so content: "Skiing fanny-first into a crevasse isn't my idea of fun. The only risk I'm taking is running out of marshmallows." Ah, sitting by a fireplace drinking hot chocolate, nothing extreme or dangerous about that. Unless, of course, the lodge clock that is precariously nailed to the wall next to Marge falls on her. The clock does fall directly on her leg and Marge suffers a compound fracture.

Seems all the Simpsons faced an extreme situation: Lisa was attacked by deer; Homer went backwards down a hill; and Marge sustained an unusual broken leg while on a ski trip. And yet, only Bart's snowboarding is considered an extreme sport!

As previously stated, younger people are more likely to participate in extreme sports than older people. Although "old" age is often a matter of one's perspective, it is generally assumed that "baby boomers" are too old to be participating in extreme sports. In fact, older people should be careful about participating in any type of "action" or contact sport. But many "baby boomers" think they can still do the things twenty-year-olds can do. For example, in January 2007, California governor Arnold Schwarzenegger injured himself in an odd way while on a ski trip. No, a clock did not fall on his leg and break it; instead, Schwarzenegger fractured his femur (thighbone) when he tripped over his own pole while standing still (Hubert 2007). Doctors described this as a highly unusual way to break such a large bone. Arnold is not alone, as amateur athletes from the baby boom generation are keeping medical offices and emergency rooms busy across the nation, studies show. In fact, injuries to this generation are so common the term "boomeritis" is now used to describe the plethora of problems that affect athletes who are past forty years old but insist on playing sports as if they were in their twenties.

Maybe there are safer sports for baby boomers, say bowling?

Homer the King Keggler

> **"Mr. Simpson bowled a perfect game without the aid of steroids, crack, angel dust, or the other narcotics that are synonymous with pro bowling."**
> —Mrs. Krabappel

Aging baby boomers are just one reason why bowling is the number one participation sport in the United States. And the writers of *The Simpsons* are clearly aware of bowling's popularity with the masses, as there are many episodes that deal with bowling.

Few people love bowling as much as Homer Simpson. After all, as Homer states, "If horseracing is the sport of kings, then surely bowling is a . . . very good sport as well." In the "And Maggie Makes Three" episode (#116), we learn that Homer's dream is to be a pin monkey—a person who works at a bowling alley, often setting up the pins (before there were automated pin resetters). In this episode, Homer and Marge tell Bart and Lisa the story of Maggie's birth. Homer explains that after having worked at the Springfield Nuclear Power Plant for eight years he was finally debt-free. Further, Homer had the pleasure of experiencing something that many workers wish they could—he quit his job and told off his boss. (Note: in *Seinfeld* they referred to this as the "march in.") In fact, he uses Mr. Burns's head as a bongo while joyfully quitting a job he hates so that he can pursue one he cherishes. As Homer leaves Mr. Burns's office for what he assumes is the last time, he proclaims, "Good-bye mind-numbing backbreaking labor forever. Hello dream job in paradise." Lisa thinks it is sort of romantic to quit an old job to pursue a dream job.

Homer secures a job as a pin monkey at Barney's Bowl-a-rama. To help celebrate his first day at his dream job, Homer takes Marge out on a romantic date. It was Homer's perfect day. A great new job, wining and dining his wife, followed by making love to his wife at home after the date. Homer tells Marge that things are perfect and he hopes things never change. Weeks go by and Homer is on top of the world. He loves everything about his job, including spraying the alley's bowling shoes and putting sanitizing cakes in the urinals. "Mmm . . . bowling fresh. Mmm . . . urinal fresh," Homer declares. What a perfect life he has. But as we all know (and as the title of this episode explains), things change. Marge informs Homer that she is pregnant (with Maggie). Homer pulls clumps of hair from his head, just as he had upon learning Marge was pregnant with Bart and Lisa. With one more mouth to feed, it will be impossible to continue working at the bowling alley and make ends meet.

Obviously, Homer does not want to give up his dream job at the bowling alley. He asks for a raise but is denied. He is told there is not enough business at the bowling alley to warrant a salary increase. Using logic that only Homer can understand, he tries to increase business by firing a shotgun into the air outside the bowling alley. As he is retelling this story to the family, Lisa says, "Mom, make Dad tell the story right!" To which Marge responds, "That's what really happened." It is clear that Homer will have to quit the job at the bowling alley if he hopes to raise a family. The crew at the bowling alley presents Homer with a satin jacket with "Sorry you had to 'Split'" on the back. Homer knows the only place he can find a job that pays a high enough salary to support his family is back at the power plant.

Dejected and demoralized, Homer heads in to see Mr. Burns about getting his job back. Not only does he have to "march back in" to beg for his old job, but Homer's prized new satin jacket is destroyed by acid rain. Mr. Burns, as with many employers in this position of complete power over an employee, takes full advantage of this situation. Homer is sent past the door marked "applicants" to a small doggy door labeled "supplicants." Homer has to literally crawl through the doggy door on his hands and knees through a tunnel that leads to Burns's office. Although some bosses might refuse to give an ex-employee his job back, Burns relishes the power it gives him over Homer. As per his company policy, Burns gives Homer a "demotivational plaque" (designed to break what is left of one's spirit) that is installed in front of his workstation. The plaque reads: "Don't Forget: You're Here Forever."

As much fun as the "march in" (when one quits a job) is, the "crawl back" (when one needs to beg for the old job back) is far worse. Homer is forced to live a life of drudgery (as he perceives it) compared to his dream life. On the day of Maggie's arrival into the world, Homer is still a little resentful toward Maggie, as he views her as responsible for the nasty turnaround in his life. During the delivery Homer exclaims, "It's wonderful, it's magical. Oh boy, here it comes. Another mouth." However, when Homer first lays eyes on Maggie he becomes overjoyed. Such are the trade-offs in life. Burns has power and wealth, but no children. Homer has a job he hates, but a wife and three kids who love him. Which option sounds better to you?

Homer no longer works at a bowling alley but he does still love to bowl. In the "Team Homer" episode (#140), Homer and Moe go to the bowling alley to bowl but they are told that there aren't any lanes available because it is "league night." Like millions of other Americans, Homer and Moe are interested in joining the league. Unfortunately, they cannot afford the five-hundred-dollar registration fee. An exasperated Homer declares, "I'm tired of being a wanna-be league bowler. I wanna be a league bowler." Thus, reluctantly, Homer decides to ask Mr. Burns for the money. When Homer arrives at Burns's office, he discovers that is boss is "out of it." Burns thinks

Homer is the Pillsbury Doughboy.

> *Homer*: Mr. Burns, I, uh, was wondering if you'd like to sponsor my bowling team for five hundred dollars.
> *Burns*: Oh, why certainly, Pop 'n Fresh. I—I owe my robust physique to your tubes of triple-bleached goo!

And with that, the registration fee is taken care of. Next, Homer and Moe recruit Apu and Otto to round out the four-person team. After a rough start, Homer's team, the Pin Pals, roll to one victory after another. They climb the standings to second place, trailing only the Holy Rollers, a team consisting of Ned Flanders, Reverend Lovejoy, and their wives.

Meanwhile, Burns has regained his senses and reviews with Smithers the recent checks he has written. He discovers a check written to the Pillsbury Doughboy for five hundred dollars and recalls Homer's visit to his office. Burns and Smithers decide to confront the Pin Pals directly at the bowling alley.

> *Burns*: Look at them, Smithers, enjoying their embezzlement.
> *Smithers*: I have a much uglier word for it sir, misappropriation.
> *Burns* (to Homer): Listen here, I want to join the team.

Obviously, the Pin Pals do not want Burns on the team; he is old and weak, and it is doubtful he can even lift a bowling ball, let alone roll it down the alley. And for poor Homer, once again, Burns is interfering with his ideal world of bowling. As previously described, Homer lost his dream job and now he fears he will lose the championship because Burns demands that he take one of the four Pin Pals members' place on the team. There is nothing Homer can do but let Burns on the team. Otto is kicked off.

On the night of the championship game pitting the Pin Pals against the Holy Rollers, Burns distributes league shirts with the Pin Pals logo emblazoned on them. Burns is a lousy bowler. The rest of the team pick up his slack but ultimately the championship comes down to Burns's last roll . . . which is two pins short. But, as Burns is bowling, Otto is in the background and tips over a novelty machine. The vibrations cause the two pins to fall over and the Pin Pals win the championship. Although Homer's championship was not perfect—he would have rather won it with Otto—as captain of the team, he is pleased to be presented with the championship trophy. Once again, however, Burns interferes. Because he paid for the registration fee, he makes claim to the trophy. Homer's moment of glory has been greatly compromised by his nemesis. It should be noted that Homer and the remaining Pin Pals break into Burns's house and steal the trophy back. However, Burns releases his hounds and they get Homer.

As in life, it seems even bowling mocks Homer. He has such a passion for it and yet any of his bowling-related victories seem to end poorly. Perhaps bowling a perfect game, a 300 score, would make Homer truly happy. Well, in the "Hello Gutter, Hello Fadder" episode (#232), Homer does roll a perfect score and achieves his fifteen minutes of fame that, apparently, each of us is guaranteed sometime in our lifetime. (Note: In the 1960s, Andy Warhol, a major figure in the pop art movement, made famous the idea that everyone will be famous for fifteen minutes. This expression also refers to the fleeting condition of celebrity.) In this episode, Homer was supposed to come home from work to have a tea party with Maggie. But when his coworkers, Lenny and Carl, invite him to go out bowling with them, Homer calls Marge to cancel his date with his infant daughter. Homer tells Marge, "The cooling tank just blew, and they're taking Lenny to the hospital." Marge is distraught when she hears that Lenny is supposedly hurt.

At the bowling alley, Homer is having a great game. He is angry at Burns yet again and pictures the pins as replicas of Burns's head. He is so focused on hitting the pins that he continues to roll strikes heading into the final frame. Kent Brockman is at the scene and reports live.

> *Brockman*: This is Kent Brockman, live from Barney's Bowl-a-rama, where local pinhead Homer Simpson is on the verge of a perfect game.
>
> (The Simpson family is at home watching TV when this live report interrupts their program.)
>
> *Lisa*: Hey! There was no accident at the plant. Dad just wanted to go bowling.
>
> *Marge*: He shouldn't have deceived me, but I'm just so relieved Lenny's okay.
>
> *Brockman*: This could be the greatest individual achievement

in the history of Springfield. Which proves just how pitiful this town really is.

Homer does it! Everyone in the bowling alley applauds and congratulates him. Apparently the bowling alley is very close to the Simpsons' home as Marge and the kids are at the alley to watch Homer roll the final of his three strikes in the tenth frame.

Although his family is upset with him for lying, and Maggie in particular becomes cold to Homer, the rest of the town treats him as a hero. He's invited to Bart's class to give a speech. Mrs. Krabappel introduces Homer to the class: "Children, today's local hero is Homer Simpson. Mr. Simpson bowled a perfect game without the aid of steroids, crack, angel dust, or the other narcotics that are synonymous with pro bowling." (Good thing they did not test for alcohol!) Next, Homer serves as a celebrity in the central chair of *Springfield Squares* (a parody of the *Hollywood Squares*) where he is referred to as Homer "Perfect Game" Simpson. Homer also makes a walk-on appearance during a Penn and Teller performance that ruins the whole illusion, causes Teller to talk (he rarely ever speaks) and endanger his life, and leads to Penn attacking him.

The "fifteen minutes" of fame Homer has enjoyed is gone. Homer learns of this while watching TV with his family. Anchors of an entertainment news show declare that Homer Simpson is "yesterday's news," a "warmed-over Fred Flintstone," and a "one-trick pony that should be put out to stud." Homer misinterprets the last comment and states that he will begin with Maude Flanders! Being "put out to stud" is not the only thing Homer is confused by; either that, or he is in a state of denial that his fame has come to an end. Lisa helps to explain what the anchorperson meant.

Lisa: Dad, what she's saying is, you've had your moment in the sun, and now it's time for you to gracefully step aside.
Homer: Lisa, I know what's going on here. They did it to Jesus, and now they're doing it to me.
Marge: Are you comparing yourself to our Lord?
Homer: Well, in bowling ability.

The sham of hero status being bestowed upon someone who rolls a perfect game in bowling (because of how common a 300 game is) aside, Homer had truly loved the limelight that his bowling accomplishment brought him. He had reached an incredible high, a thrill, a rush, that was about to be matched by an equally powerful sense of despair as he crashed to the depths of gloom. Homer walks the streets of Springfield in a deep state of depression. The Doors' eerie song "The End" plays in the background. He contemplates suicide and heads to the Springfield State Building (similar to the Empire State Building in New York City). Homer goes to the top of the building and stands on a ledge at the observation deck area. He contemplates jumping. There is a line of people behind him and the man closest to Homer states, "Less chat, more splat, pal." And then he pushes Homer!

It seems hopeless. Homer is tumbling to a certain death when, seemingly out of nowhere, Otto appears. Otto just happens to be bungee jumping (an extreme sport). In midair, Homer grabs ahold of Otto and, luckily, they both survive.

With a new outlook on life, Homer decides to spend more time with his kids. He quickly learns that Bart and Lisa have full lives of their own and so he decides to spend more time with Maggie—"the forgotten Simpson" as Homer calls her. After a rough start, father and daughter bond with each other. This episode concludes with Homer and Maggie bowling. Homer has bowled a 296 game and Maggie has managed to bowl a perfect game! But Homer penalizes her for stepping over the foul line and deducts five points from her score. Talk about insecurities! Maggie is just an infant so she is easily distracted by what just happened. Homer tickles her and she giggles. For Maggie, spending any type of quality time with her father is reward enough. Perhaps some day, Homer will learn this same lesson.

. . . AND STILL MORE SPORTS IN SPRINGFIELD!

One thing should be abundantly clear at this point. Sports have been a huge part of *The Simpsons* throughout its run. Due to space considerations, Springfield's professional sports teams are not discussed in this chapter (as stories related to them have appeared throughout this book) and neither are many of the other sports-related stories (for example, Bart was a jockey in the "Saddlesore Galactica" episode [#239]; the entire Simpson family and a number of other Springfield residents played tennis in the "Tennis the Menace" episode [#260];

Homer was a boxer in "The Homer They Fall" episode [#156]; and Grandpa Simpson participated in the Senior Olympics in the "Moe 'n' a Lisa" episode [#384]).

Further, *The Simpsons* addresses a number of important issues related to sports, such as gambling, franchise relocation, and the use of mascots, but again, to give justice to all these topics would be to double the length of this chapter. It seems an entire book could be written just on sports and *The Simpsons*. The review in this chapter was primarily limited to actual sport participation, especially by the members of the Simpson family. The attention paid to sports in *The Simpsons* reflects its importance in the United States, as well as in most societies of the world.

Chapter 12

Springfield's Educational System

Where Every Child Is Left Behind!

"I have had it with this school! The low test scores, class after class of ugly, ugly children."
—Superintendent Chalmers

E nacted by the Senate and House of Representatives, the No Child Left Behind Act of 2001 was established, among other reasons, to improve the academic achievement of disadvantaged youths and to prepare, train, and recruit high-quality teachers and principals. In January 2002, President Bush signed this act into law. Bush believes that the quality of our public schools directly affects us all as parents, students, and citizens. And further, too many children in America are segregated by low expectations, illiteracy, and self-doubt. "In a constantly changing world that is demanding increasingly complex skills from its workforce, children are literally being left behind" (Bush 2002).

Because the primary purpose of the No Child Left Behind Act is to assure quality education for all American students, accountability is an important aspect of this legislation. Every state must establish strong standards for what every child should know and learn in reading and math in grades three through eight. Student progress and achievement will be measured for every child, every year. The results from these tests are being made available in annual report cards so that parents can measure school performance and statewide progress, and evaluate the quality of their child's school, the qualifications of teachers, and their child's progress in key subjects. Individual schools are held accountable for improving performance of all student groups so that every school will be performing at proficient levels within twelve years of the act being passed.

The concept behind the No Child Left Behind legislation is a good one. Ideally, this act will afford all children equal access to a quality education. Unfortunately, this policy has not positively affected the school children of Springfield, as Bart has remained in the fourth grade for nearly two generations! Furthermore, even the academically gifted Lisa remains in the second grade. Obviously, these children have been "left behind" because the characters on *The Simpsons* do not age. However, as we shall see in this chapter, if they did age, many of the children of Springfield would suffer from the overall ineptness of Springfield's educational system.

The Institution of Education

Education is one of the most important social institutions of society. Education is so essential that it is often promoted as the solution to nearly every social problem that exists. For example, when racial and ethnic disputes arise between two distinct groups, teaching tolerance is emphasized. If a drug problem exists in a certain environment, whether it be at a workplace or a specific neighborhood, educating people on the potential dangers of drugs is promoted as the most viable solution. As it becomes ever more apparent that alternative energy sources must be developed (see chapter 9), it is up to universities, educated people, and savvy creative individuals to lead the way. In short, social policymakers generally promote education as the answer to most, if not all, social problems. But, why has the burden of solving all major social problems fallen upon the education system? And when did this occur?

As described in chapter 8, Martin Luther was one of the first proponents of mass education. However, he did not promote education as a means for solving social problems, but rather so that people could read the Bible for themselves. Nonetheless, the fact that only the social elites were afforded the opportunity to gain an education in Luther's era (1497–1560) reveals that education has not always been viewed as the tool to solve social problems. In fact, throughout most of human history, rulers had found that an ignorant mass is much easier to control than a knowledgeable one.

Universal public education never did emerge during Luther's lifetime. Instead, mass education would emerge with the rise of industrialization. Mass education began with industrialization because society needed literate people to operate machinery and to develop further technology. In the United States, mandatory education laws were finally instituted in the early 1900s. The No Child Left Behind concept discussed in the introduction to this chapter reflects the pattern established since the time of industrialization. Specifically, if people do not possess the complex skills necessary to thrive in society, they will be left behind. To avoid this social problem, school-aged children have been targeted to assure they possess the necessary academic skills to handle the demands of a technological culture.

The value of education can be measured in a variety of ways. But what grabs most people's attention is the salary discretion based on one's level of education. According to data provided by the US Census Bureau, college graduates made an average of $51,544 in 2004, compared with $28,645 for adults with a high school diploma. High school dropouts earned an average of $19,169 and those with advanced college degrees made an average of $78,093 (Ohlemacher 2006). Eighty-five percent of Americans aged twenty-five and older had at least a high school diploma or the equivalent in 2000, compared to a little more than 50 percent in 1970. Clearly, the signs are positive. Fewer children had been left behind in 2000 (before the No Child Left Behind legislation was passed in 2002) compared to 1970. Interestingly, George Bush's home state of Texas had the lowest proportion of adults with at least a high school diploma (78 percent) in 2000.

The census data reveals that as one's level of education increases, so too does one's salary. Thus, in the tradition of "knowledge is power," it should be stated that "knowledge is wealth." In this regard, it is clear that education provides a great avenue for economic upward mobility. Further, because many jobs today require specific bits of knowledge, the educational system serves as a screening and placement system to prepare people for society's occupational structure. In other words, one must have the proper credentials to work at many high-paying jobs. Homer Simpson, for example, was lucky to find a relatively high-paying job (although we do not know exactly how much money he earns) at the nuclear power plant—especially in light of the fact that his position required technical training (see chapter 9).

Realizing the relationship between education level and income, educational opportunities afforded to all Americans should serve as motivation for people to perform well in school so that they can be successful in the socioeconomic system. Unfortunately, not all school systems are created (or funded) equally, and, as a result, not all youths are on a level playing field. Unequal funding in schools is one such problem within the institution of education. The effect of teacher expectations on students may also hinder some youths in their desire to pursue an education that may lead to a high-paying career. In general, students who are *expected* by their teachers to do better than other students generally do learn more. Conversely, those school-children who are perceived as less than stellar students are likely to perform poorly in school or be "tracked" (students who are placed in classes with different content or different levels of content based on their teachers' assessment of their abilities) in less competitive classes. Teacher expectations fuel a child's self-fulfilling prophecy in education. Elementary-aged children are the most likely to be affected by teacher expectations. In this regard, Lisa will forever be tracked and perceived in a positive manner by her teachers, whereas Bart is practically doomed to failure in his future school years.

Ideally, education concerns itself with developing and providing knowledge. Competent teachers will provide information to students who are eager and prepared to learn. Parents encourage their children's pursuit of an education and assure that homework is completed in a satisfactory manner. Administrators will support teachers and students in this pursuit. And of course, funding is a nonissue.

Since education is promoted as the solution to social problems, it must have all the answers, right? And surely, the field of education is free from bickering, political agendas, and other ills that plague all the other social institutions, right? Unfortunately, as anyone in the field of education can attest, there are numerous problems in education. As a college professor, I could write a book on my observances of dysfunctional behavior and policy in higher education (but I will save that for another time). However, the creative people behind *The Simpsons* provide us with enough material to evaluate the state of education in America. From a "burnout" bus driver who occasionally places the welfare and safety of schoolchildren in jeopardy, to teachers who dread going to work, to cost-cutting administrators who care more about saving a buck than assuring a high-quality education, the Springfield educational system reflects many of the issues and problems that confront the American institution of education.

Teaching and Learning

> **"Let's get the year rolling with an all-school spelling bee!"**
> —Principal Skinner

Over the years, *The Simpsons* has provided us with numerous glimpses of the daily activities of Springfield Elementary. (Note: There are a number of *Simpsons* episodes dealing with college and adult school, but the focus of this chapter will be on elementary school.) In particular, we have come to know two of the teachers rather well. These teachers are Edna Krabappel, Bart's fourth grade teacher, and Elizabeth Hoover, Lisa's second grade teacher. Each of these women has taken upon herself the challenge of educating a group of young, middle-class children. And although they both entered the profession of teaching with the idealistic hope of positively shaping youths, they have endured their own personal crises. We have also come to know a number of other characters at Springfield Elementary School, including Groundskeeper Willie, Principal Skinner, and Superintendent Chalmers.

Teaching in Springfield

> **"It's the children I love."**
> —Mr. Bergstrom

Although they are commissioned to educate students, teachers have their own limitations. They are not perfect and they do not have perfect lives. Miss Hoover, for example, has a host of problems, some of which are revealed in the "Lisa's Substitute" episode (#32). In this episode, Hoover is late to arrive to class. All the students—except for Lisa, who is busy studying—are misbehaving by running around the room, throwing paper airplanes, and gossiping about why their teacher, Miss Hoover, is late for class. At 9:15 AM Miss Hoover is escorted into class, while crying, by Principal Skinner. Lisa comments under her breath, "God, she's been dumped again." Miss Hoover explains to the class that she will not be staying in class for long because she just came from the doctor's office and found out she has Lyme disease. She states that Principal Skinner will take over the class until a substitute teacher arrives. Naturally, the young students want to learn more about Lyme disease. Skinner eagerly explains that Lyme disease is spread by parasites called ticks.

> *Principal Skinner*: When a diseased tick attaches itself to you
>   and begins sucking your blood—
> *Miss Hoover* (nearly ready to faint): Oh . . .
> *Principal Skinner*: Malignant spirochetes inflict your blood-
>   stream, eventually spreading to your spinal fluid, and on
>   into the brain.
> *Miss Hoover*: The brain? Oh, dear God!

Skinner escorts a sobbing Miss Hoover to the door as she heads home to fight off the deadly ticks attached to her. Skinner immediately shifts into teaching mode by following Miss Hoover's lesson plan. As he begins to teach subtraction, the class is interrupted by students' gasps from another room. Skinner yells out that he knows Bart Simpson is responsible for such an outburst.

Sure enough, Bart has managed to gross out his classmates by showing a video for show-and-tell demonstrating how kittens are born. His video is entitled, "How Kittens Are Born: The Ugly Story." Bart tells the class that his family kept Snowball II: "We were going to keep the gray one (kitten) but the mother ate her." The kids yell out, "Eweee." Martin tells Mrs. Krabappel that Bart is traumatizing the kids. She agrees. But before Edna can stop Bart, he holds up the remote and says, "Oh, look, this is really cool. When I hit reverse, I can make them go back in!"

Meanwhile, back in Lisa's class, Principal Skinner is engrossed in teaching when suddenly a man dressed like a Western cowboy enters the room shooting his six-gun. Skinner, a Vietnam veteran, thinks he is under fire and "hits the deck"! Is this gun-toting person some type of a crazed maniac that periodically causes havoc in our schools? No. It is Mr. Bergstrom, the substitute teacher who is shooting blanks from his gun in an attempt to immediately grab the attention of his students. Using props is a ploy often utilized by elementary school teachers because children have limited attention spans. College professors, on the other hand, do not need to rely on such gimmicks and instead rely on providing knowledge to students who are capable of sitting at attention for hours at a time. (Although, there are some college-aged students that have not mastered this skill!)

Mr. Bergstrom has certainly caught the attention of Miss Hoover's students, and especially of Lisa, who develops an instant crush on him. (Note: Mr. Bergstrom is voiced by Dustin Hoffman, but listed in the credits as Sam Etic.) Bergstrom begins by saying, "I am a Texas cowboy and the year is 1830. And you younguns can ask me any questions you'd like." The first boy to ask a question wants to know if they can play kickball after lunch instead of science. This type of question represents one of the many challenges presented to substitute teachers, as students generally believe that when they have a substitute teacher they are not going to do "real" schoolwork. The students often challenge the substitute teacher as well because they know, sooner or later, the substitute will no longer be their teacher.

In yet another attempt to grab their attention, Mr. Bergstrom challenges the class to find three things wrong with his outfit. Lisa takes the challenge. The first mistake was his belt buckle, which read "State of Texas." As Lisa points out, Texas was not a US state in 1830. Lisa then points out that his revolver was not created until 1835. He acknowledges her as being correct.

> *Lisa*: Three, you seem to be of the Jewish faith.
> *Mr. Bergstrom*: Are you sure I'm Jewish?
> *Lisa*: Or Italian.
> *Mr. Bergstrom*: I'm Jewish.
> *Lisa*: And there weren't any Jewish cowboys.
> *Mr. Bergstrom*: Very good. (To the class) And I am also wearing a digital watch.

Mr. Bergstrom tells Lisa that her responses are "close enough" and rewards her with his cowboy hat. He also corrects Lisa by saying, "And for the record, there were a few Jewish cowboys, ladies and gentlemen. Big guys, who were great shots, and spent money freely." Mr. Bergstrom's last comment was meant to discount the negative stereotype of Jewish people as being tight with their money. Lisa proudly wears Mr. Bergstrom's hat while he continues his unorthodox approach to teaching. Her admiration for Mr. Bergstrom is cultivated by his true desire to reach his students.

Lisa's perception of Mr. Bergstrom is almost compromised when she returns to the classroom after school ends. She finds Mrs. Krabappel "putting the moves" on Mr. Bergstrom. Krabappel has become a bitter, desperate woman over the years and she views Mr. Bergstrom as a real catch. However, Bergstrom is not interested in Edna and tells her, "It's the children I love." When Lisa overhears that she nearly floats away in love with her substitute teacher. Lisa goes home and tells her mother all about her crush on her teacher. Lisa is on top of the world. She has a crush on a positive male role model and she couldn't be happier. After a couple of weeks, Marge tells Lisa to invite Mr. Bergstrom over for dinner. On the very morning Lisa plans to extend the invitation to her substitute teacher, she is alarmed to discover Miss Hoover has returned to teach her class. Miss Hoover explains her absence to her students.

Miss Hoover: You see class, my Lyme disease turned out to be
    psychosomatic. (She writes the word on the board.)
Ralph: Does that mean you were crazy?
Janey: No, that means she was faking it.
Miss Hoover: No, actually it was a little of both. Sometimes
    when a disease is in all the magazines and all the news
    shows, it's only natural to think you have it.

Although Lisa would generally show concern for Miss Hoover, right now she is devastated. All she can think of is seeing Mr. Bergstrom one last time. Lisa runs out of the school looking for him. She tries his apartment building, but Bergstrom has already moved out. A woman there, who has also fallen for Bergstrom, tells Lisa that he left for the train station. Mr. Bergstrom is on his way to his next job in Capital City. Lisa catches up to him just in time. Her little heart has been broken. Bergstrom tries to comfort her by saying it is the nature of substitute teaching for teachers to enter and leave students' lives. Lisa tells Mr. Bergstrom that he is the best teacher she has ever had, or will ever have, and pleads with him to stay. But Mr. Bergstrom tells Lisa he is needed more in the projects of Capital City.

Lisa's loss will be another student's gain. If there were enough Mr. Bergstroms to go around, perhaps no child *would* be left behind.

In the "Lisa's Substitute" episode, Bart not only tested the limits of his teacher by showing a video of the birth of his cat, but he also ran for class president, much to the chagrin of his teacher, Mrs. Krabappel. His campaign antics (which included being "pro asbestos," making promises he could not possibly keep; and telling his opponent, Martin, to "eat his shorts") were enough to challenge the patience of any teacher.

And yet, as we learn in "The Seemingly Never-Ending Story" episode (#369) Edna Krabappel stayed in Springfield in an attempt to help Bart. In this episode, Moe describes how he dated Edna Krabappel when she first arrived in Springfield as an idealistic teacher who believed she could positively influence her students. As he recounts his dating experience with Edna, they were ready to run off together at the end of her first year of teaching at Springfield Elementary. Instead, she saw Bart struggling with his schoolwork and decided to stay in order to help him and other underachievers like him. A disgruntled Moe comments, "Fate likes to play a little game— 'Up yours, Moe.'" (Note: There is a chronological storyline problem here, as Edna Krabappel is depicted as being much younger when Moe first meets her and yet, since Bart has always been in the fourth grade, only one year has passed for Edna. Further, it is implied that Edna has become more disenchanted with teaching as the years have gone by even though only one year has gone by.)

Not only is it implied that the once idealistic Mrs. Krabappel has become burned out from teaching, she has also become a bitter, lonely single woman. (Note: Mrs. Krabappel is divorced. She is sometimes referred to as Ms. Krabappel on the show, but usually as Mrs. Krabappel.) Edna is shown in a number of episodes looking for a man to marry. But it is Principal Skinner with whom she has had the longest involvement. The two have been dating (on and off) for more than half of The Simpsons run. In fact, as far back as the "Mom and Pop Art" episode (#222), Edna has impatiently waited for Seymour Skinner to propose marriage to her. But alas, Seymour is a renowned "stuffed shirt" who still lives with his mother. In the "Mom and Pop Art" episode, Seymour and Edna are romantically paddling in a rowboat through the flooded streets of Springfield.

> *Seymour*: Edna, I'm going to pop you a question. I hope the answer is "yes." (He reaches into his pocket and pulls out a jewelry box and as he opens it he asks Edna) Do you think Mother will like this hat pin?

Edna (very disappointed): Oh . . . yes.
Seymour: You've made me the happiest man on Earth.

Edna's unhappy personal life has begun to take its toll on her. This once optimistic teacher often merely goes through the motions. She manages to enjoy a few romantic moments here and there (including "secret" meeting places in the school) with Seymour Skinner (as well as a few other suitors), but for the most part she remains unfulfilled. Unfortunately, she appears to be wasting her time chasing after Seymour Skinner. Not only is he a "mamma's boy" who still lives with his mother; he is "married" to his career as an elementary school principal. In fact, as we discover in the "Sweet Seymour Skinner's Baadasssss Song" episode (#100), Skinner is "lost" without his position as principal. In this episode, Skinner gets into trouble with his boss, Superintendent Chalmers. Chalmers, as his title implies, is the superintendent of Springfield schools. He has a very threatening demeanor and dislikes Skinner and Springfield Elementary School. Chalmers often shouts "Skinner!" in a very disparaging manner. Despite the fact that Chalmers sometimes dates Skinner's mother, he is quick to blame Skinner for all sorts of problems, even those out of his control. For example, Chalmers tells Skinner, "I have had it with this school! The low test scores, class after class of ugly, ugly children."

Always looking for any excuse to fire Skinner, Chalmers finds the perfect opportunity in the "Sweet Seymour Skinner's Baadasssss Song" episode. Early in this episode, Chalmers is scolding Skinner over the phone for making an apparent anti-Semitic remark. Trying to defend himself, and sweating profusely, Skinner says, "I know the Weinsteins' parents were upset, Superintendent, but, but, ah, I was sure it was a phony excuse. I mean, it sounds so made up: 'Yom Kip-pur.'" Although Skinner may not be aware of the Jewish holiday of Yom Kippur—perhaps the most important day of the Jewish year—this is not the reason why Skinner is fired. Instead, it is an incident sparked by Skinner's nemesis Bart Simpson that leads to his ultimate downfall.

Bart has brought his dog, Santa's Little Helper, to school for show-and-tell. However, the dog wanders off from class. Sniffing the aroma of food from the cafeteria, Santa's Little Helper enters the school's venting (heating) system in search of the source of this smell. Everyone can hear the dog wandering through the vents, so

Skinner sends Groundskeeper Willie into the venting system to retrieve the dog. Willie complains.

> *Groundskeeper Willie*: What? Have ye gone waxy in yer beester? I canna fit in the wee vent, ye croquet-playin' mint-muncher!
> *Skinner*: Grease yourself up and go in, you—golf-speaking work-slacker.
> *Groundskeeper Willie*: Ooh. Good comeback.

And with that, Willie greases himself up and crawls through the venting system looking for Bart's dog. In a scene reminiscent from *Alien*, Santa's Little Helper runs quickly and eerily by Willie in adjoining vents. Willie finally catches up with the dog in the vent high above the gym floor. Unfortunately, the two of them get stuck inside the tight-fitting ducts. Their combined weight causes the ducts to sag. As a result, they have to be rescued by the fire department. At the height of the chaos in the school gym, Chalmers shows up for a sneak inspection. Chalmers walks into the gym and yells out, "Skinner!" The fire department messes up the rescue attempt. The ladder slips and crashes through a set of windows. Santa's Little Helper falls safely into Chalmers's open arms. At first, the sight of the dog calms the superintendent, but when Willie falls on top of him, that is the last straw.

> *Chalmers*: You're fired.
> *Skinner*: I'm sorry. Did you call me a liar?
> *Chalmers*: No, I said you were fired.
> *Skinner*: Oh. That's much worse.

And with that, Skinner loses his job, his life, his very identity. Many people have their very identity tied to their job position, and when that is taken away, it becomes very difficult for them to make the transition to another sphere of life. Bart and Milhouse stumble upon Skinner shopping at the Kwik-E-Mart wearing sneakers, blue jeans, and a sweater. The boys are shocked to see Skinner in a context different from what they are accustomed to. Milhouse states, "Bart, look. It's Principal Skinner, and I think he's gone crazy. He's not wearing a suit or tie or anything." Bart feels guilty for costing Skinner his job. Bart approaches Skinner and tells him he is sorry about his dog getting him fired (and biting him).

Who would have thought it? Bart actually misses his old principal. Meanwhile, Skinner has been replaced by Ned Flanders. Flanders has a much different administrative style than Skinner. Upon his introduction to the student body Ned proclaims that he hopes to put "the 'pal' back in 'principal,'" All the kids giggle. Flanders has a bowl of candy that children can help themselves to when they are sent to his office. Not surprisingly, Bart finds a way to be sent to the office on a regular basis just so he can have free candy.

Skinner, of course, misses his job. Upon a chance meeting with Bart, Skinner invites him over to his house. Bart does visit Skinner and asks him about the photo of Skinner and his army buddies taken during the Vietnam War. Skinner tells Bart about his war days. Later that afternoon, Skinner barbecues while Bart informs him about the latest doings at school. Bart informs Skinner that Flanders has instituted an "honor system" (Note: It is not explained what this means exactly) at school and has eliminated detention. Skinner, who loves a structured environment, laughs at such a notion. Bart agrees by saying the teachers are so afraid of the children that they refuse to leave the faculty lounge. Skinner laughs, "That place must be falling apart!" That night, Bart and Skinner take a walk on the beach. Skinner places a seashell to his ear but is bitten by a crab inside! From there, the two new best friends head off to Skinner's favorite place for pizza.

Springfield Elementary School *is* in chaos. Martin is inside a cage, Nelson is tearing apart textbooks, students are running around aimlessly, and Milhouse squirts ketchup over his tummy while telling Bart, "This is great. Not only am I not learning; I'm forgetting things I used to know. And it's all thanks to you, Bart." Bart is not pleased with being responsible for the total breakdown of the Springfield Elementary School system. Shockingly, even Bart realizes he has gone too far. He realizes that children must have structure, especially in school. And if Bart Simpson can figure this out, how can the administrators be so clueless?

When Bart goes over to Skinner's house the following evening, Seymour's mother hands him a note. In his letter, Skinner tells Bart how much he has enjoyed their friendship, but he needs meaning in his life. As a result, Skinner has pursued his second love, and reenlisted in the US Army. Skinner writes Bart a letter and sends him a photo of himself in uniform at Fort Springfield. Bart tells Lisa that he really misses Skinner, not just as a friend but as an enemy. Lisa replies rather philosophically, "I think you need Skinner, Bart. Everybody needs a nemesis. Sherlock Homes had his Dr. Moriarty, Mountain Dew has its Mello Yello, even Maggie has that baby with the one eyebrow."

Missing Skinner, Bart visits him at Fort Springfield. Skinner admits that the army is not what it used to be and states that he would like to get out of his new commitment and become principal again. Bart has devised a plan and shares it with Skinner.

> *Bart*: Here's the plan. Once Chalmers comes for his next inspection and sees how crappy the school has gotten, he'll fire Ned on the spot.
> *Skinner*: Uh, one question remains. How do I get out of the army?
> *Bart*: No problemo. Just make a pass at your commanding officer.
> *Skinner*: Done and done. And I mean done.

Skinner tells Bart that there is one potential flaw with his plan. If Flanders is somehow fired and he is reinstated, he will not be able to remain Bart's friend unless he becomes a good student. Bart says that will probably never happen. However, both Skinner and Bart realize that at least they were good friends once.

Chalmers shows up for his inspection and seems unconcerned by the unruly behavior. Bart tells Chalmers that he would fire Skinner under these conditions, but Chalmers admits to Bart that he really doesn't like Skinner. And besides, Chalmers believes that with the state of America's public educational system, all schools will be as bad as Springfield Elementary in just a few short months! Just as Chalmers is about to leave the school, Flanders makes his morning announcements over the intercom. Flanders begins by saying, "Let's thank the Lord for another beautiful school day. . . ." Chalmers is incensed. "Thank the Lord? Thank the Lord? That sounded like a prayer. A prayer? A prayer in a public school?! God has no place within these walls, just like facts have no place within organized religion! Simpson you get your wish. Flanders is history." So, even though Flanders is an inept administrator, that was not justification to fire him. But, as soon as he says "the Lord," Chalmers condemns him for leading a prayer.

Although this episode first aired in 1994, the debate over the role of religion and prayer in public schools continues to be a controversial topic. And, the topic of the separation of church and state will remain a heated debate in public schools for years to come.

Skinner gets his job back. Bart and Skinner meet each other in the hall, and they both realize they must return to their old roles. They give each other a quick hug and walk away. Bart snickers as he has taped a "Kick Me" sign on Skinner's back. Not to be outdone, Skinner has taped a "Teach Me" sign on Bart's back. And thus the teaching-learning saga continues at Springfield Elementary School.

School Projects and Spelling Bees: Valuable Learning Devices

> **"Lisa, every good scientist is half B. F. Skinner and half P. T. Barnum."**
> —Principal Skinner

Elementary-aged students are in school for long periods of time—far more than college students. Consider that most elementary (and high school) students attend school five days a week for approximately seven to eight hours a day compared to a "typical" full-time college student who attends for fifteen hours a *week*. Whereas college students have, ideally, mastered the art of sitting still and paying close attention to their professors, most young students have limited attention spans and are easily distracted. Consequently, many elementary school teachers find it helpful to employ such learning devices as show-and-tell, student projects, and spelling bees. A couple of examples of show-and-tell were previously discussed. An example of a "student project" is provided in the "Duffless" episode (#75).

In "Duffless," Lisa has genetically altered a tomato. She is very proud of herself because she believes her school project may end world hunger. One morning Lisa places her gigantic tomato on the breakfast table and proudly explains its importance.

Lisa: I've grown a futuristic tomato by fertilizing it with anabolic steroids.

Bart: The kind that help our Olympic athletes reach new peaks of excellence?

Lisa: The very same. I think this tomato could wipe out world hunger.

The tomato is so large that Lisa envisions it large enough to feed an entire family. Lisa brings her tomato to school and at the end of the day she intends to bring it back home with her. As she carries her tomato out of school, Lisa realizes she has forgot her math book. Lisa asks Bart to hold onto the tomato for her as she runs back into the school for her book. Originally intending no harm to Lisa's class project, Bart is tempted by the sight of Principal Skinner bending over to tie his shoe. Bart can hardly contain himself before he flings the giant genetically enhanced tomato at Skinner's butt. Pieces of tomato fly onto nearby children who laugh in joy at the sight of their principal with a giant tomato stain on his pants. Lisa rejoins Bart and the other students and to her horror discovers what Bart has done to her science project.

Lisa seeks revenge against Bart. She creates a new project comparing Bart's intelligence to that of a hamster. Lisa's proposal is to determine whether or not her brother is dumber than a hamster. Without informing Bart what she is up to, Lisa secretly conducts tests on both her brother and the hamster. For example, she places a food pellet on a high shelf within an elaborate hamster cage (similar to a living room) to ascertain whether or not the hamster can figure out a way to get the treat. The hamster pushes a miniature couch over to the shelf and successfully climbs up the couch and then the shelf. To challenge Bart, Lisa places a delicious cupcake high atop the living room bookshelf. At first, Bart repeatedly jumps in the air thinking he can retrieve it that way. Next, he climbs the bookshelf, one shelf at a time. Just as he reaches for the cupcake the bookshelf falls backwards on top of him. The hamster also knows enough not to touch an electrified food pellet machine, whereas Bart continues to get zapped while attempting to reach an electrified cupcake.

Eventually, Bart learns of Lisa's project when he reads her report. He vows that she will pay for this deceit. And the best time for Bart to exercise his revenge is the next day at the Springfield Elementary School science fair.

With the flair of a carnival showman, Bart draws the crowd's attention to his project: "Miracle of Science." In dramatic fashion, Bart proclaims that he will answer the question that has plagued mankind: "Can hamsters fly?" Bart removes a box to reveal Lisa's hamster wearing a pilot's hat, goggles, and a scarf inside the cockpit of a small motorized toy plane. The crowd is mesmerized by the very sight of the adorable-looking hamster inside an airplane. Lisa protests, "But this has no scientific merit." The crowd quickly dismisses her. Principal Skinner agrees with the sentiments of the crowd and states, "Lisa, every good scientist is half B. F. Skinner and half P. T. Barnum." And with that, Skinner hands Bart the first-prize ribbon.

Showmanship. Even in science, it is important!

Although a dramatic flair enhances scientific projects, showmanship takes a backseat to pure knowledge when it comes to spelling bees. Spelling bees are a common occurrence in elementary schools across America. Every year millions of students take part in spelling competitions. Some students dread these annual school events and are relieved to drop out in the early rounds before the stress mounts too severely. Some students, however, study for hours a day and learn the spelling "rules" in the hopes of gaining glory as a spelling bee champion. Of note, the "spelling bee" is an American term that came into use by the 1870s. The word "bee" has long been used to describe a busy gathering of people who come together for a special social purpose, such as quilting, spinning, logging, or raising a barn (Hartman and Ross 2006). The National Spelling Bee is so popular that the final round of the two-day event has been shown on ESPN since the early 1990s and is now shown on ABC. ESPN's *SportsCenter* routinely shows highlights of the spelling competition on its popular "Top Ten Plays of the Day."

Interestingly, the ability to spell words correctly seems most important in elementary school. Think about it. How often have you heard of college students participating in spelling bees? Why don't corporations and workplaces across the United States have their employees challenge each other in spelling bees? By the time youths reach high school, they are text messaging one another with abbreviations for words completely unrecognizable by the "correct spelling" community. Most people who send e-mails to each other place little importance on the spelling and correct punctuation of words. And office workers know they can always rely on their computers' spell check program to correct errors in spelling. And yet, schoolchildren are placed in the often-stressful environment of a "spelling bee."

A spelling bee is actually a wonderful academic tool designed to teach children the theory behind the correct spelling of words. Many students will memorize the spelling of thousands of words. Such a memorization exercise helps to stimulate intellectual development in young people.

After a long summer recess, many students return to school a little "rusty" in their academic habits. Realizing this, Principal Skinner, in the "I'm Spelling as Fast as I Can" episode (#303), decides to have a spelling bee on the first day of school. Skinner makes his announcement over the intercom:

> *Principal Skinner*: Let's get the year rolling with an all-school spelling bee!
> *Lisa* (happy to hear such an announcement, jumps from her desk): Woo-hoo!
> (Lisa's classmates, who clearly lack her eagerness to participate in a spelling bee, stare disbelievingly at her.)
> *Lisa*: Sigh! I guess I won't be popular this year, either.

The students meet in the school's auditorium. As we all have attended elementary school, everyone knows the routine. Students stand in line and are given a word to spell one student at a time. If they misspell the word, they sit down. If they spell the word correctly, they remain on stage for the next round. Skinner, of course, is leading the spelling bee. It is Bart's turn.

> *Principal Skinner*: Bart, your word is "imply."
> *Bart*: Imply. I-M-P . . .
> *Nelson* (interrupting): Bart said, "I am pee." He's made of pee!
> (The students laugh.)
> *Bart*: Well, I got my laugh. I'm out of here!

Bart and Nelson clearly are not in the "spirit" of the spelling bee. They prefer juvenile hijinks to the pursuit of academic excellence. Bart, the underachiever, is happy to get offstage early, especially on a high note (having made everyone laugh). Nelson makes a joke at Bart's expense to distract his schoolmates from his own less than stellar academic intellect. Lisa, on the other hand, is an entirely different story. She thrives in the academic setting and looks forward to any opportunity to shine above others. This is her way of compensating for being unpopular in school.

Lisa wins the spelling bee and, as such, qualifies for the state spelling bee finals. Skinner presents her with a prize—a crude model of the planet Mars. Upon examining the "prize," Lisa tells Skinner, "This is just a kickball with 'Mars' written on it." Skinner counters, "Behold . . . the Red Planet!" The rest of the children applaud. Lisa is very happy to have won the spelling bee. She rushes home to tell her parents. Marge tells Lisa she is very proud of her and happy that she has the spelling bee to concentrate on, rather than her crusade to "Save the Whales." As Marge informs Lisa, "Face it. They're doomed!"

Her spelling prowess continues as Lisa wins the state spelling bee contest. Lisa's family is once again proud of her.

> *Marge*: Lisa, I'm so impressed! You're the state champion!
> *Bart*: Finally! A Simpson has a trophy without a bowling ball
>   on it.

Lisa's spelling expertise also makes the local news as newscaster Kent Brockman proclaims, "And speaking of news stories, here's another. Springfield spelling phenom Lisa Simpson has qualified for spelling's answer to the Olympics: the Spellympics. In a related story, the Spellympics is being sued by the Olympics for the use of the suffix 'lympics.'"

The Spellympics are held in Calgary and the Simpsons travel there to support Lisa in her quest for the gold medal of spelling. In a hilarious spoof on grand openings for the Olympics, the Spellympics are started by the release of thousands of bees! These bees begin to sting the audience members. A military jet flies overhead to spray the bees. The bees die but the humans survive!

To this point, the spelling bees have all been about who can correctly spell the words they are given. Lisa has made it to the final three. She is ever so close to winning the Spellympics. But the Spellympics suddenly take a dark undertone. Master of Ceremonies George Plimpton informs Lisa that she must "throw" the contest so that a cute boy named Alex will win. Lisa cannot believe she has been asked to "take a dive" at a spelling contest. But Plimpton explains to her that the very survival of the Spellympics is dependent upon a cute boy winning it. (Assumingly, Lisa is not deemed cute enough for high television ratings.) As an enticement, Plimpton offers Lisa free tuition at any of the "Seven Sisters" women's colleges.

Lisa is completely distraught by the corruption of the Spellympics. She does not know what to do. On the one hand, the honorable thing to do is for her to try her best to win the competition. On the other hand, the free tuition represents her best opportunity to attend a good college. After dwelling on her dilemma all day long, Lisa dreams about the "Seven Sisters" colleges. The Seven Sisters are prestigious northeastern liberal arts institutions founded in the nineteenth century to educate women. The seven colleges officially became linked in 1926 by the Seven College Conference designed to create a united appeal for donations.

Mount Holyoke is the oldest of the Seven Sisters colleges, having opened in South Hadley, Massachusetts, in 1837. Mount Holyoke set the standard by instituting rigorous admission standards and emphasizing the sciences. Vassar opened in Poughkeepsie, New York, in 1865 and became the first institution to include an art museum among its facilities. Financial concerns prompted Vassar to open its doors to men in 1969. It was the first women's college in the country to turn coeducational. Radcliffe, located in Cambridge, Massachusetts, was founded by students seeking instruction from Harvard University. In 1999, it officially merged with Harvard. Bryn Mawr was founded in Pennsylvania by Joseph W. Taylor in 1885 to provide education to Quaker women. Barnard, located in Manhattan, opened in 1889 as an independent college affiliated with Columbia University. Smith College, located in Northampton, Massachusetts, first allowed men into its graduate programs in the 1970s, but refused men admission in its undergraduate classes. Wellesley, another Massachusetts school, opened in 1875. Hillary Rodham Clinton is a graduate of Wellesley.

In Lisa's dream, the Seven Sisters come to life, with each school being represented by a college-aged woman wearing a toga. They advise her, "Get the free ride!" Each woman attempts to entice Lisa to attend her specific college:

Barnard: We are Columbia's "girl next door."
Radcliffe: Meet Harvard men.
Wellesley: Marry Harvard men!
Mount Holyoke (a drunk woman): Party like me!
Vassar (a woman with hairy arm pits): Nonconform like me!
Smith: Play lacrosse like me!
Bryn Mawr: Or, experiment like me! (She kisses the Smith girl.)

Her dream of the Seven Sisters only further confuses Lisa. When the Spellympics finals resume the next day, Lisa makes it clear she will not take a dive. She is penalized by getting comparatively tougher words to spell. When she is near certain victory, Lisa proclaims that she was asked to "throw" the competition but she refuses to do so. She intends on winning and spelling the last word correctly. Unfortunately she misspells the word and loses the competition. She also loses the free college tuition offered to her as a bribe. Lisa is dejected. She also feels like she let her family and the residents of Springfield down by not winning the Spellympics. That is a lot of weight to carry on such small shoulders. However, when she returns home, she is thrilled to find a huge welcoming party awaiting her. The crowd offers Lisa a "hip-hip, hooray" cheer. Chief Wiggum sums up the collective sentiment of the community the best when he tells Lisa, "With second prize, you're the biggest winner this town has ever had. Before you, it was the woman who dated Charles Grodin."

And with that, Lisa's academic accomplishments bring glory and pride to her family and community.

Issues and Problems in Education

> **"Now be careful with those video cameras, children. In order to buy them, the school board had to eliminate geography."**
> —Principal Skinner

As stated in the beginning of this chapter, education is often promoted as the solution to nearly all of society's social problems. Unfortunately, there are many problematic issues associated with the American educational system. Many of these problems are reflected in *The Simpsons*'s portrayal of Springfield Elementary School. One major problem centers on the limited finances of many schools. Some do not have enough money for books for their students. Art classes and sports programs are often sacrificed in light of limited finances. Principal Skinner often complains about budget cuts as the source of Springfield Elementary's limited finances. When he finds money to fund one project, it often comes at the expense of something else. For example, in the "It's a Mad, Mad, Mad, Mad Marge" episode (#247), Skinner distributes video cameras to all the children so that they can make their own film documentaries as part of a school project. Skinner warns the students, "Now be careful with those video cameras, children. In order to buy them, the school board had to eliminate geography. (He padlocks a globe.) This globe will never spin again." Other examples of budget constraints abound in various *Simpsons* episodes.

Violence is another problem at many schools in America. Springfield Elementary School is filled with bullies who terrorize students. Nelson is the primary culprit. Another problematic issue at many schools is the lowering of academic standards. There is an alarming trend of the "dumbing" down of the curriculum at all levels of education. Examples include social promotion, the lowering of qualifying exam scores, and rewarding students for *trying* rather than *accomplishing*.

Although there are a number of issues and problems in education depicted in *The Simpsons*, the review here will be limited to standardized testing and cheating in school.

Standardized Testing

"I tell you, that standardized testing, it never lies."
—Principal Skinner

In the "Principal Charming" episode (#27), Seymour Skinner and Patty Bouvier (Marge's sister) are on a date at the Springfield Revolving Restaurant. Patty complains about the slow service. Eventually a busboy appears at their table. Skinner recognizes him as a former pupil of Springfield Elementary School.

> *Skinner*: Well, well, well, if it isn't little Jimmy Pearson. Class of '71, I believe.
> *Jimmy*: Good evening, Principal Skinner.
> *Skinner* (yelling): Pearson! Get this woman a glass of water immediately and tuck in that shirt.
> *Jimmy*: Yes sir. (He runs away.)
> *Skinner* (to Patty): Nearly thirty and still working as a busboy. I tell you, that standardized testing, it never lies.
> (Patty laughs.)

Is Principal Skinner right? Does standardized testing accurately predict the future of people while they are in elementary school? Many people in education believe so. Standardized test scores, along with grades, are the major criteria by which students are screened, tracked, and placed. The argument in favor of using standardized testing rests with the idea that all students receive the exact same test and therefore no one receives a test that is more, or less, difficult than others. The alternative to a "standardized" test is a uniquely designed test for every student. This is clearly not a viable option. Standardized tests are easier to administer (numerous copies are made, instead of numerous versions of a test) and easier to grade (only one answer key is needed).

Other arguments in favor of standardized testing include the idea that they improve the accountability of students and schools. In line with the mandates of the No Child Left Behind Act, standardized tests will be implemented in reading, math, and science to assure that no child is failing to meet minimum government requirements in these vital subject areas. (Some people argue that standardized testing should be extended to other subjects as well.) With test data results, schools can measure how well teachers, school programs, and individual students are doing compared to others.

Proponents of standardized testing also believe that such tests motivate students to actually learn the material rather than just memorize materials for tests. Standardized tests cover such a broad area that it is nearly impossible to memorize all the material. However, if students have actually learned the subject area, they should be able to answer a wide range of questions that may appear on a standardized test. Further, proponents of standardized testing argue that such tests help to screen out students who are not prepared for the next level of education. This is important, they argue, because knowledge is cumulative. In other words, students who struggle at their current grade will certainly struggle at the next stage.

Standardized testing has its detractors as well. There are many arguments put forth to end standardized testing. For example, standardized tests can be culturally biased, or unfair. It is often argued that standardized tests are written for middle-class students and not inner-city or culturally diverse youths. A strong argument against standardized testing rests with the reality that all school districts are not equally funded nor are all students equally prepared (by teachers and administrators) to do well on standardized tests. Opponents of standardized testing also worry that teachers may spend too much time conducting tests rather than teaching diverse subjects.

Many people worry that the importance placed on standardized tests causes too much stress for children. Test-takers may feel nauseated, go into a cold sweat, or even "freeze up." Psychologists refer to this as "test anxiety." Furthermore, if a student does poorly on a standardized test, he or she may develop a negative self-attitude. This negative sense of self may trigger a negative self-fulfilling prophecy, leading to an even greater downward spiral.

Perhaps most troubling to opponents of standardized testing is their knowledge of the fact that any test given is a measurement of that student's knowledge level on that specific test. And therefore, standardized test results are not always accurate predictors of a student's future (whether it is in college or a career).

Among the variations of standardized testing to be conducted at Springfield Elementary School are the "Career Aptitude Normalizing Test" (CANT) and the general intelligence aptitude (IQ) test. The students of Springfield take the CANT test in the "Separate Vocations" episode (#53). The CANT test is designed to pinpoint the children's future careers. Lisa is highly disappointed to discover that her test results indicate she is best suited to be a "homemaker." Among the seemingly limitless opportunities for Lisa, she envisions herself as a jazz musician. Lisa explains, "I've got it all figured out. I'll be unappreciated in my own country, but my gutsy blues stylings will electrify the French. I'll avoid the horrors of drug abuse, but I do plan to have several torrid love affairs. And, I may or may not die young, I haven't decided." Lisa's future aspirations take a greater hit when she is told by a teacher at the "Li'l Ludwig's Music Studio" that she will never be a great jazz musician because she has inherited a finger condition know as "stubbiness" (her fingers are too stubby). The teacher adds that this gene usually comes from the father's side of the family! Considering Lisa has never aged past second grade, we may never know what the future actually holds for her; and therefore, we will never be able to judge the accuracy of the CANT results.

As for Bart, his test results indicate that he should be a policeman. Most viewers of *The Simpsons* are certainly not surprised that Bart's future is connected to the law, although many of us would presume he would be on the "wrong" side of the law. In an attempt to foster his interest in law enforcement, Bart is offered an opportunity to do a "ride-along" with officers Lou and Eddie. Bart's idea of police work is shaped by media portrayals and not reality.

> *Bart*: Hey, fellas, let's go shoot some bad guys.
> *Lou* (laughs): Well, it doesn't quite work that way, son.
> *Eddie*: People see movies like *McBain* and they think its all bang bang, shoot-'em-up, cops-'n'-robbers.

Both Bart and Lisa are affected by their standardized tests results. Lisa has become disinterested in school and starts to act out in negative ways. Bart, who received an "honorary badge" after helping Eddie and Lou make an arrest, has a taste for the power that comes with wearing a badge. As a result, Principal Skinner enlists Bart as a hall monitor. Bart does such a good job of maintaining law and order that the school has been transformed into a "police state." As Milhouse quips, "Sure, we have order—but at what price?"

Lisa becomes upset with her teacher, Miss Hoover, after she is scolded for misbehaving. Seeking revenge, Lisa steals all the teacher's edition textbooks—rendering the teachers inept without the answers. (A truly sad state of affairs is depicted here, as the teachers are unable to teach without the answers in their books.) Lisa hides the books and Principal Skinner places Bart in charge of finding them. Bart orders a locker-to-locker search. When he discovers that the books are in Lisa's locker, he takes the blame for her and ultimately receives six hundred days of detention. Lisa is shocked by Bart's wonderful gesture.

> *Lisa*: Bart, why did you take the blame?
> *Bart*: 'Cause I didn't want you to wreck your life. You got the brains and the talent to go as far as you want, no matter what anyone says. And when you do, I'll be right there to borrow money.

It seems Bart is more in tune to his and Lisa's future than the standardized testing results from CANT. The lesson here is you "CANT" let standardized test results dictate your future. Instead, pursue your dreams. But this is not the only time standardized testing comes into question on *The Simpsons*.

In the "Bart the Genius" (#2) episode, the Simpson family plays Scrabble in an attempt to improve Bart's verbal abilities for his impending aptitude test. As a fourth grader, Bart is scheduled to take a standardized intelligence test. Bart plays the word "kwyjibo" and claims victory in the game of Scrabble. Homer, munching on a banana, questions the legitimacy of the word and asks Bart to explain the meaning of "kwyjibo."

> *Bart*: Kwyjibo, ah . . . a big, dumb, balding North American ape with no chin.
>
> *Marge* (recognizing this description fits Homer): And a short temper.
>
> *Homer*: I'll show you a big, dumb, balding ape. (He chases after Bart.)
>
> *Bart* (running away): Ah, oh. Kwyjibo on the loose!

Creating words for the game of Scrabble will not help Bart on his IQ test. Mrs. Krabappel is about to distribute the standardized tests to her students and makes the following statement: "Now, I don't want you to worry, class. These tests will have no effect on your grades. They merely determine your future social status and financial success. If any." And with these stress-producing words, the students take the test. Bart is stumped by the very first question. He struggles to comprehend its very meaning. Martin Prince, the smartest kid in the fourth grade, finishes his test early and is allowed to read a book under a shady tree outside. While Mrs. Krabappel is distracted, Bart switches his test with Martin's.

Homer and Marge Simpson are called to the principal's office to discuss Bart's earlier misbehavior—he painted graffiti on the school walls. While the Simpsons are in Skinner's office, they receive Bart's IQ test results from district psychologist Dr. Pryor. The news is shocking, as Bart has scored a 216—a score so high that Bart is labeled a genius. Marge and Homer are at a loss. Bart is called into Skinner's office. The psychologist asks Bart if he is often bored in class, feels frustrated with the assigned schoolwork, and whether he dreams of leaving the class to pursue his own independent studies. Dr. Pryor explains to Homer, Marge, and Principal Skinner that "gifted" students are often bored with "normal" class work assignments and that they tend to act out because of this boredom.

Education experts agree with this analysis. The Education Department believes that many of America's brightest youngsters are bored and unchallenged in school. The curriculum offered to top students in the United States is less rigorous than that in other countries. It is estimated that about two million children nationwide (about 5 percent of enrollment) are considered gifted. When a schoolchild has mastered 35 to 50 percent of the grade curriculum in five basic subject areas before starting the school year, that child is labeled "gifted" (*Las Vegas Review-Journal* 1993). Failing to challenge our brightest students is akin to ignoring one of our greatest natural assets.

Dr. Pryor wants to enroll Bart in a school that does not rely on grades, assignments, and deadlines. This is music to Bart's ears! He envisions a kick-back school where anything goes. Skinner is so happy to be rid of Bart that he does not insist on retesting Bart's IQ. Bart is excited, but Homer remains unconvinced.

> *Homer*: Doc, this is all too much. I mean, my son a genius—
> how does it happen?
> *Dr. Pryor*: Well, genius-level intelligence is usually the result of
> heredity and environment. . . .
> (Pryor examines the dumbfounded look on Homer's face and
> searches in mind for other alternatives.)
> *Dr. Pryor*: Uh . . . although in some cases, it's a total mystery.

Homer drives Bart to his new school, the Enriched Learning Center for Gifted Children. Bart realizes right away how different this school is from his previous one. The teacher starts the day by saying, "Discover your desks, people." Bart is lost. He tries to cover up the fact that he does not belong at this school. The students discuss paradoxes that affect their lives. When it is Bart's turn, all he can think to say is, "Well, you're damned if you do, damned if you don't." Bart's new classmates quickly figure out that he is not too bright, certainly not a genius. Growing tired of the new school, Bart eventually admits to the truth, that he switched tests with Martin.

This episode teaches us that although highly intelligent students may not be properly challenged in school, all students who act out in mischievous ways are not necessarily geniuses!

Cheating

"I cheated! Cheated, cheated, cheated, cheated, cheated!"
—Lisa Simpson

The fact that Bart cheated on his IQ test should not have surprised anyone. Not only has he failed to show academic promise throughout his life, cheating itself is quite common in school (at all levels of education). In fact, dishonesty of all sorts is common in adulthood. People cheat on their spouses and their taxes, and dishonesty runs rampant in many corporate workplaces (from Enron to Tyco). And don't expect things to change any time soon. The Josephson Institute of Ethics—a nonprofit organization that conducts training in business ethics and character education—has found that cheating is common among America's high school students. Sixty-one percent of students surveyed admitted to cheating on an exam in the past year; 28 percent stole from a store; 23 percent stole from a relative; and 39 percent lied to save money (*Parade* 2006). Michael Josephson, president of the institute, notes that fewer than 2 percent of cheaters are caught and only half of those are punished.

In the case of Lisa Simpson, even when she admits to cheating, she is not punished. In fact, in the "Lisa Gets an 'A'" episode (#210), she is told to keep her cheating a secret so that Springfield Elementary School can receive government funds now that they have reached the minimum state requirement on grade averages. (This is the result of Lisa receiving an A+++ on a test she purchased from Nelson.) (Note: As the bully of the school, Nelson has collected a wide assortment of student exams. He then sells copies of the exams to students who need them. Thus, Nelson is not only a bully [which qualifies him as a "street criminal"], he is also a white-collar criminal!) As a result of this score, the school's overall average climbs above the state minimum requirement.

But why would Lisa, or anyone for that matter, cheat? Cheating occurs most often when students don't think they can get caught, or when the penalties are mild if they do get caught. Students cheat because of the pressure placed on them to do well. As quoted earlier in this chapter, Mrs. Krabappel underscored the importance of certain tests, especially standardized tests, when she said, "they merely determine your future social status and financial success. If any."

As a rule, Lisa would never cheat. She is smart and she likes schoolwork. But in the "Lisa Gets an 'A'" episode, she is too sick to go to school and stays home. Lisa starts to play video games and becomes distracted from her schoolwork. Before long, she is ignoring her studies completely. Fearing that her grade point average will fall,

Lisa resorts to buying a copy of her exam from Nelson (the teachers use the same tests year after year at Springfield). Principal Skinner heaps a great deal of praise on Lisa, but her guilty conscience gets the better of her. She tries to come clean to Principal Skinner.

> *Lisa*: I cheated! Cheated, cheated, cheated, cheated, cheated!
> *Skinner*: Lisa, what are you trying to say?
> *Lisa*: I cheated!

Skinner is flabbergasted that Lisa would cheat. But he and a very pleased Superintendent Chalmers (who has arrived at Springfield Elementary) want the government aid money for a new scoreboard and many needed school supplies. Skinner, Chalmers, and Lisa look out a window and watch two kids playing tetherball with a cement block (instead of a ball) tied to a rope.

> *Chalmers*: Don't you think those youngsters deserve a regulation tetherball?
> (Skinner, Chalmers, and Lisa walk down a school hallway and look inside the fourth grade class where Mrs. Krabappel is using the "Oscar Mayer" periodic table. They listen in on her lesson plan.)
> *Mrs. Krabappel*: Now, who can tell me the atomic weight of Bolongium?
> *Martin*: Oooh! Delicious?
> *Mrs. Krabappel*: Correct. I would have also accepted snacktacular.
> (Skinner, Chalmers, and Lisa reflect.)
> *Skinner*: We can buy real periodical tables instead of the promotional ones from Oscar Mayer. (They open a door with a sign that says "Computer Room.")
> *Skinner*: And for the first time ever, our computer lab actually has a computer in it.

Ralph is using the computer and says hello to "Super Nintendo Chalmers." Chalmers and Skinner have successfully pressured Lisa to keep her cheating a secret for the good of the school and her classmates. A big ceremony is held where the school receives an oversized novelty check from State Comptroller Atkins. The check is to be presented to Lisa. Sure enough, however, Lisa's conscience gets the better of her.

> *Lisa*: I know this giant check is very important to everyone here. But what's more important is the truth. Because, after all, education is the search for the truth.
>
> *Skinner*: No, no, it isn't! Don't listen to her; she's out of her mind!

And with that, Lisa walks off the stage, feeling better about herself. Her family takes her home. Meanwhile, Skinner and Chalmers had assumed that Lisa would change her mind and had actually set up a dummy award presentation with a fake State Comptroller Atkins. The real Atkins appears and ceremoniously hands over the check.

We learn a rather deceitful lesson here. Education may ideally be the "search for truth," but it takes cheating to pay the bills! On a more serious note, it is sad that budget constraints and overall poor grades lead to Skinner covering up the serious infraction of cheating on a school test. Is it any wonder that America's educational system is no longer the best in the world?

Chapter 13

Physical and Mental Health in Springfield

"All my life I have been an obese man trapped inside a fat man's body."
—Homer Simpson

There is an old cliché that people use to make others feel better when they have faced some sort of setback: "At least you have your health!" This expression implies that any problem can be faced as long as one has good health. Logic alone would seem to dictate that good health should be a goal for everyone. But what about people without good health or affordable health insurance? What expression do we use to get them encouraged about their lives when facing difficulty?

From a functional perspective, the normal and natural state of affairs is for people to be healthy and contribute to society. As a result, the opposite situation, ill health, can be seen as a dysfunction. In capitalistic social systems it is especially important for people to be healthy enough to work so that they produce goods and services to be consumed. This helps to explain, in part, why employers offer health insurance to their employees. In the "King-Size Homer" episode (#135), Monty Burns institutes a mandatory fitness program for his workers at the Springfield Nuclear Power Plant. The exercises consist of a mere five minutes of calisthenics and yet some employees complain about this health requirement. Homer, for example, tries hiding in a bathroom stall to avoid working out. Smithers and a couple of "goons" track him down and literally drag the crying and kicking Homer to the exercise area. Homer screams out, as if in extreme pain, at the mere thought of participating in a conditioning program, "NO! NO! Oh for the love of . . ." Smithers comments, "Boy, I've never seen a man so desperate to avoid five minutes of calisthenics."

Wearing a Yale letterman's jacket, Burns leads the exercise program by barking out commands: "Raise your right hock. Aerate! [Breathe] Raise your left hock. Aerate! I want to see more Teddy Roosevelts and less Franklin Roosevelts!"

As we shall see (later in this chapter), Homer fails to embrace the exercise program and resorts to extreme measures to escape the well-intentioned health curriculum at his workplace.

HEALTHCARE IN AMERICA

The United States spends more money per person on healthcare a year ($5,700), and a greater percentage of its gross domestic product (more than 15 percent) than any other country in the world (Wallechinsky 2007). Unfortunately, every citizen does not have equal access to the best facilities and care available. For those who can afford it, the United States offers the best healthcare in the world. Yet, the United States lags behind many other countries in significant areas of healthcare. Consider the following:

- Forty-three countries have more doctors per capita.
- Forty-nine nations have more hospital beds per capita.
- Thirty-three countries have a lower infant death rate.
- Twenty-eight countries have a lower maternal death rate.
- Twenty-nine nations have a higher life expectancy for women and twenty-seven have a higher life expectancy for men. (Note: the average life expectancy for an American woman is 79.5 years and 74.1 years for an American man.)
- In all of the above healthcare categories, the United States' position has steadily declined over the last twenty years (Wallechinsky 2007).

The leading cause for America's rapid descent in overall health rests with the fact that Americans consume more calories per capita than the citizens of any other nation. Not surprisingly, the United States leads the world in the predominance of obesity. (Note: obesity will be discussed in greater detail later in this chapter. Obesity is a running theme in *The Simpsons*.)

The word "health" has been used numerous times already in this chapter. But what is health? According to the World Health Organization (WHO), the United Nations agency that specializes in health around the world, health is defined as "a state of complete physical, mental and social well-being and not merely the absence of disease or infirmity" (World Health Organization 2007A). Considering the major health problems around the world (e.g., disease, famine, and extreme poverty), the WHO faces many major obstacles in reaching its seven-point "global health agenda" by 2015. Established in 2006, the seven points of emphasis established in the WHO's "Engaging for Health" plan are:

1. Investing in health to reduce poverty.
2. Building individual and global health security.
3. Promoting universal coverage, gender equality, and health-related human rights.
4. Tackling the determinants of health.
5. Strengthening health systems and equitable access.
6. Harnessing knowledge, science, and technology.
7. Strengthening governance, leadership, and accountability. (World Health Organization 2007C)

A great number of assets will have to be allocated in order for WHO to reach its idealistic goals of reducing global poverty, developing technology that ends disease, and providing medicine to those who need it (and cannot afford it). Medicine and affordable healthcare for all are superb goals, especially for an agency such as WHO.

Medicine is often in short supply both globally and in the United States. But what is medicine? Medicine is both an area of knowledge (a science) and the application of that knowledge as a means of maintaining health and restoring it by treating disease. Medicine, then, involves a social system designed to treat illness and sustain good health. The provision of medicine is a fundamental aspect of general healthcare.

Many people believe the US government should provide healthcare for all American citizens. This money, of course, would come from taxpayers. Proponents of some sort of universal healthcare coverage cite the fact that over forty million Americans are without health insurance and many millions more do not have affordable full-coverage healthcare. Other people worry that if a government-backed healthcare program was implemented, employers would dramatically (or completely) cut back on the coverage they provide their employees. On the other hand, there are some people who do not believe the government should be obligated to provide healthcare to its citizens and, consequently, they endorse the idea that every person is responsible to take care of his or her own personal needs.

The conflict perspective on the study of healthcare focuses on the inequalities within the system. For example, as previously mentioned, the United States (like many Western societies) provides wonderful healthcare for those who can afford it. This often leaves the poor and people of rural areas underserved because the best medical services are found where people are numerous and/or wealthy. Obviously, being wealthy is always better than being poor, but this is especially true when it comes to healthcare. Whereas the wealthy can afford preventive care and participate in "regular" doctor visits, the poor and/or uninsured usually only visit a doctor when they are sick. This dramatically different approach to medicine and healthcare can lead to deadly results. It is a sad reality that many people die every day simply because they cannot afford healthcare. How does a civil society allow such a thing?

PHYSICAL HEALTH

"You see, Lisa, it's been an unlucky year for Laramie. A lot of the people who smoke our product have been, well . . . dying."
—Jack Larson

Casual observers might be surprised by the large number of diverse health-related topics found in *Simpsons* episodes over the years. Among the topics discussed are blood transfusions, organ transplants and organ donation, health insurance fraud, the harmful effects of smoking, peanut butter allergies, and even "helper monkeys" for disabled people. (Note: Discussion will be limited to the two leading preventable causes of death: smoking tobacco and obesity.)

Despite the wide variety of physical health topics covered by *The Simpsons*, it is the topic of obesity that comes to the forefront most often. This includes spoofs of beer-guzzling couch potato adults (e.g., Homer Simpson) who risk their health due to obesity and a glimpse of the ever-growing problem of child obesity (e.g., Bart Simpson, Milhouse Van Houten, and Nelson Muntz).

The Growing Problem of Obesity

> **"Obesity is really unhealthy. Any doctor will tell you that."**
> —Lisa Simpson

Let's revisit the "King-Size Homer" episode previously introduced in this chapter's opening story. Burns has instituted a mandatory health program at the nuclear power plant. Homer has difficulty performing the most basic of exercises, including push-ups. Turning red in the face and panting heavily, Homer struggles with his first push-up. When he reaches the top of the push-up, he moans out, "Two." His friend and co-worker, Lenny, points out his error in counting: "Mmm, actually Homer that was just one. See, each push-up includes both an up part and a down part." Homer replies with his typical "D'oh!" Someone Homer's age (assumed to be within the category of thirty to thirty-nine years) should be able to do twenty-five to thirty-five full-body (not from the knees) "real" push-ups (where neither the chin nor chest touch the ground) in a minute. Homer was exhausted after just one push-up! Clearly he has strength issues, as the only requirement for successfully doing a push-up involves one's ability to lift one's own weight. In this regard, a person's age and gender should be irrelevant aspects in doing push-ups.

Homer has more than strength issues as he flirts with potentially deadly physical health dangers every day due to his obesity. Instead of embracing the exercise program at work, he seeks to find a way out of it. Homer notices that his co-worker Charlie is not with the rest of the plant's workers exercising.

Homer: Hey, where's Charlie? How'd he get out of this?
Carl: Aw, he's at home on disability.

> *Lenny*: Yeah, he got injured on the job and they sent him home
>   with pay. Pftt. It's like a lottery that rewards stupidity.
> *Homer*: Stupidity, eh?

It dawns on Homer that he would rather be at home as well. He is
willing to do almost anything to avoid doing physical exercise.
Homer walks around the nuclear plant trying to get injured. Surprisingly, he is unsuccessful at getting injured. Homer decides to take a
different approach. He reads a book titled *Am I Disabled?*: "Carpal
Tunnel Syndrome? No. Lumber lung? No. Juggler's despair? No.
Achy-breaky pelvis? No. Oh, I'm never going to be disabled. I'm sick
of being so healthy! Hey wait—'Hyper-obesity.' If you weigh more
than 300 pounds, you qualify as disabled."

Already obese for his height of six feet tall at 239 pounds, Homer
decides to gain 61 pounds just so that he can work at home. Bart tells
his father that he is happy to help him gain weight. Lisa, however,
protests her father's wish to gain weight just so that he is labeled as
"disabled."

> *Lisa*: "Daaad! I must protest. You're abusing a program in-
>   tended to help the unfortunate.
> *Homer*: I'm not saying it's not sleazy, honey. But try to see it
>   my way. All my life I have been an obese man trapped
>   inside a fat man's body.

Lisa tries to discourage Homer. She points out, "Obesity is really
unhealthy. Any doctor will tell you that." Instead of heeding Lisa's
warning, Homer seeks out a doctor who will help him gain weight. He
finds Dr. Nick Riviera (a recurring character), Springfield's most
unscrupulous doctor. Dr. Nick advises Homer to "focus on the neg-
lected food groups, such as the whipped group, the congealed group,
and the choc-o-tastic." Dr. Nick also tells Homer to be creative: "Instead
of making sandwiches with bread, use Pop-Tarts. Instead of chewing
gum, chew bacon." In short, Dr. Nick gives the worst bit of advice that
a medical professional should give to an already obese man.

Homer gorges on food continuously until he finally cracks the
three-hundred-pound barrier. His dream of being disabled so that he
can stay at home has been fulfilled. As a legally recognized disabled
person, Mr. Burns is obligated to set up a workstation for Homer at

his home. In a formal proclamation, Mr. Burns states, "I am pleased to dedicate this remote work terminal. It will allow our safety inspector here to perform his duties from home." Yes, remember? Homer is a nuclear power plant safety inspector—who is now working from home!

Homer is happy that he does not have to drive to work. He is actually on time now. But Homer also begins to face discrimination and humiliation as a result of his obesity. For example, when he goes to the movie theater, he is told that he is too fat for the theater seats. When Homer begins to complain, the manager offers him a garbage bag full of popcorn if he will just quiet down. Homer is offended that the theater manager has offered him food to calm down. Homer claims to take a stand for all obese people and states, "Overweight people are not undisciplined, lazy, and irresponsible." Lulu Hunt Peters first proposed the idea that fat people suffered from a lack of willpower. In her book, *Diet and Health, with Key to the Calories* (1918), Peters, a physician, proclaimed that extra pounds on the body were not only unattractive but immoral. She advised people to watch their caloric input and exercise regularly. Peters also warned her readers that reducing and staying slim meant a lifetime of struggle (Smith and Kiger 2004).

By the end of this episode, Homer sees the error of his purposely putting on weight just so that he can work at home. He asks Mr. Burns for help. Burns agrees to put Homer through an advanced regimen of exercises. However, Burns quickly realizes that Homer is incapable of basic physical exercise (due to his extreme atrophy) and agrees to pay for his liposuction.

Health problems associated with obesity are such a real crisis that they constitute the second-leading cause of preventable deaths in the United States. Tobacco is the leading cause. However, according to the Centers for Disease Control and Prevention (CDC), obesity is rapidly approaching tobacco as the number one culprit of preventable death. In 2000, poor diet including obesity and physical inactivity caused four hundred thousand deaths in the United States. This figure represents more than 16 percent of all deaths. Tobacco, the leading killer of Americans, was responsible for the death of 435,000 Americans in 2000. Obesity and inactivity strongly increase the risk of diabetes, the sixth-leading cause of death in the United States. Further, like tobacco, obesity and inactivity increase the risks for heart disease, cancer, and cerebrovascular ailments, including strokes. The Homer Simpsons of the world, and there are many of them, need to be far more concerned about their weight and physical inactivity.

As stated previously, when Homer was at his original weight of 239 pounds, he was obese. (The three-hundred barrier qualified him as "hyper-obese," meaning he was extremely obese.) Although it is quite easy to distinguish a thin person from an extremely obese person, one's perception often influences the dividing line between being "overweight" and "obese." Thus, a number of overweight people fail to acknowledge it and many obese people attempt to convince themselves that they are simply overweight. It is important, then, to define such terms. Being "overweight" generally refers to weighing more than normal or necessary, especially when considering what is typical for someone's age, height, and build. Someone is obese when his or her increased weight is the result an excessive accumulation of fat. According to the CDC (2004), 34 percent of US adults are considered overweight and an additional 31 percent are obese.

Presently, the most commonly used measurement to determine whether someone is overweight or obese is the Body Mass Index (BMI). The BMI is an index of weight adjusted for the height of an individual. The BMI formula is calculated by dividing a person's weight by his or her height squared and multiplying by 703. (Note: Numerous links are available online that will calculate one's BMI score. Simply conduct a Google search under "BMI" and such sites will appear.) Adults with a BMI of 25 or more are considered "overweight," and those with a BMI score of 30 or more are considered "obese."

At six feet and 239 pounds, Homer Simpson has a BMI score of 32.4—which makes him officially "obese." His BMI score at 300 pounds was a whopping 40.7. As a point of interest, the "average" American male is five feet nine and a half inches and weighs 191 pounds. This equates to a BMI score of 27.8, which equates to an "overweight" status. The "average" American female is five feet four inches and weighs 164 pounds. This equates to a BMI score of 28.2, which equates to an "overweight" status. In short, the average American, male or female, is overweight.

A major criticism of the BMI is the fact that it does not allow for a distinction between muscle weight and weight as a result of fat. As a result, some people, such as weight lifters, may record a BMI score that categorizes them as "overweight" (or in some cases even "obese") when in actuality their above-average weight is the result of muscle mass and not body fat. Anyone with an above-average amount of muscle is likely to score high on the BMI. Thus, even though this author will admit to a BMI score of 26.7 ("overweight"), he is quick to point out that most of the excess is due to muscle!

There are a number of reasons why the waistline of the average American is growing in size. Failing to exercise is often coupled with physically inactive behaviors such as watching television, playing video games, and an increasing number of hours spent in front of the computer. Junk food, which stays fresh for a longer period of time than fruits and vegetables, has become a staple of many Americans' diet. Further, many people eat at fast-food restaurants on a regular basis. The increased food portion sizes offered by many fast-food places increase the number of calories and fat that consumers ingest.

In the "Diatribe of a Mad Housewife" episode (#323), the occurrence of supersizing an order at a fast-food restaurant is hilariously presented when Homer places his order at the drive-thru at Krusty Burger.

> *Homer*: Let's see, I'll have sixteen gravy scrape'ems, a bucket of twisty lard, two super choker breakfast burritos with macho sauce, and megasize it, please.
> *Krusty Burger employee*: I can also deep-fry that, sir.
> *Homer*: Great. And, I'll have a Diet Coke—deep fried.
> (The Krusty Burger employee hands the food to Homer through the drive-thru window. He has deep-fried the entire bag!)

Despite the fact that some of the food items ordered by Homer are unique to Krusty Burger (what the heck is a scrape'em or a twisty lard?), Homer presents a common scenario wherein people supersize an order and attempt to counteract it with a diet soda. Ordering a diet soda, although commendable perhaps, does not detract from the large intake of calories and fat from deep-fried foods. Supersized orders of greasy food are a major contributor to the obesity epidemic plaguing the United States.

An increasing number of Americans are becoming overweight and obese. One might think that, because of this, people would be more sensitive to heavy people. And yet, if you ask any obese person whether or not they have been victimized or mocked because of being overweight, chances are they can provide many examples. Negative slurs directed toward fat people include, "fat slob," "big mouth," and "el Gordo." Obese people face many forms of discrimination. For example, they need to ask for an "extender" for their seatbelt on an airplane; rides at amusement parks cannot accommodate them; booths at restaurants are too tight to fit into; seats at the theater are usually too small (as Homer Simpson found out when he weighed three hundred pounds); employers are sometimes hesitant to hire obese people; visits to the doctor's office are met with such obstacles as scales that cannot weigh them and hospital gowns that are too small to fit; and the occasional public joke or insensitive comment that is directed toward them. *The Simpsons* provides numerous examples of insensitive treatment directed at the obese. Two examples are provided below.

In the "Brush with Greatness" episode (#31), the hefty Homer Simpson gets stuck inside the water slide at the Mount Splashmore theme park. The tunnel slide is not equipped to handle someone as large as Homer. But why isn't it? Didn't the designers of Mount Splashmore realize that many theme park visitors are overweight? The theme park employee initially sends numerous kids behind Homer in an attempt to get him unstuck. It does not work. Instead, there is a pile up of kids stuck behind Homer inside the water slide tunnel. Eventually the park workers remove a section of the tunnel to free everyone. Homer is humiliated. And, at least for this episode, he becomes inspired to lose weight.

Homer is shamed because of his weight in the "King of the Hill" episode (#201) as well. In this episode, Homer has teamed up with Bart in the "Capture the Flag" game at the church picnic. As Homer attempts to run to the finish line, he becomes winded and falls. Because he is so fat he cannot run the short distance necessary to win the race. Things only get worse as the other kids throw eggs at Homer. Still too tired to get up or defend himself, Homer rolls over and the kids pelt him with eggs on the other side of his body. Watching this, Bart becomes humiliated by Homer. Once again, Homer is temporarily motivated to go on a diet. But like every other time, his diet will not last long.

Although Bart was humiliated by Homer's poor physical performance at the church picnic, there are many occasions where he is portrayed as being just as lazy as his father. For example, in the "When Flanders Failed" episode (#38), Marge worries that Bart is becoming too fat from sitting around watching too much television and encourages him to get some exercise. Bart decides to give karate a try. But like his father, Bart decides there is too much work involved in taking karate lessons and he sneaks off to the arcade instead. Aside from his occasional skateboarding, Bart lives a rather inactive lifestyle. He eats a lot of junk food and sits around watching TV. Bart's behavior is reflective of many children in Springfield who resemble many children in the United States. And this introduces us to another huge and growing physical health problem—childhood obesity.

It is important that children engage in regular exercise. It is the obligation of both parents and the education system to ensure that all children engage in regular physical activity. Unfortunately, there are some school districts that do not require physical education programs, and in some cases, they have actually eliminated gym. Imagine, in this age of growing obesity there are schools that do not require daily exercise. Running around at recess, kicking a ball, and a number of other simple physical forms of activity can benefit the general health of children. Parents also need to ensure that their children exercise and eat right. Parents should provide children with healthy snacks, such as fruit, healthy grain cereals, or trail mix, instead of junk food like potato chips and candy.

Unfortunately, and to no one's surprise, the childhood obesity rate is increasing in the United States. As with adults, a BMI is utilized to determine the number of overweight and obese children and adolescents. According to the American Obesity Association (2002) about 15.5 percent of adolescents (ages twelve to nineteen) and 15.3 percent of children (ages six to eleven) are obese. The number of obese American children has increased dramatically over the past two decades and trends would indicate that the problem is only going to get worse.

The consequences of childhood obesity are potentially grave. Among other things, overweight children have a greater risk for diabetes, asthma, and hypertension. The odds of an American child becoming a diabetic are now one in three; for Latino children it is one in two. In addition to these dangers, obese children have an increased risk of heart failure and digestive problems, and have more chronic medical conditions than an excessive smoker or drinker. The chronic nature of health problems is directly tied to the reality that an obese child is more likely to become an obese adult and, thus, suffer from health ailments for a longer period of time than children who are not overweight.

The United States is not the only country in the world facing a rapidly growing number of obese children and adults. Virtually every nation characterized by modernization (which brings with it a less active physical existence combined with a diet that includes "junk" food) is facing an increasing number of obese people and diabetics. The International Obesity Task Force, a section of the International Association for the Study of Obesity, blames the agricultural policies of the world's top producing nations as contributing to the increasing problem of obesity in developing nations. Such polices favor high-fat, high-energy products over basic fruits and vegetables (Syracuse *Post-Standard* September 5, 2006).

In the "Bart's Friend Falls in Love" episode (#58), which aired nearly two decades ago, Kent Brockman sounds the alarm about the growing threat of obesity: "Did you know that 34 million American adults are obese? Taken together, that excess blubber could fill the Grand Canyon two-fifths of the way up. That may not sound impressive, but keep in mind it is a very big canyon." Although the image of the Grand Canyon being filled by excess human blubber is a little disturbing, it is likely filled by now.

Tobacco: The Leading Preventable Cause of Death

"What a feeling! I'm as happy as a smoker taking that first puff in the morning."
—TV daughter

Marge Simpson's sisters, Patty and Selma, are both chain-smokers. As a result, they are endangering both their own health and the health of all the people who must endure their secondhand smoke. And yet, if they wish to do something about this, "all" they have to do is stop smoking. The word "all" is placed in quotation marks because, as any smoker who has attempted to quit can tell you, it is very difficult to simply say "no." And yet, as easy as it is to understand why it is so difficult to quit smoking, it is far more difficult to understand why anyone would *start* smoking. The days of looking at a smoker as being "cool" are long gone. No one, except perhaps young rebellious kids, view a smoker as being "cool." After all, how cool can it be to have a "cancer stick" attached to one's mouth? Most people start smoking when they are young (high school age). They often do this as a means of displaying their independence from the rules established by adults. Ironically, once they become adults, most smokers wish they had never started. As with many lessons in life, the decision to start smoking is nearly always regretted later in life.

By now everyone knows that smoking tobacco is the leading preventable cause of premature death. In other words, if smokers had simply decided never to start smoking, they would not face the array of health problems associated with smoking. Further, they would not harm others with their secondhand smoke. Every year more than 440,000 Americans die from tobacco use; most of these deaths are caused by smoking cigarettes. (Note: Nearly twice as many men die from smoking compared to women. This is attributed to the fact that historically men were more likely to smoke than women. Today, females are just as likely to start smoking as males.) In the United States, one in five deaths is smoking related (Centers for Disease Control 2001). Smoking triples the risk of dying from heart disease among middle-aged men and women. In short, the average smoker's life expectancy is reduced by eight to twelve years. The smoker has to weigh the possible benefits that smoking provides against the extreme risk of dying prematurely.

The largest number of smoking-related deaths is caused by cardiovascular diseases (heart disease, hypertension, and stroke), followed by various cancers (e.g., lung and throat), respiratory diseases (e.g., chronic airway obstruction, pneumonia, and bronchitis/emphysema), and other causes, such as burn deaths. Cigarette smoking is harmful because of the drug nicotine found in tobacco. Nicotine is a drug that stimulates the brain. Regular users will experience withdrawal symptoms such as craving, anxiety, restlessness, headaches, irritability, hunger, difficulty with concentration, and feeling awful when they try to give up or go any length of time without smoking. Nicotine is not the only harmful drug found in tobacco. Tar, at least fifty known carcinogens (causes of cancer), and thousands of other chemicals are found in every cigarette. Generally speaking, most people would go out of their way to avoid the dangerous chemicals found in tobacco products.

Tobacco smoking is not just a problem in the United States. Cigarette smoking is the single leading cause of illness and premature death in the United Kingdom (UK) as well. More than 100,000 people in the UK die each year due to smoking. (Note: the UK has a much smaller total population than the US.) The World Health Organization estimates that nearly 5 million people die each year from smoking worldwide. They also estimate that this number will increase to 10 million deaths annually by 2030 (CBSNews.com 2002).

The harm caused by smoking tobacco products is not limited to the user. Secondhand smoke (the smoke that is exhaled from the user along with the smoke from the burning cigarette being held by the user) causes harm to nonsmokers. US surgeon general Richard H. Carmona announced in 2006 that there is no risk-free level of exposure to secondhand smoke. "Nonsmokers exposed to secondhand smoke at home or work increase their risk of developing heart disease by 25 to 30 percent and lung cancer by 20 to 30 percent. The finding is of major public health concern due to the fact that nearly half of all non-smoking Americans are still regularly exposed to secondhand smoke" (United States Department of Health and Human Services 2006, 1). Secondhand smoke is especially harmful to children, who are victimized by being around people (e.g., their parents) who smoke. Recently, a number of states have proposed legislation to ban smoking inside cars with infants and/or young children. Legislation such as this follows the trend of smoking restrictions placed on smokers for the past decade. For example, many states have enacted smoking bans in public buildings, workplaces, restaurants, and bars. Smokers are forced to smoke outside (and at a certain distance from building entrances).

As one of the leading causes of death, preventable or otherwise, it is a wonder that tobacco is still legal. The United States engages in a war on terrorism in an attempt to safeguard the lives of Americans, and yet allows tobacco to be sold legally! How can the government justify this? Among the simpler explanations for tobacco's continuing legal status is economics. Tobacco has been a cash crop since colonial days. Many southern states and especially powerful corporations still profit from this killer drug. And, apparently, they do so relatively guilt-free. Tobacco companies are guilty of targeting young people. They do this because older users die off and need to be replaced by younger consumers and because young people are far more impressionable than older adults. (They are more likely to view smoking as "cool.") Greatly restricted in the manner they may advertise, tobacco companies sponsor a variety of events to make sure that their brand name remains recognizable. Such is the case in the "Lisa the Beauty Queen" episode (#63).

In this episode, Laramie Cigarettes, along with Krusty the Clown, sponsor the Little Miss Springfield pageant. Homer enters Lisa in the contest because he is influenced by a Little Miss Springfield commercial he views on television. In this commercial a father and daughter are enjoying each other's company when they are joined by Jack Larson.

Father: Wow! President of Laramie Cigarettes, Jack Larson!

Larson: This year, Laramie is sponsoring the Little Miss Springfield Pageant. You see, government regulations prohibit us from advertising on TV. (He takes a puff on a cigarette and holds up a box of Laramies.) Ah, that sweet Carolina smoke! But, they can't prohibit us from holding a beauty pageant for little girls aged seven to nine.

Homer: Lisa's aged seven to nine!

Jack Larson: Your daughter could be crowned Little Miss Springfield by our host, the maitre d' of glee, Krusty the Clown!

Krusty (file footage tape): I heartily endorse this event or product.

TV daughter (dressed as a pageant winner): What a feeling! I'm as happy as a smoker taking that first puff in the morning.

Homer: That could be Lisa!

Initially, Lisa is reluctant to participate in the contest (see chapter 6 for an explanation). Lisa changes her mind when she realizes that her father really believes in her and wants her to feel good about herself. Although Lisa comes in second place, she is later crowned Miss Springfield when the winner, Amber Dempsey, is injured by a bolt of lightning.

As with most beauty contest winners, Lisa is expected to make a number of public appearances. By default, she becomes a representative of the corporate sponsors. As an advocate against tobacco, Lisa wants nothing to do with promoting cigarettes. Unfortunately for her, Lisa's first scheduled public appearance as Little Miss Springfield is the Springfield Founders Festival Parade. She is asked to ride on the Laramie Cigarettes float that is decorated with, among other things, a giant pack of cigarettes and the Menthol Moose (a spoof of "Joe Camel"). Larson explains the importance of her riding on the float:

"You see, Lisa, it's been an unlucky year for Laramie. A lot of the people who smoke our product have been, well . . . dying." As the float moves along the parade route, Lisa and the Menthol Moose toss free samples of cigarettes to the crowd. Lisa is shocked to see everyone smoking, even children. Lisa is especially upset when she sees her baby sister, Maggie, replace her pacifier with a cigarette.

Lisa has seen enough. She yells out, "Stop this float!" The float comes to a sudden halt, causing Santa Claus, riding in the float behind her, to crash into them. Lisa refuses to be a corporate representative for Laramie. She kicks the pack of cigarettes off the float and vows to speak out against the evils in society: "From dog-napping to cigarettes." The headline in the next morning's *Springfield Shopper* reads: "Lisa Kicks Butt."

Her next appearance is at a college football game. Lisa considers football an evil of society as well and proclaims, "Before I sing the national anthem, I'd like to say that college football diverts funds that are badly needed for education and the arts!" Inspired by this, a number of nerds charge the football field. The headline in the next morning's *Springfield Shopper* reads: "Nerds Pummeled in Football Melee."

The Little Miss Springfield sponsors and organizers are very displeased with Lisa's behavior. In a smoke-filled room they try to figure out a way to have Lisa dethroned and Amber Dempsey restored. Jack Larson bursts into the room with incriminating evidence—Lisa's pageant application. As it turns out, in the area of the application that warned, "Do not write in this space," Homer wrote "OK." The corporate executives decide that this was a violation of the application form and have Lisa stripped of her crown. Kent Brockman breaks the news to Springfield residents during his news report. Lisa and Homer watch the footage together. Homer feels guilty and takes full responsibility. But Lisa is okay with it.

> *Lisa*: Dad, do you remember why you entered me in that pageant?
> *Homer*: I dunno. Was I drunk?
> *Lisa*: Possibly. But the point is, you wanted me to feel better about myself, and I do.

Thus, Lisa teaches us a valuable lesson. It is better to live by one's code of ethics than be a beauty queen and sell out for corporate "big shots."

The numerous chemicals added to tobacco increase the addictive quality of smoking and make it more difficult for users to quit. In the "E-I-E-I (Annoyed Grunt)" episode (#231), *The Simpsons* provides social commentary on the addictive nature of tobacco. In this episode, Homer has offended a southern colonel by failing to honor a pistol duel initiated by Homer. Fearing for his life, Homer takes his family to his childhood home—Grandpa Simpson's farm. Homer's plan is to start a new life centered on farming. Unfortunately, the old family farm is rundown. The neighboring farmers warn Homer that he'll never be able to grow anything on his farm because the soil is lacking in nutrients.

Homer plants a variety of seeds hoping that something will grow. Alas, the farmers' warnings are proven accurate as nothing grows on the Simpson farm. One night Homer comes up with an idea. He calls Lenny at the nuclear plant and asks him to ship some plutonium to the farm. When the plutonium arrives, Homer loads it into a pesticide sprayer. "Time to give Mother Nature a little goose," Homer comments. At night, the fields literally glow due to the plutonium. Marge tells Homer that the fields are "eerily beautiful." The next day little sprouts begin to appear. Because Homer has planted a mixture of seeds he has no idea what might grow in his fields. He is hoping for corn, carrots, peas, or tomatoes. He will be shocked by what is actually growing.

Shortly after the first sprouts appear, tomato plants quickly spring to life. Homer dreams about the different types of ketchup his tomatoes will become. Bart takes a bite out of a tomato and quickly spits it out.

Bart: Bleh! Tastes like cigarette butts.

Marge (looking at the tomato tossed by Bart): That's odd. The outside looks like a tomato, but the inside is brown.

Lisa: Maybe the tomato seeds crossbred with the tobacco seeds.

Homer: Oh, great. I've got a field full of mutants.

Bart: Gimme! I want more. (He grabs the tomato back and eats it.)

Lisa: I thought you said it tasted terrible

Bart: It does. But it's smooth and mild. (He grabs another crossbred tomato.) And refreshingly addictive.

Homer: Addictive, eh?

Homer realizes the value of an addictive product. Once people sample an addictive product they become "hooked." Homer sets up a roadside stand with a sign that reads: "ToMacco."

> *Lisa*: Tomacco? That's pretty clever, Dad. I mean, for a product that's evil and deadly.
>
> *Homer*: Aw, thanks honey.
>
> *Marge*: Well, I'm not crazy about the plutonium or nicotine, but it is very nice to see Bart eating his vegetables.
>
> (At this time, Chief Wiggum drives up and gets out of his car with his son, Ralph.)
>
> *Wiggum*: Excuse me, Mr. Farmer Man? I promised my son he could tip over his first cow, and I . . . (he notices the sign) tomacco?
>
> *Homer*: Yes, it's the latest craze. Try some, won't you? (He offers Ralph a free sample.)
>
> *Wiggum*: Go ahead, Ralphie. The stranger is offering you a treat.
>
> *Ralph* (takes a bite and then spits out the tomacco): Oh, Daddy, this tastes like Grandma.
>
> *Wiggum* (tries a bite and also spits it out): Holy Moses, it does taste like Grandma!
>
> *Ralph*: I want more.
>
> *Wiggum*: Yeah, me too. We'll take a bushel or a pack or just— just give it to me.

Homer giggles evilly. He knows what a valuable product he has created. People cannot stand the taste of it (think about kissing someone right after they have smoked a cigarette—yuck!) and yet they purchase as much as they can with no regard to the financial or health costs. Indeed, a long line of people wait in front of Homer's tomacco stand.

Before long, Homer is contacted, in person, by representatives from Laramie Cigarettes. One of the reps, Mindy, explains to Homer that tobacco companies are in a bit of a pickle in regard to selling tobacco to children.

> *Mindy*: Kids are crazy about tobacco, but the politicians won't let us sell it to them.
>
> *Homer*: Those dirty, rotten—
>
> *Mindy*: Tell me about it. But there's no law against selling kids

tomacco. That little "m" is worth a lot of money to us—
and to you.

The Laramie executives offer Homer $150 million for his tomacco product. He talks it over with his family. Lisa attempts to stop her father.

> *Lisa*: Dad, it's a tobacco company. They make billions off the suffering and death of others.
> *Bart*: She's right, Dad. They can afford a lot more.

Inspired more by Bart's line of thinking than by Lisa's, Homer asks the executives for $150 billion. The executives refuse his counteroffer. Homer remains confident as he is the only person with tomacco. However, while the Simpsons are away from their farm negotiating with the Laramie executives, animals from the neighboring farms have trampled down the Simpsons' fence and begin eating the tomacco plants. They become addicted to the tomacco just as humans have. The Simpsons return to their farm just in time to save the last tomacco plant. Homer cuddles the plant and speaks to it.

> *Homer*: There, there. We had quite a scare today, but you're going to make us millions. Yes you are.
> *Lisa*: You're about to launch a terrible evil on the world. You've got to destroy this plant.
> *Homer*: I know, honey, but what can I do as an individual? I wouldn't know where to begin.
> *Lisa*: Just burn that plant right now and end this madness.
> *Homer*: I wish I could make a difference, Lisa, but I'm just one man.
> *Lisa*: (Growls.)
> *Homer*: I agree, but how?

Lisa is obviously frustrated because Homer can end the tomacco craze by simply destroying the last plant. The Laramie executives manage to steal the plant from Homer and fly away in a helicopter. However, a crazed sheep boards the helicopter in order to eat the plant. During the shuffle to safeguard the plant the helicopter crashes and the last tomacco plant is destroyed. With nothing else to do, the Simpsons move back to Springfield. The southern colonel is waiting for Homer. Marge attempts to mellow out the gunslinger by offering him some mincemeat pie—his favorite. The colonel is pleased enough to merely shoot Homer in the arm. After enjoying his own slice of pie, Homer heads off to the hospital.

The "E-I-E-I (Annoyed Grunt)" episode is a blatant attempt by the creators of *The Simpsons* to provide social commentary on tobacco: Imagine if someone had simply destroyed the first tobacco crop. If this had been the case, the leading preventable cause of death would be eliminated and healthcare costs would go down for all of us. Instead, millions of people consume a deadly drug on a daily basis. And every year, millions of people worldwide die because of this deadly weed.

The Simpsons reminds us that the leading causes of death are preventable. If people simply avoid smoking tobacco, cut back on the junk food they eat, and exercise regularly, they will add numerous years to their life expectancies.

In an odd bit of humor, *The Simpsons* provides another piece of advice in regard to preventable causes of death. Specifically, if you are an old man with a weak heart, avoid physical contact with a gorgeous young woman. In "The Mansion Family" episode (#238), Cornelius Chapman, Springfield's oldest man, is honored for his longevity as part of the "Springfield Pride Awards." The 108-year-old Chapman is called onstage by co-hosts Kent Brockman and Britney Spears. Britney gives Cornelius a kiss and his old ticker cannot handle the rush of excitement from the 18-year-old beauty. One might argue that once a man has reached the century mark, dying as a result of a kiss from a hot young woman is a better way to go than dying prematurely due to smoking or obesity.

MENTAL HEALTH AND MENTAL ILLNESS

"Which one of us is truly crazy?"
—Leon Kompowsky/Michael Jackson

Mental health is a state of emotional and psychological well-being that allows an individual to function, both cognitively and emotionally, in society and meet the regular demands of everyday life. Good physical health is an important ingredient of mental health. Other aspects of mental health include the absence of mental illness, how we feel about ourselves, how we feel about others, and how we are able to meet the demands of life.

Mental health also refers to a branch of medicine that deals with achievement and maintenance of psychological well-being. This field has made many advances in the past few decades. During this time, the mental health profession has developed an increased understanding of the brain's function through the study of neuroscience, developed new effective medications and therapies, and has standardized diagnostic codes for mental illness. And yet, there is much more to be learned about mental health. Social factors such as stress and self-esteem may cause poor mental health. If stress is caused by financial difficulties, medical and psychological treatment will be far less effective than gainful employment as a means to stimulate recovery.

Globally, a large number of people suffer from some sort of mental illness. The World Health Organization (2007D) claims that 450 million people worldwide are affected by mental, neurological, or behavioral problems at any time. Some problems become so serious that people commit suicide. WHO estimates that 873,000 people die by suicide every year (worldwide). Mental illness, therefore, is common to all nations and causes a great deal of suffering, especially when left untreated.

Treatment can be costly. Presently there is considerable debate as to who should be held responsible to cover the costs of mental healthcare. At one time the government took responsibility for the care of the mentally ill. This changed during the Reagan era. In an attempt to cut spending, Reagan eliminated many of the programs designed to help the severely mentally ill. Many facilities were closed and patients were released. Without supervision or a home to return to, many of these people became homeless and occasionally committed serious crimes. Some people believe that the government should shoulder the responsibility for the care of the mentally ill. Others, however, believe that employers should provide mental healthcare just as they provide physical healthcare.

For example, on December 22, 2006, New York governor George Pataki signed legislation known as Timothy's Law, or the Mental Health Parity Bill that requires mental and emotional illnesses be included in health insurance policies written in New York State. The legislation calls for the state's insurance superintendent to figure out a way of providing financial relief to businesses that pay for employees' (and their families') mental health needs (*Business Review* 2006). Timothy's Law was named in honor of Timothy O'Clair, a twelve-year-old who committed suicide in 2001. He would most likely be alive today if he had been able to receive the treatment he so urgently needed. Unfortunately, the cost of his treatment was not covered under his parents' health insurance. In an act of desperation, Timothy's parents, Tom and Donna, had given up custody of their son in hopes that the state would take care of him. Fate intervened and time ran out for Timothy. The O'Clairs have been pushing for mental healthcare coverage ever since this tragedy took place.

Suicidal deaths are just one of the many social costs related to poor mental health and mental illness. The quality of life for those who suffer from a mental illness is greatly compromised. The quality of life for those who are closely associated with individuals with a mental illness is also (potentially) compromised. Mental illness is as responsible for job absenteeism as the physical illness of cancer, heart attacks, and back problems combined. It is estimated that mental illnesses cost US businesses $79 billion annually in lost productivity (*Timothy's Law* 2006).

The more mental health professionals learn about mental health, the more they realize how preponderant mental illness really is. Biases against mental illness and the lack of public knowledge are among the barriers that limit proper diagnosis and treatment of many mental illnesses from which people silently suffer. Although in "real" life, people are likely to receive a credible diagnosis from mental health professionals, in Springfield, this is not always the case.

Identifying Mental Illness, Springfield Style

> **"You're a credit to dementia."**
> —Lisa Simpson

In the "Stark Raving Dad" episode (#36), Homer is identified by Mr. Burns and Waylon Smithers as being "abnormal" and, therefore, subject to a mental evaluation. They come to this conclusion because Homer wears a pink shirt to work. All the other men wear white shirts. Being singled out at work is what Homer had feared earlier that morning. When Marge retrieved the wash, she discovered that everything was pink. It turns out Bart had placed his red hat in the wash without Marge's knowledge. Homer immediately chokes Bart, and utters his classic line, "Why you little—." Homer is especially mad at Bart because he does not want to wear pink at work. He realizes all the guys at work will mock him (see chapter 6 for a discussion on pink clothing). Marge tries to reassure Homer by saying, "Nobody's going to notice if you wear a pink shirt to work."

The scene shifts to Homer and the other drones marching into work at the power plant. Burns and Smithers are watching the workers on their security monitors. Wearing a pink shirt, Homer clearly stands out. Burns comments to Smithers, "Judging by his outlandish attire, he must be some sort of freethinking anarchist." Smithers responds, "I'll call security, sir." Before security arrives, the workers do indeed mock Homer. They offer him a pink donut. Security shows up and takes Homer away. They even conduct a full-body search (including a cavity search!). Homer tries to explain to Burns that he is only wearing a pink shirt because of Bart's red hat in the wash. Burns does not believe him and orders Homer to see a psychiatrist, Dr. Monroe. Monroe states that it used to take months to establish a patient's sanity but that has all changed now, thanks to "The Marvin Monroe Take-Home Personality Test." Monroe states, "Twenty simple questions that determine exactly how crazy, or 'meshuggenah,' someone is." Reluctantly, Homer takes the test home with him.

At home, Homer tries to get Marge to fill out his exam for him. She refuses. Next, Homer turns to Lisa to take his test for him, but she wants Homer to listen to her poem first. After she starts to read the poem, Homer changes his mind. Finally, he turns to Bart. As one might suspect, the answers that Bart provides will only get Homer into trouble. Sure enough, when Burns learns of his test results, he has Homer institutionalized at the New Bedlam Rest Home for the Emotionally Interesting.

Homer is given the classic inkblot stain test. He becomes frustrated when one ink blot resembles Bart. The doctor's attendants constrain Homer while he asks, "How can you tell who's sane and who's insane?" The doctor says, "Well, we have a very simple method. Whoever has that stamp on his hand is 'Insane.'" And with that, Homer's hand is stamped "Insane." They place Homer in a room with a big white guy named Leon Kompowsky who thinks he is *the* Michael Jackson. (Note: because of contractual issues, *The Simpsons* originally credited "John Jay Smith" as the voice of Leon Kompowsky. The real Michael Jackson did provide the voice for this episode.) Homer explains to Leon that he was labeled as "Insane" because of what he wore. Leon tells Homer that he too was labeled "Insane" for what he wore—one white glove with rhinestones.

Reflecting the concerns that many people have, especially men, about admitting to their families that they have a mental ailment, Homer is afraid to call home. Leon Kompowsky volunteers to call for him. While taking a message from him, Bart believes Leon Kompowsky to be the *real* Michael Jackson. After he gets off the phone, and before he tells all his friends he spoke with Michael Jackson, Bart tells Marge that Homer is in a mental institution. Marge replies, "Oh, my God, Mother was right!" Marge calls New Bedlam and is put on hold. The "on hold" music is Patsy Cline's "Crazy." Marge makes an appointment to meet with the doctor at the institution. She is told that Homer suffers from "a persecution complex, extreme paranoia, and bladder hostility." Marge attempts to assure the medical staff that if they avoid using Bart's name for at least five minutes, they will find that Homer is "sane." Upon hearing this, a nurse proclaims, "You mean there really is a Bart? Good Lord!"

Convinced that Homer is no threat to himself or others, the medical staff decides to let him go home. Homer wants something in writing from New Bedlam. They issue him a certificate that states: "Homer J. Simpson is not insane." This is quite interesting; instead of labeling Homer as "sane," he is listed as "not insane." This is similar to the judicial system, which finds exonerated accused criminals to be "not guilty" rather than "innocent." Think about it!

Homer credits Leon Kompowsky with helping him make it through his ordeal at the institution. He tells Leon that if he ever "regains his marbles" he is welcomed at the Simpson home anytime. Leon tells Homer that he voluntarily checked himself into the institution and is therefore free to accept his offer. Meanwhile, the rumors have spread throughout town and everyone is waiting for Michael Jackson at the Simpsons home. Everyone, especially Bart, is disappointed that Leon is not the real Michael Jackson. But Bart and Leon bond over writing a birthday song for Lisa. (A classic moment of *The Simpsons* involves Michael Jackson and Bart singing "Happy Birthday" to Lisa.)

The episode ends with Lisa extremely happy with her birthday present and Michael revealing himself as Leon Kompowsky, a former bricklayer from Paterson, New Jersey. He speaks in his real, deep voice, and explains to the Simpson family that all his life he was really angry until one day he just started talking like Michael Jackson. From that point on, everyone was smiling at him and treating him nicely. So he kept on doing it. He then asks a rhetorical question, "Which one of us is truly crazy?" Holding onto his certificate from the New Bedlam institute, Homer blurts out, "Not me, I have this!" He leaves the Simpson home singing the "Happy Birthday Lisa" song as a happy Leon Kompowsky, and Lisa yells out, "You're a credit to dementia."

Dementia is a type of mental illness that involves the progressive decline of cognitive functioning of the brain beyond what might be typically expected from normal aging. Dementia may be caused by depression, as in the case of Leon Kompowsky.

Depression and Nervous Breakdowns

"Poor Maggie. How many insanity hearings have you been to in your short little life?"
—Lisa Simpson

Depression can be a serious problem. According to the World Health Organization (2007B), depression is a common mental disorder that is characterized by a "depressed mood, loss of interest or pleasure, feelings of guilt or low self-esteem, disturbed sleep or appetite, low energy, and poor concentration." Depression is a fairly common mental disorder affecting about 121 million people worldwide. Depression is also among the leading causes of disability worldwide. Depression can be treated with antidepressant medications and/or structured forms of psychotherapy. If left untreated, depression can become chronic. In extreme cases it can lead to suicide. In other instances, depression can trigger a nervous breakdown.

"Nervous breakdown" is a popular term—not a clinical term—that is generally used to describe a mental disorder. There are a number of disorders that fit under the "nervous breakdown" umbrella, but the most common are anxiety, panic disorder and panic attacks, trauma disorders (e.g., post-traumatic stress disorder and acute stress disorder), psychotic disorders (e.g., schizophrenia), and mood disorders (e.g., depression and bipolar disorder). In short, a "nervous breakdown" is a severe or incapacitating emotional disorder that generally occurs suddenly and is marked by depression.

Although there have been times when Homer has been depressed, it is Marge Simpson who has been repeatedly sent "over the edge." And is it any wonder Marge sometimes struggles to maintain her sanity? Her husband is enough of a handful for any woman, and Bart, well, we all know what a handful he can be. Taking care of an infant is never easy, but add two more kids and the challenge increases. Even Lisa presents her own unique problems for Marge. Lisa expects a great deal from her mother. As a result, there are times when Marge simply cannot handle all the stress and anxiety. For example, in the "Homer Alone" episode (#50), Marge reaches the limits of her sanity and has a nervous breakdown on the Springfield Bridge. She stops her car in the middle of the bridge, blocking traffic in both directions. The honking horns and the arrival of the police only fuel her anxiety. In a bit of comic relief, the police use cautionary tape to block off Marge's car that reads: "Distressed Mother—Stay Clear." Realizing she needs a vacation from Homer and the kids, she checks herself into Rancho Relaxo, a spa designed to pamper her. Chances are, there are many people out there who could benefit from a relaxing weekend (or week!) spa, free from the daily worries that confront them.

In the "It's a Mad, Mad, Mad, Mad Marge" episode (#247), Marge has the usual sources of stress—her husband and kids—along with a new source of anxiety, Becky. Becky (guest voice by Parker Posey) is a cute young woman who has been left at the altar by Otto (the bus driver) who chose heavy metal over her. (Becky had given the heavy metal–loving Otto the option of choosing her or his love for loud music.) Bart invites Becky to live with the family without consulting with them first. Because Marge advised Becky to confront Otto about his music (Becky does not like heavy metal music), she felt a little responsible for Becky's marriage being called off. As a result, Marge allows the young and attractive Becky to temporarily move in with the Simpsons.

Before long, Marge becomes jealous of Becky. Becky has managed to bond with Lisa and Bart. She is also a better cook than Marge so Homer instantly likes Becky. As the conversation below illustrates, it seems Becky can do just about everything better than Marge.

Lisa: Isn't it wonderful to have a hip female influence in the house?

Marge: Yes. Well, I guess I'll go roll socks. It's not hip, but it has to be done.

Becky: Actually, you could just tie them at the ends. That way the elastic doesn't wear out.

Marge: Yes. I hate when things get worn out. Mmm . . . socks . . . welcomes . . .

Marge has made a not-so-subtle hint to Becky to move on. And perhaps for good reason, as her sisters warn her about the dangers of allowing a gorgeous young woman in the house.

Patty: Look, honey. Never let an attractive woman into your house. All they ever do is usurp your family and then kill you.

Selma: Like that documentary, *The Hand That Rocks the Cradle*.

Although Marge points out that *The Hand That Rocks the Cradle* was a movie, Becky is a real threat to her home and family. Unbeknownst at this point in time, Becky is indeed planning on killing Marge and taking her family from her. Before this happens, however, Marge snaps while at a restaurant and is arrested by Chief Wiggum for assault. Marge had walked in on Becky giving Homer mouth-to-mouth in order to save him from choking. Marge thought Becky was kissing Homer.

A board of psychiatrists declare Marge legally "insane." The Simpson family, along with Becky, is at the hearing. Lisa asks her little sister, "Poor Maggie. How many insanity hearings have you been to in your short little life?" Before the authorities are able to transfer Marge to a mental hospital, she escapes. Hoping to find evidence that Becky is up to no good, Marge returns to the Simpson home. Becky admits to her deviant plan to steal Marge's home and family. Marge is relieved to find out she was not "crazy." (Note: Marge is presumably cleared of all charges and not sent to a mental institution.)

Just as anyone can suffer from a physical illness, it is important to realize that we are all potentially subject to mental illness. It is important for people to maintain physical *and* mental health. Just as physical exercise and a good diet can help most people maintain physical fitness, seeking therapy and dealing with stress and anxiety are important when dealing with mental illness.

Here's wishing everyone good physical health and serenity!

Chapter 14

Tricks and Treats

"Well, I'll be a son of a witch."
—Bart Simpson

One morning, Bart Simpson wakes up with a scary feeling and shouts from his bed, "Oh no, I can't see! I'm blind!" In actuality, there is a piece of duct tape covering his eyes. Homer walks into his son's room and, while yanking the tape from Bart's eyes, proudly proclaims, "Ha-ha! April Fools'!" A few moments later, Bart opens the refrigerator door and retrieves a carton of milk for his breakfast. Unbeknownst to Bart, his father has replaced the good milk with sour milk. Bart drinks from the carton and immediately spits out the foul-tasting beverage. Again, Homer appears and mocks Bart: "Ha-ha! April Fools'! I've been keeping that carton of milk next to the furnace for six weeks. Sucker!" Bart threatens to get even with Homer by fooling him later in the day. Homer ups the ante by taunting his son, "You couldn't fool your mother on the foolingest day of your life if you had an electrified fooling machine."

THE TRICK OF THE PRANK

"Mrs. Simpson, I'm afraid your husband is dead. Ha-ha! April Fools'! He's not dead!"
—Dr. Hibbert

The scenes described in the introductory story are from "So It's Come to This: A Simpsons Clip Show" episode (#77). Homer is one of those people who enjoys the holiday tradition of fooling people on April 1, otherwise known as "April Fools' Day." In this episode, Homer also contemplates the origin of April Fools' Day. As usual, Lisa is readily available to offer an explanation. Let's compare her answer to other popular explanations.

April Fools' Day: A Trickster's "Holy" Day

> **"Like Halloween and Christmas, April Fools' Day traces its origins to pagan rituals."**
> —Lisa Simpson

Sitting at the breakfast table and feeling proud about fooling Bart, not just once but twice, Homer wonders aloud, "Ah, what noble visionary thought up April Fools' Day?"

> *Lisa* (answering Homer's query): Like Halloween and Christmas, April Fools' Day traces its origins to pagan rituals.
> *Homer*: God bless those pagans.
> *Lisa*: April 1 used to be the pagan New Year.

In the "So It's Come to This . . ." episode, Lisa tells the story of the first prank pulled on April 1. The scene shifts back to a pagan Simpson family, April 1, 1022. The family chants "Blood for Ba'al!" as they dance around a pagan god. Standing nearby watching this pagan ritual is a 1022 Christian Flanders family. The pagan Simpsons offer a "New Year's" greeting to the Flanders family. As Lisa narrates her story to present-day Homer, she points out that the Christians had just changed their calendars, making January 1 the start of the new year. Meanwhile, back to the 1022 story, Ned mocks pagan Homer by saying New Year's Day was three months prior. Even so, Ned offers the pagan Simpsons a gift. Rod Flanders, Ned's youngest son, states, "It's ram's blood for your God-less ceremony." Homer eagerly opens the jar anticipating it to be ceremonial blood. Instead, the jar is filled with rubber snakes that fling into the air, scaring the unsuspecting Simpsons. A laughing Ned Flanders says, "April Fools'!"

Homer interrupts Lisa's storytelling by adding his own ending. He claims that after being shamed by the prank pulled by the Flanders family, the pagan Simpsons tie them to a burning stake while chanting, "Now, who's laughing? Now, who's laughing?" (Note: The Lisa character does not participate in the ritual, but sits off to the side.)

The true origin of April Fools' Day, sometimes called "All Fools' Day," is uncertain. Lisa's claim that April Fools' Day has its roots with pagan rituals would seem to be accurate. It is likely that any direct connection to present-day ritualistic April Fools' antics is linked to the 1500s when the Gregorian calendar took over from the Julian. Those who forgot to acknowledge the change and attempted to celebrate New Year's Day on the previously celebrated first day of the year (April 1) were teased as "April fools."

Many ancient cultures recognized April 1, or days near the vernal equinox (March 20 or March 21), as the first day of the new year. The Romans held end-of-the-winter celebrations (Hilaria celebration) typically around late March or early April and viewed spring as the start of the new year. In medieval Europe, March 25, the Feast of the Annunciation, marked the beginning of the new year. However, because the last week of March was "holy week" the new year was not celebrated until April 1. Considering the fact that most people associate spring with rebirth, or new birth, it seems more logical to consider the first day of the new year around April 1. So, how and why did this change?

As previously stated, the change occurred when Pope Gregory XIII ordered a new calendar (in 1582), the Gregorian calendar, to replace the old Julian calendar. The new calendar decreed that New Year's Day was to be celebrated on January 1. France adopted the calendar immediately. Eventually, the new calendar format was accepted by a growing number of nations. However, a number of people either refused to accept the new date or simply never heard about the new calendar, and continued to celebrate New Year's Day on April 1. Those who accepted the new calendar were known to mock the traditionalists. They would often send the traditionalists on "fools' errands" in an attempt to trick them into believing something false (e.g., like the 1022 Flanderses convinced the pagan Simpsons that their gift was a jar of ram's blood when instead it was filled with rubber snakes).

Although the change in calendar is a plausible explanation as to why people pull pranks and tricks on each other on April 1, this account is not complete. People from many cultures have celebrated

April 1 as a day of foolishness long before they were introduced to the Gregorian calendar. England, for example, did not adopt the Gregorian calendar until 1752, but April Fools' Day was already established there (Christianson 2000). Another theory about April Fools' is tied to the idea that people simply act a little giddier at the start of spring because they are happy that winter is finally over. This "spring fever" has undoubtedly affected people for centuries. Furthermore, ancient holidays such as the Roman Hilaria celebration, the Indian (Hindu) Holi festival of color (people celebrate in the streets by throwing different tints of powder on each other until eventually everyone is covered in different colors), and the northern European festival to honor Lud, a Celtic god of humor, could have all served as forerunners to celebrating April Fools' Day (McEntire 2003). We may never know the true history of April Fools' Day because much of this tradition is rooted in folk culture, rather than elite culture, and ancient folk culture is seldom documented. Regardless of its origin, April Fools' Day is a day often full of pranks and tricks being played among friends and family.

Homer and Bart certainly enjoy April Fools' Day hijinks. Turning our attention back to the "So It's Come to This . . ." episode, we should remember that Bart has vowed revenge against his father. Bart searches for ideas about the perfect prank when an idea is handed to him by his intended victim. Bart watches as Homer reaches for a Duff beer out of the refrigerator. Homer drops the can, picks it up, and opens it. As a result of its being shaken, a small amount of the beer spills on Homer. Homer says aloud, "It's a good thing that beer wasn't shaken up any more, or I'd have looked quite the fool." While Homer is not looking, Bart steals a can of beer and takes it to the Springfield Hardware store to shake the can up in a paint shaker.

The contents are so explosive that Bart is barely able to return the can of beer to the fridge. When Homer goes to the fridge for his next beer, he opens the can that Bart has modified. At the same time Homer opens the beer Bart emerges to yell, "April F—!" But before he can finish his statement the combustible can of beer explodes, ripping the roof off the house! Homer is rushed to Springfield General Hospital. His concerned family waits for a prognosis. Dr. Hibbert solemnly informs Marge, "Mrs. Simpson, I'm afraid your husband is dead. Ha-ha! April Fools'! He's not dead!"

Dr. Hibbert's very unprofessional behavior is only one reason why some people dread this day of foolery. For as much fun as April Fools' jokes can be, there are many people who do not care to be victimized by a practical joke. On the other hand, April Fools' Day is a prankster's delight.

Pranks and Practical Jokes

"Oh, now don't fret. These days, the victims of comedy trauma, or 'traumedies,' can still lead rich, full lives."
—Dr. Hibbert

April Fools' Day, of course, only comes once a year. What are pranksters to do the other 364 days of the year? The truth is people can pull pranks and practical jokes whenever they want—bearing in mind there are potential negative consequences for pulling a prank or practical joke on certain people or in certain circumstances. For example, placing a "fart" device on the seat of a conservative, uptight boss just prior to an important meeting when he or she is about to determine your continued employment with the company is ill advised. Despite the potential pitfalls, there are many people who like to fool others. Practical jokes are usually set up to produce what the perpetrator views as a humorous outcome at the expense of the victim, or target.

Victims of practical jokes are not always amused by the tactics of some perpetrators. The Simpson family was not amused when Dr. Hibbert informed them that Homer died as the result of an exploding can of beer. In "The Springfield Connection" episode (#126), Ned Flanders does not find the humor in Homer's practical joke. In this episode, Homer strings "Police Line Do Not Cross" yellow tape around the Flanderses' home. When Ned returns home from grocery shopping and sees the police tape, he immediately thinks the worst. Ned states, "Oh my Lord. Something horrible has happened." Emerging from behind a bush, Homer (laughing) tells Ned, "Fooled you, Flanders. I made you think your family was dead." Homer continues to laugh, but Ned does not find the humor in the "joke." Common decency (and "common sense") should be reason enough for any perpetrator of a practical joke to realize that making someone believe that their loved ones are dead is outside the bounds of an acceptable prank.

When someone tells a joke, the jokester usually relies on words to make her point. However, a practical joke is a type of humor that involves someone doing something, meaning there is an act or a "practice." Doing "something" physical involves a "setup" or deception, which is (generally) eventually revealed to the target. The victim then is made to be the butt of the joke and he or she is thereby made to feel foolish, or humiliated. While jokes may or may not be cruel or mean, there is an inherent strain of malice in most practical jokes. Putting someone at risk as part of a practical joke borders on sadism or vindictiveness. For example, in the "Mr. Plow" episode (#68), Homer pulls a practical joke on Barney that nearly costs his friend's life.

In this episode, Homer and Barney are snowplowing rivals. As Mr. Plow, Homer is making a nice income by plowing for businesses and residential homes. Homer even earns the "key" to the city after his plowing prowess allowed the Springfield schools to stay open. (The children of Springfield were not nearly as forthcoming with praise!) Homer's friend Barney becomes jealous of all the positive attention Homer is receiving. Homer attempts to inspire his friend to make something of himself, just as he did. However, instead of coming up with his own idea, Barney decides to plow snow also. Only Barney purchases a bigger truck and plow than Homer. Barney calls himself the Plow King. Shortly thereafter, Barney has "stolen" nearly all of Homer's clients. In an act of revenge, Homer decides to pull a prank on Barney by making a phony call to the Plow King asking him to plow a driveway atop Widow's Peak. Barney accepts the job and heads up the hazardous mountain.

Homer realizes the inherent danger of Widow's Peak, as it is avalanche-prone, but he is proud of his practical joke nonetheless. While Barney is away, Homer reclaims his lost clients. Meanwhile, the Plow King becomes trapped under an avalanche—one that he set off himself as a result of a loud burp. Even though he is making a lot of money plowing, Homer feels guilty when he learns that his prank has led to Barney being trapped under an avalanche. Homer drives up Widow's Peak and is able to save his friend. Homer also suggests that he and Barney become plowing partners. Barney agrees.

> *Homer*: When two best friends work together, not even God himself can stop them.
> (The sky opens above Homer and Barney.)
> *God*: Oh, no? (Suddenly all the snow melts.)

In the "Faith Off" episode (#237), Homer becomes upset that a cocktail party he was invited to at Springfield University was nothing more than a fund-raiser designed to solicit donations for the university. Homer beseeches help from some college buddies to pull a prank on the dean—who is viewed as the perpetrator of this fund-raiser. They attempt the classic "bucket over a door" practical joke. The joke was designed so that when the dean opens his door the contents of the bucket would spill all over him. This line of thinking falls directly under the realm of practical jokes, where the victim is made to be the butt of the joke and is thereby made to feel foolish. However, it is Homer who ends up with a bucket of super glue over his head. The practical joke has backfired! Later, Marge takes Homer to see Dr. Hibbert about removing the bucket from Homer's head.

> *Dr. Hibbert*: Hmm . . . I'm afraid it's hopeless. Beneath that bucket he's more glue than man.
> *Marge*: So he's stuck like this forever?
> *Dr. Hibbert*: Oh, now don't fret. These days, the victims of comedy trauma, or "traumedies," can still lead rich, full lives.

Practical jokes involve physical comedy. In some cases the intended victim is at risk of physical (and potentially mental) harm. On other occasions, however, a good practical joke is simply funny, even if everyone does not "get the joke." For example, in the "Bart Sells His Soul" episode (#132), Bart has targeted the members of the Springfield Community Church. He has replaced the hymn lyrics in all the prayer books with the classic "In-A-Gadda-Da-Vida" by the Iron Butterfly. The parishioners sing the song as if it were a religious hymn: "In the Garden of Eden . . ." The elderly woman playing the church organ has a hard time keeping up with her long solo. (Note: For those unfamiliar with this 1960s song, there is an extremely long [guitar] solo in the seventeen-minute album version of the song that challenges the most adept rockers. The term "heavy metal" was first used to describe this song.) And while the elderly organist, who plays this solo because of the lack of a guitarist in church, nearly collapses at the end of the song, Bart is quite pleased with his prank. Reverend Lovejoy, needless to say, was less amused! However, despite the organist nearly collapsing, no one was harmed by this practical joke.

Prank Phone Calls

> **"Ivana Tinkle? Just a sec. Ivana Tinkle! All right everybody, put down your glasses—Ivana Tinkle!"**
> —Moe Szyslak

In the early years of *The Simpsons*, it was quite common for Moe to be the victim of a prank phone call, usually perpetrated by Bart. A prank phone call, also known as a crank call, is a form of practical joke performed via the telephone. Prank phone calls are a juvenile form of humor generally perpetrated by kids and radio talk show hosts who rely on such immature forms of entertainment. As with any type of practical joke, however, prank calls can quickly cross over a thin line between humor and harassment. People who receive crank calls certainly do not appreciate being victimized by such antics.

Certain types of prank phone calls can jeopardize the safety of others. For example, calling a 9-1-1 operator to report a false accident can divert emergency services away from real emergencies. Such was the case in South Glen Falls, New York. An eight-year-old girl (name withheld from news reports), the same age as Lisa Simpson, placed 135 prank phone calls to 9-1-1 operators. The juvenile prankster called to report false accidents, leading officers on wild goose chases. Sheriff's deputies and 9-1-1 dispatchers used surveillance equipment that trace cell phone calls using satellite technology. The deputies traced a prank call to the girl's home while she was on the phone with a 9-1-1 operator (Syracuse *Post-Standard* February 10, 2007).

Whereas most forms of practical jokes and pranks can be viewed by an audience, prank phone calls are usually enjoyed by the caller only, although it is possible for others to listen in on the conversation. Pranksters, however, may record the hoax call and play it back to others. In cases such as these, the pranksters risk possible legal repercussions from such overseeing organizations as the Federal Communications Commission (FCC). Nonetheless, the television show *Crank Yankers* involved a series of real-life prank calls made by celebrities and then reenacted onscreen by puppets for an entertaining effect.

The prank phone calls utilized in *The Simpsons* are inspired by the famous recorded prank calls from the Tube Bar tapes. Louis "Red" Deutsch, a no-nonsense type of guy, opened the Tube Bar in Jersey City, New Jersey, after Prohibition. Among his rules were no women allowed (until the 1970s) and only serious whiskey-and-mixed-drink patrons were allowed in the bar. Food was not served and reading the newspaper was not allowed inside the bar. Patrons leaned against walls while drinking. John Davidson and Jim Elmo began making prank calls to the Tube Bar (named after the nearby Manhattan–New Jersey subway) and infuriated Red Deutsch. The pranksters would ask Red to call out fictitious names, which, when said aloud, sounded like something else. For example, the pranksters would ask for a Mr. Koholic, first name Al. When the bartender yelled out to the bar patrons, "I am looking for Al Koholic" it sounded like "alcoholic." What came out of those phone calls was an incredible collection of the taped telephone torments of an old man with a "red" hot temper. As soon as Deutsch would catch on to the prank, he would respond with extreme hostility. Red shouted obscenities (mostly "mother" insults) at the pranksters, threatening them with bodily harm if he ever found out who they are.

In *The Simpsons*, Moe's Tavern serves as the Tube Bar, and hot-tempered Moe represents Deutsch and his short fuse. There are some obvious differences between Moe's and the Tube Bar, most notably, Moe serves Duff beer and no mixed drinks, and the patrons sit at the bar. However, Moe does insist that his patrons drink and drink continuously, otherwise they are simply taking up space. This is clearly in the tradition of Red Deutsch at the Tube Bar. A few examples of crank phone calls made to Moe's are listed below:

Moe: Moe's Tavern.
Bart: Is Mr. Freely, there?
Moe: Who?
Bart: Freely. First initials, I. P.
Moe: Hold on, I'll check. (He calls out to the bar patrons.) Is I. P. Freely here? I. P. Freely!
(Moe catches on, gets angry, and complains to Homer about receiving prank phone calls.)
Homer: You'll get that punk someday, Moe.
Moe: I don't know. He's tough to catch. He keeps changing his name. (From the "Homer's Odyssey" episode [#3]).

Bart: Is Jacques there?
Moe: Who?

Bart: Jacques. Last name, Strap.

Moe: Hold on. (He calls out.) Jacques Strap! Hey, guys, I'm looking for a Jacques Strap! (From the "Moaning Lisa" episode [#6]).

Bart: Hello, is Al there?

Moe: Al?

Bart: Yeah, Al. Last name, Koholic.

Moe: Phone call for Al. Al Koholic. Is there an Al Koholic here? (From the "Some Enchanting Evening" episode [#13]).

Moe: Hello, Moe's Tavern—birthplace of the Rob Roy.

Bart: Is Seymour there? Last name, Butts.

Moe: Just a sec. (He calls out to the bar patrons.) Hey, is there a Butts here? Seymour Butts? Hey, everybody, I wanna Seymour Butts!

Moe (after it finally dawns on him that he is being pranked): Hey, wait a minute. Listen, you little scum-sucking pus bucket. When I get my hands on you, I'm gonna pull out your eyeballs with a corkscrew. (From the "One Fish, Two Fish, Blowfish, Blue Fish" episode [#24]).

Bart: Hello. Is Homer there?

Moe: Homer who?

Bart: Homer Sexual.

Moe: Wait one second, let me check. (He yells out to the bar patrons.) Homer Sexual. Ah, come on, come on, one of you guys has gotta be Homer Sexual.

Moe (it dawns on Moe he has been pranked): Oh no, you rotten little punk! If I ever get ahold of you, I'll sink my teeth into your cheek and rip your face off! (From the "Principal Charming" episode [#27]).

Bart: Uh, hello. Is Mike there? Last name, Rotch.

Moe: Hold on, I'll check. Mike Rotch. Mike Rotch! Hey, has anybody seen Mike Rotch lately? (From the "Blood Feud" episode [#35]).

Interestingly, *The Simpsons* explains the origin of Moe's victimization of prank phone calls in the episode, "The Way We Weren't" (#333). In this episode, Homer and Marge retell the story of their first kiss to their children. The kiss occurred when they were ten years old and at summer camp. Due to a series of mishaps, the young Homer tells Marge that his name is Elvis Jagger Abdul Jabbar. When Homer fails to show up at the girls' camp for his second date, Marge phones the boys' camp looking for him. Moe, who is unofficially serving as a junior counselor, answers the phone. Marge asks to speak to Elvis Jagger Abdul Jabbar. Realizing immediately that this is a fake name, Moe gets angry and yells at Marge. Moe then turns toward the camera and explains, "That's the origin of that!" (Implying, of course, that Moe has just explained to the TV viewing audience why he dislikes prank phone calls as an adult.)

There are times when prank phone calls misfire. For example, when the fictitious name turns out to be the real name of a bar patron. On other occasions, an honest request to find someone may be misinterpreted as a prank call. For example, in the "Homer the Smithers" episode (#145), Mr. Burns dials a phone (apparently for the first time) looking for Smithers. Mr. Burns punches in numbers that spell out "S-M-I-T-H-E-R-S." He reaches Moe's Tavern instead and says, "I'm looking for Smithers, first name Whalen." Moe repeats Mr. Burns's request but becomes angry, thinking it is a prank call. This is understandable, in that Burns used the same formula utilized by Bart so many times before. Moe, who has no idea this is a genuine request and that the caller is Mr. Burns, the richest man in Springfield, threatens to physically harm the caller. In another example of a prank phone call that backfires, Homer, in the "Bart on the Road" episode (#148), attempts to pull a prank on Moe. As the dialogue below illustrates, Homer is no "prank yanker" master.

> *Homer*: Hello, I'd like to speak with a Mr. Snotball, first name, Ura.
> *Moe*: Ura Snotball?
> *Homer*: What? How dare you! If I find out who this is, I'll staple a flag to your butt and mail you to Iran!

In the "New Kid on the Block" episode (#67), Bart meets Laura Powers and immediately becomes smitten with her. However, as we learned in chapter 4, Laura does not share Bart's feelings. Things get worse for Bart when Laura starts to date Jimbo Jones. Jimbo is one of the bullies at school who picks on younger kids like Bart. Now Jimbo is in his house while Laura babysits the Simpson children. When Jimbo and Laura begin making out, Bart cannot take it any longer. He devises a plan that starts with a prank phone call to Moe's. Moe answers the phone call.

> *Moe*: Hey, just a sec, I'll check. (He turns to the bar patrons.) Amanda Huggenkiss. Hey, I'm looking for Amanda Huggenkiss! Why can't I find Amanda Huggenkiss? (As usual, the bar patrons laugh at Moe for being a victim of a prank phone call.)
> *Barney*: Maybe your standards are too high!
> *Moe* (on the phone): Why you SOB. If I ever find out who you are, I'm going to shove a sausage down your throat and stick starving dogs in your butt.
> *Bart*: My name is Jimbo Jones and I live at 1094 Evergreen Terrace.
> *Moe*: Ah-ha! Big mistake pal. (He hangs up the phone.) I knew he'd slip up sooner or later.

And with that, Moe reaches for a huge butcher's knife ("rusty and dull") ready to cause bodily harm to his tormentor. Moe runs off to 1094 Evergreen Terrace—the Simpsons' home address. He opens the door as Laura and Jimbo are making out. Moe yells out, "Who's Jimbo Jones?" Jimbo is so frightened that he begins to cry. Moe says, "I wasn't really gonna kill you. I was just gonna cut ya." Moe returns to his bar. Laura breaks up with Jimbo. And, as a means of bonding with Bart, Laura makes a prank phone call to Moe's. (Assumingly, Moe has had enough time to return to the bar.)

> *Laura*: Hello. I'd like to talk to Ms. Tinkle. (Bart whispers a first name for Laura to use.) First name, Ivana.
> *Moe*: Ivana Tinkle? Just a sec. (He turns to the bar patrons.) Ivana Tinkle! All right everybody, put down your glasses— Ivana Tinkle!

Once again the bar patrons mock Moe. Laura and Bart solidify their friendship as pranksters.

It should be noted that today it is a little more difficult to pull prank phone calls as they can be traced through caller ID and *69. However, pranksters still have at least two options at their disposal. One, they can "block" their phone number from the view of those who receive the call. And, pranksters can use pay phones (yes, there are still a few of them left!) and not worry whether or not anyone can trace the call. It should also be noted that in some cases, prank calls are treated as criminal offenses. Examples include calling in a "bomb threat" or falsely reporting a crime or emergency.

HALLOWEEN AND OTHER TREATS

"Scaring people into giving us treats is fun. We should do this every year."
—Selma Bouvier

One of the many traditions associated with Halloween involves telling ghost stories. To this end, *The Simpsons* annually airs its "Treehouse of Horror" episodes. These episodes generally involve three separate stories within one episode. In the introduction to the first "Treehouse of Horror" episode (#16), Marge Simpson provides a lengthy warning to viewers:

> Hello, everyone. You know, Halloween is a very strange holiday. Personally, I don't understand it. Kids worshiping ghosts, pretending to be devils . . . things on TV that are completely inappropriate for younger viewers. Things like the following half hour. Nothing seems to bother my kids, but tonight's show—which I totally wash my hands of—is really scary. So, if you have sensitive children, maybe you should tuck them into bed early tonight instead of writing us angry letters tomorrow. Thanks for your attention.

Despite this warning, some viewers were not prepared for this Halloween special. A number of people did write angry letters in protest of the scary content. Despite this, for most viewers, the Halloween episodes represent an ultimate treat from *The Simpsons*.

Marge does, however, raise an interesting point. That is, Halloween does seem like a strange holiday. Every other day of the year, parents warn their children not to take candy from strangers. And yet, on Halloween night, children by the millions go door-to-door in disguise, asking relatives, friends, neighbors, and strangers for free candy! Further, these disguises are often outrageous, scandalous, supernatural, and paganistic in design. This strange holiday and the ritualistic behaviors associated with it begs the question, "How did this all get started?"

Halloween's Rituals and Origins

Halloween (October 31) represents many things to many people. For children, it is a night to dress in costumes (e.g., a superhero character, a ghost, a princess, and so on) and go door-to-door soliciting treats. This ritualistic behavior involves children knocking on a door (or ringing a doorbell) and saying, "Trick or Treat" when someone opens the door. The children, or trick-or-treaters as they are known, expect to be handed some sort of treat, preferably candy. Generally, by the end of the evening, kids take in quite a haul of goodies. Most of us can remember going through a sack of candy sorting out the "good" candy from the "cheap" or "bad" candy; or God forbid, fruit! (Note to people who distribute treats at Halloween: Children do not want fruit for Halloween; they get that all year from their parents and at school! Caramel apples are an exception to this rule.) Some kids will eat so much candy on Halloween that they get sick. Others will store candy like a chipmunk preparing for a long winter and eat a little bit at a time. And it is not unheard of for parents to sneak some candy from their children's goodie bag.

People who do not provide treats may expect to be victimized by some sort of prank such as having their door and/or windows pelted by eggs, or their house "TPed"—rolls of toilet paper thrown on the trees in the yard or around the house itself. In this manner, people who do not provide treats to kids expecting them will have to deal with some sort of cleaning-up process the next day. Interestingly, some homeowners turn the tables on trick or treaters by creating scary scenarios that ultimately lead to children running away in fear.

This author can remember as a young child trick-or-treating for one of his first Halloweens and upon excitedly saying, "trick or treat" (and expecting immediate gratification of candy being placed in his Halloween plastic pumpkin) having the homeowner say, "What sort of tricks are you prepared to do?" I was dumbfounded by this! I remember thinking to myself, with my older brother and younger sister at my side, "Just give me the candy!" The homeowner was relentless. He said, "If you want a treat, I want to see a trick!" With my mother standing at the end of the driveway (safeguarding her children) my options of what type of tricks to deliver were limited. After mercilessly embarrassing us, the homeowner eventually gave us each a small candy bar. Now, if he had pulled this trick on me during my rebellious adolescent years, he would not have been happy with the tricks I was capable of committing—just think of what Bart Simpson might do if placed in this scenario!

A worse scenario than being "tricked" by a homeowner is being dangerously victimized. There are "sickos" who attempt to harm children who trick or treat at their homes by doing such things as placing razor blades inside an apple or an orange. Many adults have their children's candy x-rayed at a hospital or some designated place that has set up x-ray machines for this very purpose. Other mean-spirited people may tamper with candy by adding poison. In short, Halloween is not all fun and games.

Halloween, of course, is not just for kids. Adults enjoy this odd holiday as well. They attend Halloween parties and often wear outrageous or "naughty" costumes, such as pregnant nuns; short-skirted nurses or private-schoolgirl outfits; devil costumes with full props; and a wide variety of creative outfits. Bars often have contests and award people for their costume based on some sort of criteria (e.g., most original, sexiest, or best couple costume). As someone who has lived throughout the country, I have discovered that warm-weather cities and cities known for their promiscuity have the wildest adult-themed Halloween parties. Among the most scandalous annual Holiday parties is the Exotic Erotic Halloween in San Francisco. This strictly adult-themed party often resembles an orgy of erotica with enough outrageous behavior to meet everyone's wildest dreams. In line with the contemporary meaning of Halloween, this party, like with most Halloween parties across the United States, is all about humor and good times.

The contemporary celebration of Halloween has drifted quite a distance from its pagan origins. Halloween, also known as All Hallows' Eve, originated as a pagan festival among the Celts of Ireland and Great Britain. Around the fifth century BCE, October 31 marked the end of the Celtic calender. (Samhain literally means "summer's end.") Thus, the Celts celebrated November 1 as the first day of the new year. Legend has it that, on October 31, the spirits of all those who had died throughout the preceding year came back in search of living bodies to possess for the next year. The Celts believed this was the only way "lost souls" could be saved in the afterlife. Because the still-living did not want to be possessed, they would dress and act outrageously the night before New Year's day. The Celtic people would dress in costume, such as wearing the head of a dead animal, to trick the spirits into thinking they were spirits as well. This tradition is directly tied to why Americans dress up in costume on Halloween.

After the Romans invaded Ireland and conquered the Celtic people (first century CE), two new holidays were introduced in conjunction with the Samhain celebrations. The first of these was called "Feralia" and took place in late October as a celebration in honor of the dead. The second holiday was held in honor of the Roman goddess Pomona, the mythical goddess of fruit and fruit trees, gardens, and orchards. (Pomona is associated with the harvest.) It is believed that the tradition of bobbing for apples on Halloween is related to the celebrations of this Roman/Celtic holiday as one of Pomona's symbols is an apple. The Celts continued their pagan rituals until the time of the arrival of Christianity in the sixth century CE.

Although dressing in costume and acting outrageously originates with the Celts, the idea of "trick-or-treating" did not. Instead, the practice of walking from door to door asking for treats originates with Christianity. November 2, the Christian holy day of All Souls' Day, involved early Christians walking from village to village begging for "soul cakes"—square pieces of bread and currants. In return for the "soul cakes," beggars promised to offer up prayers on behalf of the dead relatives of the donors. At this time, the Christians believed that the souls of dead people remained in limbo until they received enough prayers to enter Heaven. Influenced by Celtic tradition and early Christian practices, Pope Gregory IV standardized November 1 as the date for "All Saints Day," or "All Hallows' Day" for the entire Western Church in 835 CE.

Today, most Western countries celebrate Halloween as the Americans do. But this celebration is certainly not universal. Americans living in Australia are surprised to find that Australians do not celebrate Halloween. However, because of American influence, the holiday is catching on. Halloween is not celebrated in Russia, either. A

Russian colleague of mine visited the United States in late October and was amazed by the Halloween-related items found in department stores. Fake teeth, fake blood, ghoulish costumes, and free candy for anyone who knocks on your door is not a tradition that has found its way to this former Soviet nation. However, just as a variety of aspects of American popular culture have found their way into Russia, it is just a matter of time before Russians enjoy this uniquely strange holiday.

Treehouses of Horror

> **"Well, look who it is! If I knew you were coming, I'd have baked a cat!"**
> —Selma Bouvier

Every year beginning with the second season, *The Simpsons* has aired its "Treehouse of Horror" Halloween special. In the first "Treehouse of Horror" episode (#16), Lisa and Bart tell scary stories to each other in their tree house. Maggie is with them. Homer eavesdrops and becomes frightened by their tales of horror.

One of the stories, "Hungry Are the Damned," introduces viewers to space aliens from Rigel-4. The space aliens are one-eyed octopi and appear every year in the annual "Treehouse of Horror" episodes. The story begins with the Simpson family barbecuing in their backyard. Suddenly a spaceship hovers overhead. A tractor beam lifts members of the Simpson family to the ship one at a time. Because of his weight, it takes two tractor beams to lift Homer. Once the family members are aboard, the ship heads off to outer space. The Simpsons are greeted by Kang, one of the space aliens.

Kang: Greetings, Earthlings. I am Kang. Do not be frightened. We mean you no harm.
Marge: You speak English?
Kang: I am actually speaking Rigellian. By an astonishing coincidence, both of our languages are exactly the same.
Bart: Well, what are you gonna do with us, man?
Kang: Kodos and I are taking you to Rigel-4, a world of infinite delights to tantalize your senses and challenge your intellectual limitations.

Lisa pleads with Kang and Kodos. Lisa informs the aliens that she realizes the Simpsons are inferior forms of life and that they face that prejudice on Earth every day; and yet they are relatively happy. She gets on her knees to beg for mercy. While Lisa makes her proclamation, a huge buffet is brought to them. The Simpsons are told to eat as much as they want, but to eat everything they take. All of their favorite foods are presented to them, including fried shrimp, pork chops, and sloppy Joes. The Simpsons eagerly gorge themselves on a seemingly endless supply of food.

While the rest of her family continues to eat, Lisa wanders around the spaceship. She sneaks into the food preparation room and discovers a book titled *How to Cook Humans*. (Note: This is a parody of the *Twilight Zone* episode "To Serve Man.") Lisa immediately becomes alarmed. She warns her family to stop eating because she believes the aliens are merely fattening them up for their own consumption. She shows them the cookbook she found in the kitchen. Homer confronts Kang. Kang is taken aback by the accusation. He blows off some dust to reveal that the title of the book is *How to Cook For Humans*. Not convinced by Kang's explanation, Lisa blows more dust off the book to reveal that the title now reads, *How to Cook Forty Humans*. The Simpsons are alarmed again. That is, until Kang says there is still more space dust on the book. He blows off the remaining dust to show the full title of the book, *How to Cook For Forty Humans*. Kang feels insulted by the Simpsons' accusations.

> *Kang*: Let me get this straight; you thought—
> *Kodos*: They thought we were going to eat them!
> *Kang*: Good god! Is this some kind of joke?
> *Kodos*: No! They're serious!
> *Lisa*: Well, why were you trying to make us eat all the time?
> *Kodos*: Make you eat? We merely provided a sumptuous banquet, and frankly, you people make pigs of yourselves!
> *Serak*: I slaved in the kitchen for days and days for you people and— (Serak begins to sob.)
> *Kodos*: Well, if you wanted to make Serak the Preparer cry, mission accomplished.

The space aliens fly back to Earth and drop off the Simpsons at their home. As the Simpsons disembark from the spaceship, Kang scolds them. He informs the Simpsons that they could have lived in paradise, forever, experiencing emotions they never could on Earth, and they would have been treated like gods. Marge comments, "For a superior race, they really rub it in." The spaceship takes off. Lisa says, "There were monsters on that ship. And surely we were them."

In the "Treehouse of Horror II" episode (#42), Marge offers another warning at the start. (Note: The warnings would only continue for a few more years.) Marge reminds viewers that she warned people not to let their children watch last year's show and yet children watched it anyway. Marge adds, "Well, this year's episode is even worse; it's scarier and more violent and I think they snuck in some bad language, too."

This episode begins with Homer answering the door to find two older kids, Dolph and Kearney, trick-or-treating at the Simpson home. They are not wearing costumes.

> *Dolph and Kearney* (simultaneously): Trick or treat, man.
> *Homer*: Hey aren't you a little old for this? You're not even wearing costumes.
> *Dolph*: Hand over the candy, old dude, or we'll egg your house back to the Stone Age.
> *Homer* (emptying his bowl of candy into their bags): Here you go, kids.

As previously mentioned, there are consequences for not cooperating with kids expecting candy on Halloween. Egging the house of a noncompliant is the standard way of dealing with someone who refuses to hand out treats. Homer does not want to clean the house of eggs, so he willingly gives in to the demands of Kearney and Dolph. Unfortunately for Homer, even after meeting with their demands, Kearney and Dolph egg his front door.

Marge and the kids return home. Homer inquires about their haul. Bart proudly dumps a huge bag of candy on the floor. Homer says he is proud of him. Marge tells the kids they can have one piece of candy, but she wants them to save the rest. She is too late, as Homer and the kids are munching away on one piece of candy after another. She warns them, "If you eat too much, you'll have nightmares." Sure enough, Homer, Lisa, and Bart all have nightmares. And thus, the three storylines for this "Treehouse of Horror" episode are set.

Lisa's nightmare involves the Simpson family on vacation in Marrakech, Morocco. The family walks through an open market. Homer is tempted to purchase a magic monkey's paw. The monkey's paw grants four wishes. However, the seller of the monkey's paw warns Homer that grave misfortune accompanies each wish made. Naturally, Homer buys the monkey's paw anyway. Homer brings the paw back to Springfield before making any wishes. Maggie grabs the monkey's paw while no one is looking and apparently makes a wish. Shortly afterwards, a new pacifier is delivered to the front door for Maggie. Bart makes a wish for the Simpsons to be rich and famous. Shortly afterwards, their living room is filled with money. A number of townspeople discuss how sick and tired they are with the Simpsons (the first sign of the curse).

Lisa, meanwhile, makes a wish for world peace. The scene shifts to the United Nations where England apologizes to Argentina for the Falklands War.

> *British Ambassador*: Eh, sorry about the Falklands, old boy.
> *Argentinean Ambassador*: Oh, forget it. We kind of knew they were yours.
> (Note: the Falklands War first started in 1982 after Argentina took control of the South Georgia Island. The British government was completely caught off guard by this and retaliated with military force, driving the Argentines off the island.)

Lisa's wish does come true, as peace is declared around the world. Without the threat of war, all the weapons on planet Earth are destroyed. People everywhere rejoice. Americans join hands (similar to the popular "Hands Across America" that occurred in 1986) and make a giant peace sign. The space aliens Kang and Kodos see this peace sign and realize that Earth is easy prey for a hostile takeover. They enslave all the Earthlings and humanity appears doomed. Lisa's wish surely did have negative consequences. Once again, the townspeople blame the Simpsons.

But there is still one wish remaining on the monkey's paw. Unfortunately, Homer wastes it by wishing for a turkey sandwich. Homer's simple wish backfires as he complains that the turkey is a "little dry." Just as Homer is about to throw the monkey's paw in the trash, Ned

Flanders walks by. He takes the monkey's paw and wishes that the space aliens will leave Earth. Ned's wish comes true and he is treated as a hero.

The Halloween symbols of witchcraft and black cats come to the forefront in the "Treehouse of Horror VIII" episode (#182). Witchcraft is associated with the supernatural and magical powers. Those who practice witchcraft are known as witches. Since medieval times, witchcraft has been associated with evil and the devil. Witches are generally female, although male equivalents, such as wizards, sorcerers, and warlocks, are also believed to exist. During the Puritan age of colonial America, witches were sometimes burned at the stake (other witches were hanged or stoned to death) by religious zealots who feared their presumed supernatural power. People have feared witches because they believe that witches can conjure spells to make them do things against their will. Further, the Bible warns against witches, "Thou shalt not suffer a witch to live" (Exodus 22:18). This is an expression used to describe a person who should be killed.

Black cats are often associated with witches and have played a major role for centuries in folklore, superstition, and mythology. Black cats are believed by some to be witches incarnate. As a result, superstitious people may fear black cats. This is especially true at Halloween. The primary reason that black cats and not some other color of cat are associated with witches is because the color black is often associated with the color of night and of "evil." Add to this, the color black is generally worn at funerals and thus becomes associated with sorrow or mourning.

The Easy Bake Coven story of the "Treehouse of Horror VIII" episode highlights many of the myths associated with witchcraft and black cats at Halloween. This story takes place in 1649 with Springfield as a puritanical society. The townspeople are burning women at the stake who are suspected of being witches. The mayor, who resembles present-day Quimby states, "You are hereby found guilty of the crime of witchcraft. I sentence you hags to be burned at the stake until you are deemed fit to reenter society!" Clearly, once a woman is burned to death at the stake, she will not be able to reenter society. And such was the illogic of burning witches at the stake. The 1649 Lisa Simpson points out the flaws of accusing a woman of being a witch.

Lisa: If they're really witches, why don't they use their powers to escape?

Homer: That sounds like witch-talk to me, Lisa.

Lisa: Never mind.

Flanders: That's seventy-five witches we've processed. That oughtta show God whose side we're on, eh, Pastor?

Reverend Lovejoy: Yes, Nedwin, but we have many more strumpets to incinerate.

Reverend Lovejoy proclaims that there is still one other witch among them. The townspeople turn to Marge and accuse her of being a witch. Marge denies being a witch, but everyone yells out, "Burn her!" Chief Wiggum places Marge on a broom (an instrument associated with witches) and shoves her off a cliff. Wiggum reinforces the illogic associated with sacrificing women accused of being witches by saying, "If you're innocent, you will fall to an honorable Christian death. If you are, however, the bride of Satan, you will surely fly your broom to safety. At that point you will report back here for torture and beheading." The rest of the townspeople go along with this line of thinking. Women are especially reluctant to complain because they realize they run the risk of being accused as a witch. In actuality, the real reason women were burned at the stake in the 1600s was because of the patriarchical nature of society. The men of power feared any woman who displayed any form of independent thinking. They were especially troubled by a woman who was willing to live a life without a man. Surely, they thought, such a woman must be a witch.

The 1649 Marge is thrown from the cliff. However, as she falls, she suddenly turns into a witch and flies to safety. Upon seeing such a sight Bart proclaims, "Well, I'll be a son of a witch!" Marge flies over the townspeople and admits to being a witch. "That's right. I'm a witch! And I'm the one who withered your livestock, soured your sheep's milk, and made your shirts itchy." In an act of revenge, Marge turns Eddie and Lou into snowmen. She then commands a swarm of bats to attack the remaining townspeople. Marge flies away and joins her sisters, Patty and Selma, who are in a cave cooking over a cauldron. Upon seeing Marge flying to their cave, Selma states, "Well, look who it is! If I knew you were coming, I'd have baked a cat!" Marge explains to her sisters that the townsfolk found out she is a witch and that she was forced to leave her family.

The townspeople worry that the three witches will seek revenge.

A worried Maude tells Ned that she has heard tales of witches coming to normal folks' homes and eating their children. In a desperate attempt to protect their children, the Flanderses offer the witches freshly baked gingerbread children instead. Ned points out the advantage of gingerbread children—they are boneless! The witches are pleased with the treats offered to them by the Flanderses and other townspeople and fly back to their hideaway. Selma states, "Scaring people into giving us treats is fun. We should do this every year!"

And with that, the tradition of giving out treats to those dressed as witches becomes an annual event. At least according to *The Simpsons*!

Each of the successive "Treehouse of Horror" episodes provides viewers with a variety of treats. Kang and Kodos continue their yearly visits to Earth, at times wreaking havoc. For example, as described in chapter 10, in the "Treehouse of Horror XVII" episode (#382), Kang and Kodos invade Earth under the pretense of being "liberators" as part of their Operation Enduring Occupation—a political statement about the Iraq War. And, in "Treehouse of Horror IX" (episode #207), viewers of *The Simpsons* are led to believe that Maggie may actually be the by-product of Marge's love with one of the space aliens.

The "Treehouse of Horror" episodes are indeed an annual treat for all of us trick-or-treaters who enjoy *The Simpsons*.

OTHER TREATS: COUCH GAGS AND CHALKBOARD MESSAGES

"Nobody reads these anymore."
—Bart's chalkboard message

The "Treehouse of Horror" episodes are annual treats for our viewing enjoyment. However, the pleasure of watching *The Simpsons* is certainly not limited to the Halloween specials, or even the regular sketches. Many viewers look forward to the special little treats provided in the chalkboard messages scrawled by Bart and the couch sequences at the start of each episode. There are literally hundreds of examples of chalkboard messages and couch sequences. In fact, it appears the writers of *The Simpsons* sometimes grow tired of these little treats, as there are occasions where the chalkboard messages are nonexistent and the couch sequences have been repeated. As a means of displaying their lack of interest in these tedious treats, the writers of *The Simpsons* once had Bart write on the board: "Nobody reads these anymore." Loyal viewers will attest that is not true. After all, they are treats!

The chalkboard messages are a running visual treat that occur during the opening credits of most *Simpsons* episodes. The audience finds a frowning Bart Simpson writing a unique phrase on the school's chalkboard as a part of some sort of punishment. When the school bell rings, ending the day, he immediately runs out of the classroom, a happy boy. Once outside the school, Bart jumps on his skateboard and heads home. The rest of the Simpson family is also heading home. Marge and Maggie, after finishing their shopping, drive home. Homer, after finishing a day at work, also drives home. Lisa is shown riding her bike home from school. They all converge at home at the same time, narrowly missing hitting each other in the driveway. Finally, they all head to the couch where the final opening sequence occurs—the couch gag.

The chalkboard phrases are usually written in uppercase. Generally, the phrases written on the chalkboard have nothing to do with the episode itself. In that manner, it is understandable why the writers may consider such a task as pointless. A mere sampling of these chalkboard messages are provided below:

I WILL NOT WASTE CHALK ("Bart the Genius" [#2])
I WILL NOT INSTIGATE REVOLUTION ("Moaning Lisa" [#6])
I WILL NOT PLEDGE ALLEGIANCE TO BART ("Itchy & Scratchy & Marge" [#22])
I WILL NOT SELL MIRACLE CURES ("The Front" [#78])
I AM NOT DELIGHTFULLY SAUCY ("Homer Loves Flanders" [#97])
I WILL REMEMBER TO TAKE MY MEDICATION ("Homer vs. Patty and Selma" [#120])
A FIRE DRILL DOES NOT DEMAND A FIRE ("The Canine Mutiny" [#173])
I NO LONGER WANT MY MTV ("Lisa's Sax" [#181])
I WILL NOT MESS WITH THE OPENING CREDITS ("Trash of the Titans" [#200])
BUTT.BUTT IS NOT MY E-MAIL ADDRESS ("When You Dish upon a Star" [#208])
MY MOM IS NOT DATING JERRY SEINFELD ("Viva Ned Flan-

ders" [#213])

GRAMMAR IS NOT A TIME OF WASTE ("Marge Simpson In: 'Screaming Yellow Bonkers'" [#218])

I CAN'T SEE DEAD PEOPLE ("Take My Wife, Sleaze" [#234])

I WAS NOT THE SIXTH BEATLE ("Homer vs. Dignity" [#253])

I SHOULD NOT BE TWENTY-ONE BY NOW ("Simpsons Tall Tales" [#269])

NOBODY READS THESE ANYMORE ("The Parent Rap" [#271])

I WILL NEVER LIE ABOUT BEING CANCELLED AGAIN ("The Sweetest Apu" [#288])

FISH DO NOT LIKE COFFEE ("Bart vs. Lisa vs. the Third Grade" [#294])

SPONGEBOB IS NOT A CONTRACEPTIVE ("Pray Anything" [#301])

SANDWICHES SHOULD NOT CONTAIN SAND ("The Bart of War" [#312])

As the opening credits end, the entire Simpson family converges, from different directions, into the family living room. They are aiming for their position on the couch in front of the television. Their positioning is anything but routine. A sampling of couch gags is provided below:

- The couch falls apart when everyone sits on it. ("Homer's Odyssey" [#3])
- The couch falls through the floor. ("Bart Gets an 'F'" [#14])
- The family safely parachutes into the living room. Homer's chute, however, does not open and he crashes to the floor. ("Homer's Enemy" [#176])
- After each family member sits on the couch, hairdryers come from behind and give each of them a hairstyle of a different family member. ("Lisa Gets an 'A'" [#210])
- The Simpsons are frogs and the living room is a swamp. ("Homer Simpson in Kidney Trouble" [#211])
- After the family members sit on the couch, an animated human hand spins them around, leaving the characters diffused. ("Viva Ned Flanders" [#213])
- Numerous townspeople are already in the Simpson living room

when the Simpson family enters. ("The Old Man and the 'C' Student" [#223])

- The living room is flooded by a melting iceberg. ("They Saved Lisa's Brain" [#225])
- The Simpsons are poured out of a cement truck backed up in the living room. ("Hello Gutter, Hello Fadder" [#232])
- After the Simpsons are seated, they fall into a crack of the couch, which turns into a "shredder" with the characters coming out as if they went through a paper shredder. ("Take My Wife, Sleaze" [#234]).
- The Simpsons enter the living room in bumper cars and there is no couch. ("Alone Again Natura-Diddly" [#240])
- The Simpsons all have Moe's face. ("She Used to Be My Girl" [#339])
- A newspaper headline proclaims: "Couch Gag Thrills Nation." ("Simpsons Christmas Stories" [#365])
- An animated human hand with a pair of scissors makes paper cutouts shaped like the Simpson family. ("The Haw-Hawked" [#386])

Perhaps the most elaborate couch gag comes from "The Ziff Who Came to Dinner" episode (#327). In this episode the Simpsons find their positions on the couch and the camera angle zooms outward beyond the living room, then beyond the Simpson house, beyond Springfield, beyond Earth, and then beyond the galaxy. The expanded scene finally ends inside Homer's head. Sitting on the couch Homer exclaims, "Wow!" Wow, indeed, Homer! This couch gag is reminiscent of the philosophical question, "What if our entire galaxy was merely a cell of a giant's hand?"

And with that in mind, what if *The Simpsons* is merely a figment of our collective imaginations? Would that make *The Simpsons* a trick, or a treat?!

Chapter 15

The Animation Domination of The Simpsons

**"Oh, Marge, cartoons don't have any deep meaning.
They're just stupid drawings that give you a cheap laugh."**
—Homer Simpson

As described in chapter 1, Homer, Marge, Bart, Lisa, and Maggie Simpson were first introduced to the viewing public on April 19, 1987, as a comic short on *The Tracey Ullman Show*. On December 17, 1989, the first full-length episode of *The Simpsons* debuted.

Matt Groening was in the right place at the right time when he first presented his idea of an animated dysfunctional family to the executives at the FOX Broadcasting Company. FOX was a relatively new and unestablished fledging network that arose from Channel 11 in Los Angeles. Since its inception, FOX has been willing to take a gamble on a number of controversial shows including one of the best shows ever broadcast, *Married . . . with Children. Married . . . with Children*, starring the gorgeous Christina Applegate, was also a show about a dysfunctional family.

The Simpsons often makes fun of its parent network, FOX, and its willingness to broadcast shows that other networks pass on. For example, in the "Today, I Am a Clown" episode (#319), Krusty pitches reality TV show ideas to the executives of FOX. They pass on all his initial ideas. Surprised by this, Krusty says to the FOX executives, "C'mon, you people are known for taking chances on crappy shows."

As it turns out, the FOX executives agree to broadcast Krusty's bar mitzvah under the title, "Krusty the Klown's Wet 'n' Wild Bar Mitzvah." The bar mitzvah special features Mr. T as a guest. The show is a huge ratings success but Krusty manages to disappoint his father because he has made a mockery of a religious ceremony on TV.

Although FOX has never aired such a show as a *Wet 'n' Wild Bar Mitzvah*, it has certainly demonstrated a willingness to broadcast questionable shows. However, as a viewer of FOX TV, I can honestly state that I am a huge fan of more FOX shows than just *The Simpsons* and *Married . . . with Children* (for example, *21 Jump Street*, *Melrose Place*, *In Living Color*, *The Adventures of Brisco County, Jr.*, *King of the Hill*, and *Family Guy*). As a former resident of Los Angeles, I remember watching a lot of the FOX shows on the local Channel 11 long before the FOX "network" extended nationwide. Shows such as *The Simpsons* and *Married . . . with Children* were the face of FOX TV in the late 1980s and early 1990s. And although the Bundy family is long gone (but still available in syndication), the Simpson family and the other residents of fictional Springfield continue to entertain audiences with original episodes.

THE SIMPSONS AS A MICROCOSM OF SOCIETY

The Simpsons is a satirical parody of the values of a stereotypical middle-class American family. In essence, the show lampoons many elements of the human condition and the American way of life. As demonstrated throughout this book, *The Simpsons* touches upon many cultural aspects, including religion; politics; environmentalism; economics; education; health and aging; gender; race and ethnicity; friendship; and of course, romance, marriage, and family. In this regard, it could be argued that *The Simpsons* is a microcosm of society. That is, nearly all the elements of the greater American society are found in *The Simpsons*.

A microcosm is a small world, or a world within itself. When a particular social entity is said to be "a microcosm of society," it means that the elements within this microcosm mirror the elements of the greater society. The institution of sports, for example, is often argued to be a microcosm of the greater society. *The Simpsons* may be viewed as a microcosm of the human experience, as the residents of

Springfield reflect or mirror the residents of many cities, suburbs, and towns across America. By depicting the behavioral patterns of the Springfield residents and articulating upon their interactions with the various social institutions of American society, viewers are able to place themselves in the position of *The Simpsons* characters because their experiences mirror our experiences. As demonstrated throughout this book, the Springfield characters are capable of great feats of courage, strength, and heroism, just as they are capable of making many mistakes. Consequently, *The Simpsons* is a domain occupied by the same social constructions that are found in the greater society. The study of *The Simpsons* ("Simpsonology"), then, helps us to better understand the greater society.

THE SIMPSONS AND POPULAR CULTURE

The Simpsons has entertained millions of people around the world for a generation. Once considered a radical animated television program, *The Simpsons* has been surpassed by a number of fringe shows designed to push the envelope of television acceptability. However, this does not mean that *The Simpsons* is no longer cutting edge; rather, the show is now viewed as a mainstream product of American popular culture. As illustrated throughout this book, many of the expressions uttered by *The Simpsons* characters, especially those of Homer and Bart, have become common in popular culture. But what is "popular culture"?

"Popular culture" is a generic term that has many different meanings depending upon who is defining it. In contrast to "high culture," popular culture is generally viewed as the "people's culture." That is, elements of popular culture most directly impact the masses, or the "public." Because it is the culture of the people, popular culture both reflects and influences people's everyday life (Petracca and Sorapure 1998). Popular culture may be defined as the items (products), ideas, and forms of expression and identity that are frequently encountered or widely accepted, commonly liked, or approved, that are characteristic of a particular society at a given time. A key feature of popular culture is its accessibility to the masses as it is, after all, the culture of the people. Thus, popular culture is a vehicle that allows large heterogeneous masses of people to identify collectively with others (Delaney 2007). Urbanization, industrialization, the mass media, and the continuous growth in technology since the late 1700s have all been significant factors in the formation of popular culture. These social forces continue to be factors in shaping popular culture today (Delaney 2007).

Sources of Popular Culture

As described above, a number of social forces (urbanization, industrialization, and the growth of technology) have directly influenced the formation of popular culture. In contemporary society, however, it is the mass media that serves as the greatest source of popular culture. The mass media includes the print media (especially newspapers, magazines, and books), film, radio, video games, the Internet, and perhaps most important, television. Television is a particularly powerful medium for spreading an ideology. TV shows provide concise bits of information neatly packaged with built-in break periods (commercials) that afford viewers enough time to digest the information viewed, bathroom breaks, and timeouts to retrieve snacks from the kitchen. The commercial breaks themselves are important, as advertisers hope to sell products to a "captured" audience.

People around the world watch numerous hours of television daily. Some people watch so much television that they resemble Homer Simpson's "couch potato" persona. Considering the vast array of television programs available via cable or satellite, combined with high-density, large-screen, viewing capacity, is there any wonder we watch as much television as we do? Television brings news, weather, sports, information, and entertainment into the comfort of our own homes.

Animation Domination

Although animated cartoons were once considered the domain of Saturday morning viewing by children, the contemporary era has witnessed a great number of animated shows (e.g., *South Park*, *Family Guy*, *King of the Hill*, *Futurama*, and *American Dad*) broadcast at night and directed toward adult audiences. Despite the many pretenders to the throne, however, it is *The Simpsons* that remains the clear-cut king of cartoons. And although there is often great meaning behind many cartoons (as demonstrated throughout *Simpsonology*), the primary intent is always to entertain the masses. Homer Simpson explains this reality to his wife in the "Mr. Lisa Goes to Washington" episode (#37), "Oh, Marge, cartoons don't have any deep meaning. They're just stupid drawings that give you a cheap laugh."

The Simpsons are an animated middle-class family that survives week-to-week by Homer's paycheck. In this regard, the Simpson family is fairly typical of many American families. For those of us who are not married with children, or living from paycheck to paycheck, there are plenty of other characters to relate to in Springfield. Then again, because *The Simpsons* is a cartoon, the situations that the characters find themselves in are often exaggerated and their insane stunts never permanently harm them. We mere mortals would feel the pain of Homer falling off a cliff which he simply shrugs off. Further, while the characters on *The Simpsons* never age, we viewers do. Perhaps that is another important reason why we love *The Simpsons* so much. We are able to watch the show from a time perspective of choice. That is, we can remember when we first watched the show and how we related to various characters, or we can watch the show from our current life status.

There are critics who believe that television, especially cartoons, is responsible for the "dumbing down" of society. They also argue that certain media presentations, especially violent cartoons and films, serve no redeeming value. (Note: In *The Simpsons* it is common for the Springfield children, and occasionally the adults, to watch the ultraviolent *Itchy & Scratchy* cartoon. *The Simpsons* writers do this in order to draw attention to violent cartoons and their effect on children.) Not surprisingly, Homer Simpson disagrees with those who would argue that violent cartoons and movies serve no purpose. In the "The Ziff Who Came to Dinner" episode (#327), the Simpson and Flanders families watch an ultraviolent film (*The Deadening*) at the movies. All the children, even Bart, are afraid and want to leave the theater. But Homer insists that they stay put. Later that evening at the dinner table, Bart and Lisa are still frightened and Marge is upset with Homer for allowing them to watch such a scary horror movie. Homer dismisses Marge's concerns and justifies his actions with this response: "Scaring kids is good for them. It hardens them against future terrors." And so there you have it, based on the logic of Homer Simpson, children who watch violent, scary, and perhaps "inappropriate" television shows and movies will be better prepared for the harsh realities of life.

Even so, the realization of the power behind cartoons is in itself potentially scary. Bart discovers this in the "Yokel Chords" episode (#392). In this episode, Bart is talking to his school-appointed psychologist, Dr. Stacey Swanson (voiced by Meg Ryan). While sitting on Dr. Swanson's couch, Bart describes his dream to her: "And then, I had this dream that my whole family was just cartoon characters and that our success had led to some crazy propaganda network called FOX News." Cartoons cannot possibly be that powerful, can they? That would make them potentially very scary!

In February 2003, Todd Leopold of CNN wrote an article praising *The Simpsons*'s three-hundredth episode. Leopold (2003) states that *The Simpsons* is a major part of American and Western culture because millions of people outside the United States also identify with the Springfield characters. Indeed, the show is broadcast around the world including such countries as Australia, Canada, France, Germany, Japan, Belgium, Brazil, the Philippines, Israel, and the United Kingdom. In Australia, *The Simpsons* airs on Saturdays and Sundays. The FOX8 Sunday broadcast includes the airing of five episodes during a segment called "The Super *Simpsons* Weekends." In Brazil, *The Simpsons* is aired daily in both English and Portuguese.

Mass merchandising has a tremendous effect on popular culture. Being a cartoon certainly has its advantages when it comes to merchandising products. Children are immediately drawn to the cartoon *Simpsons* characters. And for twenty years, children have grown up loving *The Simpsons*. This helps to explain the dramatic impact on popular culture that this show possesses. In 2003 for example, FOX had arrangements with more than five hundred licensees worldwide and each license included up to two hundred commercial *Simpsons* products. As anyone who has traveled abroad can attest, *Simpsons* merchandise (for example, arcade pinball machines, T-shirts, lunch boxes, collective figurines, video games, puzzles, posters, cell phones, and so on) is popular throughout much of the world. William LaRue, author of *Collecting Simpsons!* (1999), argues that kids love the wacky appearance of *The Simpsons* merchandise; teens love the rebellious spirit it represents; "baby boomers" see novelty appeal; and merchants love making lots of money by selling it.

With billions of dollars in worldwide merchandise sales, *The Simpsons* is clearly much more than just a cartoon. LaRue (2007) suggests that the top eight *Simpsons* collectibles for die-hard fans are: *The*

Simpsons Slushee Machine; plush Maggie Simpson (a collectible doll); plush Lisa Simpson; *The Simpsons* Sez Game; *The Simpsons* Flashback Playset; *The Simpsons* Wall Calendar; *The Simpsons* Pinball; and *The Simpsons* Animation Cells. *The Simpsons* is so popular worldwide that nearly any item with its brand name attached to it will sell.

On May 20, 2007, *The Simpsons*, a series *Time* (1999) magazine named the twentieth century's best television show, reached the four hundred–episode barrier and became one of the longest-running television shows in American history. Only a handful of prime-time scripted television series surpass the total number of episodes aired by *The Simpsons*. They include: *Gunsmoke* (633), *Lassie* (588), *The Adventures of Ozzie and Harriett* (435), and *Bonanza* (430). Cracking the four hundred barrier in this era is amazing, especially in light of the great diversity of shows available to viewing audiences via cable and the Internet. Dan Castellaneta, the "voice" of Homer Simpson, argues that the Homer character has endeared himself to millions of viewers for twenty years because, "He enjoys life. He enjoys his TV. He enjoys his food . . . [and] he doesn't really want anything to bother or shake up what he's got going" (Morrow 2007). In other words, Homer is a lot like most of us would like to be—focused on having fun and enjoying life. And what can possibly be wrong with that?

The four hundredth episode, "You Kent Always Say What You Want," continued the prevailing theme of the eighteenth season—an attack on censorship and highlighting the extreme difference between the relatively liberal FOX TV and the ultraconservative FOX News. In this episode, newsman Kent Brockman utters a forbidden word on the air while interviewing Homer. (Homer accidentally spilled hot coffee on Kent's lap.) Kent was upset that he had to waste time on his *Smartline* show for something so trivial as Homer purchasing the one-millionth ice cream cone at a local ice cream store. His scheduled "provocative" discussion of the Middle East was preempted in lieu of this fluff piece. Brockman sarcastically states, "Of course this has nothing to do with the fact that this station and the ice cream company are owned by the same corporation."

Immediately upon realizing his gaffe, Brockman apologizes while still on-the-air for using a swear word. Kent informs the public that he will make a huge donation to a number of charities that are set up to stop teen cursing. Kent is worried that he might get into trouble but is relatively happy to realize that the typical person on the street had no clue he goofed up. Apparently, no one watched his news show. This scene was written to indicate the shrinking market for network news. Brockman thinks he might be in the clear.

The next day, the Simpson family discusses Brockman's interview with Homer. Grandpa is upset that Brockman got away with saying a curse word on-the-air. He begins a tirade with a typical old-man's rant, "Back in my day . . ." Lisa is worried that Brockman may still get into trouble and sarcastically states, "There are a lot of religious watchdog groups out there, keeping the world safe from the horror of free expression." Bart adds, "You mean there are losers who spend all day watching TV looking for stuff to complain about? Who would be lame enough to do that?" Well, in Springfield, we all know who is lame enough to sit around and watch TV looking for something to complain about. Sure enough, Ned Flanders is sitting at home reviewing tapes of all televised programs. When he hears Brockman's "bad" word, he goes into a tirade. Ned goes online and summons his "Online Christian soldiers" into action. Ned's sons ask their father what he is doing and why he is so upset. Flanders replies that he is "Deploring people I never met to pressure a government with better things to do than punish a man who meant no harm for something nobody even saw." His son Todd replies, "Daddy, we think you need a new mommy." Ah, from the mouths of babes. Even Ned's young sons realize he just needs to get—well, you can fill in the rest, I don't want to get censored!

Ned finishes his online directive with this signature: God's little bellyacher, Ned Flanders. His activism initiates an FCC investigation. The FCC levies a $10 million fine against Channel 6 for Brockman's shameful language. The station responds by firing Brockman. (Note: The station's firing of Kent Brockman mirrors the firing of Don Imus for his outrageous comments on the radio just weeks before this *Simpsons* broadcast.) Outside the studio, Nelson shames Brockman with his typical "Ha-ha" and adds, "Your distinguished career is over."

Worried that Kent might commit suicide because his career is destroyed, Marge invites him to stay at the Simpson home. Homer does not want Kent in his house because, as he states, "I'm sorry Marge, but I won't live under the same roof with a member of the *liberal* media." Trying to make an excuse for Homer's uncharitable conduct, Marge apologizes to Kent by saying, "You'll have to excuse him. He's been watching a lot of FOX News." Homer counters Marge's comment by saying, "Did you know that every day, Mexican gays sneak into this country and unplug our brain dead old ladies?" Homer has clearly touched upon a lot of "hot button" topics in contemporary American culture that separate liberal and conservative viewpoints. What's amazing is that *The Simpsons* continues to get away with slamming FOX News even though FOX TV is owned by the same corporation that owns FOX News.

Although the incongruence between FOX TV and FOX News have been discussed previously on several *Simpsons* episodes (as well as in this chapter), the writers take another stab at it in this episode. Homer, Kent, and Lisa are watching television. On one channel is FOX TV airing a show (*Landing Strip*) about strippers running an airline. Homer loves this show because it's about *real* people—hot young women. On the other channel a FOX News anchor is condemning liberals—on its "Liberal Outrage" segment—for their willingness to allow NASA to "abort" space missions whenever they feel like it. Homer is outraged and mutters, "Liberals. I hate them so much." In this regard, Homer is demonstrating the sentiments of both liberal and conservative people. He likes "liberal" mindless television that highlights "T and A," but he promotes a conservative viewpoint that is antiabortion. Lisa points out the incongruency between FOX TV and FOX News by saying, "One thing I've always wondered. How can FOX News be so conservative when the FOX network keeps airing raunchy shows? They don't fit together."

Kent expresses his outrage over political censorship by saying, "FOX deliberately runs shows that will earn them huge fines which is then funneled through the FCC and goes straight to funding the Republican Party and everyone in the media knows it but no one has the guts to say it." Inspired by his activism, Lisa decides to help Kent. She introduces him to the wonders of the Internet. Lisa helps him create a short video on "real" news and uploads the video on YouTube.com. As Brockman mingles with community members, he learns that young people are getting their news and information online instead of from network television. Brockman becomes an instant hero because of his YouTube videos. At the same time, however, network executives view Kent as a radical challenge to the conservative status quo that attempts to control the news media. They offer Kent his old job back plus a 50 percent pay increase if he agrees to return to the network. Brockman obliges. It seems he cares more about his own personal status and security than he cares about fighting the good fight.

In yet another example of fighting censorship in this four hundredth episode, Homer asks Lisa, "Do you want to hear something really bad that Kent told me about the FOX network?" Lisa is eager to hear and says, "Of course." Homer's hands start to shake; he warns his daughter that this news is *really* bad. Homer states, "For years now, FOX has been . . ." Homer is cut off by a narrative voice-over proclaiming the glory of FOX and its fine programming, like *American Idol* and the *American Idol* results show. Lisa's response to Homer's shocking news is also dubbed. Homer says he will not be silenced, but the episode ends. Damn conservative (or is it liberal?) media!

Fighting censorship and the war in Iraq, *The Simpsons* remains as relevant as ever. The "You Kent Always Say What You Want" episode also includes a cameo appearance from Ludacris (real name, Chris Bridges). Ludacris, a rapper-actor in real life, plays a tube of toothpaste, Luda-Crest, which performs a public service on the *Menace Tooth Society* instructional video that Lisa's dentist shows her before her scheduled dental appointment. Luda-Crest raps an anticavity song and although the lyrics are quite lame, Ludacris is an active part of popular culture. His guest appearance keeps alive the tradition of famous people willing to do cameos on this still very socially relevant TV show.

The year 2007 also marked *The Simpsons*'s first major motion picture, *The Simpsons Movie*. *The Simpsons* has earned twenty-three Emmys (to date) and praise from critics for its continued cutting-edge social commentary and humor. Clearly, *The Simpsons* has made an impression on popular culture.

THE SIMPSONS AND THE FUTURE

It is premature to discuss the finality of *The Simpsons* since the show is still airing new episodes. But just how long will *The Simpsons* characters remain as popular culture icons? It would seem that the best answer is "indefinitely." As of this writing, creator Matt Groening has expressed his interest in continuing *The Simpsons* series for the foreseeable future. And despite predictions of doom and gloom from "media experts" that people will stop watching TV because of such alternatives as video games and the Internet, more people are watching TV than ever before. According to a 2007 report by Nielsen Media Research, the average American spends four hours and thirty-five minutes a day in front of the tube—the highest recorded figure ever for television viewership (*Parade* March 18, 2007). Further, it is highly likely that additional *Simpsons* films will be released in the future. But even if the creators decide not to make any new episodes, *The Simpsons* will continue to see life in syndication and DVD for generations to come. With over four hundred episodes and new audiences (those outside the United States and future generations) to tackle, *The Simpsons* characters will remain as popular cultural icons for a long time to come.

Simpsons fans might be interested to know that on Matt Groening's "wish list" is a series spin-off centered on Homer Simpson "in all stages of his life" (Keveney 2007). This is good news for all *Simpsons* fans but especially for aging fans who have related to Homer for a generation already.

The Simpsons provides us with a much-needed diversion from everyday life. Millions of viewers look forward to Sunday evenings in anticipation of great comedic relief provided by those wacky characters who reside in Springfield, Somewhere, USA. We can't imagine a Halloween without a "Treehouse of Horror" episode. And, listening to the opening theme music of *The Simpsons* is akin to Pavlov's dogs hearing the ringing of the experimental bell. We don't salivate to this sound (I presume!) but we smile with glee, realizing we are about to be entertained by Homer, Marge, Bart, Lisa, Maggie, and the rest of our favorite Springfield characters.

The Simpsons definitely deserves to be recognized for its impact on popular culture. And this recognition should extend beyond such mainstream museums as the Smithsonian, to include the Museum of Television and TV (MTTV). The MTTV, a fictional museum that parodies the Museum of Television and Radio, was introduced to fans of *The Simpsons* in the "Milhouse Doesn't Live Here Anymore" episode (#325). In this episode, the Springfield schoolchildren visit the MTTV. There are a number of interesting wings in this museum, including the "Hall of Nosy Neighbors." Among the honored nosy neighbors are Ned Flanders (*The Simpsons*), Mr. Roper (*Three's Company*), and Mrs. Kravitz (*Bewitched*). Another wing pays tribute to "Things That Talk, but Shouldn't." Included in this display are the chimpanzee from *Lancelot Link*, the robot from *Lost in Space*, Kitt (the car) from *Night Rider*, and the horse from *Mr. Ed*. Although such a wing was not shown in this episode, I suggest that *The Simpsons* would be a feature in the "Influences on Popular Culture" wing.

Simpsonology represents an attempt to reveal the impact of *The Simpsons* on popular culture, and demonstrates the many ways the show mirrors and parodies everyday social life. Some people will appreciate this book more than others, just as some people appreciate *The Simpsons* more than others do. Homer echoes these sentiments in the "Diatribe of a Mad Housewife" episode (#323), when he provides Marge with a review of her recently published novel.

> *Homer*: The end of your book was the wake-up call I needed after falling asleep at the beginning of your book.
>
> *Marge*: That's the best review I've gotten. Seriously, these reviews are terrible.
>
> *Homer*: Don't worry about those losers, Marge!

And that's the beauty of popular culture. While some members of society may not find enjoyment in a particular aspect of the popular culture, many others will. *The Simpsons* may have its detractors, but it has countless millions of supporters in the United States and around the world.

As Homer Simpson himself might say, "Mmm, there really is a bit of Springfield in all of us!"

Bibliography

American Obesity Association. 2002. "Childhood Obesity." http://www
.obesity.org/subs/childhood/prevalence.shtml.

Bender, Thomas. 1991. *Community and Social Change in America*. Baltimore:
Johns Hopkins University Press.

Bodenheimer, George. 2006. Live discussion at the State University of New
York at Oswego's "Sports Media Summit," held October 21.

Bush, George W. 2002. "Foreword by President George W. Bush." *The White
House Press Release for the "No Child Left Behind Act of 2001."* http://www
.whitehouse.gov/news/reports/no-child-left-behind.html.

Business Review. 2006. "Pataki to Sign Timothy's Law on Mental Health Coverage." http://albany.bizjournals.com/albany/stories/12/18/daily/67
.html.

Catton, W. R. 1980. *Overshoot: The Ecological Basis of Revolutionary Change*.
Urbana: University of Illinois Press.

CBS. 2002. "Smoking-Related Death Estimate Rises." http://www.cbsnews
.com/stories/2002/10/11/health/main525264.shtml.

Centers for Disease Control. 2001. "Cigarette Smoking-Related Mortality."
http://www.cdc.gov/.

———. 2004. "Obesity Approaching Tobacco as Top Preventable Cause of
Death." http://www.doctorslounge.com/primary/articles/obesity_death/.

Christianson, Stephen G., ed. 2000. *The American Book of Days*, 4th ed. New
York: H. W. Wilson.

Couvrette, Phil. 2006. "Killer Played Columbine Game." Syracuse *Post-Standard*, September 15, p. A6.

Crenson, Matt. 2006. "Two Americans Win Nobel Prize for Physics." Syracuse *Post-Standard*, October 4, p. A9.

401

Danton, Eric R. 2003. "Study Links Violent Lyrics to Aggressive Behavior." *Buffalo News,* May 7, p. D7.

Davidson, Keay. 2006. "Global Warming Warnings Just Got a Lot Worse." *San Francisco Chronicle,* June 26, p. A10.

Delaney, Tim. 2002A. "Religious Doomsday Cults: The Sky Is Falling!" In *Values, Society & Evolution*, edited by Harry J. Birx and Tim Delaney, 153–67. Auburn, NY: Legend Books.

———. 2002B. "The Value of Multiculturalism." In *Values, Society & Evolution,* edited by Harry Birx and Tim Delaney, 169–82. Auburn, NY: Legend Books.

———. 2004. *Classical Social Theory: Investigation and Application.* Upper Saddle River, NJ: Pearson.

———. 2005. *Contemporary Social Theory: Investigation and Application.* Upper Saddle River, NJ: Pearson.

———. 2006. *American Street Gangs.* Upper Saddle River, NJ: Pearson.

———. 2007. "Popular Culture: An Overview." *Philosophy Now* 64 (November/December): 12–13.

Delaney, Tim, and Tim Madigan. 2008 (forthcoming). *Sports: Why We Love Them.*

Dobson, Hugo. 2006. "Mister Sparkle Meets the Yakuza: Depictions of Japan in *The Simpsons.*" *Journal of Popular Culture* 39, no. 1: 44–68.

Elber, Lynn. 2004. "Life with 'The Simpsons.'" Syracuse *Post-Standard,* November 10, p. G2.

Elias, Marilyn. 2007. "Study: Real Fathers Fail to Measure Up to Televised Versions." *USA Today,* June 14, p. 11D.

Entertainment Weekly. 2007. "The Simpsons Movie," April 27/May 4, pp. 67–69.

Gonzalez, Erika. 2007. "What You Don't Know About 'The Simpsons.'" Syracuse *Post-Standard,* June 28, p. E4.

Greyhound Rescue, Inc. 2006. "Home Page." http://www.greyrescue.org.

Hartman, Holly, and Shmuel Ross. 2006. "Spelling Buzz." http://www.factmonster.com/spot/spellingbee1.html.

Hayden, Tom. 2004. *Street Wars: Gangs and the Future of Violence.* New York: New Press.

Hubert, Cynthia. 2007. "Fall Down, Go Boomer." *Sacramento Bee* (appearing in Syracuse *Post-Standard*), January 11, p. E2.

Hyde, Justin. 1999. "'Jenny Jones Show' Found Negligent in Guest's Slaying." *Buffalo News,* May 7, p. A1.

Keating, Thomas. 1994. *Intimacy with God.* New York: Crossroad.

Keveney, Bill. 2007. "Sunday Episodes Take 'Simpsons' to No. 400." *USA Today,* May 18.

Lakshmanan, Indira A. R. 2006. "A Living Tree Emits Oxygen. A Dead One Emits Carbon Dioxide." *Boston Globe,* December 6, p. A9.

LaRue, William D. 1999. *Collecting Simpsons! An Unofficial Guide to Merchandise from* The Simpsons. Liverpool, NY: KML Enterprises.

———. 2007. "Top 8 *Simpsons* Gifts." *About: Animated TV*. http://animated tv.about.com/cs/merchandise/tp/simpgifts03.htm?=1.

Lasswell, Harold. 1936. *Who Gets What, When, How*. New York: McGraw-Hill.

Las Vegas Review-Journal. 1993. "School Bores Gifted Children, Says Report," November 5, p. 8A.

Leopold, Todd. 2003. "A Milestone for '*The Simpsons*.'" CNN.com. http://www.cnn.com/2003/SHOWBIZ/TV/02/13/simpsons.300/index.html.

Lindersmith, Alfred R., Anselm L. Strauss, and Norman K. Denzin. 1991. *Social Psychology*, 7th ed. Englewood Cliffs, NJ: Prentice Hall.

McConnaughery, Janet. 1998. "Initially Biased: Study Says Names Shorten or Lengthen Life." *Los Angeles Times*, March 28, p. A10.

McEntire, Cassell Nancy. 2003. "Purposeful Deceptions of the April Fool." *Western Folklore* 61, no. 2: 133–51.

Melvin, Don. 2005. "To Dutch, Global Warming Not a Theory." *Cleveland Plain Dealer*, September 11, p. A7.

Morrow, Terry. 2007. "Celebrating 400 '*Simpsons*' Episodes." Syracuse *Post-Standard*, May 18, p. E4.

Newman, Brian. 2003. "Integrity and Political Approval." *American Association for Public Opinion Research* 67: 335–67.

Nisbet, Robert. 1969. *The Quest for Community*. New York: Oxford University Press.

O'Connor, Anahad. 2005. "Do Violent Video Games Make Kids Aggressive?" Syracuse *Post-Standard*, September 6, p. D2.

Ohlemacher, Stephen. 2006. "College Degree's Value: $23,000 a Year." Syracuse *Post-Standard*, October 26, p. C1.

Olsen, Jan M. 2005. "Greenland's Big Thaw Worries Scientists." *Cleveland Plain Dealer*, September 11, p. A8.

Ortved, John. 2007. "Simpson Family Values." *Vanity Fair*, August, pp. 94, 96, 98, 100, 102–104.

Parade. 2006. "Cheating Nation," October 15, p. 20.

———. 2007. "Media News: TV Time Again," March 18, p. 18.

Pasko, Jessica M. 2006. "Is Feminism Dead?" Syracuse *Post-Standard*, July 23, p. A12.

Playboy. 2007. "Playboy Interview: Matt Groening," June, pp. 57–60, 145–46.

Petracca, Michael, and Madeleine Sorapure, eds. 1998. *Common Culture*, 2nd ed. Upper Saddle River, NJ: Prentice Hall.

Post-Standard. 2006. "Expert Blames Ag Policies for Fat in Developing Lands," September 5, p. A4.

————. 2007. "Don't Get Up Yet, Another Great Moment in Sports History Is Only Hours Away," January 3, p. A2.

————. 2007. "Man Retains His Throne," January 4, p. A2.

————. 2007. "8-Year-Old Girl Allegedly Made 135 Fake 911 Calls," February 10, p. A8.

Rose, Peter. 1981. *They and We*, 3rd ed. New York: Random House.

Salary.com. 2006A. "What Is a Mom Worth? Working Mom vs. Stay at Home Mom Salaries for 2006." May 3, 2006. http://www.salary.com/.

————. 2006B. "What Is a Stay-at-Home Dad's Work Worth?" June 16, 2007. http://www.salary.com/.

Seinfeld. 1991. "The Stranded" First air date, November 27.

Shibutani, T., and K. Kwan. 1965. *Ethnic Stratification: A Comparative Approach.* New York: Macmillan.

Smith, Martin J., and Patrick J. Kiger. 2004. *Poplorica: A Popular History of the Fads, Mavericks, Inventions, and Lore That Shaped Modern America.* New York: HarperCollins.

Solomon, Jack. 1998. "Masters of Desire." In *Common Culture: Reading and Writing About American Popular Culture*, 2nd ed. Michael Petracca and Madeleine Sorapure, eds., 46-59. Upper Saddle River, NJ: Prentice Hall.

Tilove, Jonathan. 2006. "End of an Era for 200,000,000th American." *Cleveland Plain Dealer,* September 24, p. A1.

Time. 1999. "The Best of the Century." December 31. http://www.time.com/time/magazine/article/0,9171,993039,00.html.

Timothy's Law. 2006. "Facts about Timothy's Law." http://timothyslaw.org/facts.htm.

Turnquist, Kristi. 2007. "The Wrong Springfield." Syracuse *Post-Standard*, August 8, p. E4.

United States Department of Health & Human Services. 2006. "New Surgeon General's Report Focuses on the Effects of Secondhand Smoke." http://www.hhs.gov/news/press/2006pres/20060627.html.

United States Environmental Protection Agency. 2007. "About the EPA." http://www.epa.gov/epahome/aboutepa.htm.

United States Nuclear Regulatory Commission. 2007A. "Inspection." http://www.nrc.gov/who-we-are.html.

————. 2007B. "Who We Are." http://www.nrc.gov/what-we-do/regulatory/safety-oversight.html.

Vedantam, Shankar. 2002. "New Study Again Links TV, Violent Behavior." *Buffalo News,* March 29, p. A1.

Vogel, Charity. 2003. "Pink-Collar Job." *Buffalo News,* May 22, pp. A1, A7.

Wallechinsky, David. 2007. "Is America Still No. 1?" *Parade,* January 14, pp. 4–6.

Waters, Mike. 2006. "Drexel Ready to Step into the Spot Light." *Syracuse Post-Standard,* December 19, p. D4.

World Health Organization. 2007A. "About WHO." http://www.who.int/about/en/.

———. 2007B. "Depression." http://www.who.int/mental_health/managment/depression/defintion/en/.

———. 2007C. "Engaging for Health: A Global Health Agenda." http://www.who.int/.

———. 2007D. "Mental Health." http://www.who.int/mental_health/en/.

Index of Cited Episodes